# ANONYMOUS NOISE

Ryoko
Fukuyama

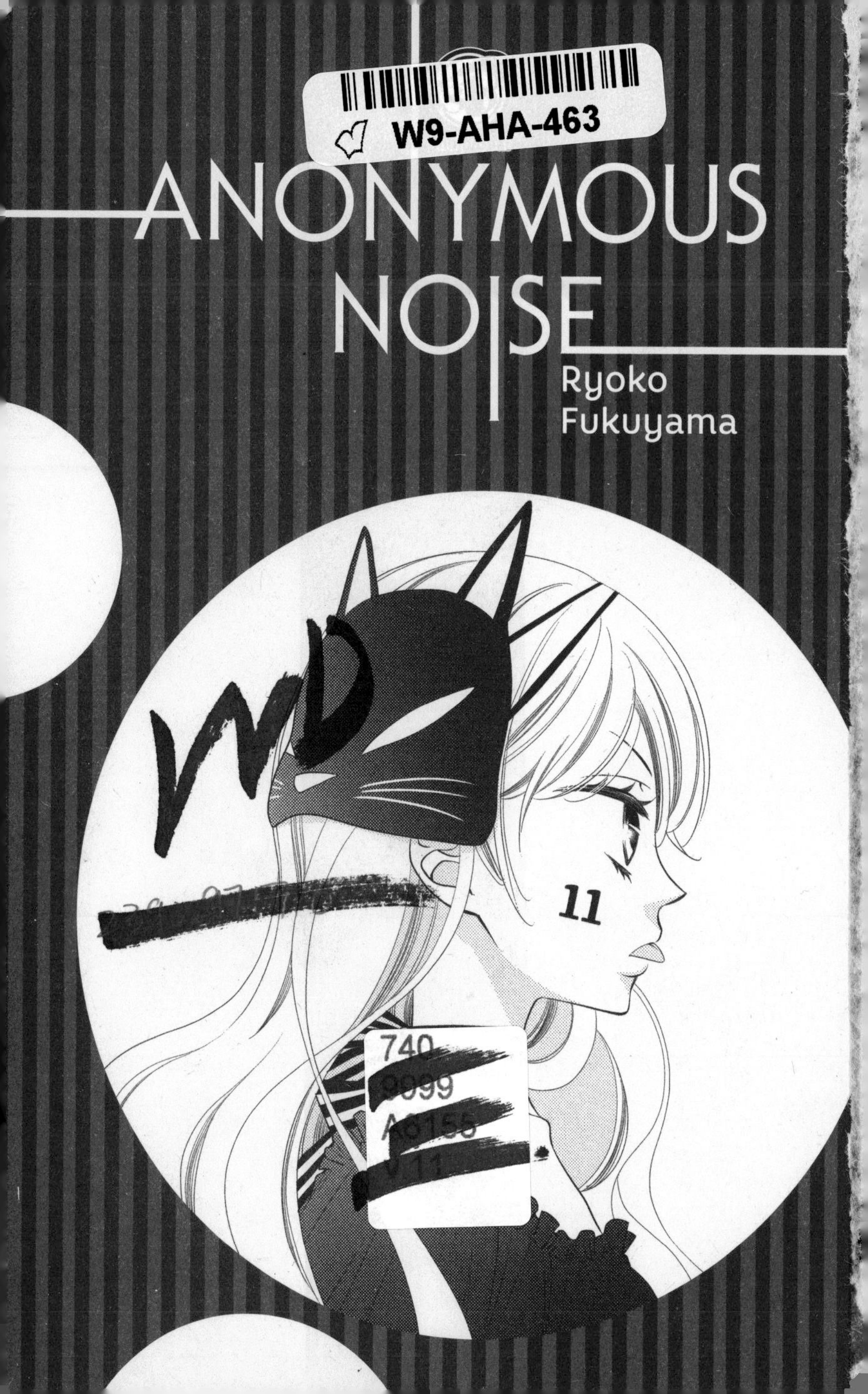
11

# Anonymous Noise
## Volume 11

### CONTENTS

SONG 59

# IN NO HURRY TO SHOUT

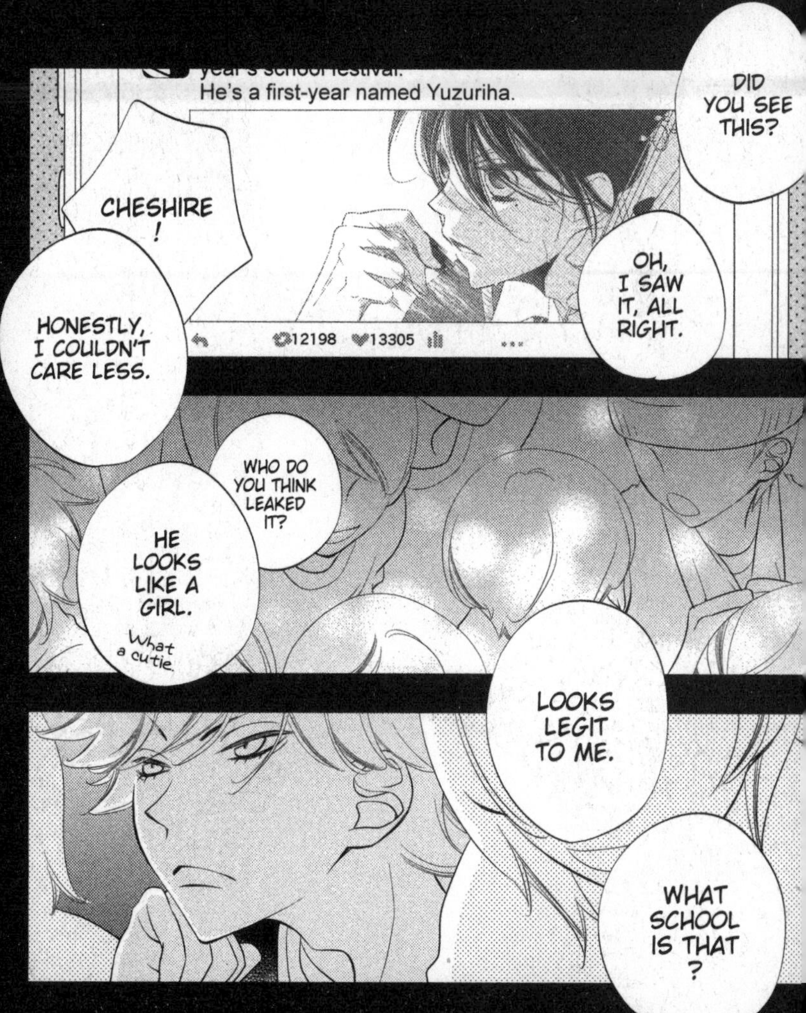
DID YOU SEE THIS?
OH, I SAW IT, ALL RIGHT.
year's school festival.
He's a first-year named Yuzuriha.
12198
13305
CHESHIRE!
HONESTLY, I COULDN'T CARE LESS.
WHO DO YOU THINK LEAKED IT?
HE LOOKS LIKE A GIRL.
What a cutie.
LOOKS LEGIT TO ME.
WHAT SCHOOL IS THAT?

FIRST LIVE TOUR

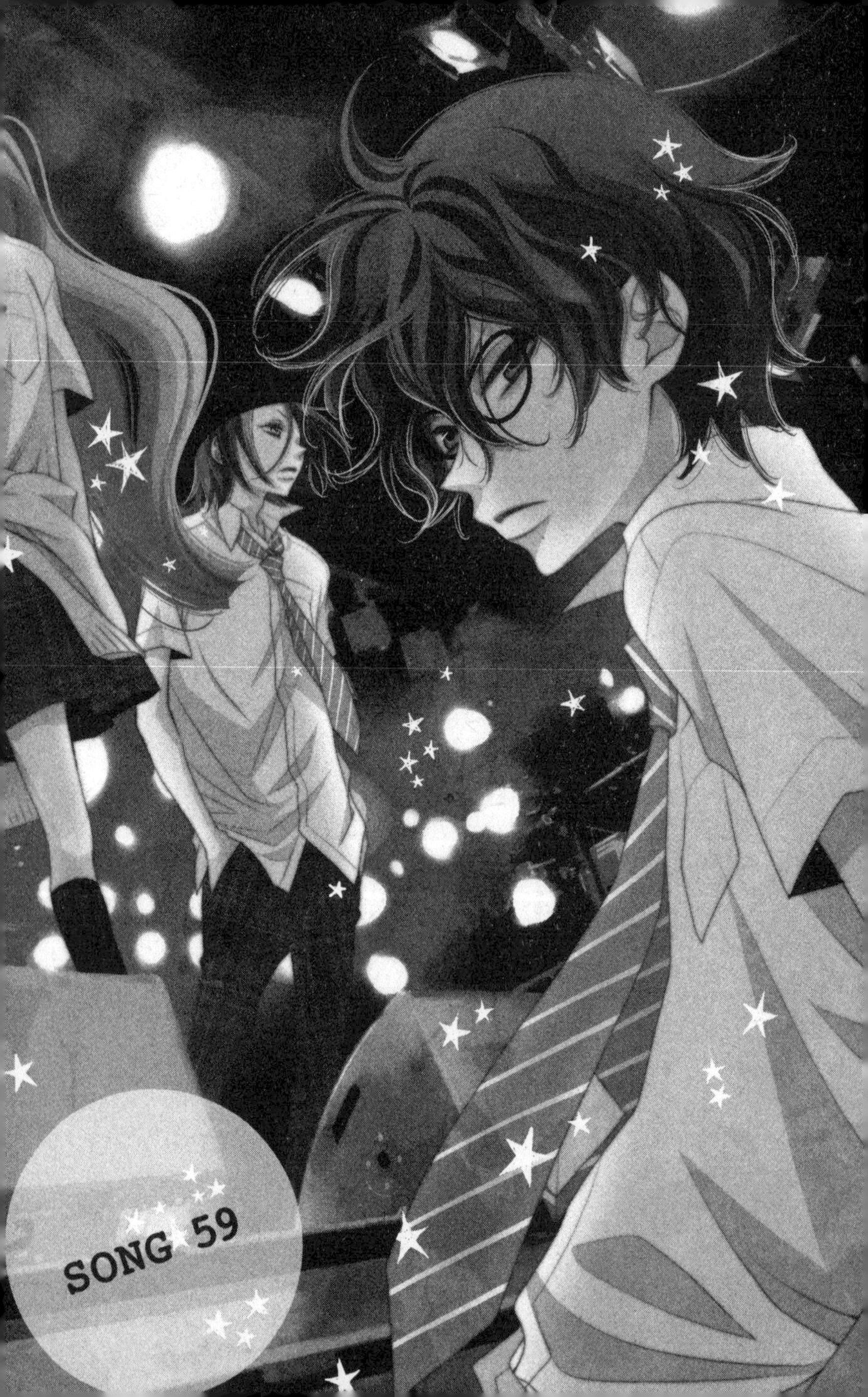
SONG 59

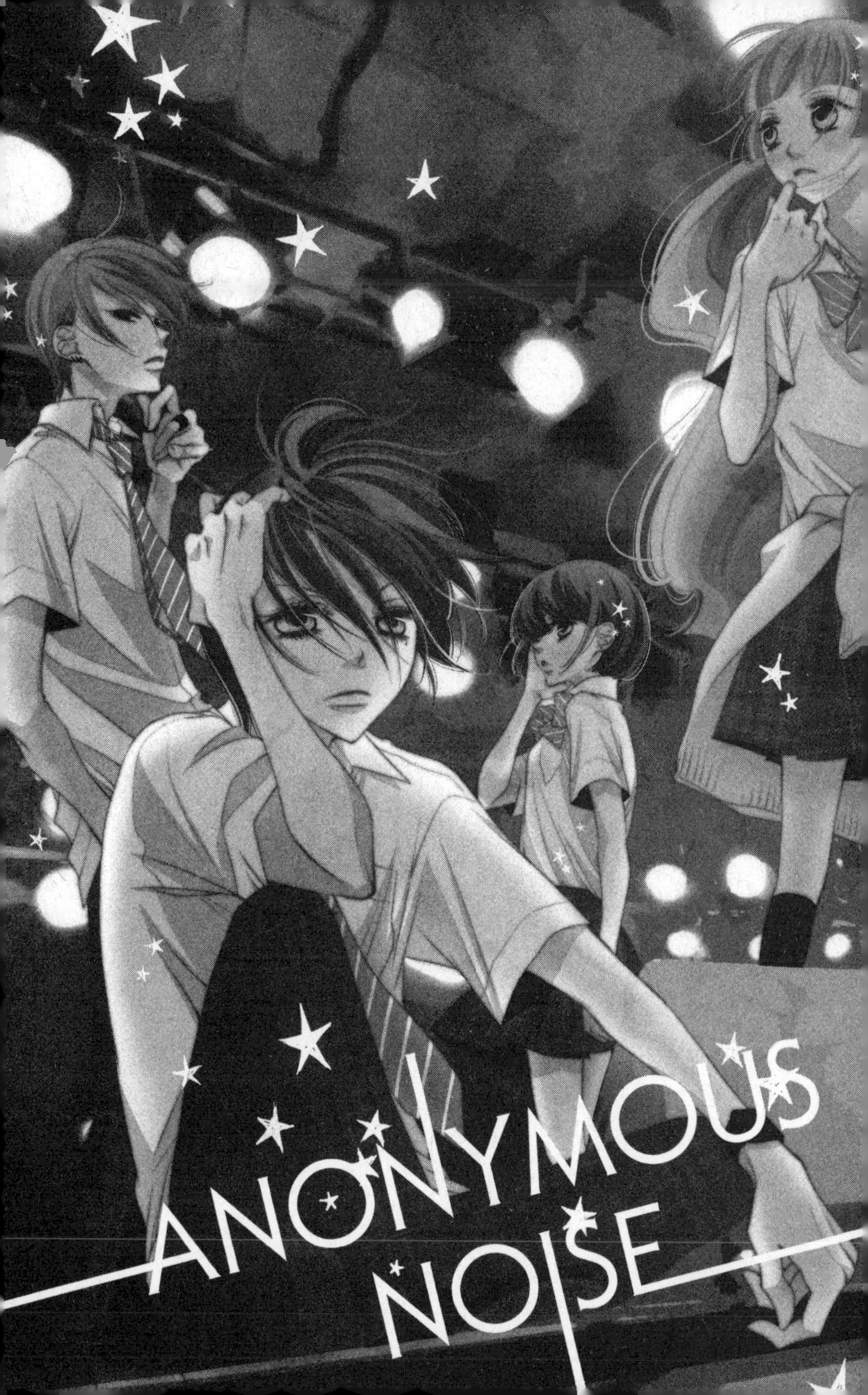
ANONYMOUS
NOISE

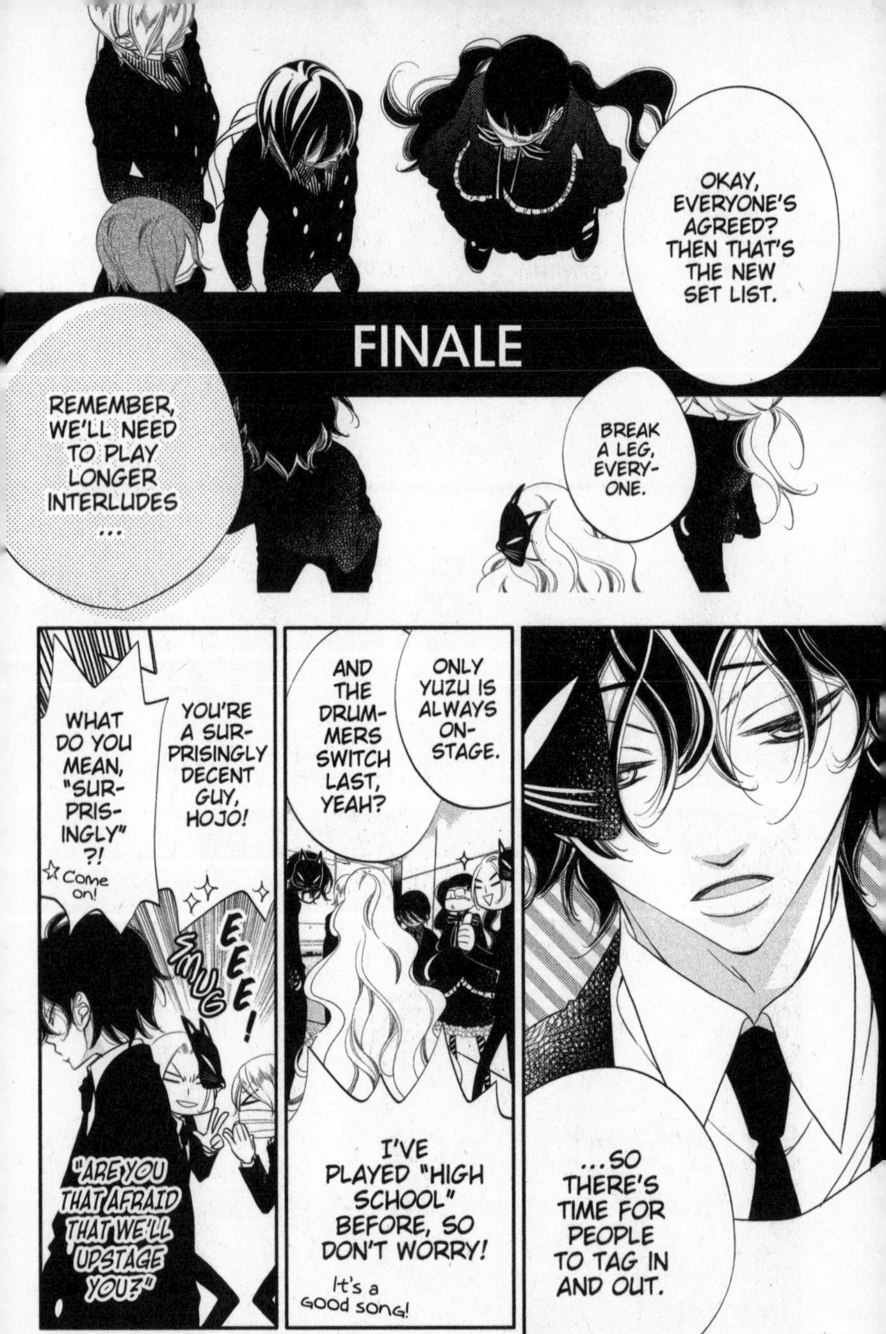
OKAY, EVERYONE'S AGREED? THEN THAT'S THE NEW SET LIST.
FINALE
BREAK A LEG, EVERY-ONE.
REMEMBER, WE'LL NEED TO PLAY LONGER INTERLUDES ...
...SO THERE'S TIME FOR PEOPLE TO TAG IN AND OUT.
ONLY YUZU IS ALWAYS ON-STAGE.
AND THE DRUM-MERS SWITCH LAST, YEAH?
I'VE PLAYED "HIGH SCHOOL" BEFORE, SO DON'T WORRY!
It's a good song!
YOU'RE A SUR-PRISINGLY DECENT GUY, HOJO!
WHAT DO YOU MEAN, "SUR-PRIS-INGLY"?!
☆ Come on!
EEE!
SMUG
"ARE YOU THAT AFRAID THAT WE'LL UPSTAGE YOU?"

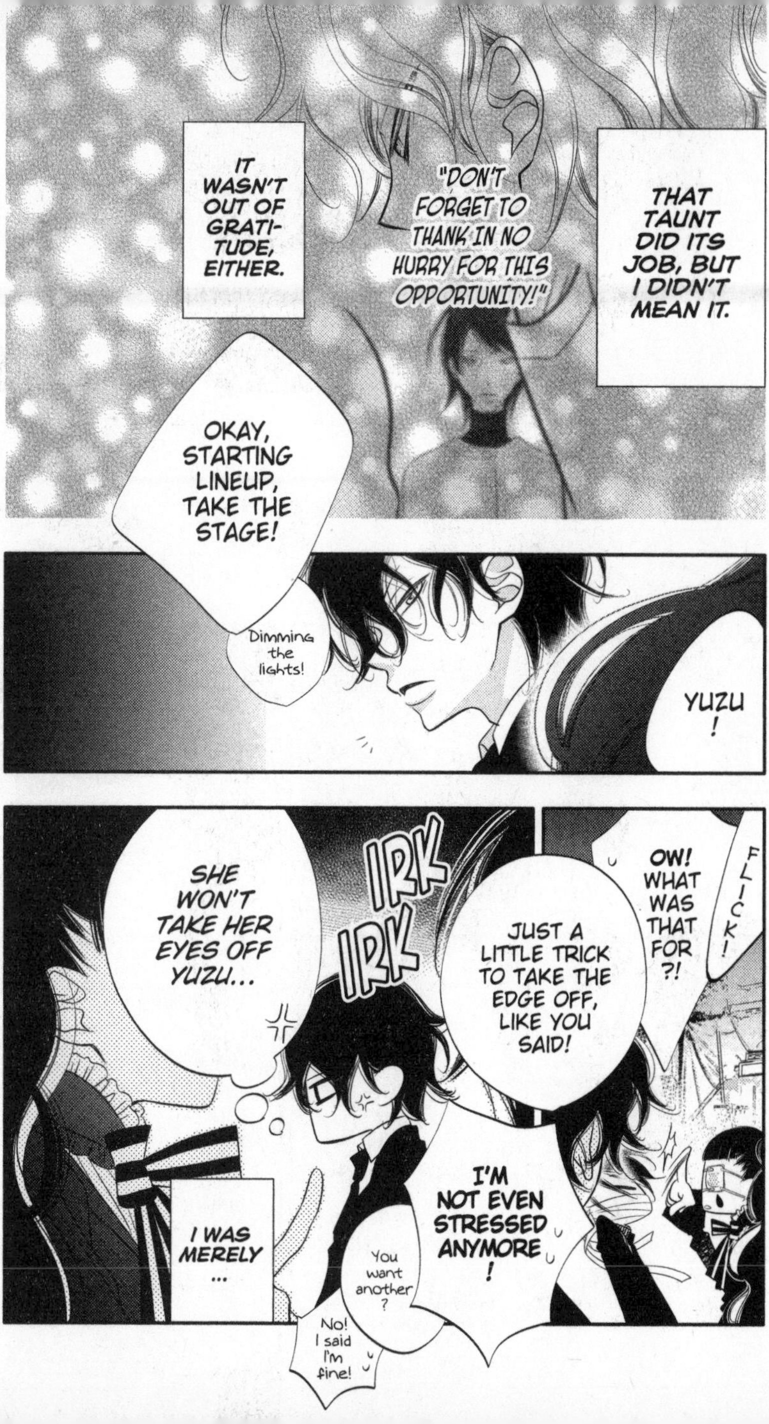
THAT TAUNT DID ITS JOB, BUT I DIDN'T MEAN IT.
"DON'T FORGET TO THANK IN NO HURRY FOR THIS OPPORTUNITY!"
IT WASN'T OUT OF GRATITUDE, EITHER.
OKAY, STARTING LINEUP, TAKE THE STAGE!
YUZU!
Dimming the lights!
FLICK!
OW! WHAT WAS THAT FOR?!
JUST A LITTLE TRICK TO TAKE THE EDGE OFF, LIKE YOU SAID!
IRK IRK
SHE WON'T TAKE HER EYES OFF YUZU...
I'M NOT EVEN STRESSED ANYMORE!
You want another?
No! I said I'm fine!
I WAS MERELY...

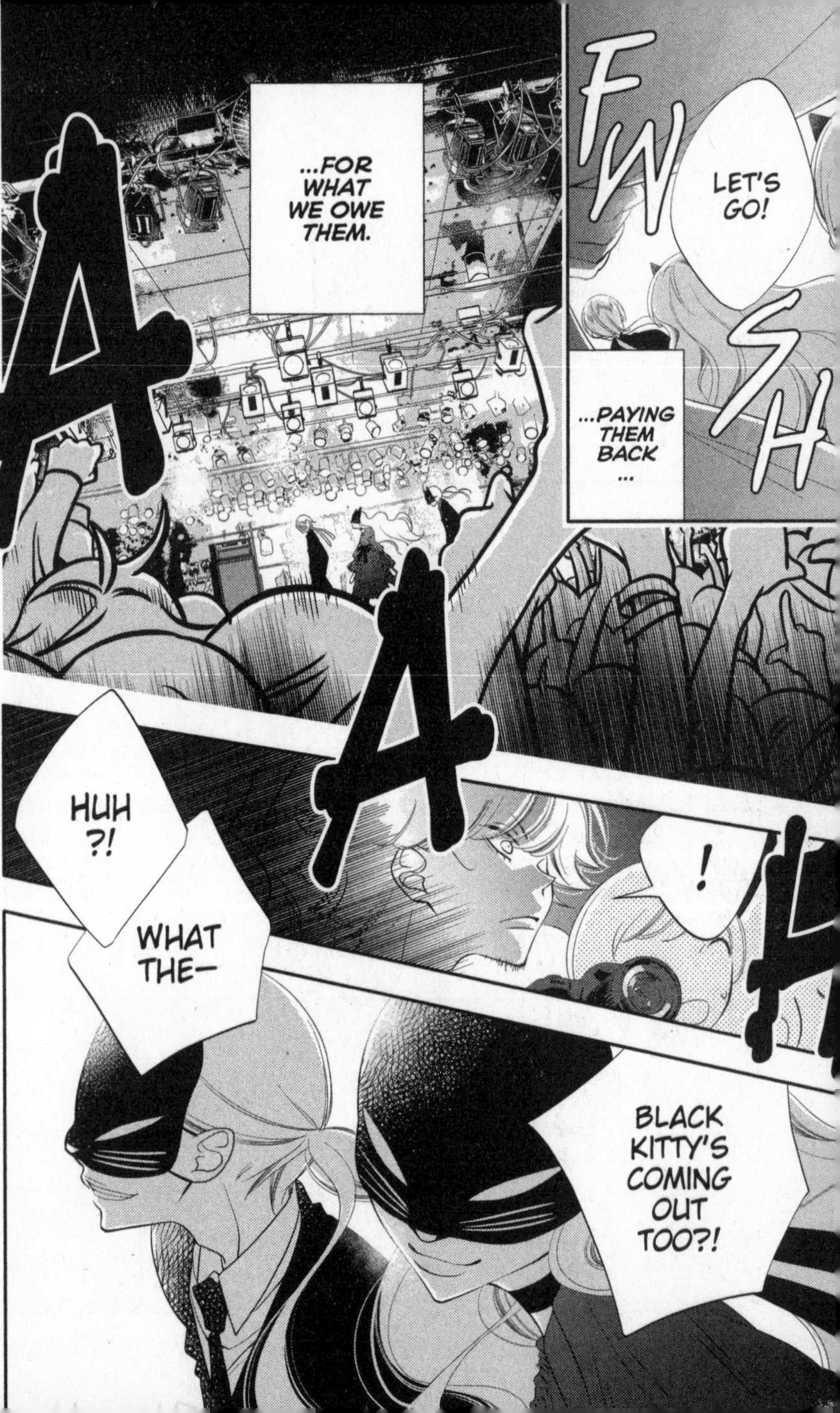
FWSH
LET'S GO!
...PAYING THEM BACK ...
...FOR WHAT WE OWE THEM.
!
HUH ?!
WHAT THE—
BLACK KITTY'S COMING OUT TOO?!

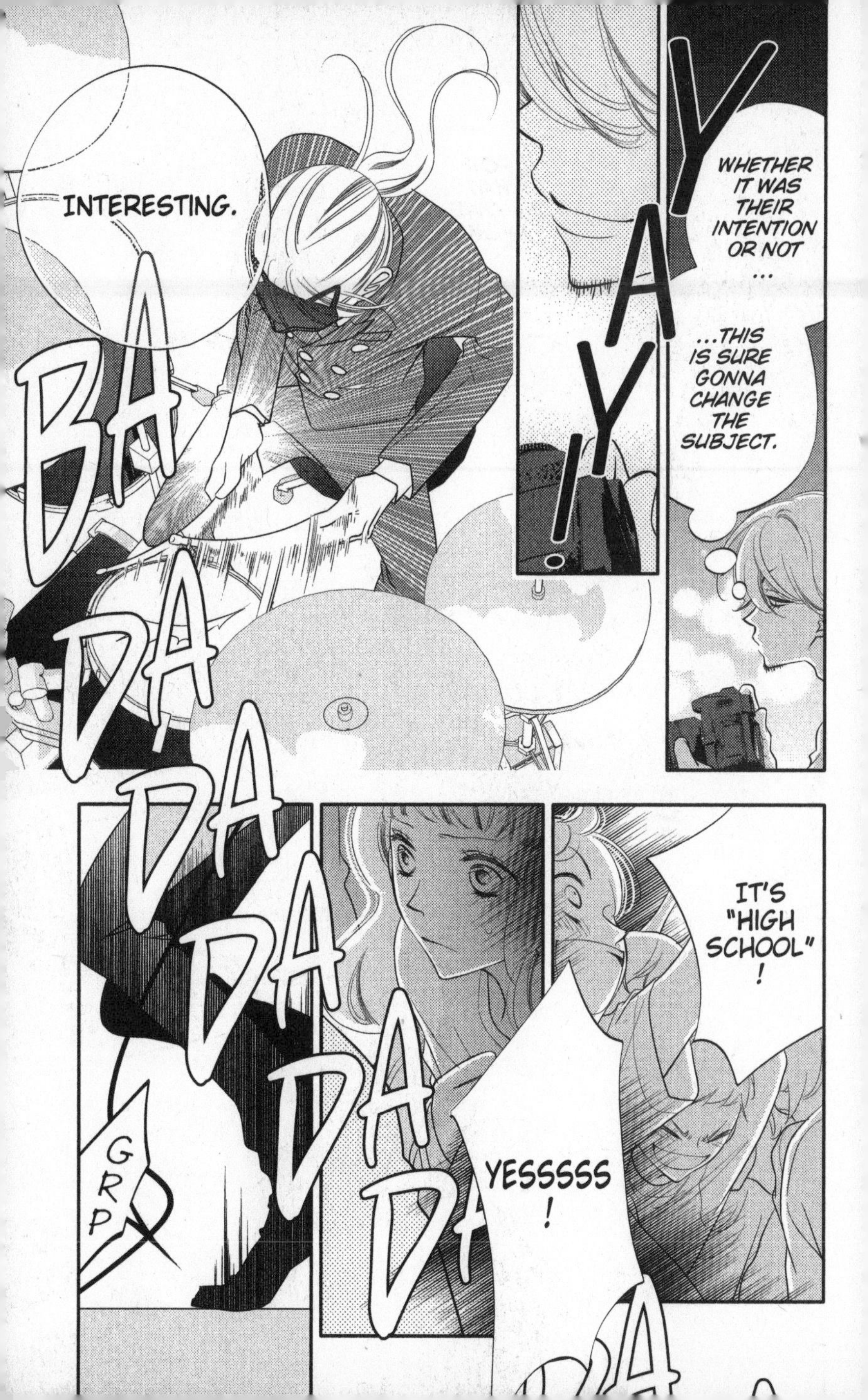
WHETHER IT WAS THEIR INTENTION OR NOT ...
...THIS IS SURE GONNA CHANGE THE SUBJECT.
YAY!
INTERESTING.
BADADADADADADA
IT'S "HIGH SCHOOL" !
YESSSSS !
GRP

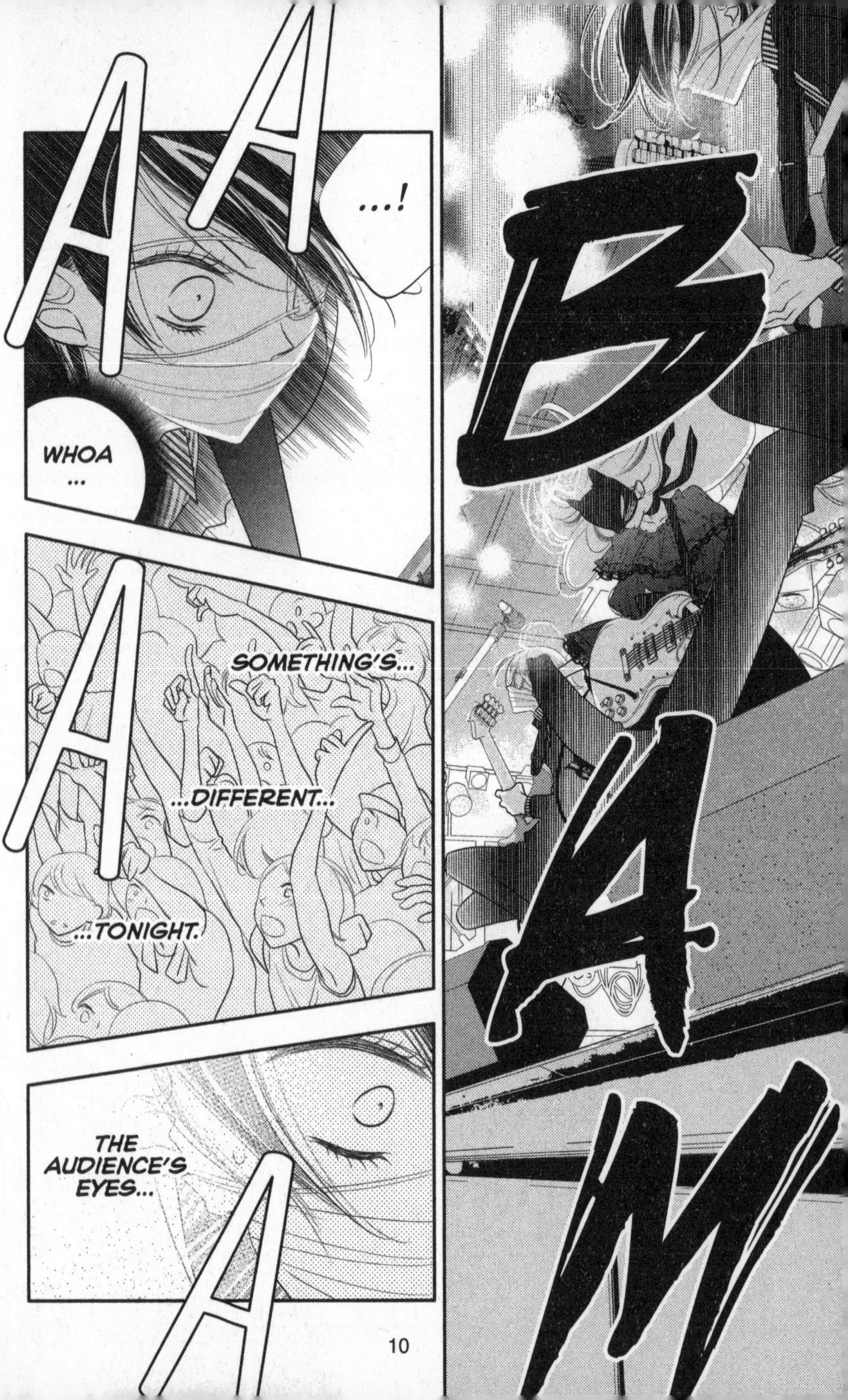
BAM
AAAA
...!
WHOA ...
SOMETHING'S...
...DIFFERENT...
...TONIGHT.
THE AUDIENCE'S EYES...

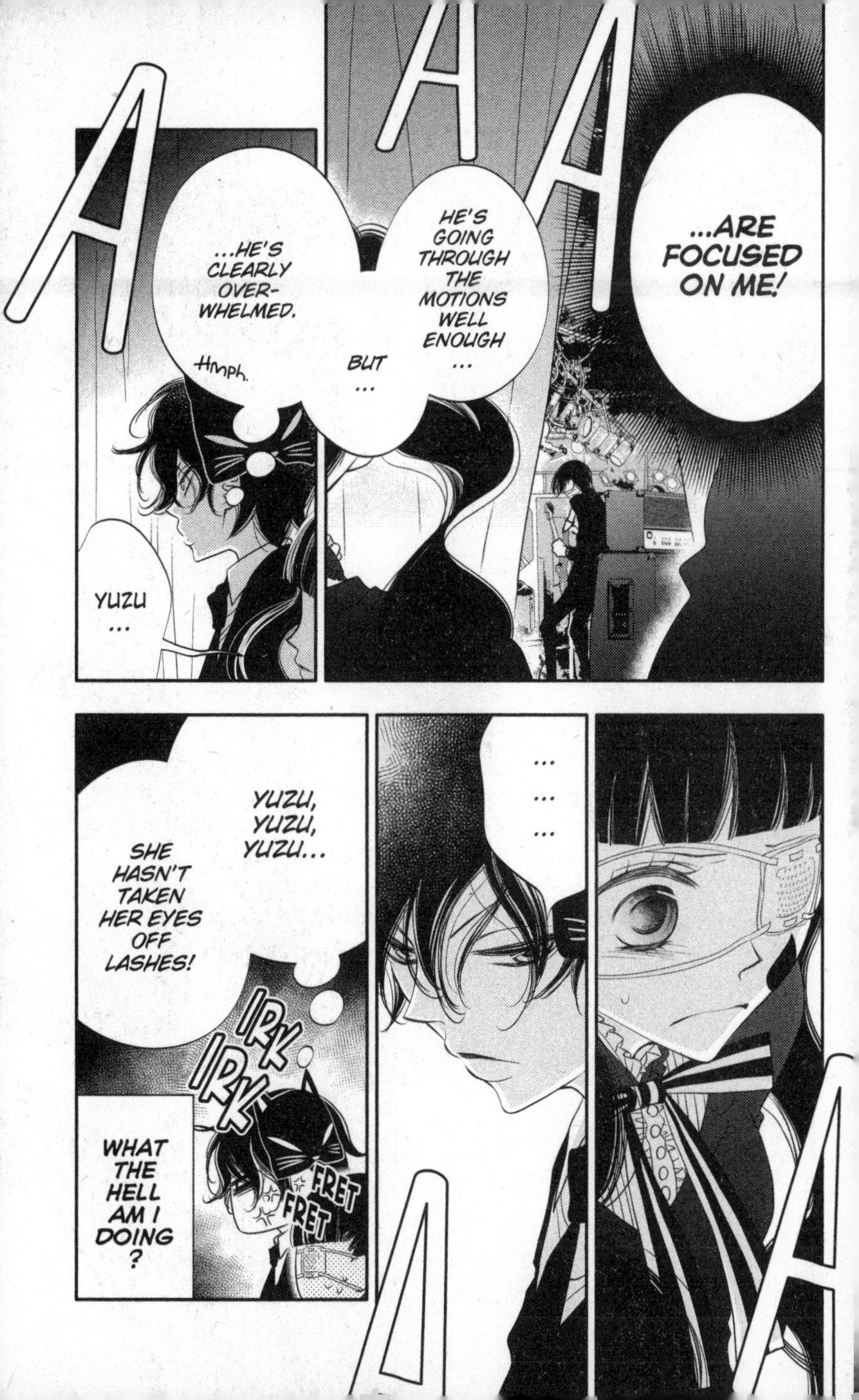

A A A
...ARE FOCUSED ON ME!
HE'S GOING THROUGH THE MOTIONS WELL ENOUGH ...
BUT ...
...HE'S CLEARLY OVER-WHELMED.
Hmph.
YUZU ...
... ... ...
YUZU, YUZU, YUZU...
SHE HASN'T TAKEN HER EYES OFF LASHES!
IRK IRK
WHAT THE HELL AM I DOING?
FRET FRET
A A A

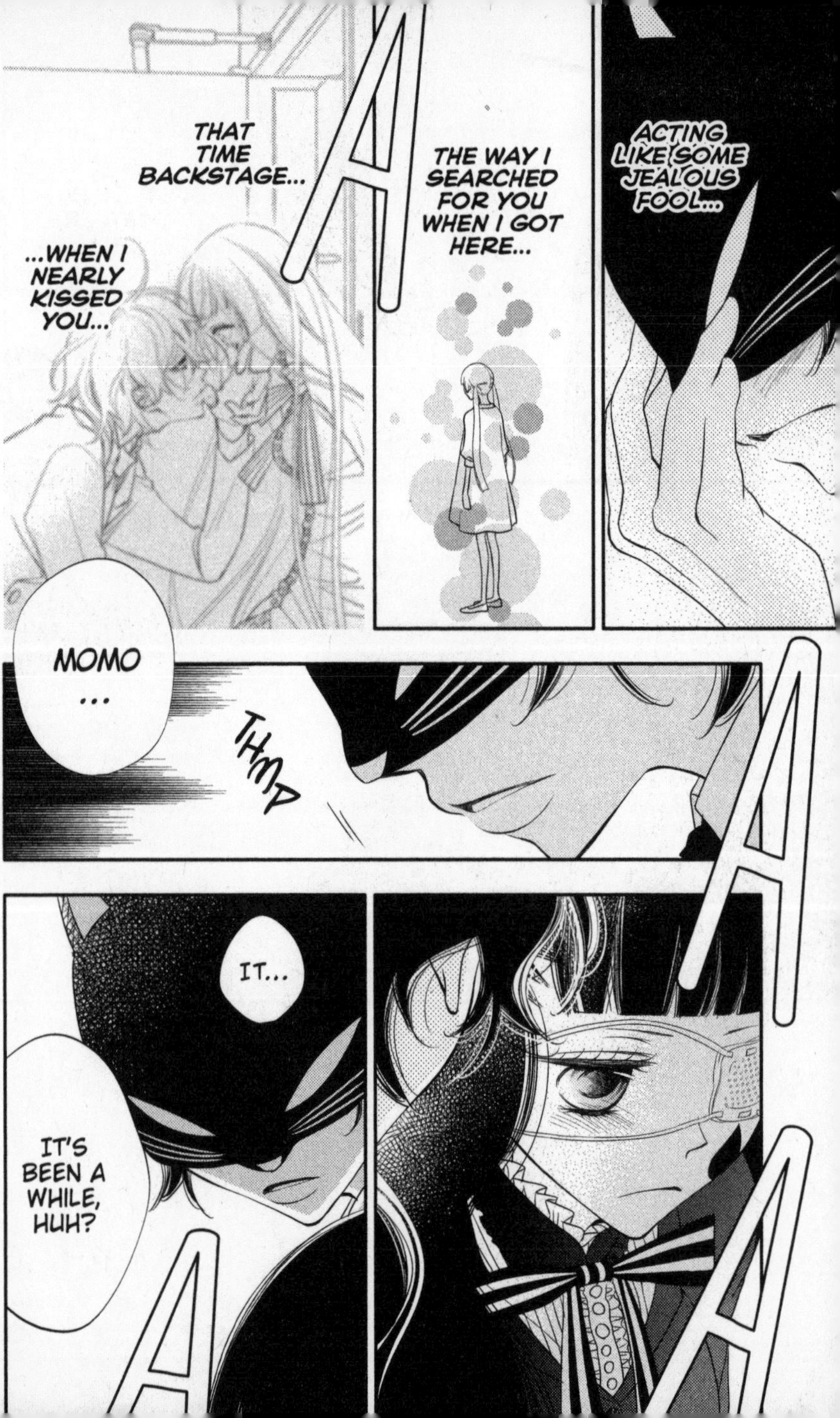
ACTING LIKE SOME JEALOUS FOOL...
THE WAY I SEARCHED FOR YOU WHEN I GOT HERE...
THAT TIME BACKSTAGE...
...WHEN I NEARLY KISSED YOU...
MOMO ...
THMP
IT...
IT'S BEEN A WHILE, HUH?

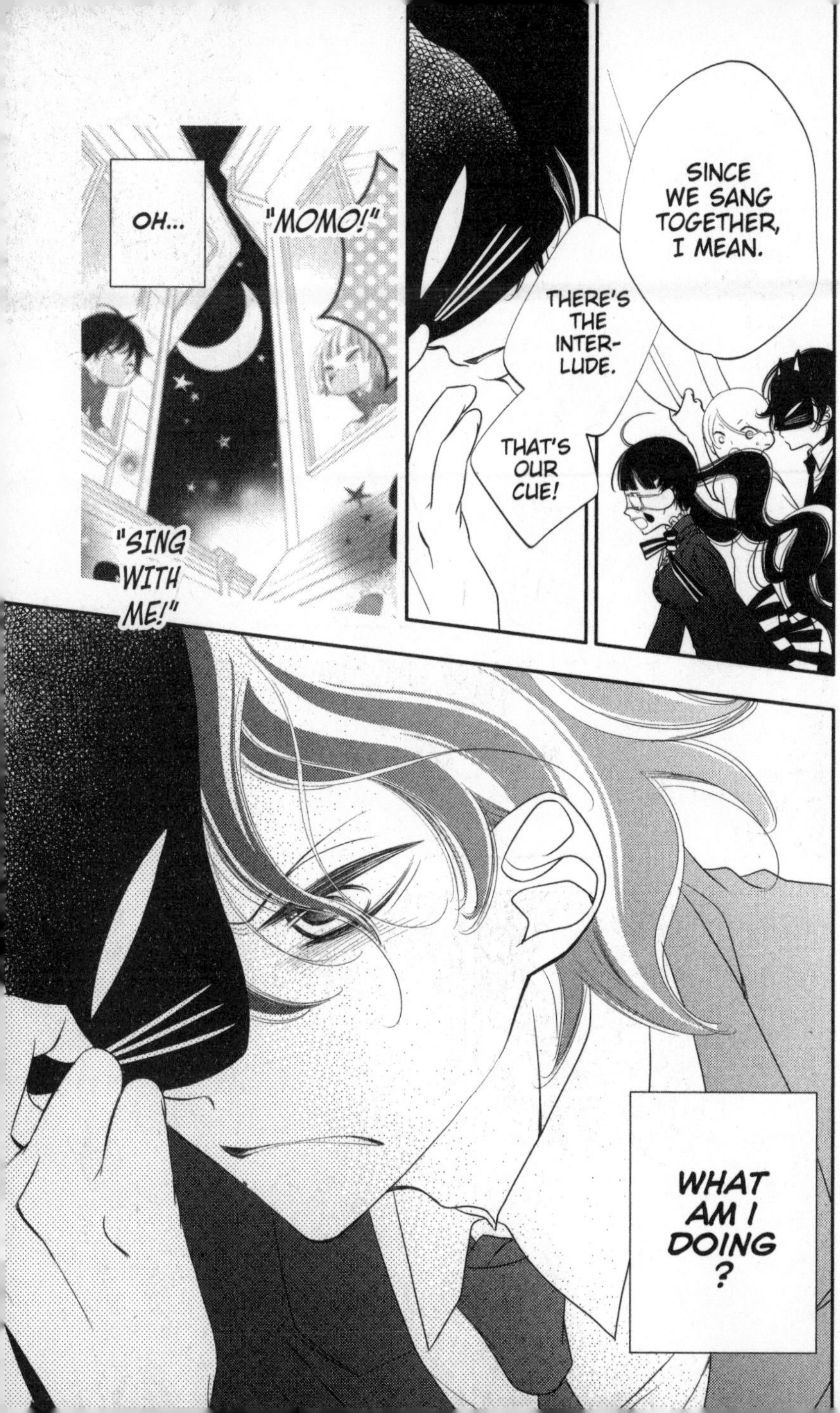
SINCE WE SANG TOGETHER, I MEAN.
THERE'S THE INTER-LUDE.
THAT'S OUR CUE!
"MOMO!"
OH...
"SING WITH ME!"
WHAT AM I DOING?

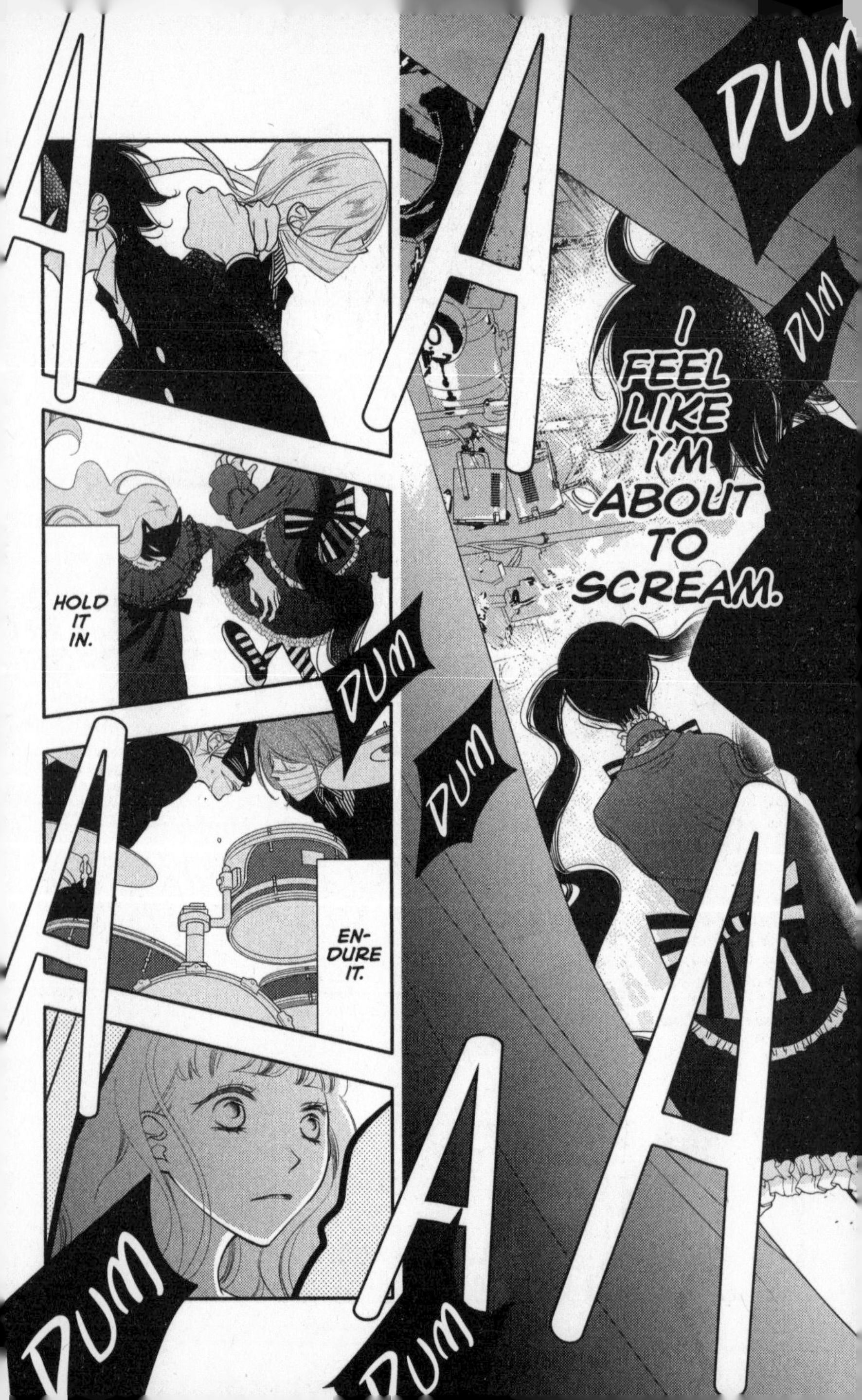
DUM
A
DUM
I FEEL LIKE I'M ABOUT TO SCREAM.
DUM
A
A
DUM
A
HOLD IT IN.
DUM
A
EN-DURE IT.
DUM

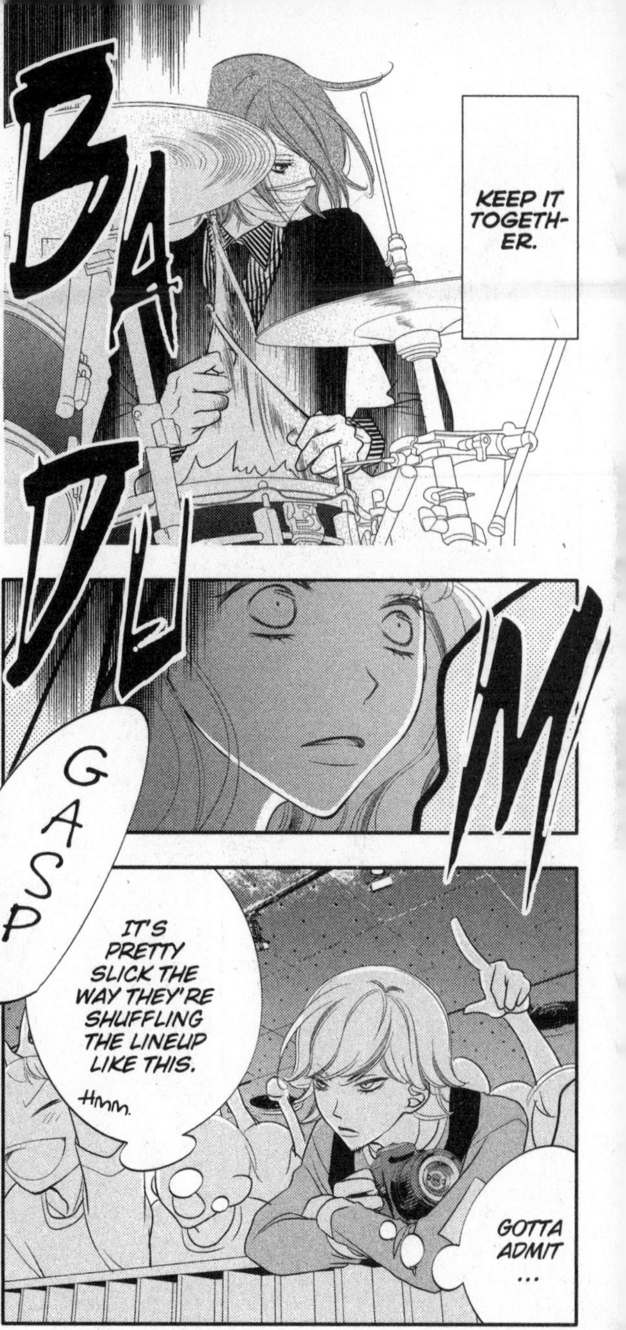
KEEP IT TOGETHER.
BADUM
GASP
GOTTA ADMIT...
IT'S PRETTY SLICK THE WAY THEY'RE SHUFFLING THE LINEUP LIKE THIS.
Hmm.

1

It's great to see you! I'm Ryoko Fukuyama. YAY!

Thank you so much for picking up volume 11 of Anonymous Noise.

This volume's cover is A—better known as Miou. As I was drawing it, I got so excited about how good she looked in purple and black! It turned out dark yet beautiful, and I had a ton of fun drawing it.

My heart's already racing thinking about what I'm going to do with Kuro for volume 12. Anyway, I hope you'll enjoy volume 11!

I LOANED OUT ALL THE OTHERS. NOW I JUST HAVE THE STRAT!

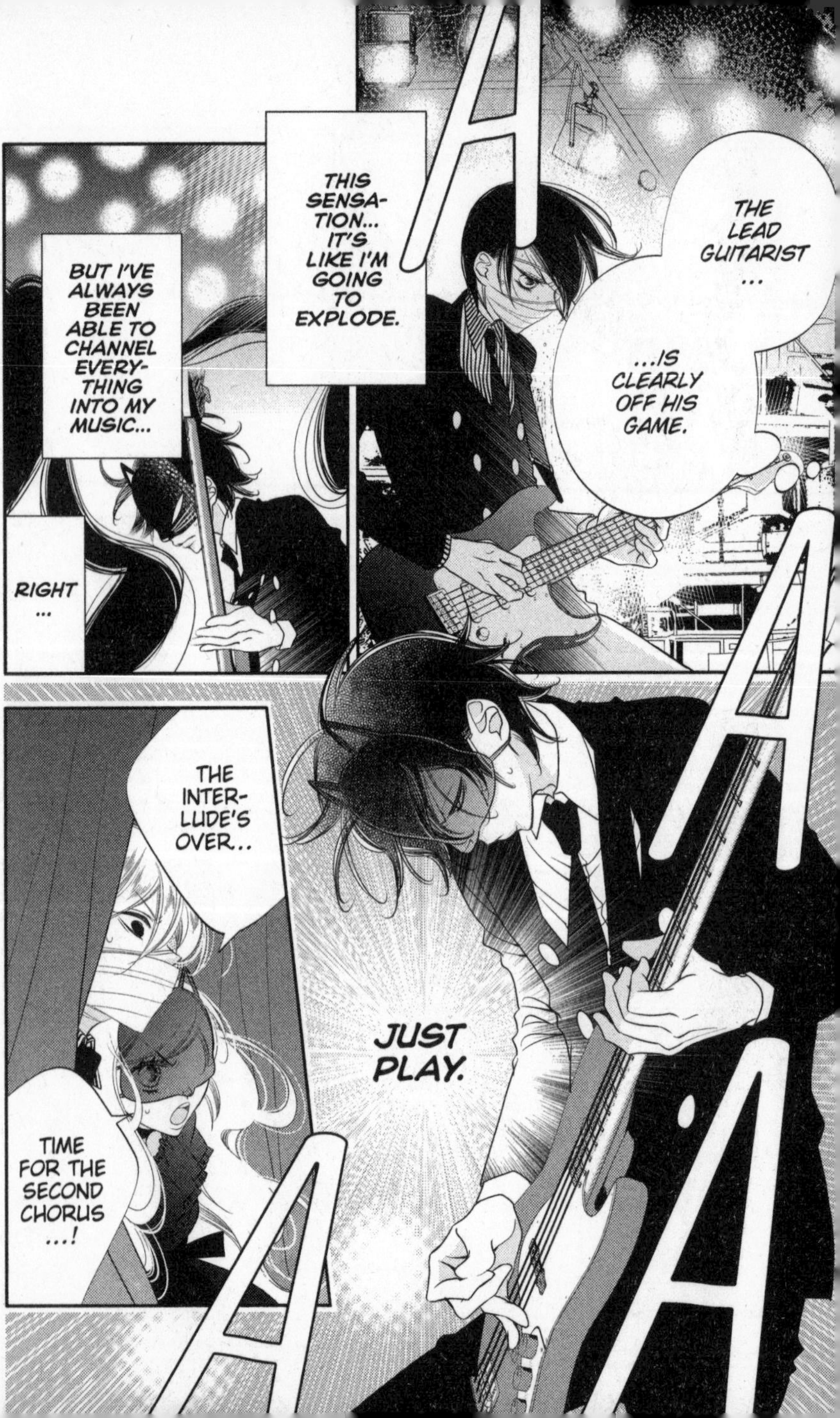
THE LEAD GUITARIST...
...IS CLEARLY OFF HIS GAME.
THIS SENSATION... IT'S LIKE I'M GOING TO EXPLODE.
BUT I'VE ALWAYS BEEN ABLE TO CHANNEL EVERYTHING INTO MY MUSIC...
RIGHT...
AAAAAA
JUST PLAY.
THE INTERLUDE'S OVER...
TIME FOR THE SECOND CHORUS...!

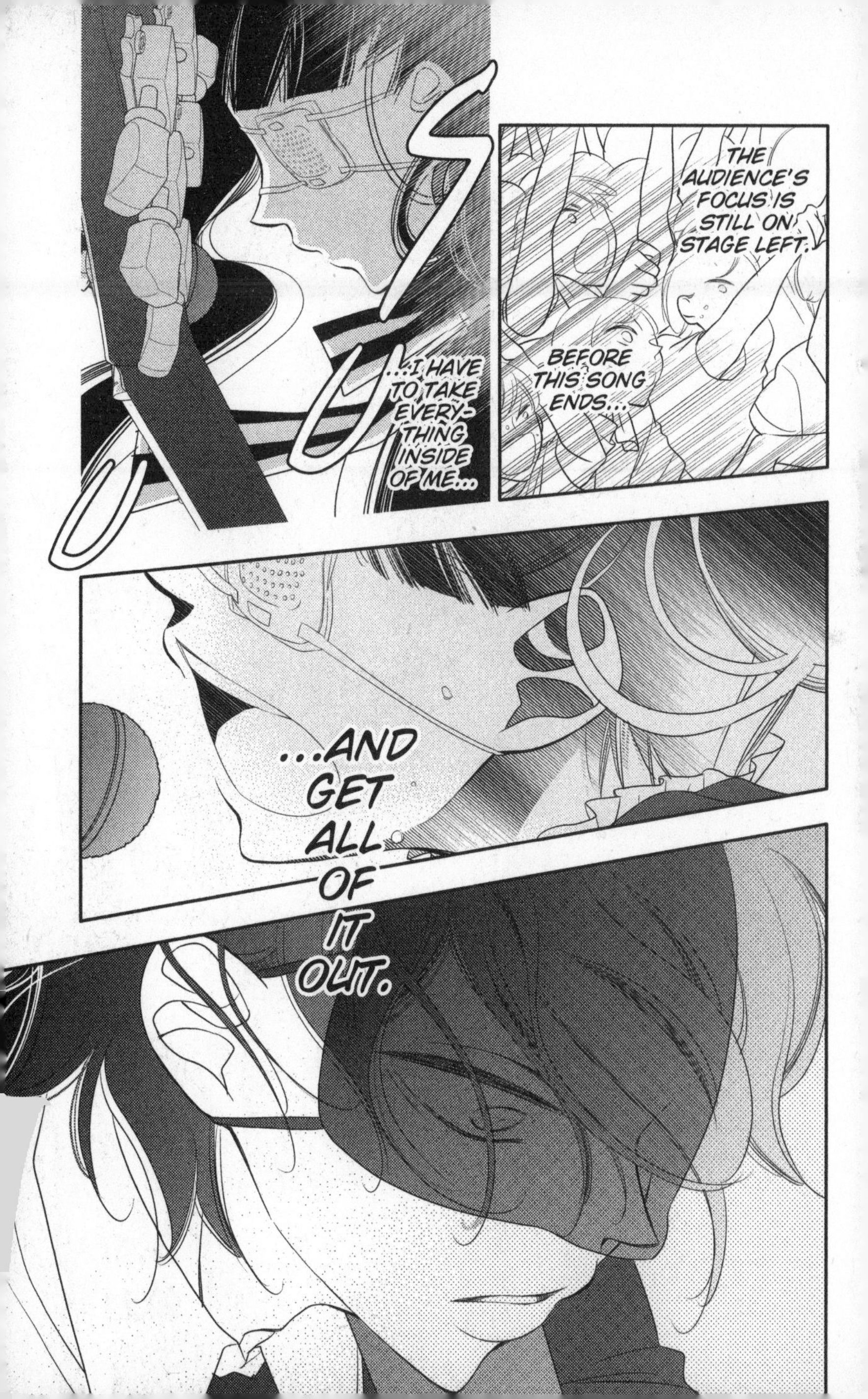
THE AUDIENCE'S FOCUS IS STILL ON STAGE LEFT.
BEFORE THIS SONG ENDS...
...I HAVE TO TAKE EVERY-THING INSIDE OF ME...
SUU
...AND GET ALL OF IT OUT.

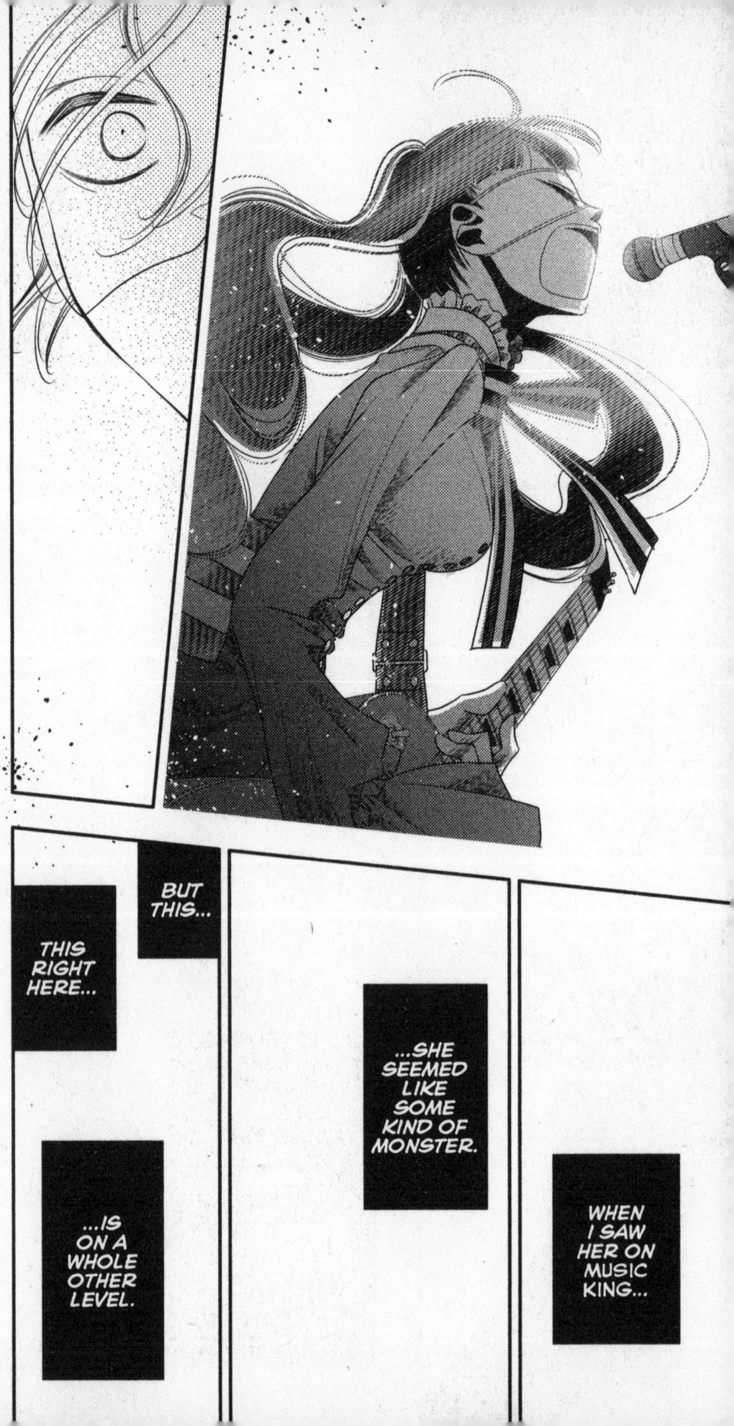
WHEN I SAW HER ON MUSIC KING...
...SHE SEEMED LIKE SOME KIND OF MONSTER.
BUT THIS...
THIS RIGHT HERE...
...IS ON A WHOLE OTHER LEVEL.

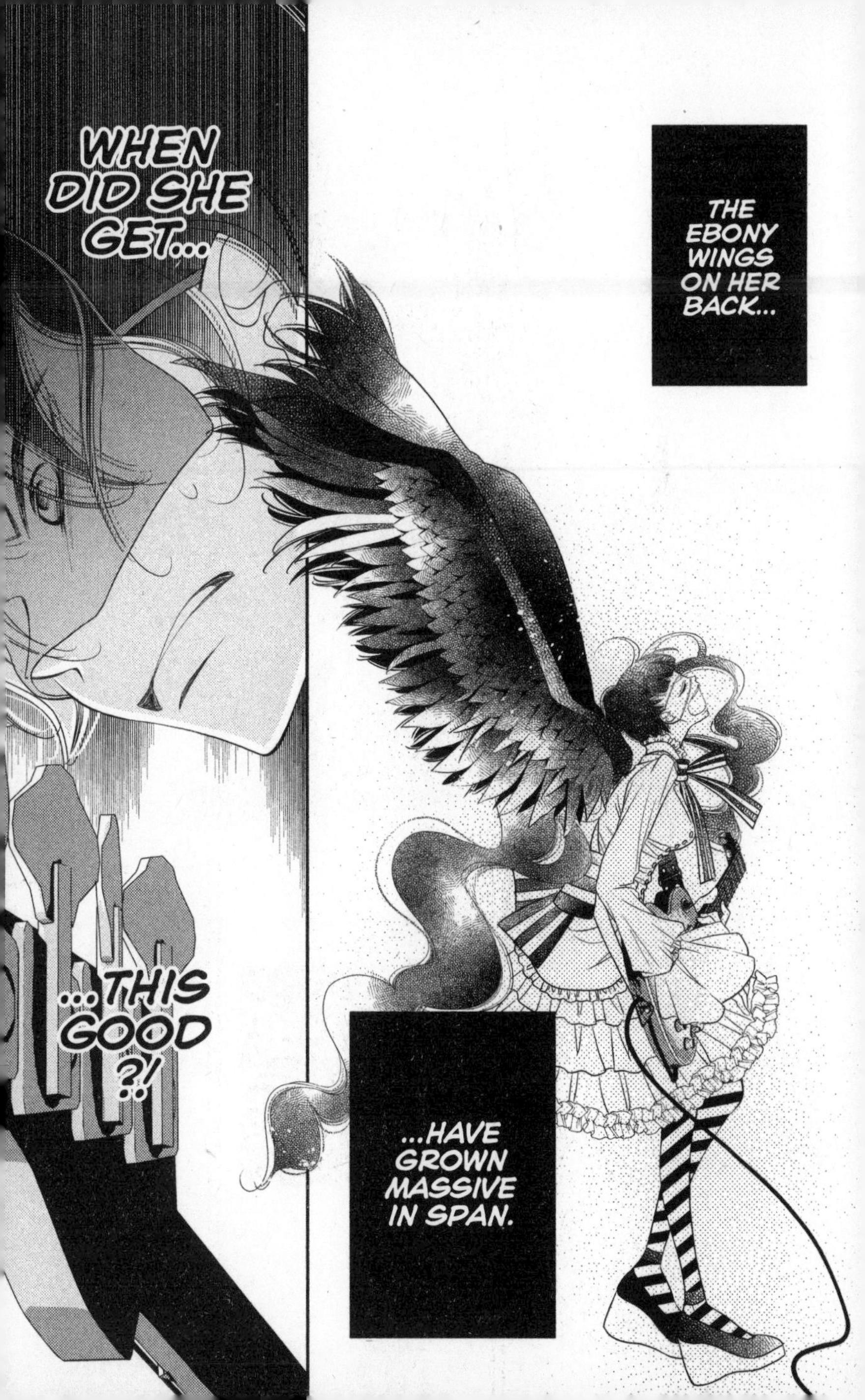
THE EBONY WINGS ON HER BACK...
...HAVE GROWN MASSIVE IN SPAN.
WHEN DID SHE GET...
...THIS GOOD?!

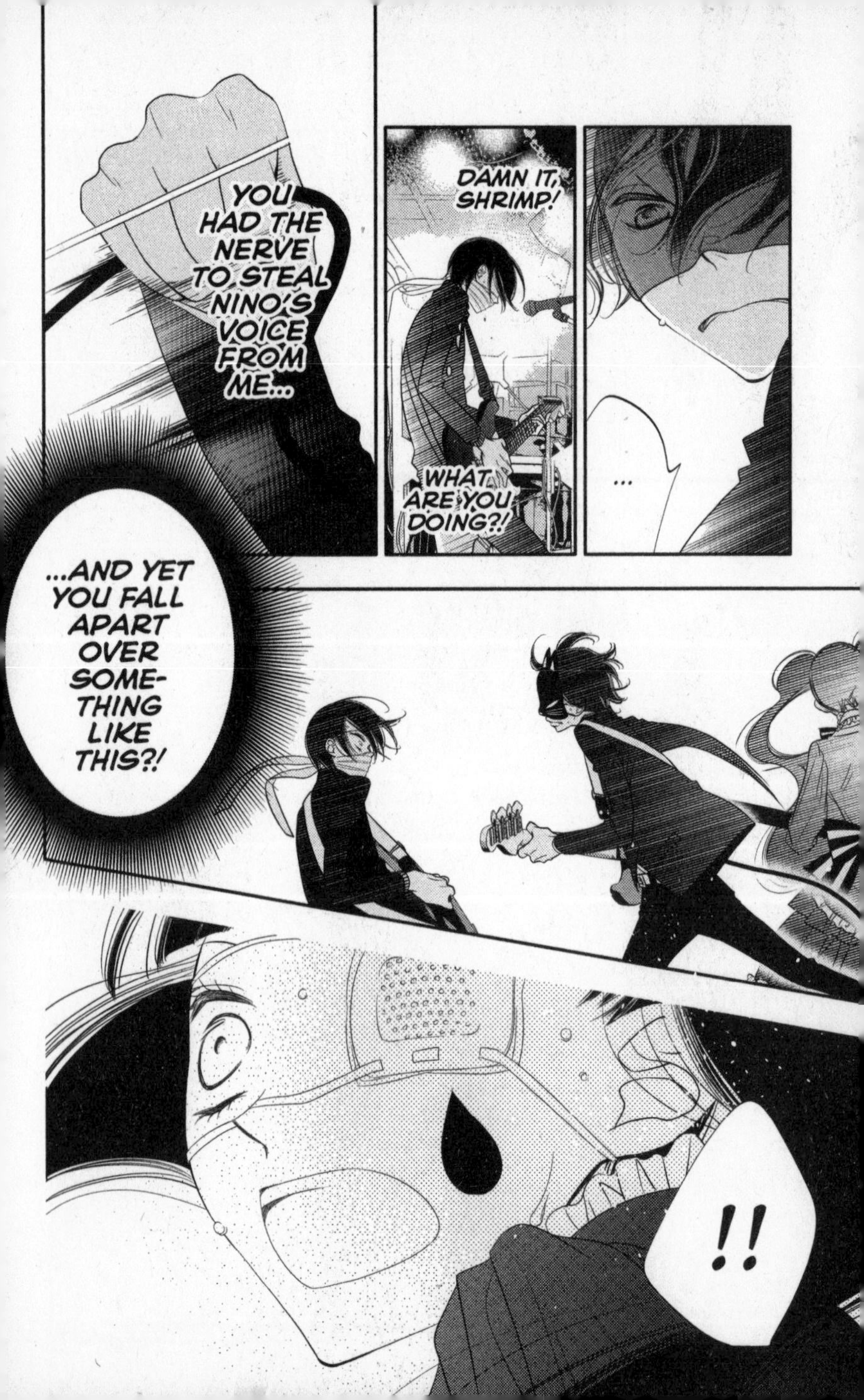
...
DAMN IT, SHRIMP!
WHAT ARE YOU DOING?!
YOU HAD THE NERVE TO STEAL NINO'S VOICE FROM ME...
...AND YET YOU FALL APART OVER SOME-THING LIKE THIS?!
!!

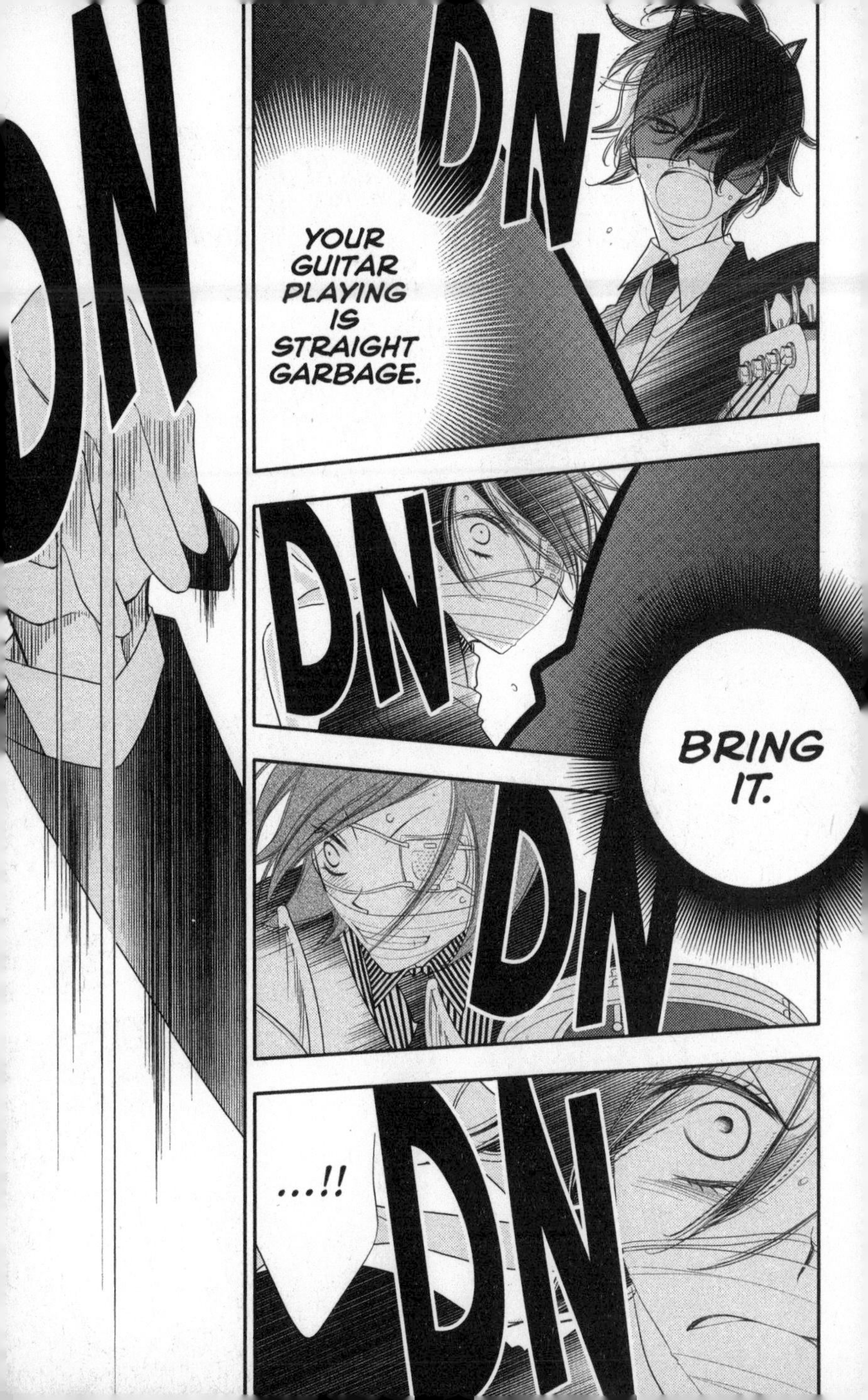
DN
YOUR GUITAR PLAYING IS STRAIGHT GARBAGE.
DN
BRING IT.
DN
DN
...!!
DN

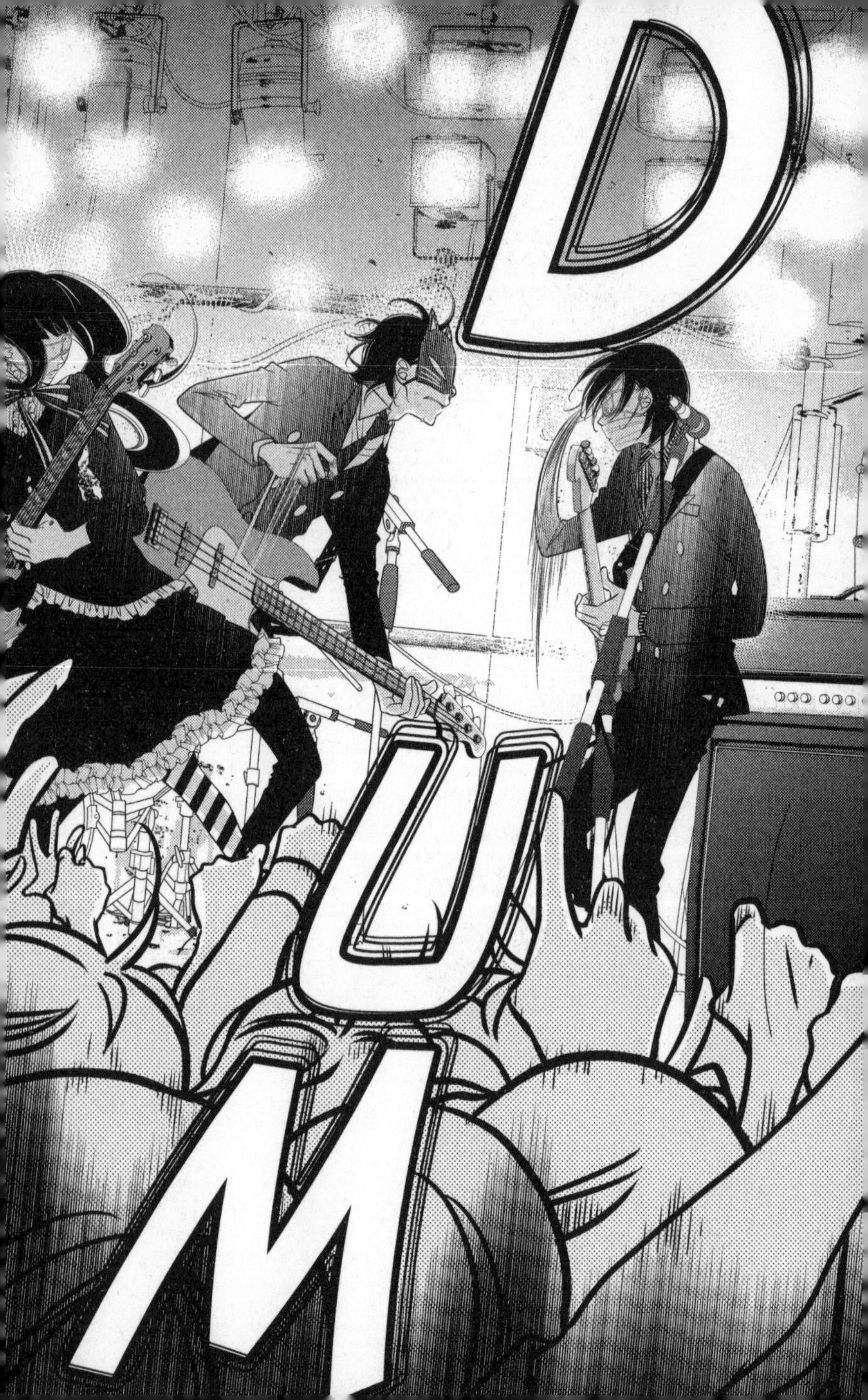
DUM

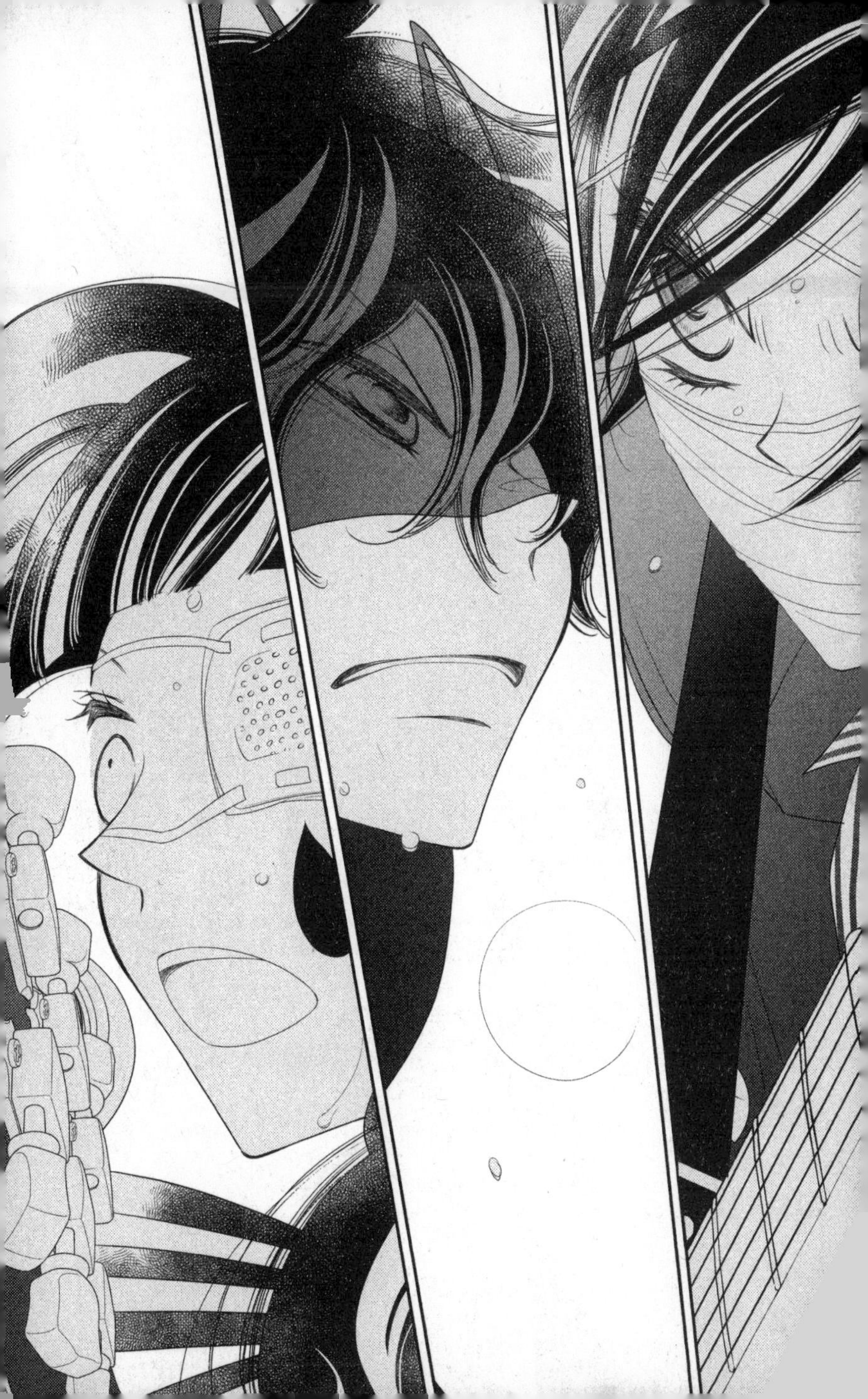

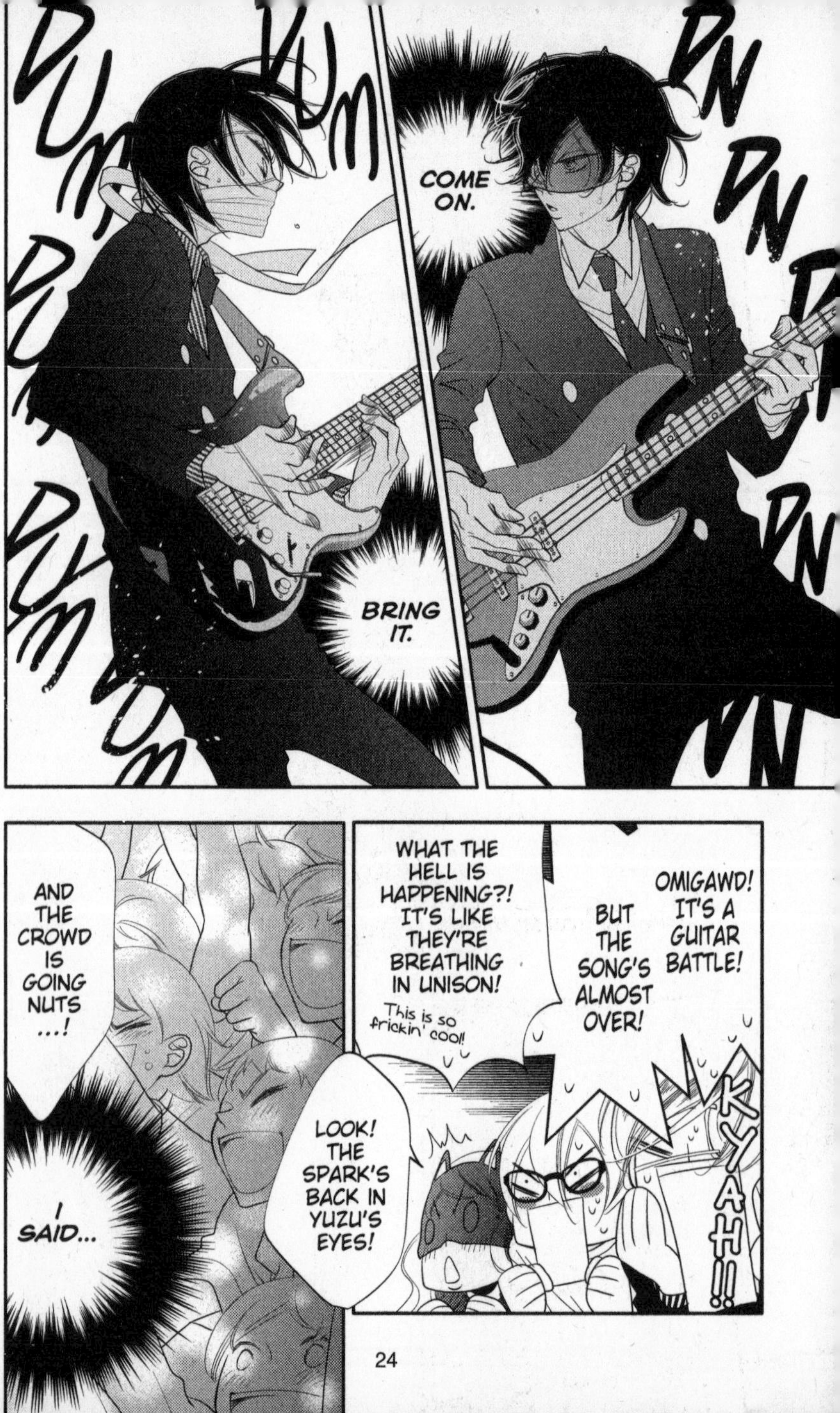
DN DN DN DN DN
COME ON.
DUM DUM DUM DUM DUM
BRING IT.
OMIGAWD! IT'S A GUITAR BATTLE!
BUT THE SONG'S ALMOST OVER!
WHAT THE HELL IS HAPPENING?! IT'S LIKE THEY'RE BREATHING IN UNISON!
This is so frickin' cool!
KYAAH!!
LOOK! THE SPARK'S BACK IN YUZU'S EYES!
AND THE CROWD IS GOING NUTS...!
I SAID...

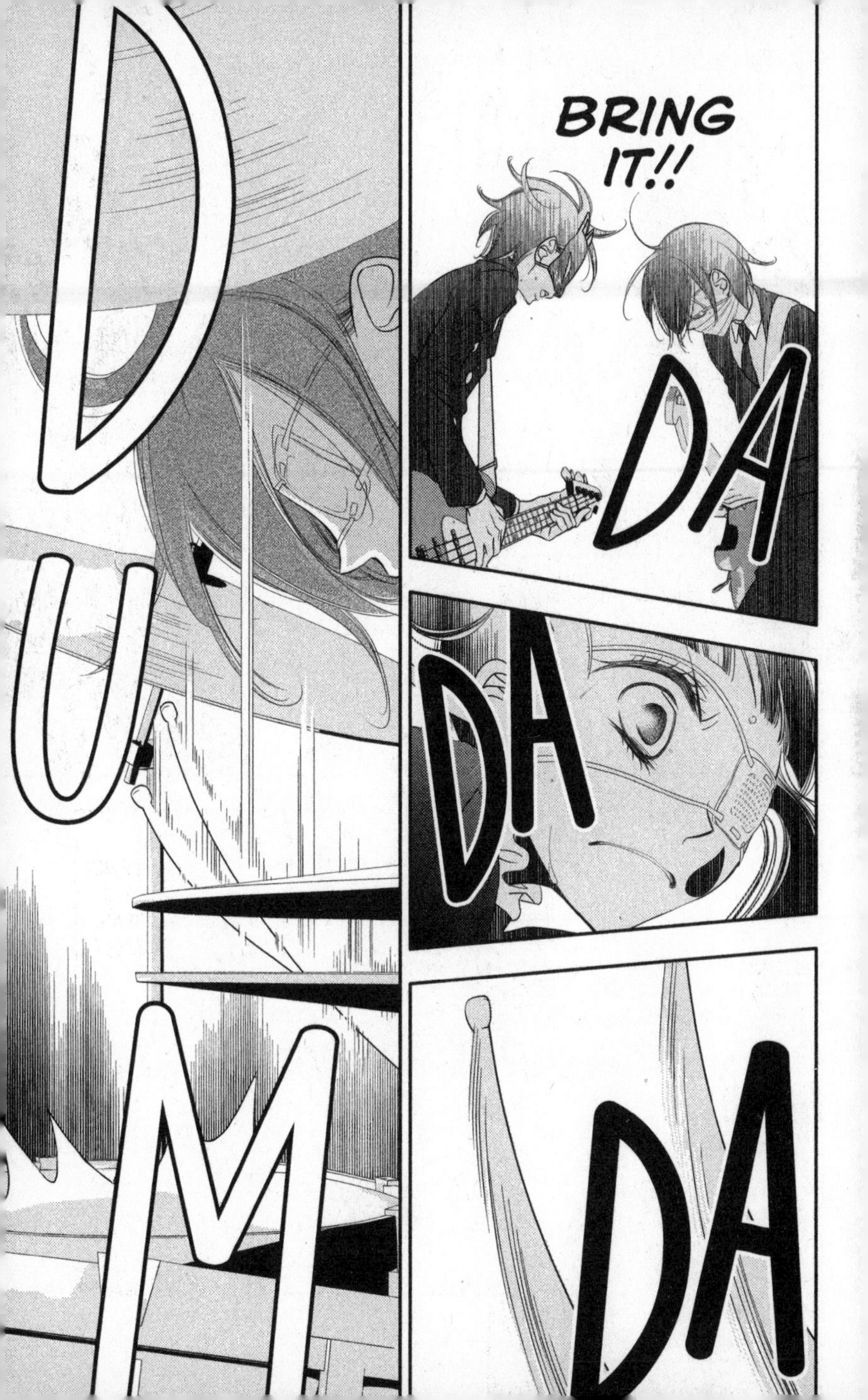
BRING IT!!
DA
DA
DA
DUM

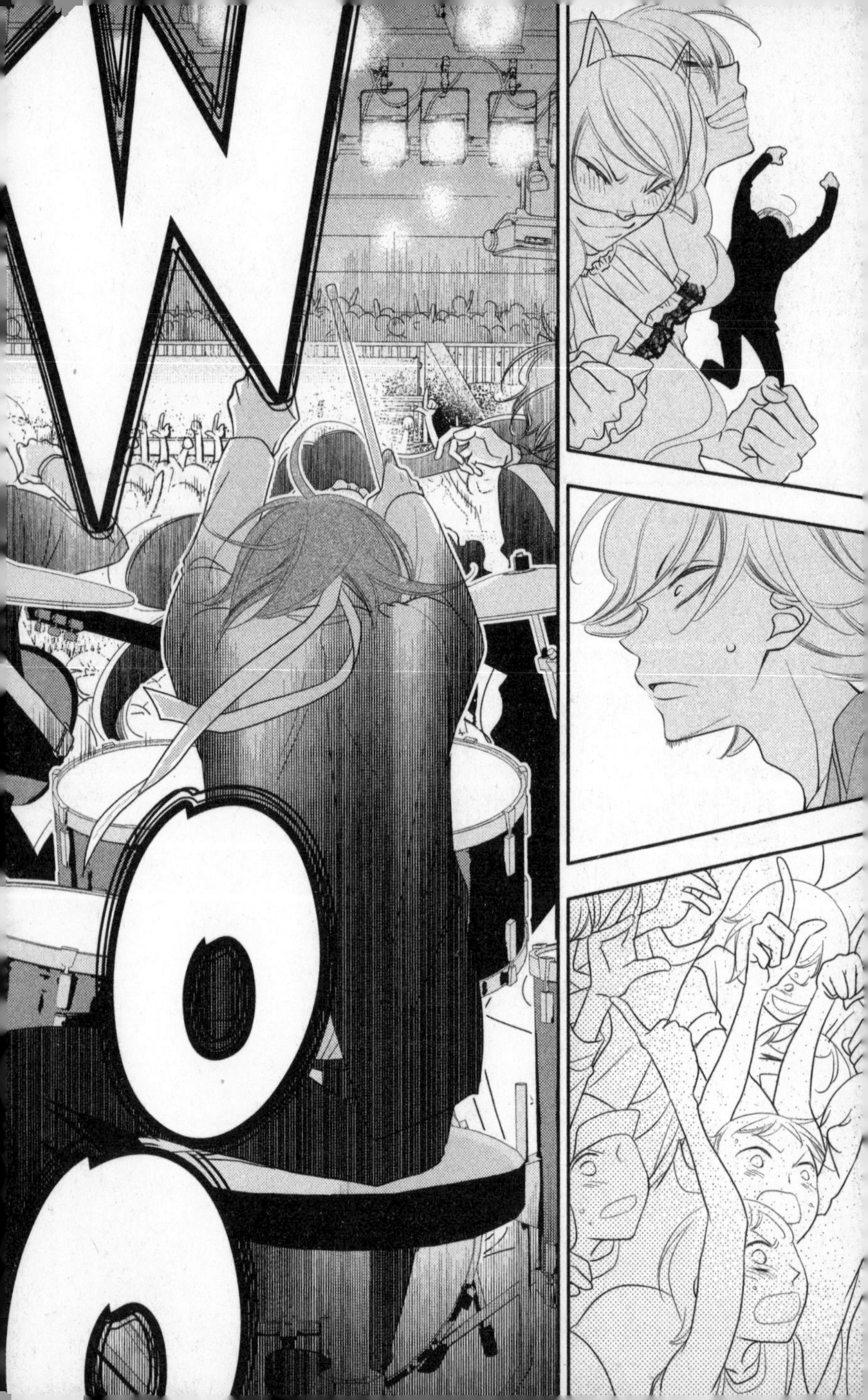
WOO

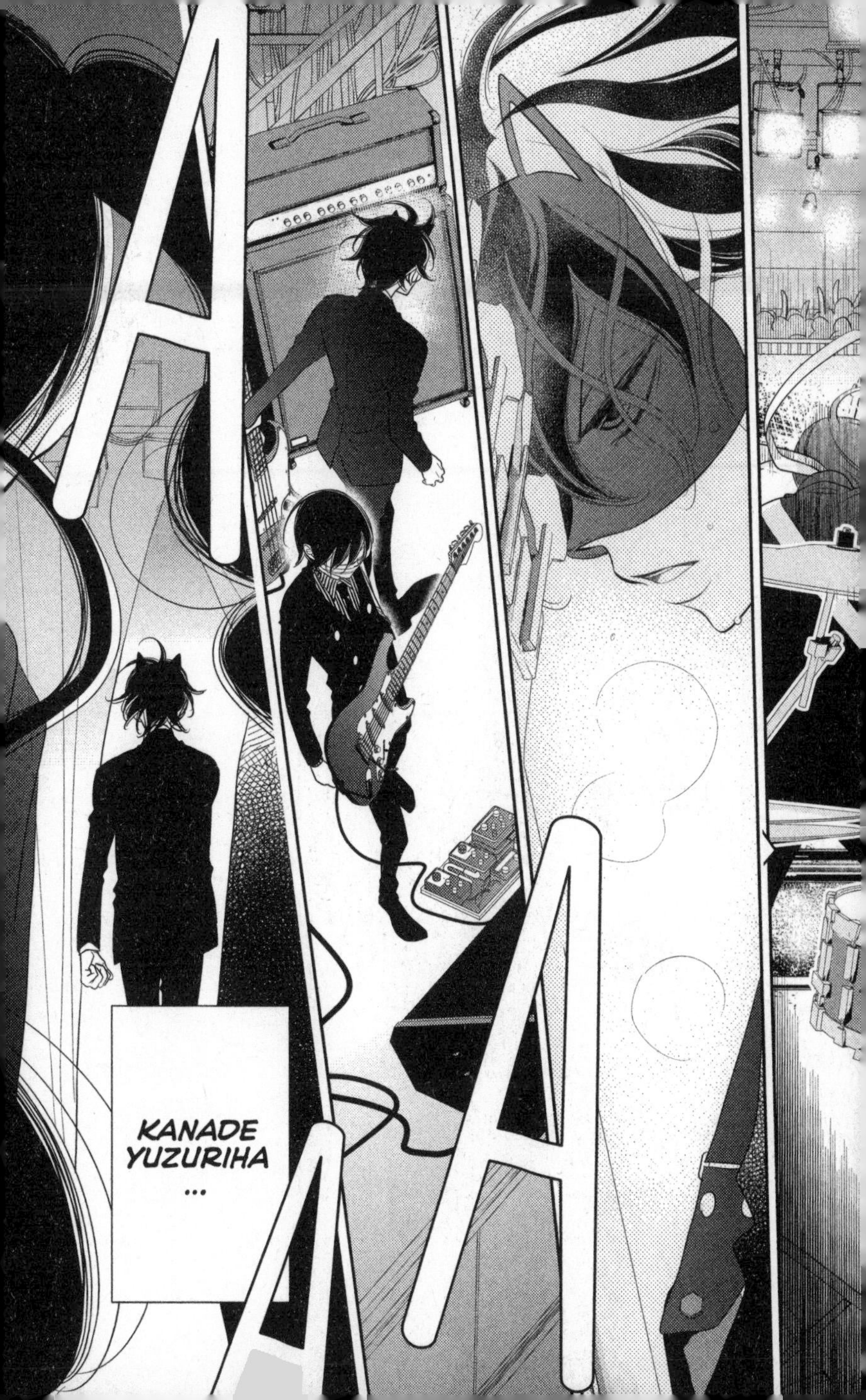
A
A
A
A
KANADE YUZURIHA ...

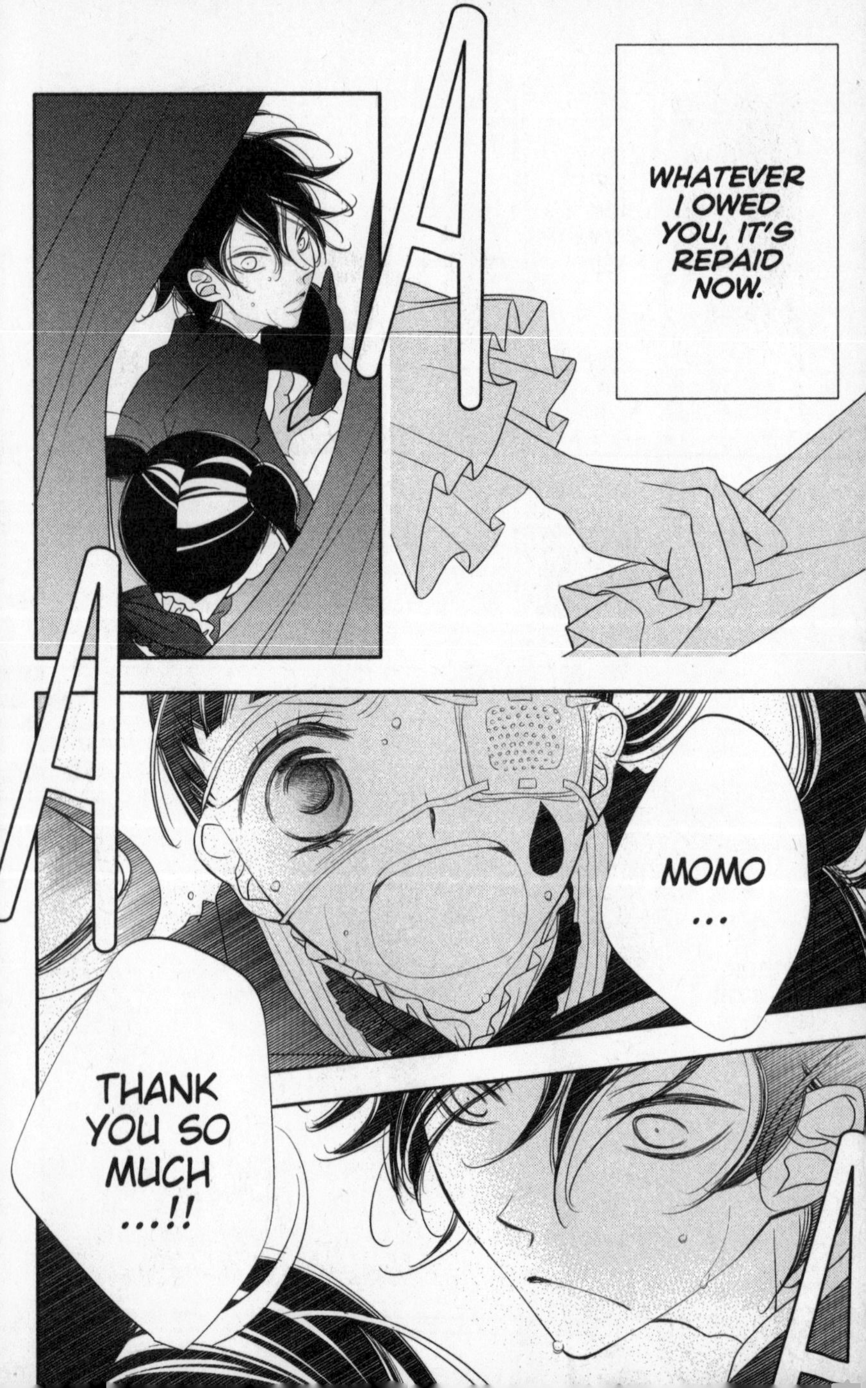
WHATEVER I OWED YOU, IT'S REPAID NOW.
AAAA
MOMO ...
THANK YOU SO MUCH ...!!

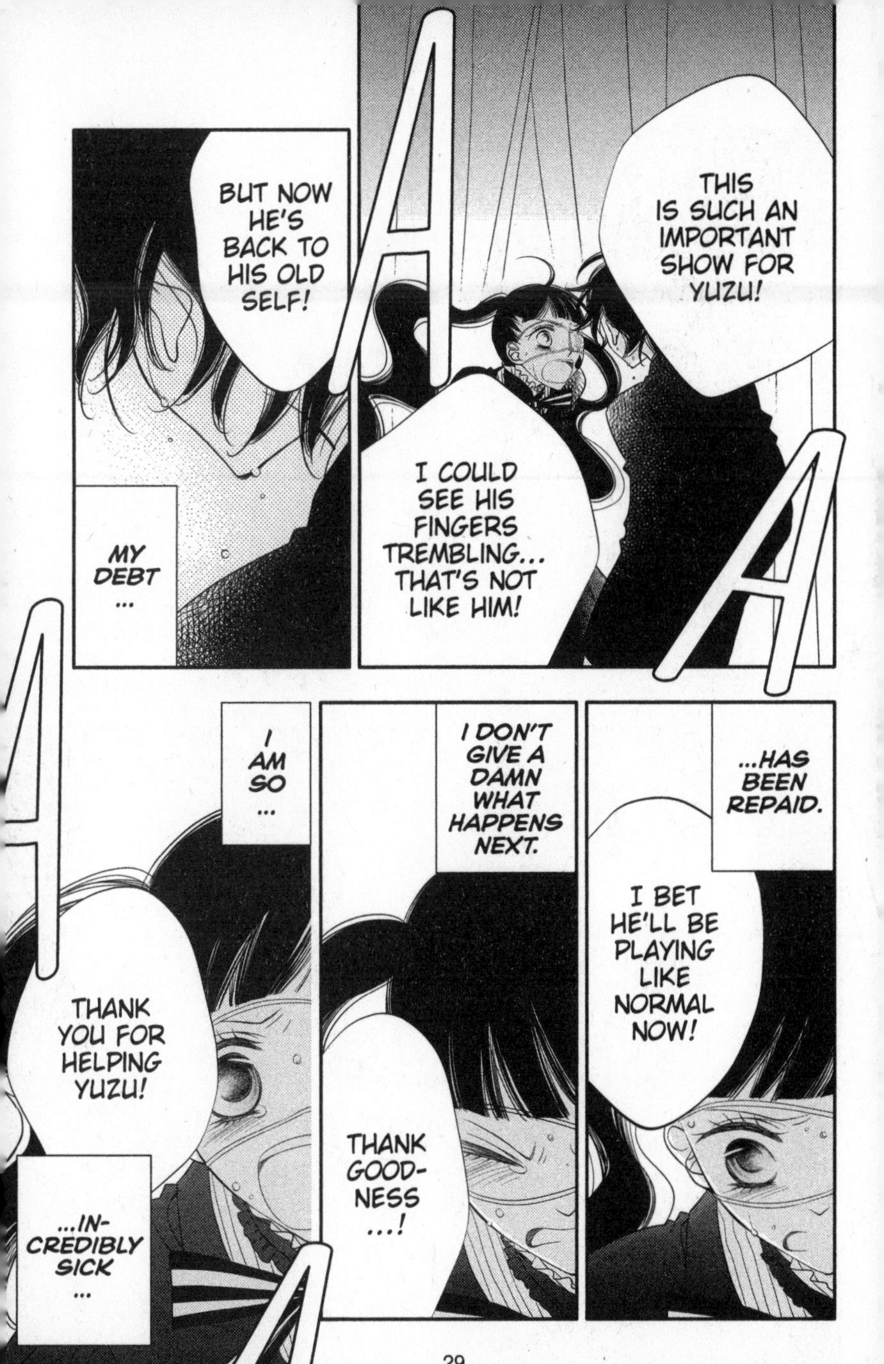
THIS IS SUCH AN IMPORTANT SHOW FOR YUZU!
I COULD SEE HIS FINGERS TREMBLING... THAT'S NOT LIKE HIM!
BUT NOW HE'S BACK TO HIS OLD SELF!
MY DEBT ...
...HAS BEEN REPAID.
I BET HE'LL BE PLAYING LIKE NORMAL NOW!
I DON'T GIVE A DAMN WHAT HAPPENS NEXT.
THANK GOOD-NESS ...!
I AM SO ...
THANK YOU FOR HELPING YUZU!
...IN-CREDIBLY SICK ...

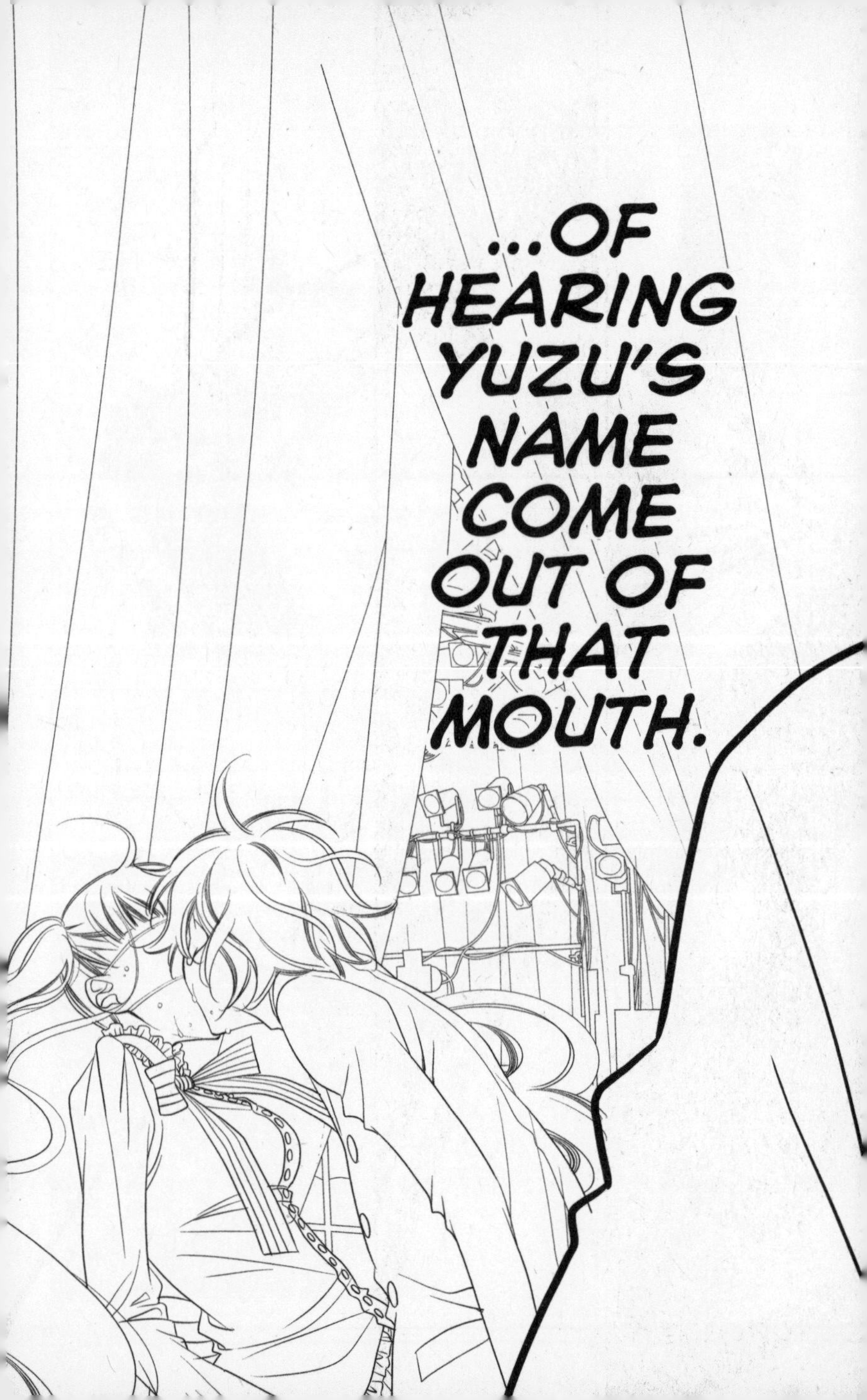
...OF HEARING YUZU'S NAME COME OUT OF THAT MOUTH.

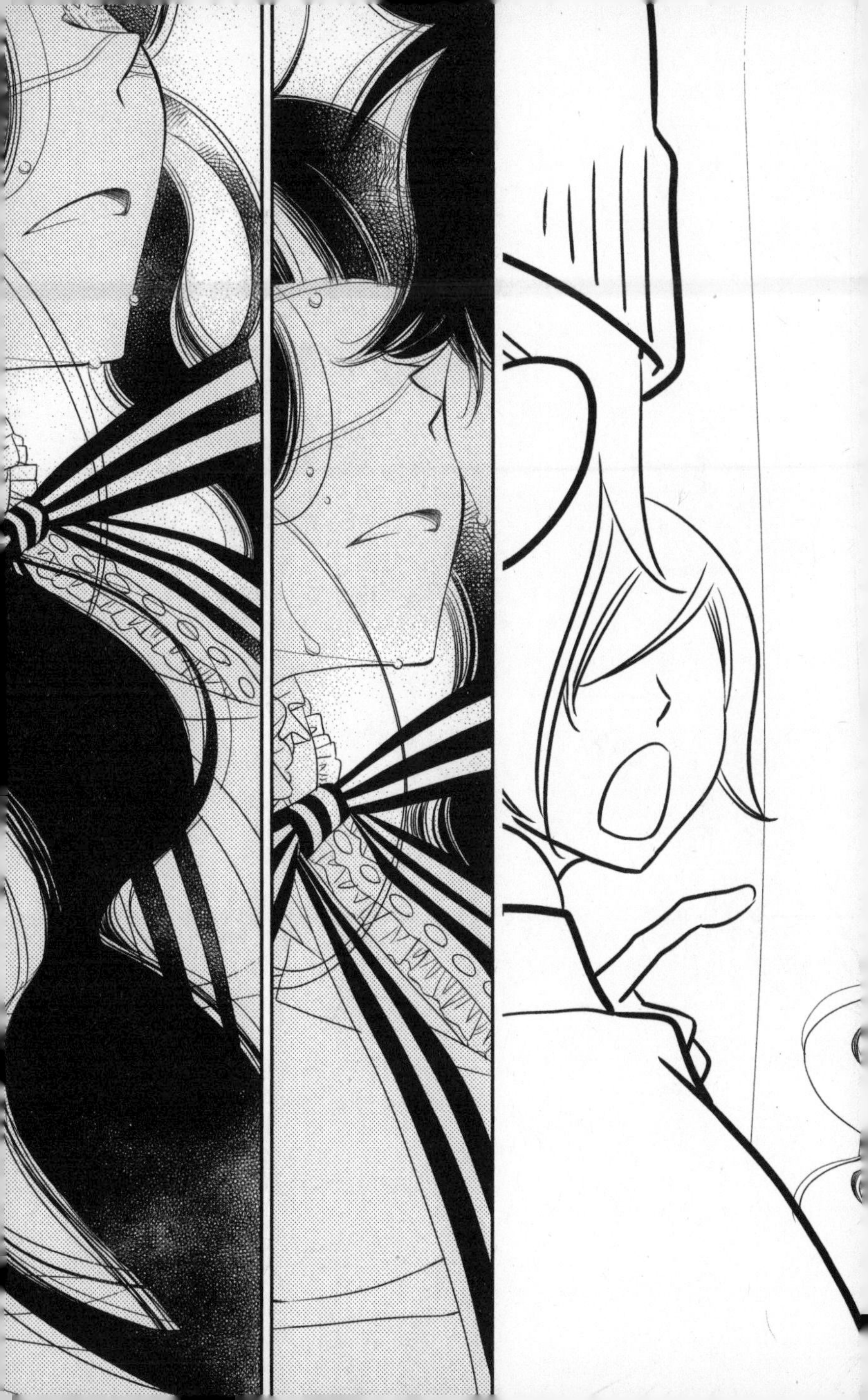

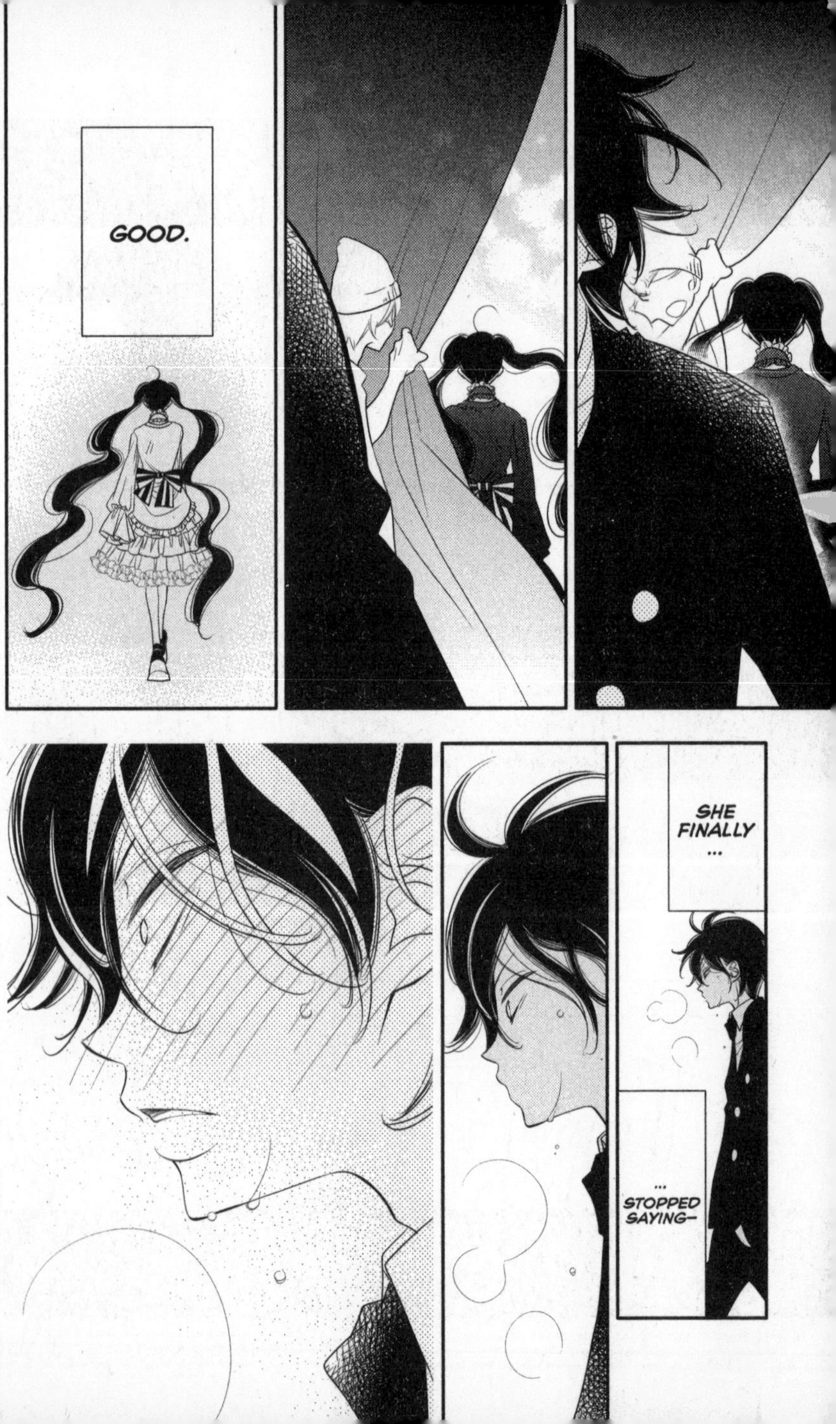
GOOD.
SHE FINALLY ...
... STOPPED SAYING–

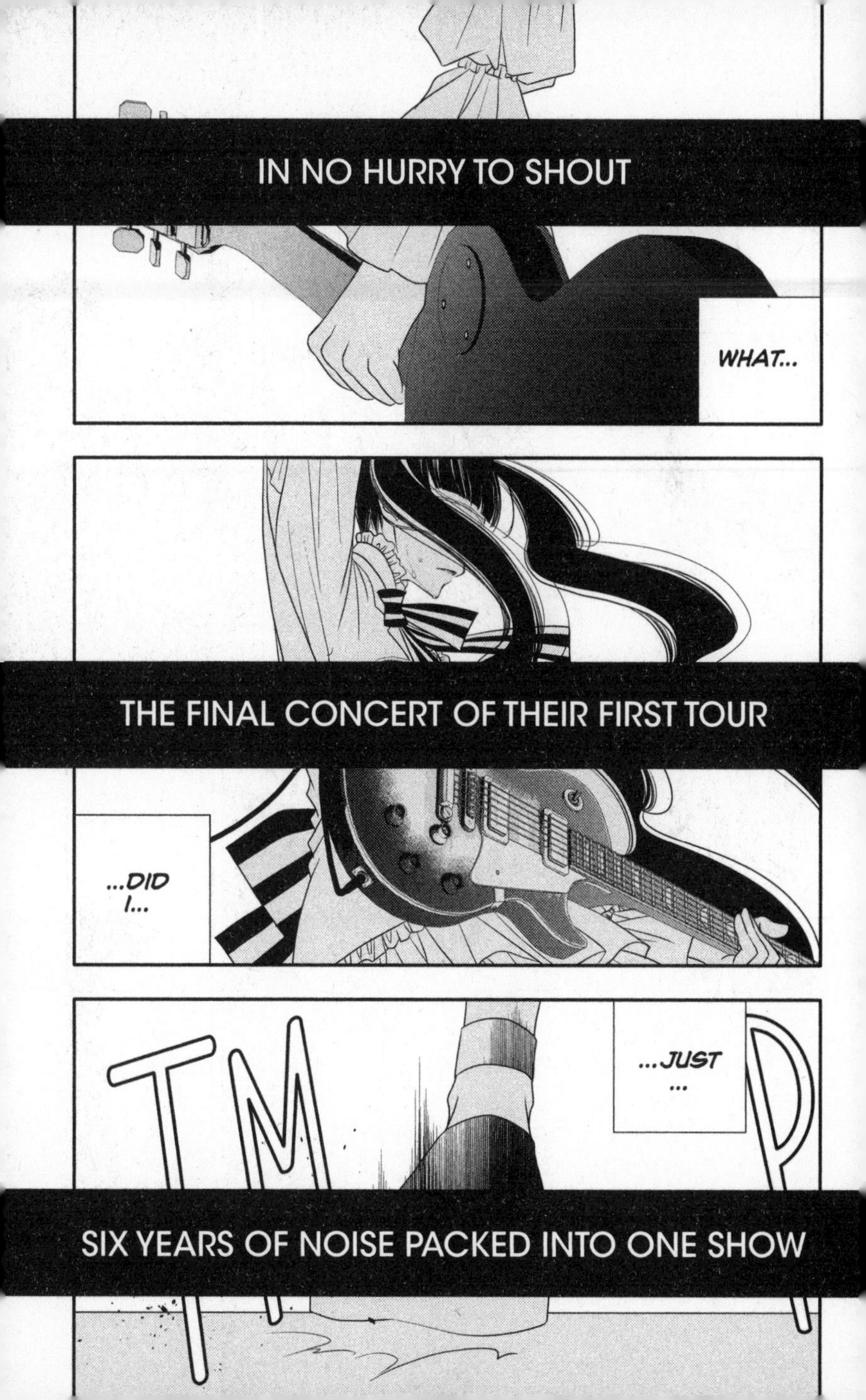
IN NO HURRY TO SHOUT
WHAT...
THE FINAL CONCERT OF THEIR FIRST TOUR
...DID I...
...JUST ...
SIX YEARS OF NOISE PACKED INTO ONE SHOW

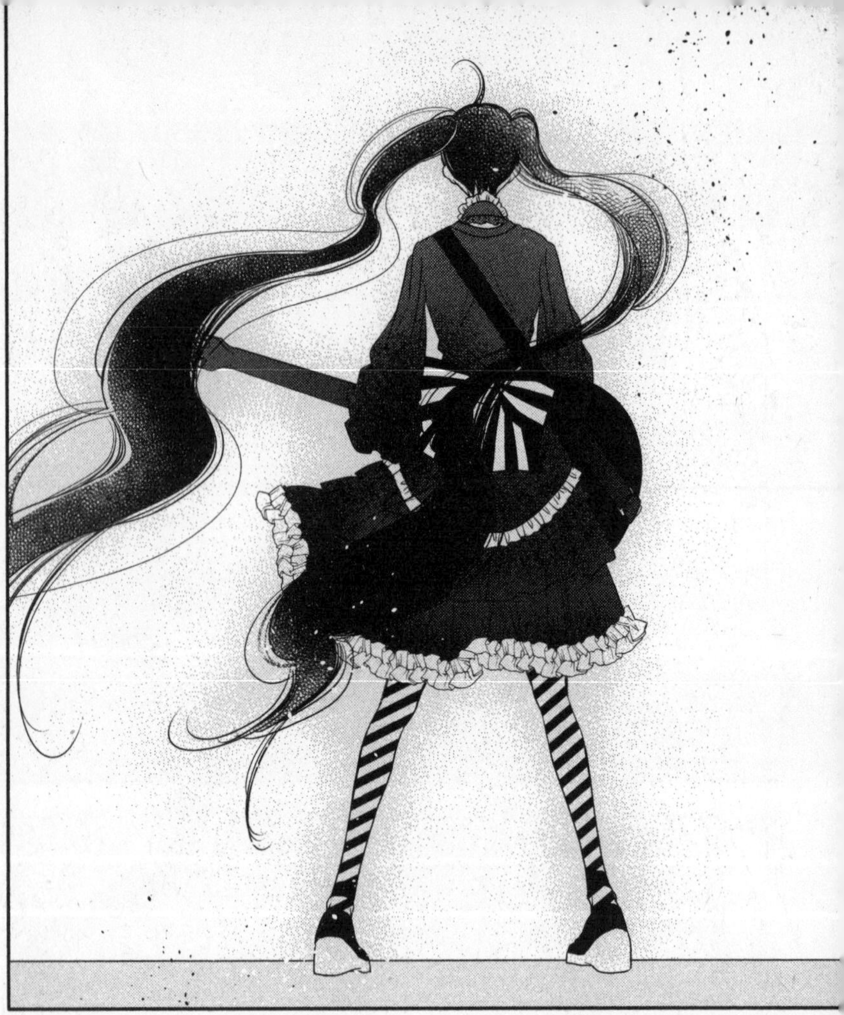

IT BEGINS.

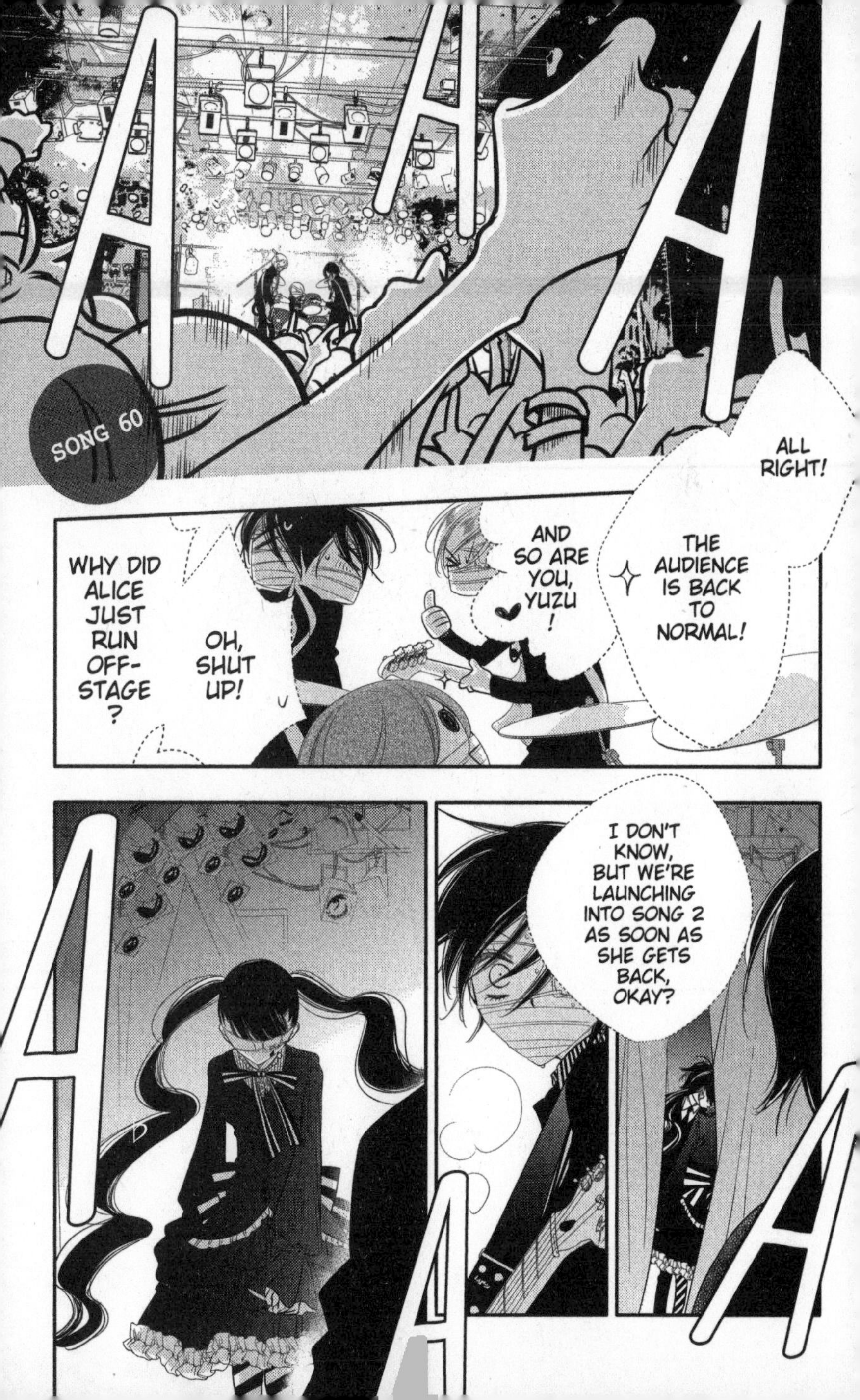
AAAA
SONG 60
ALL RIGHT!
THE AUDIENCE IS BACK TO NORMAL!
AND SO ARE YOU, YUZU!
OH, SHUT UP!
WHY DID ALICE JUST RUN OFF-STAGE?
I DON'T KNOW, BUT WE'RE LAUNCHING INTO SONG 2 AS SOON AS SHE GETS BACK, OKAY?
AAAA

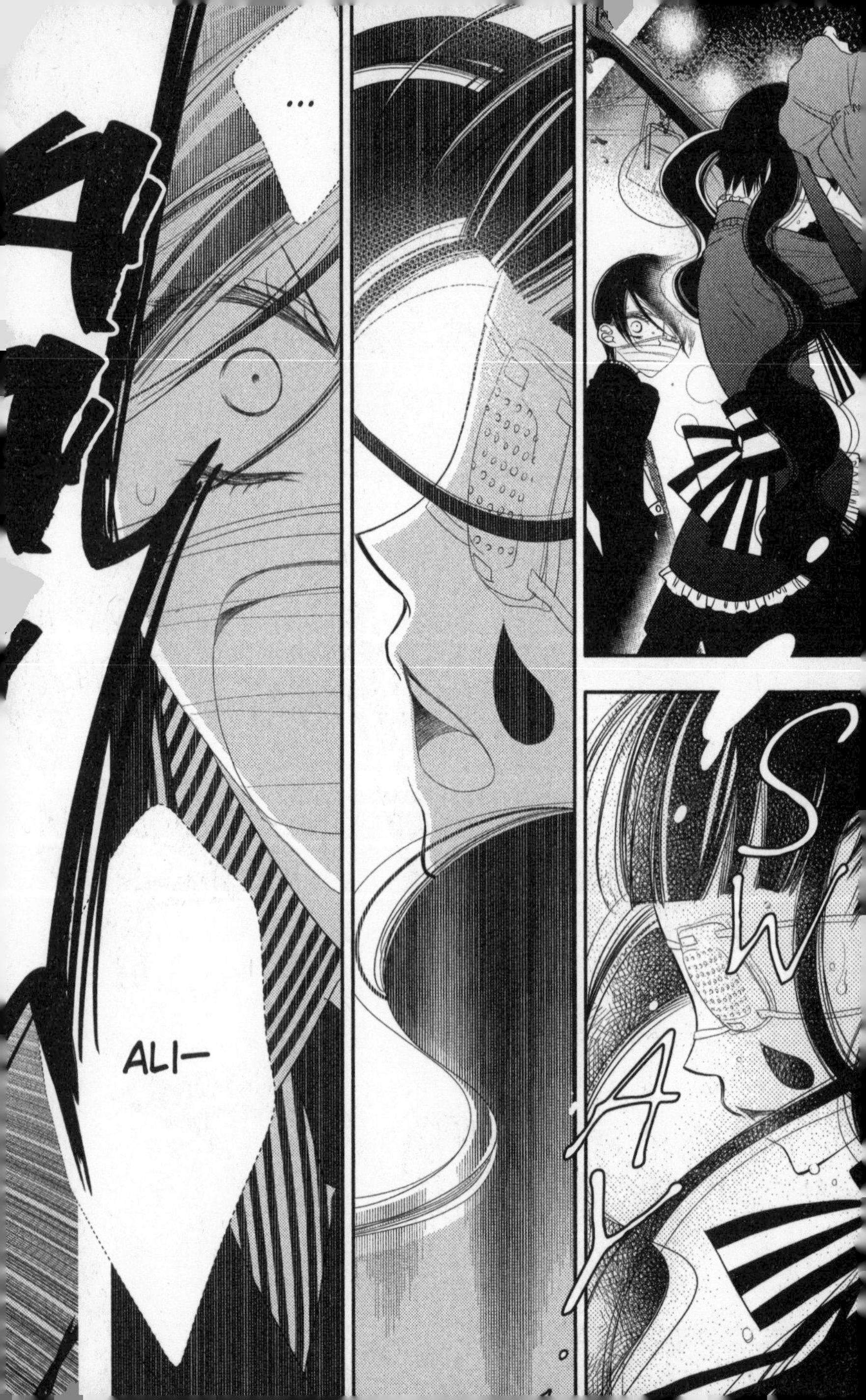
SWAY
...
ALI—

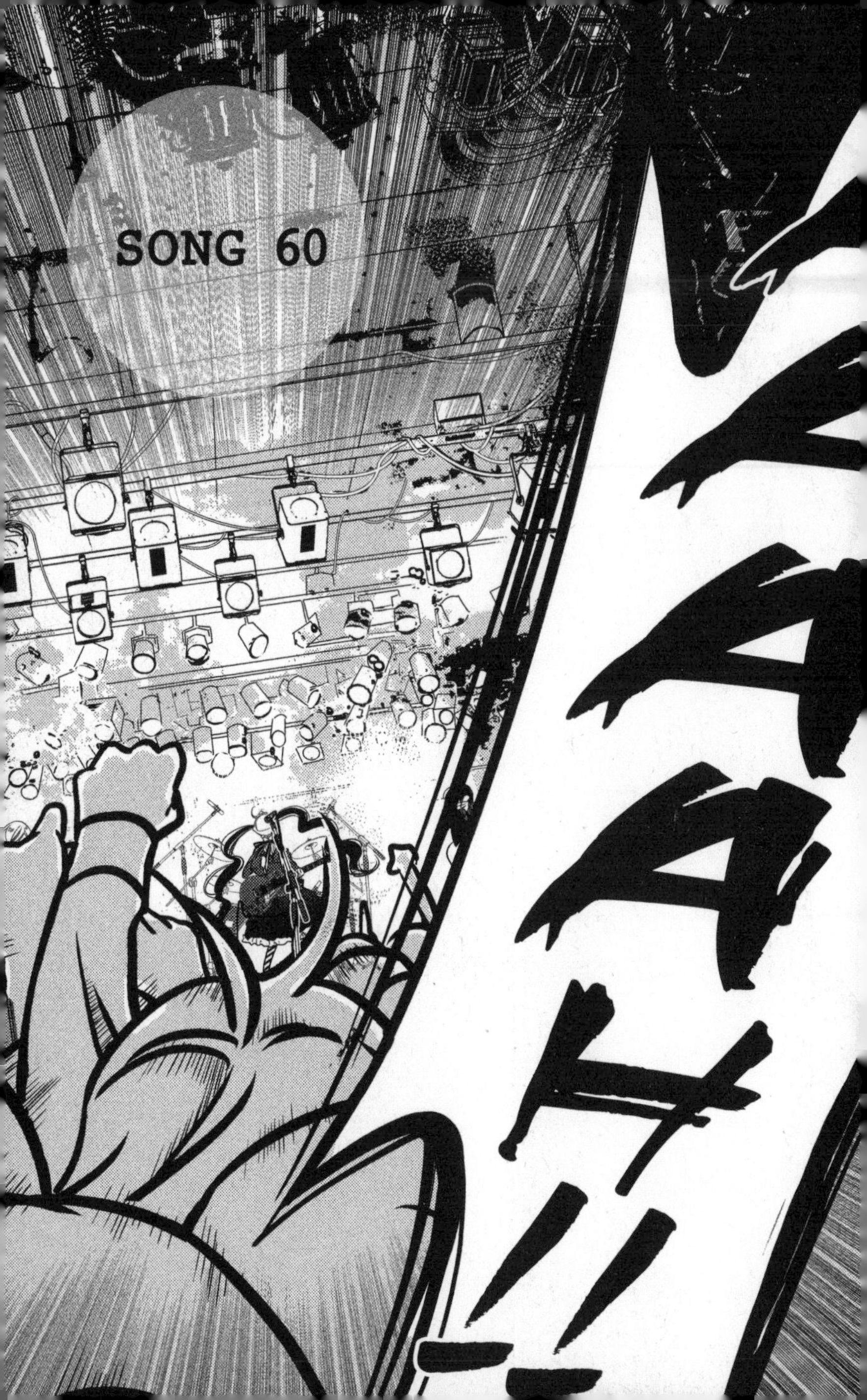
SONG 60

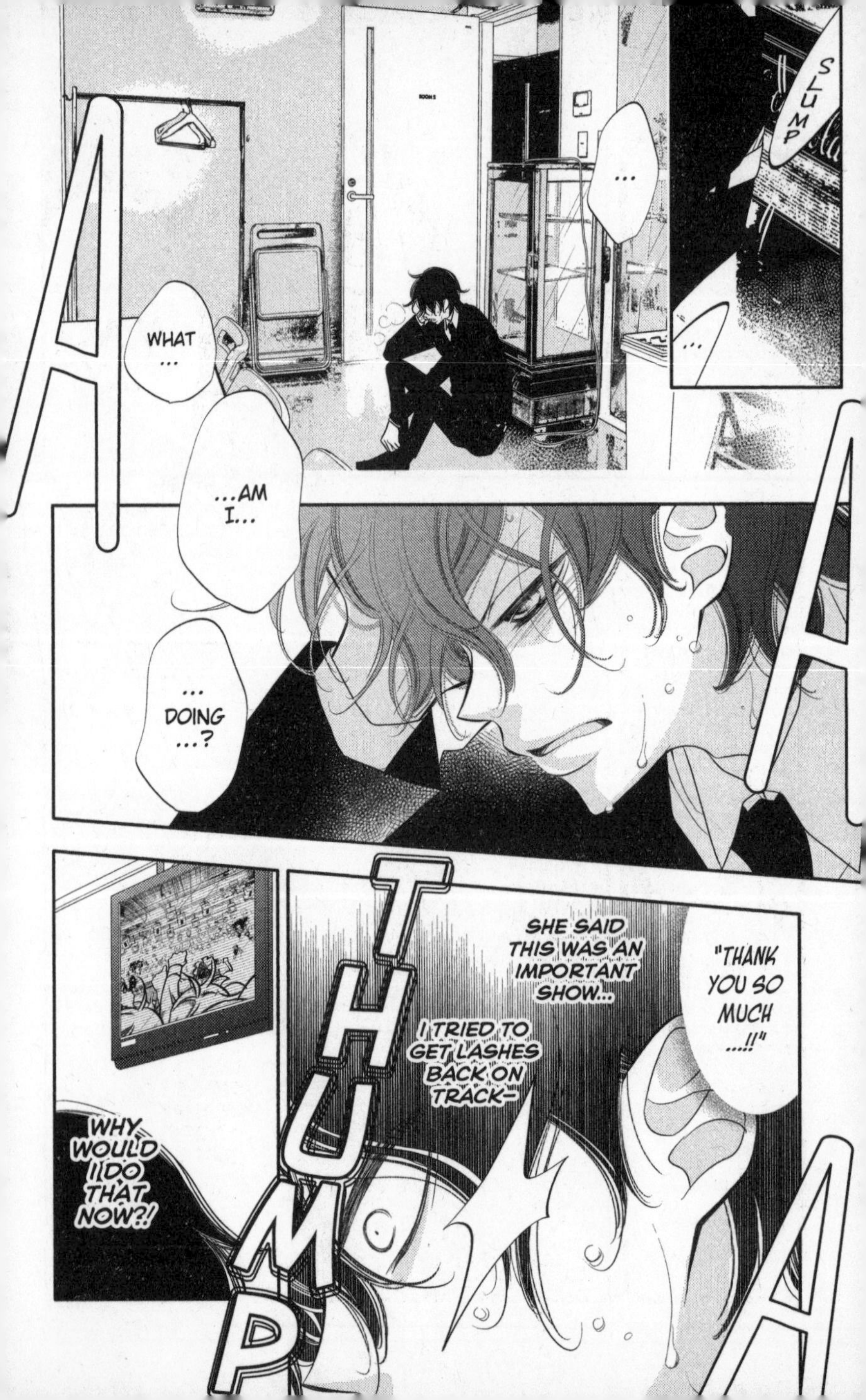
SLUMP
...
...
WHAT ...
...AM I...
... DOING ...?
AAAA
"THANK YOU SO MUCH ...!!"
SHE SAID THIS WAS AN IMPORTANT SHOW...
I TRIED TO GET LASHES BACK ON TRACK—
WHY WOULD I DO THAT NOW?!
THUMP

2

We've announced this in the magazine and online already, but if you haven't heard... Anonymous Noise is going to be a live-action movie! Can you believe that? I still can't believe it myself! I actually heard about it even before I knew about the anime, just a few days after Sora went to heaven.

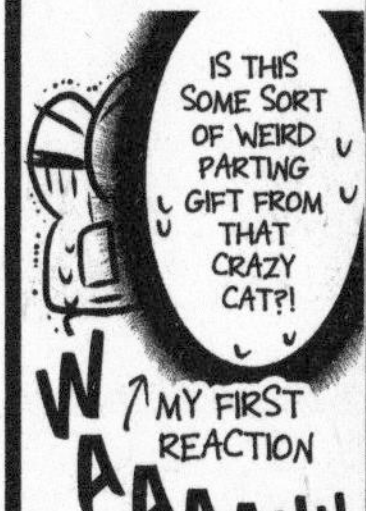
IS THIS SOME SORT OF WEIRD PARTING GIFT FROM THAT CRAZY CAT?!
WAAAAAHH
↑MY FIRST REACTION

We had all sorts of companies expressing interest in the anime and movie rights, and I am so grateful to all of them. Honestly, I still can't believe it.

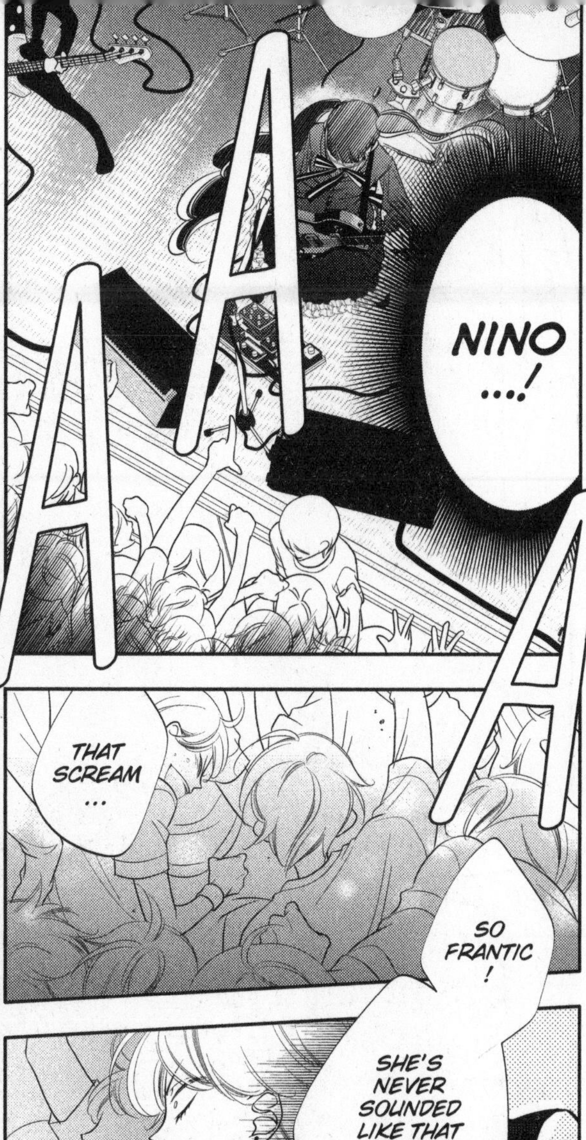
AAAA
NINO ...!
THAT SCREAM ...
SO FRANTIC!
SHE'S NEVER SOUNDED LIKE THAT BEFORE TODAY!

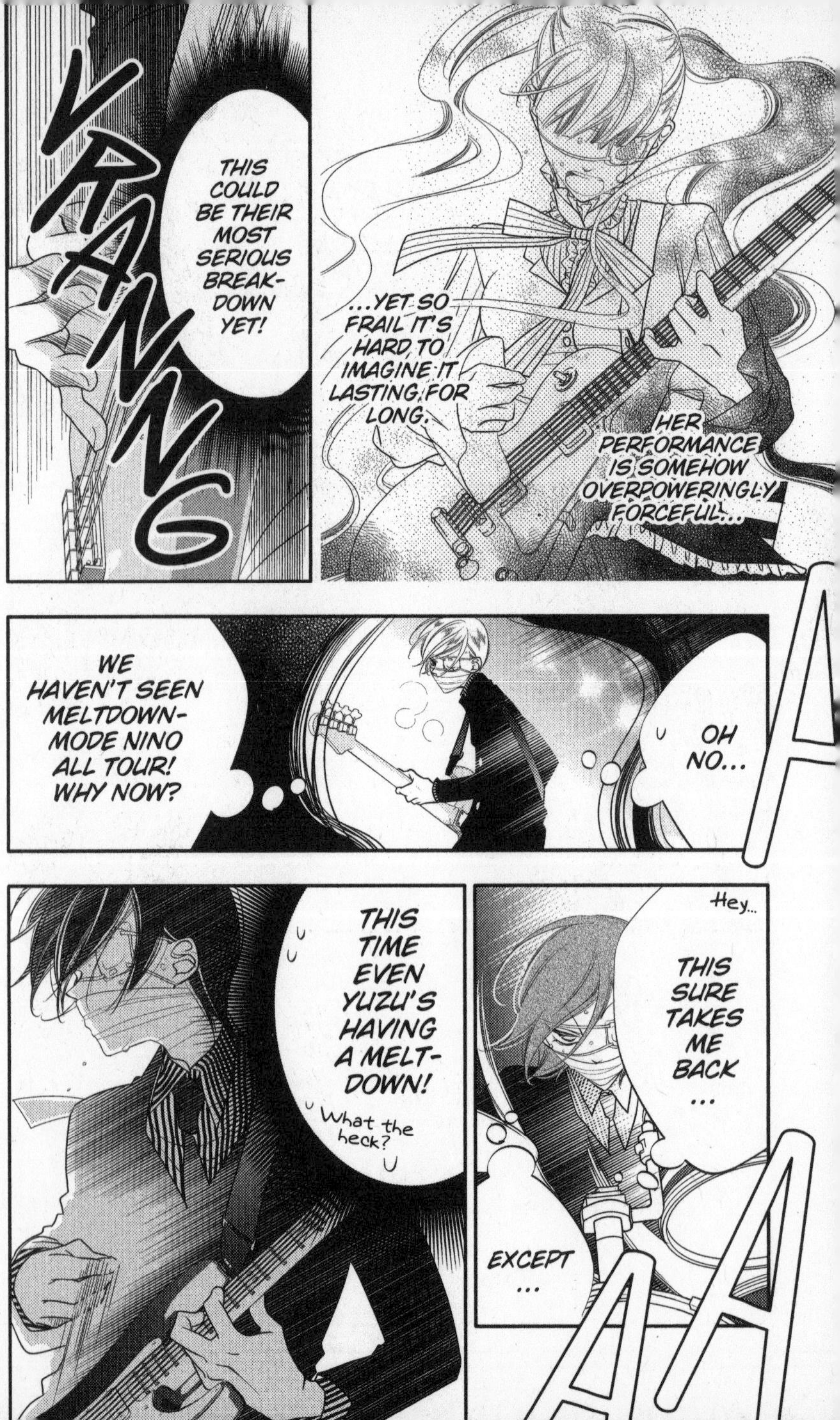
HER PERFORMANCE IS SOMEHOW OVERPOWERINGLY FORCEFUL...
...YET SO FRAIL IT'S HARD TO IMAGINE IT LASTING FOR LONG.
VRANNG
THIS COULD BE THEIR MOST SERIOUS BREAK-DOWN YET!
OH NO...
WE HAVEN'T SEEN MELTDOWN-MODE NINO ALL TOUR! WHY NOW?
AAAAA
Hey...
THIS SURE TAKES ME BACK...
EXCEPT...
THIS TIME EVEN YUZU'S HAVING A MELT-DOWN!
What the heck?

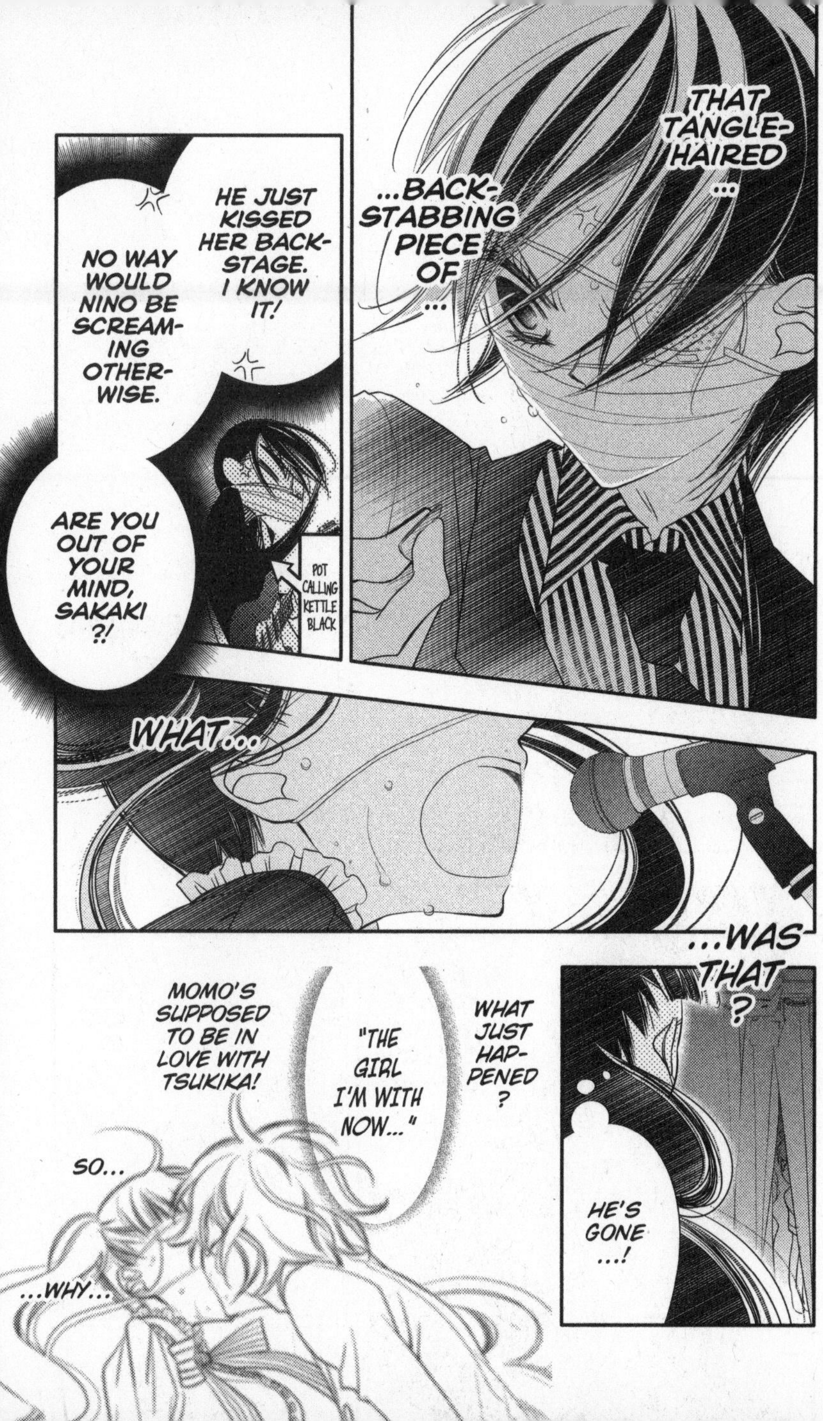
THAT TANGLE-HAIRED...
...BACK-STABBING PIECE OF...
HE JUST KISSED HER BACK-STAGE. I KNOW IT!
NO WAY WOULD NINO BE SCREAMING OTHERWISE.
ARE YOU OUT OF YOUR MIND, SAKAKI?!
POT CALLING KETTLE BLACK
WHAT...
...WAS THAT?
WHAT JUST HAPPENED?
HE'S GONE...!
"THE GIRL I'M WITH NOW..."
MOMO'S SUPPOSED TO BE IN LOVE WITH TSUKIKA!
SO...
...WHY...

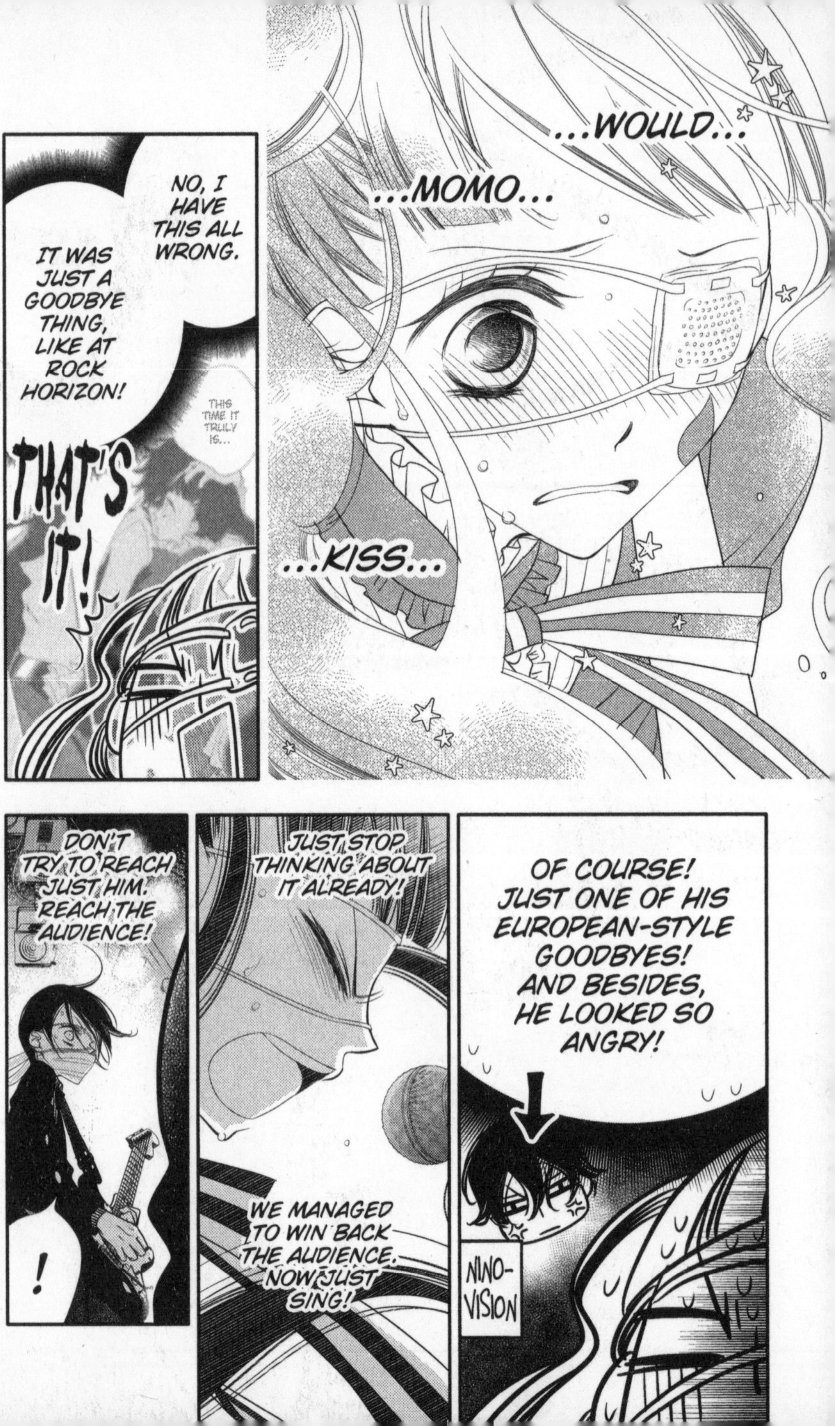
...WOULD...
...MOMO...
...KISS...
NO, I HAVE THIS ALL WRONG.
IT WAS JUST A GOODBYE THING, LIKE AT ROCK HORIZON!
THIS TIME IT TRULY IS...
THAT'S IT!
OF COURSE! JUST ONE OF HIS EUROPEAN-STYLE GOODBYES! AND BESIDES, HE LOOKED SO ANGRY!
NINO-VISION
JUST STOP THINKING ABOUT IT ALREADY!
WE MANAGED TO WIN BACK THE AUDIENCE. NOW JUST SING!
DON'T TRY TO REACH JUST HIM. REACH THE AUDIENCE!
!

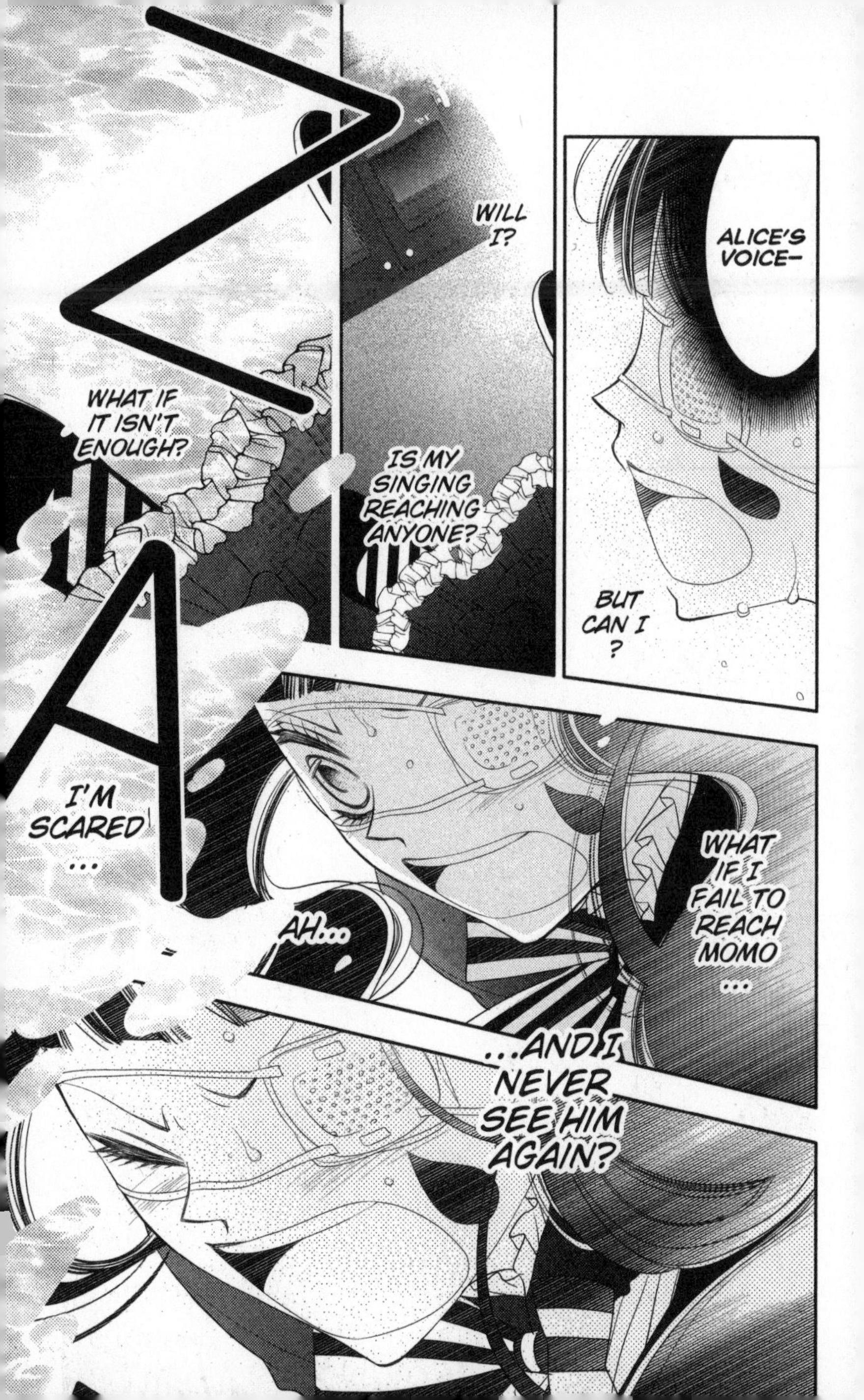
ALICE'S VOICE—
BUT CAN I ?
WILL I?
IS MY SINGING REACHING ANYONE?
WHAT IF I FAIL TO REACH MOMO...
AH...
...AND I NEVER SEE HIM AGAIN?
WHAT IF IT ISN'T ENOUGH?
I'M SCARED...

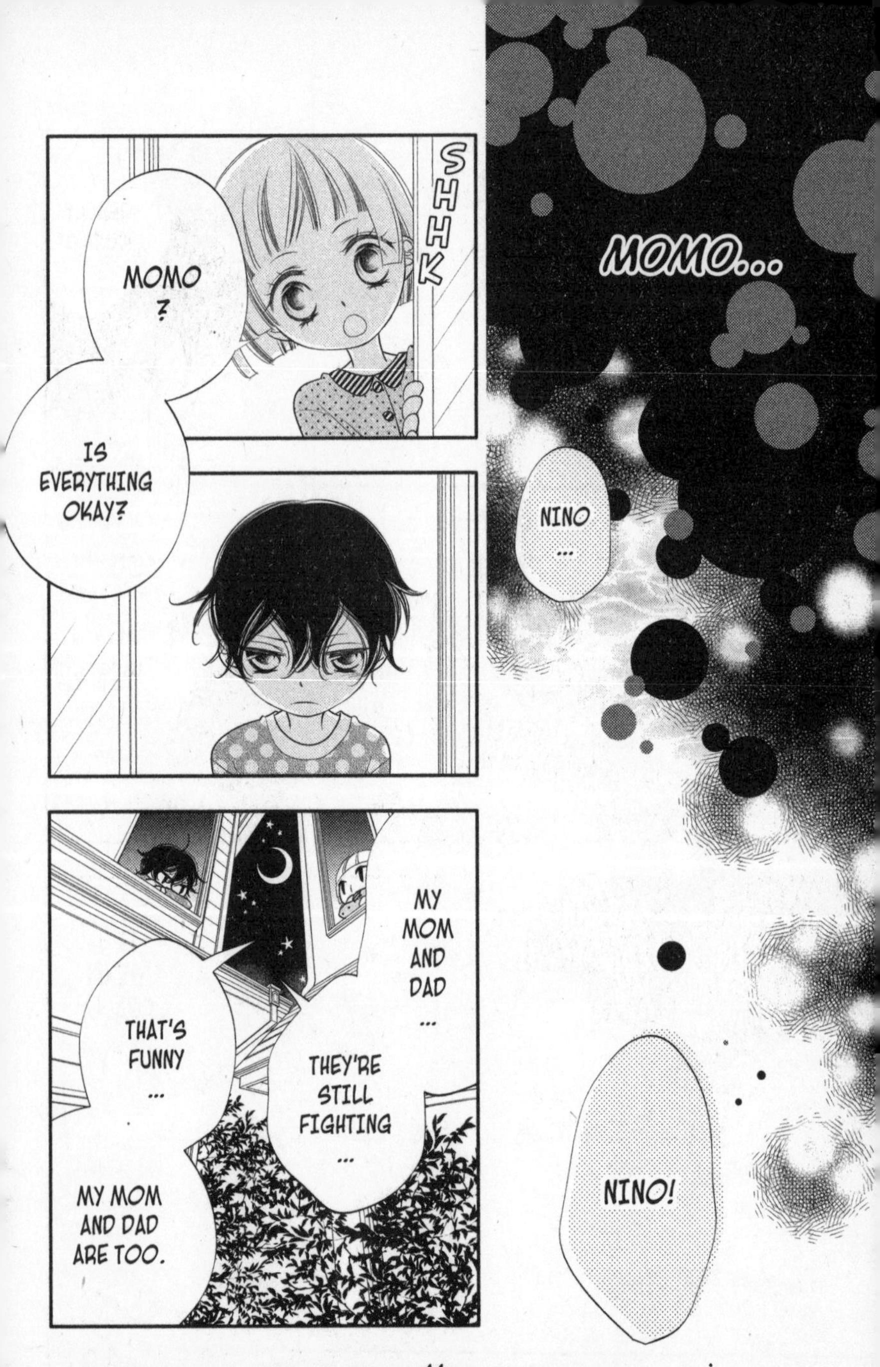
MOMO...
NINO ...
NINO!
SHHK
MOMO ?
IS EVERYTHING OKAY?
MY MOM AND DAD ...
THEY'RE STILL FIGHTING ...
THAT'S FUNNY ...
MY MOM AND DAD ARE TOO.

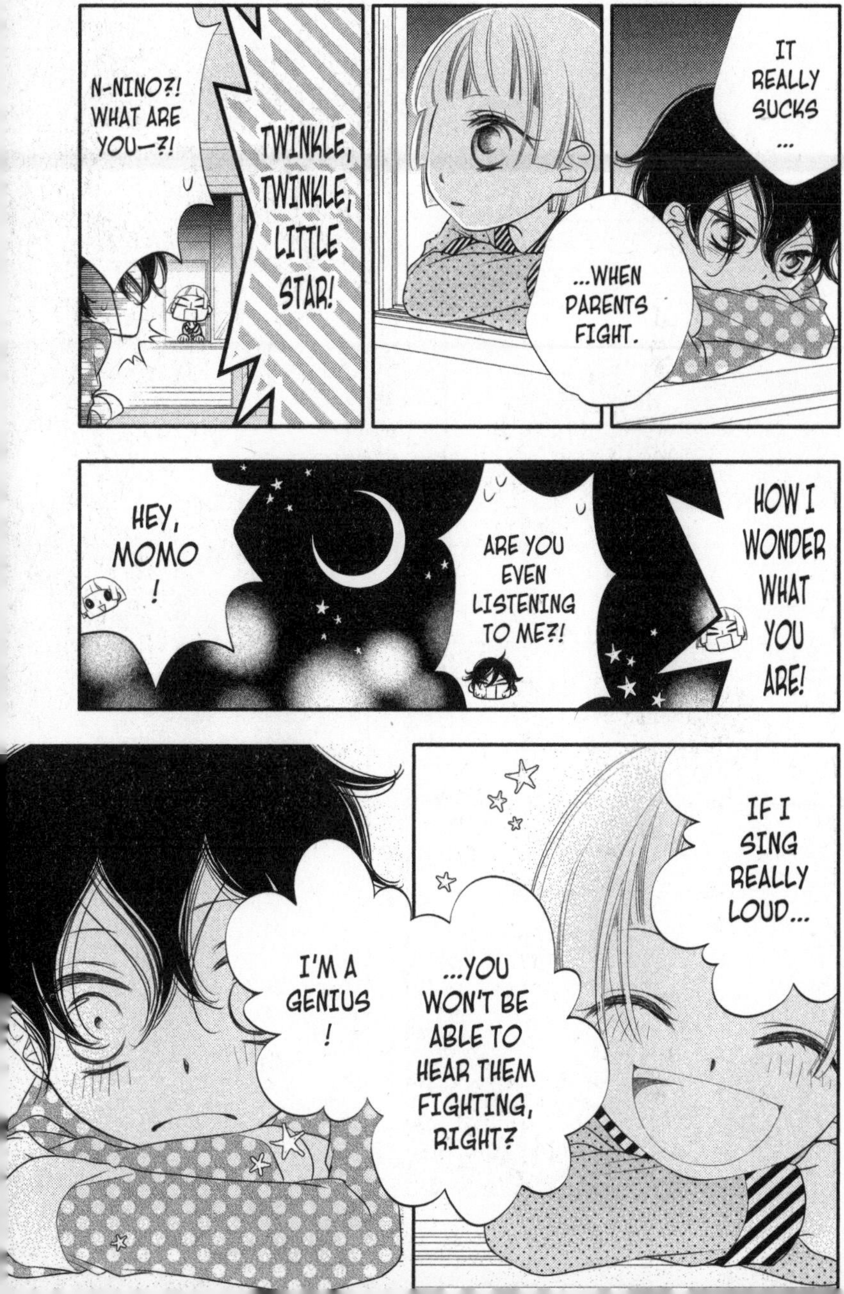
IT REALLY SUCKS...
...WHEN PARENTS FIGHT.
TWINKLE, TWINKLE, LITTLE STAR!
N-NINO?! WHAT ARE YOU—?!
HOW I WONDER WHAT YOU ARE!
ARE YOU EVEN LISTENING TO ME?!
HEY, MOMO!
IF I SING REALLY LOUD...
...YOU WON'T BE ABLE TO HEAR THEM FIGHTING, RIGHT?
I'M A GENIUS!

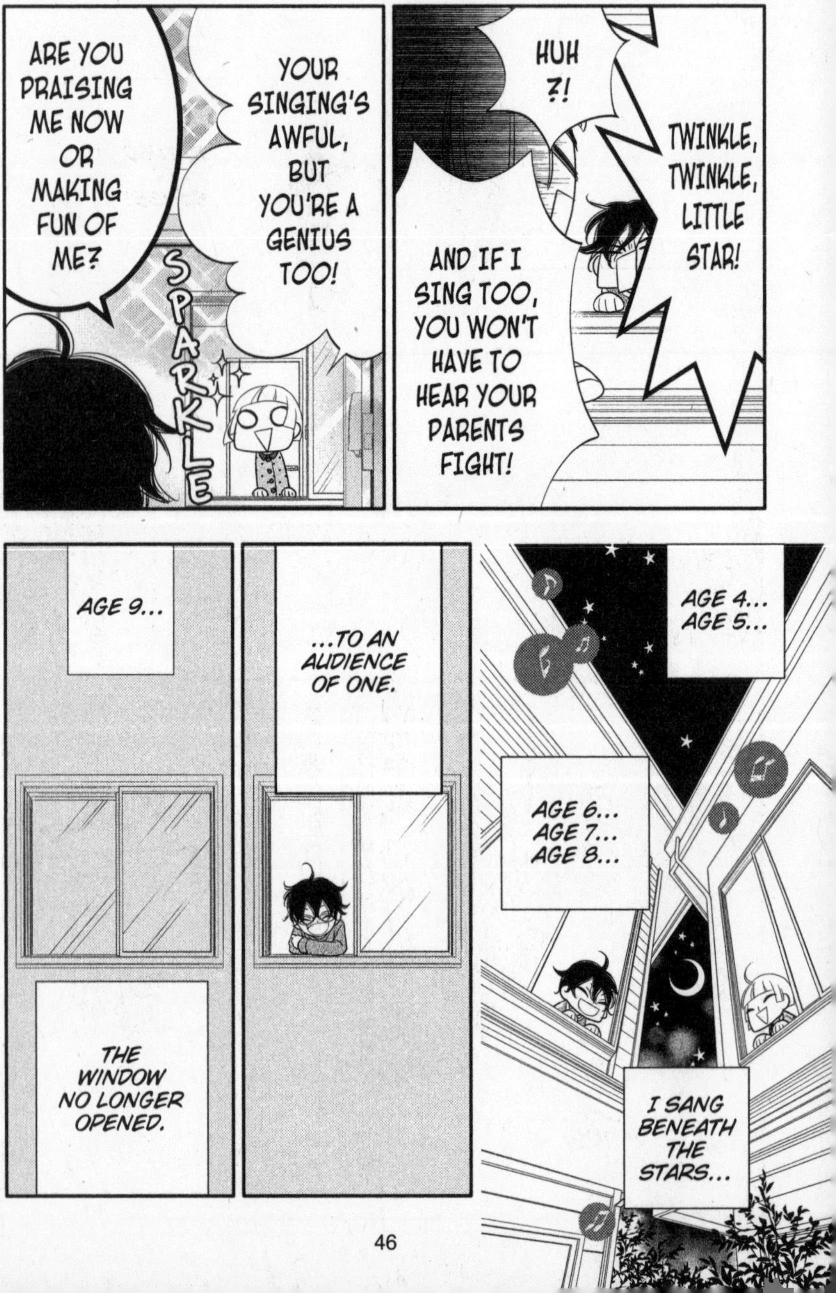
TWINKLE, TWINKLE, LITTLE STAR!
HUH ?!
AND IF I SING TOO, YOU WON'T HAVE TO HEAR YOUR PARENTS FIGHT!
YOUR SINGING'S AWFUL, BUT YOU'RE A GENIUS TOO!
SPARKLE
ARE YOU PRAISING ME NOW OR MAKING FUN OF ME?
AGE 4... AGE 5...
AGE 6... AGE 7... AGE 8...
I SANG BENEATH THE STARS...
...TO AN AUDIENCE OF ONE.
AGE 9...
THE WINDOW NO LONGER OPENED.

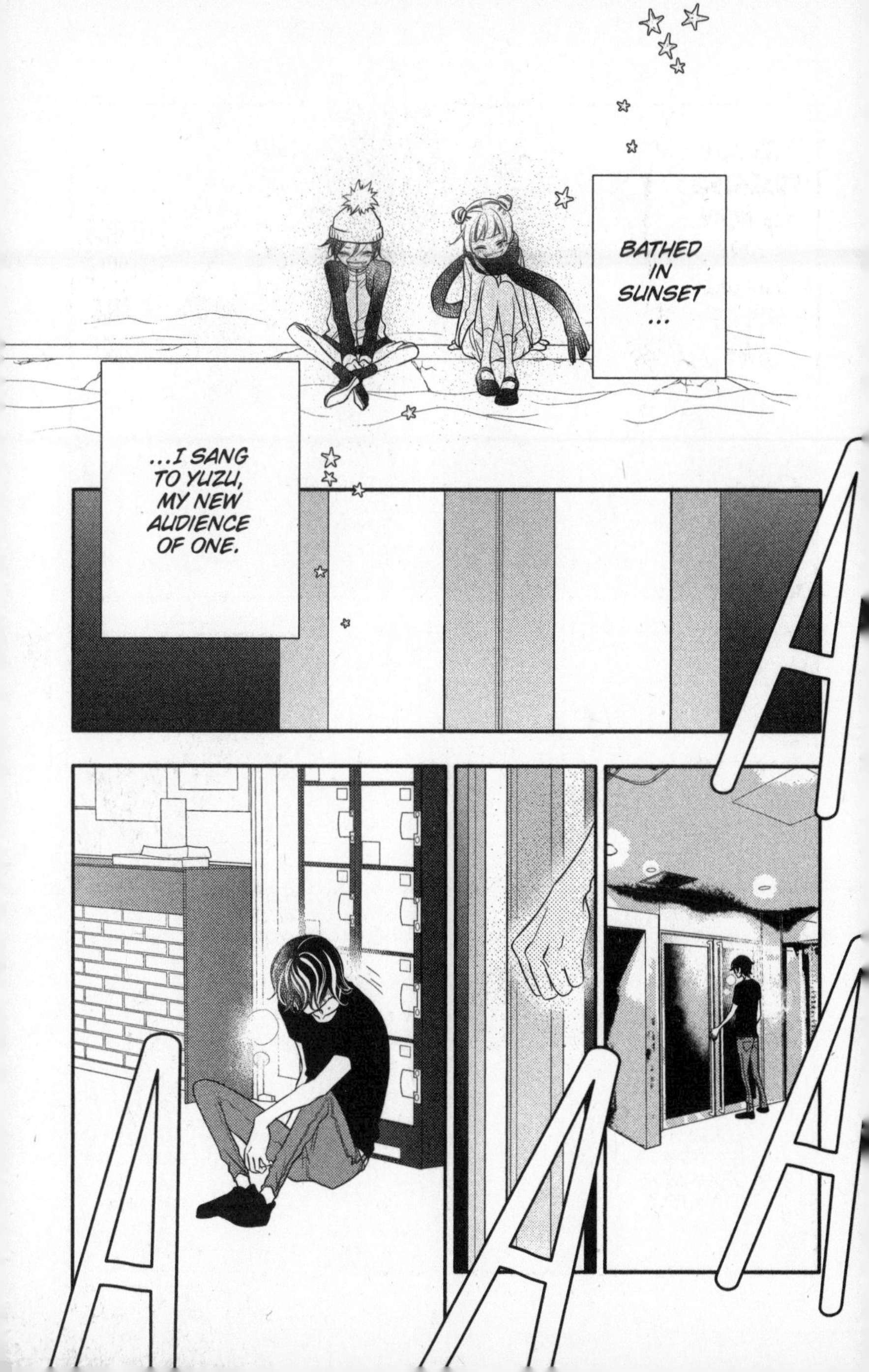
BATHED IN SUNSET ...
...I SANG TO YUZU, MY NEW AUDIENCE OF ONE.

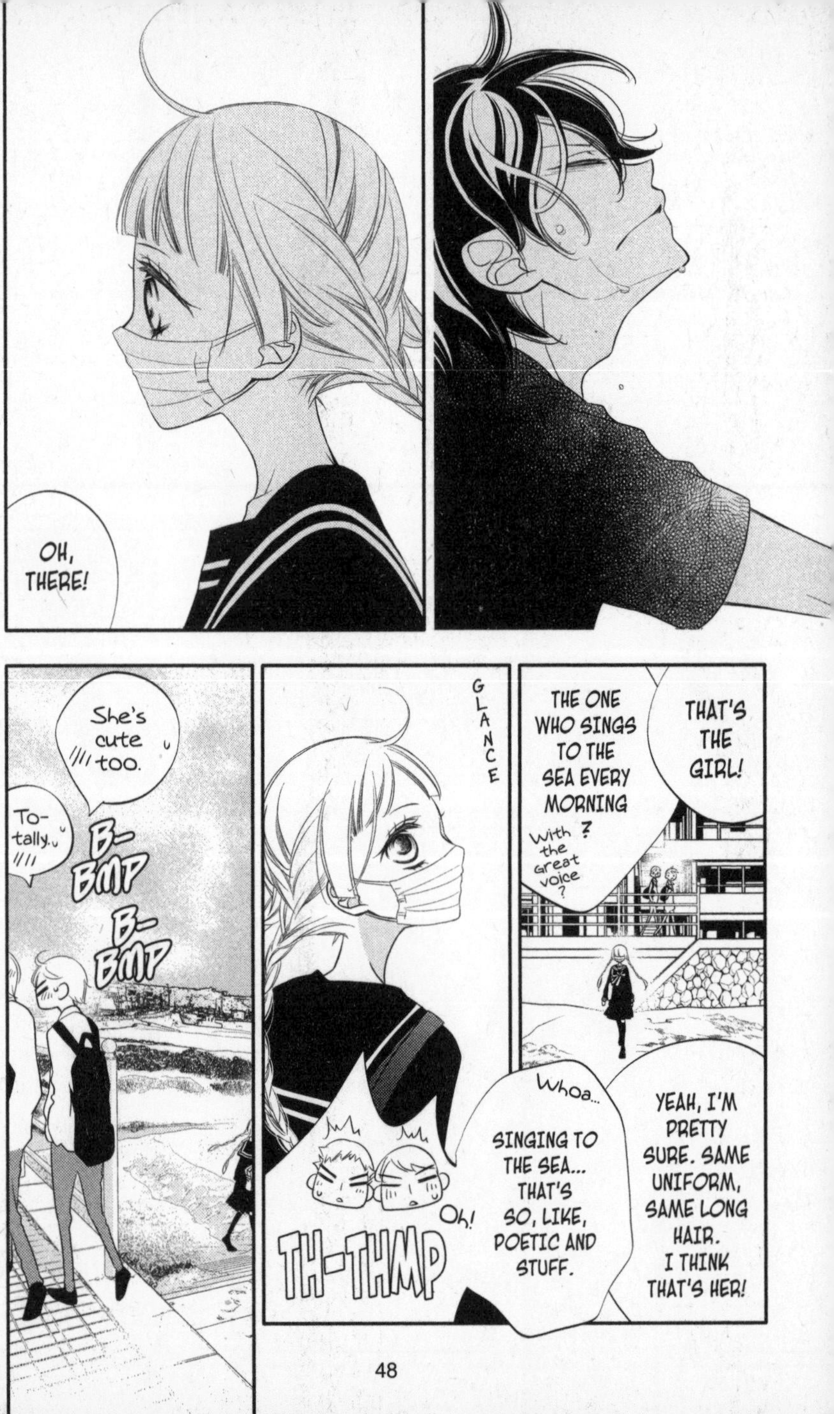
OH, THERE!
THAT'S THE GIRL!
THE ONE WHO SINGS TO THE SEA EVERY MORNING?
With the great voice?
YEAH, I'M PRETTY SURE. SAME UNIFORM, SAME LONG HAIR. I THINK THAT'S HER!
Whoa...
SINGING TO THE SEA... THAT'S SO, LIKE, POETIC AND STUFF.
GLANCE
Oh!
TH-THMP
She's cute too.
To-tally.
B-BMP
B-BMP

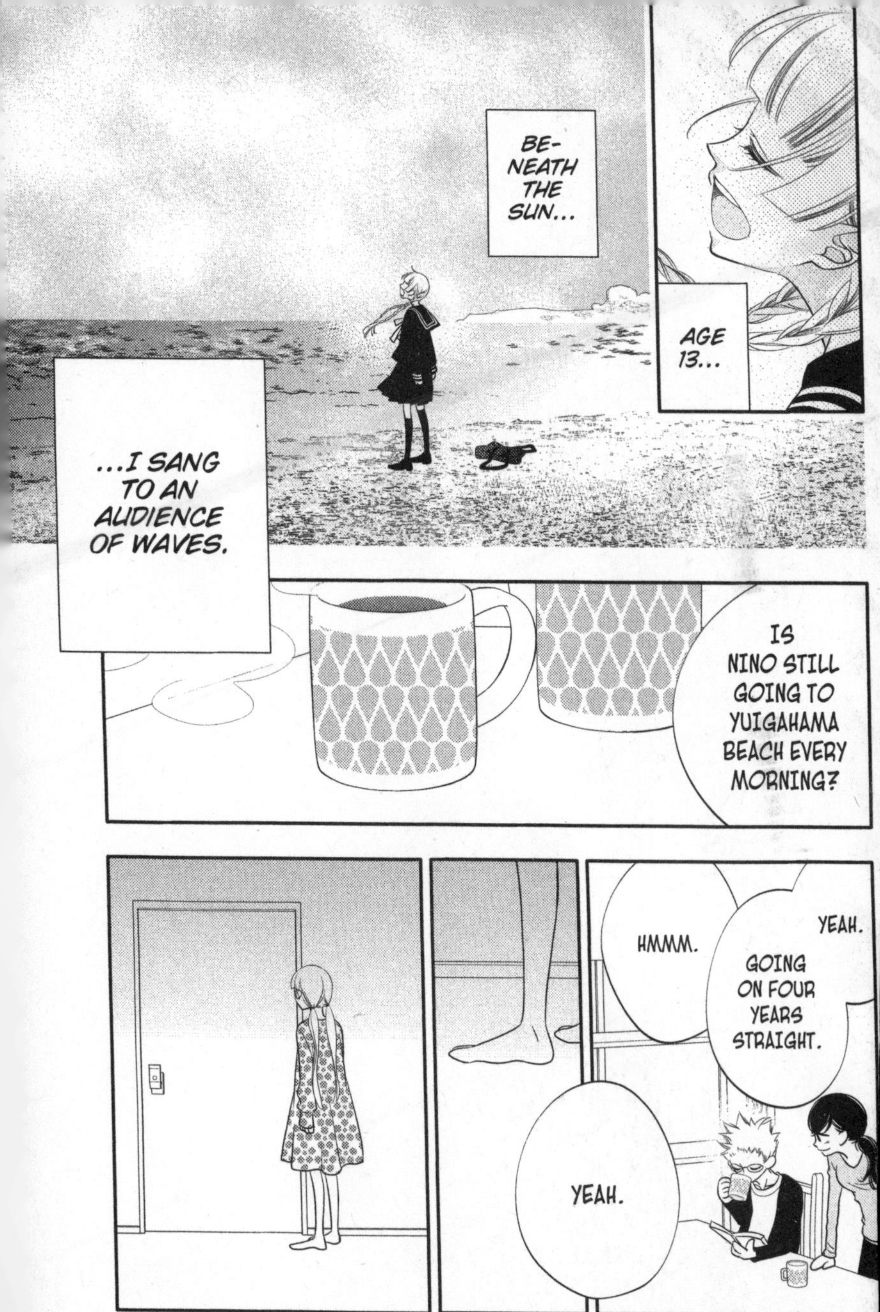
AGE 13...
BE-NEATH THE SUN...
...I SANG TO AN AUDIENCE OF WAVES.
IS NINO STILL GOING TO YUIGAHAMA BEACH EVERY MORNING?
YEAH. GOING ON FOUR YEARS STRAIGHT.
HMMM.
YEAH.

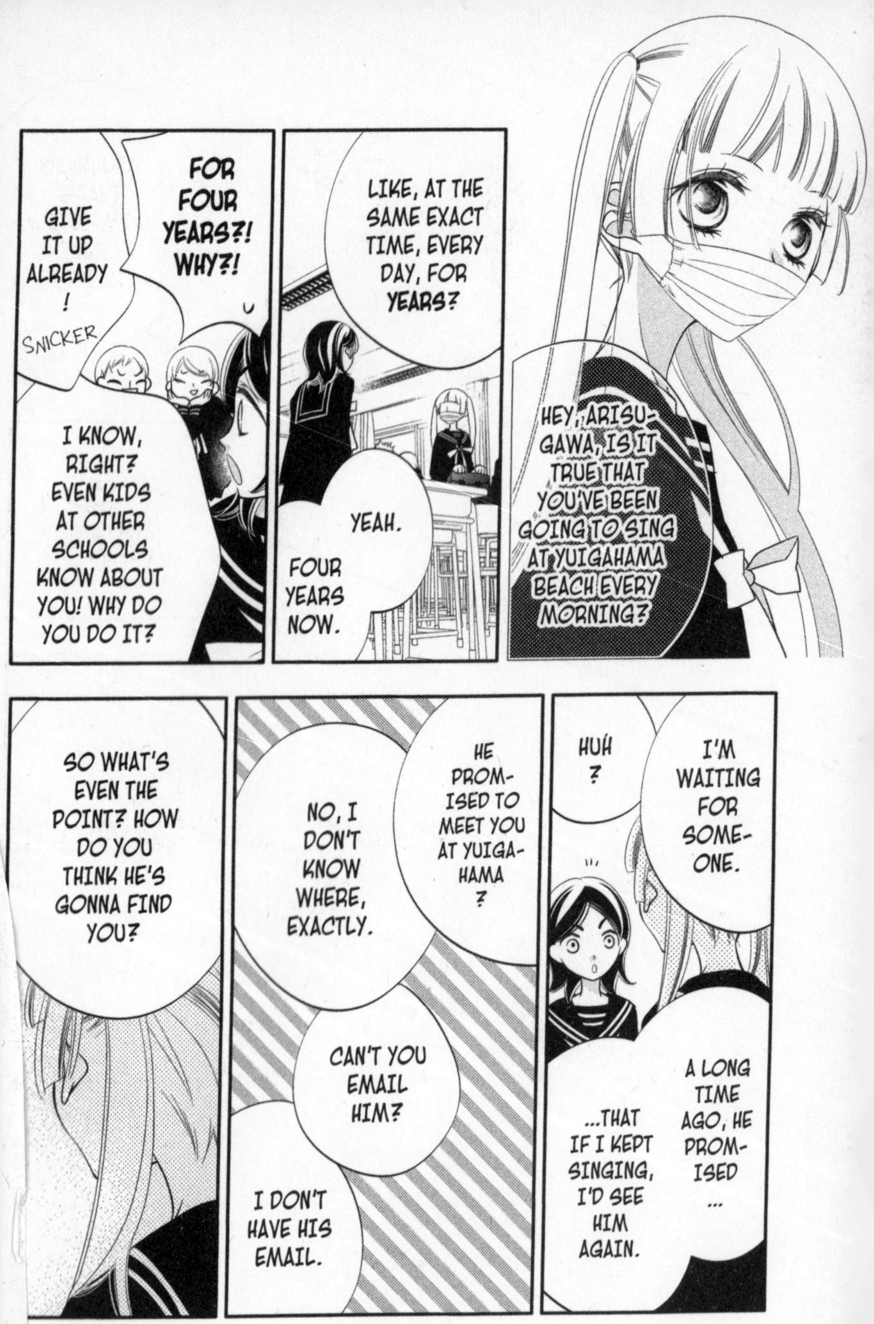
HEY, ARISUGAWA, IS IT TRUE THAT YOU'VE BEEN GOING TO SING AT YUIGAHAMA BEACH EVERY MORNING?
LIKE, AT THE SAME EXACT TIME, EVERY DAY, FOR YEARS?
YEAH.
FOUR YEARS NOW.
FOR FOUR YEARS?! WHY?!
GIVE IT UP ALREADY!
SNICKER
I KNOW, RIGHT? EVEN KIDS AT OTHER SCHOOLS KNOW ABOUT YOU! WHY DO YOU DO IT?
I'M WAITING FOR SOMEONE.
HUH?
A LONG TIME AGO, HE PROMISED...
...THAT IF I KEPT SINGING, I'D SEE HIM AGAIN.
HE PROMISED TO MEET YOU AT YUIGAHAMA?
NO, I DON'T KNOW WHERE, EXACTLY.
CAN'T YOU EMAIL HIM?
I DON'T HAVE HIS EMAIL.
SO WHAT'S EVEN THE POINT? HOW DO YOU THINK HE'S GONNA FIND YOU?

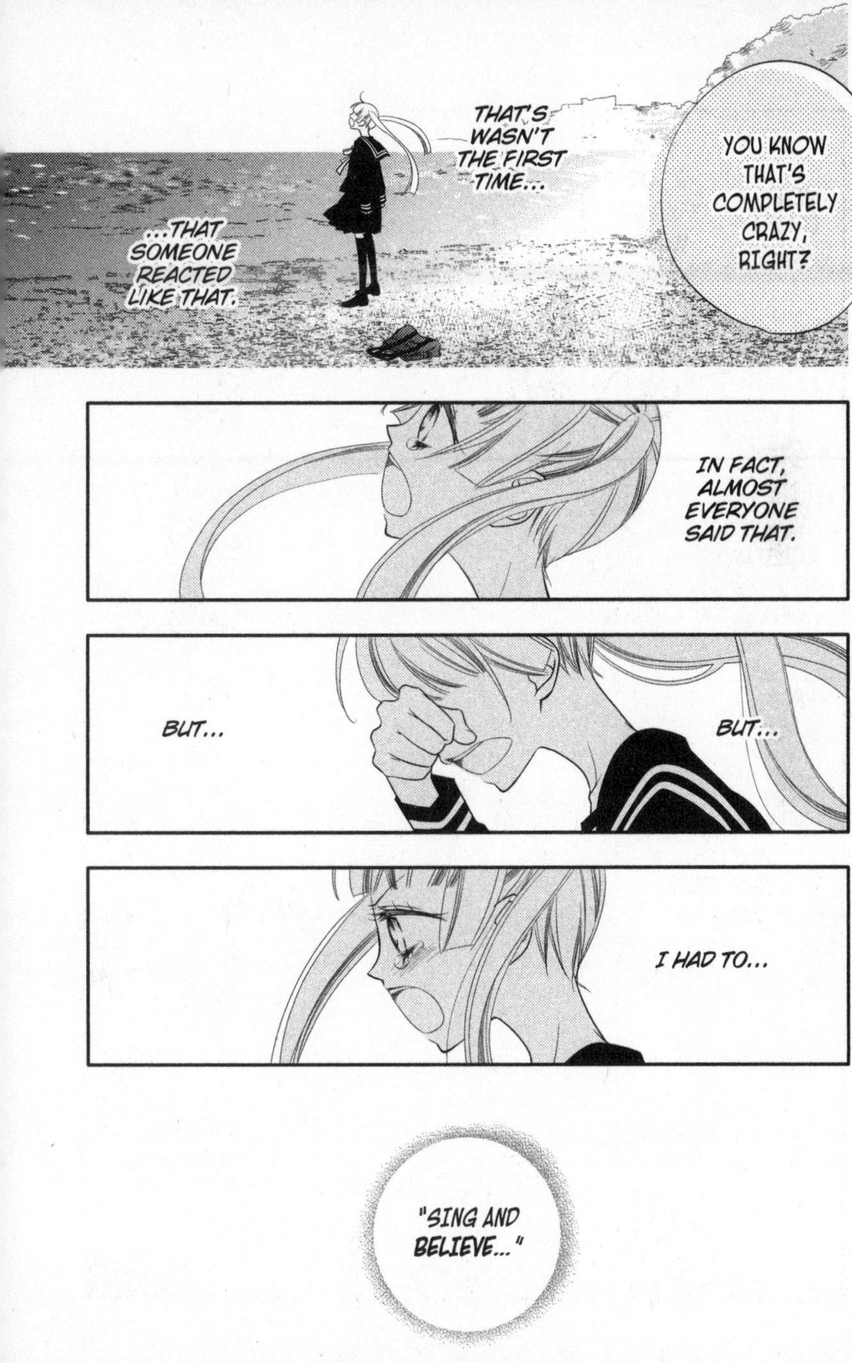
YOU KNOW THAT'S COMPLETELY CRAZY, RIGHT?
THAT'S WASN'T THE FIRST TIME...
...THAT SOMEONE REACTED LIKE THAT.
IN FACT, ALMOST EVERYONE SAID THAT.
BUT...
BUT...
I HAD TO...
"SING AND BELIEVE..."

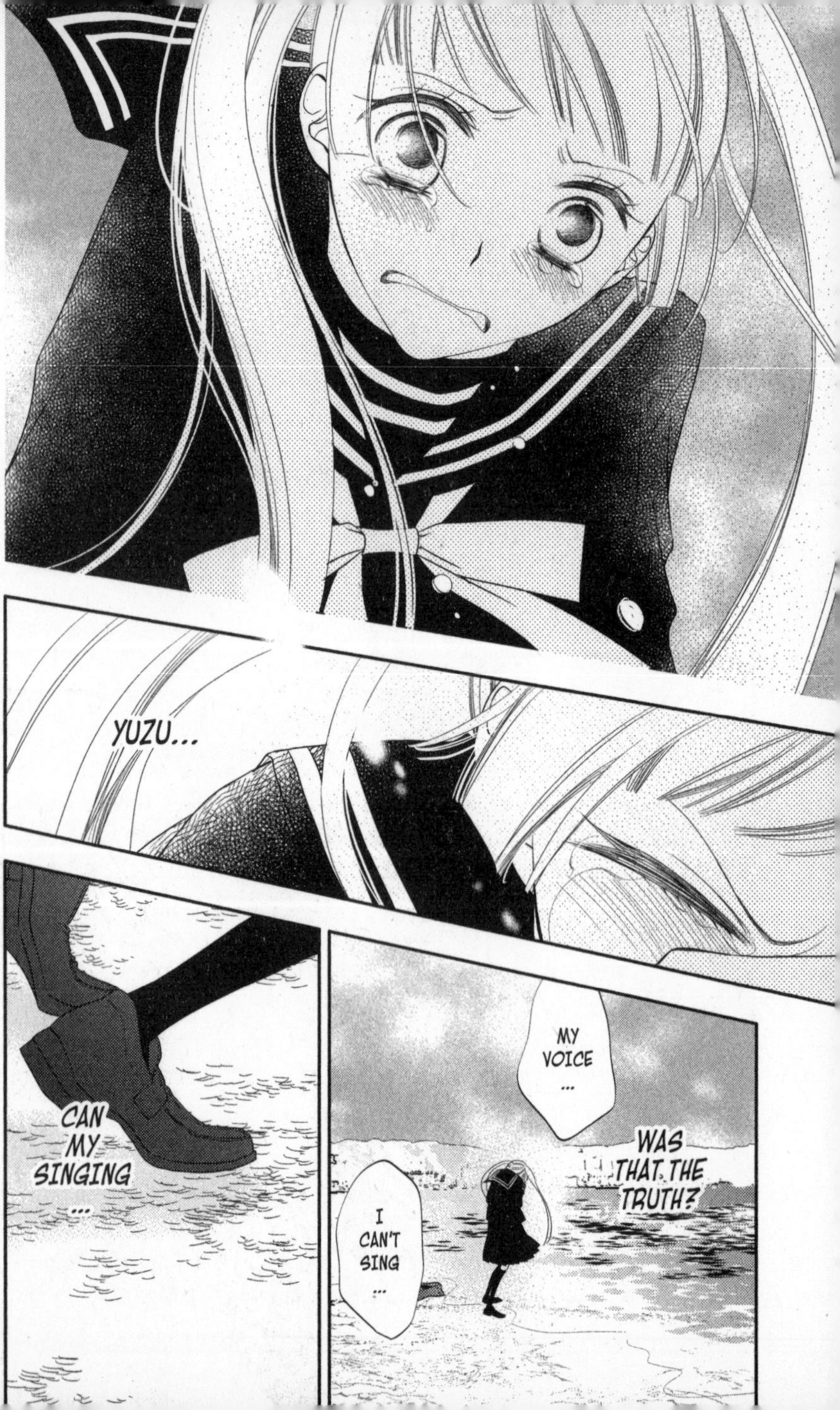
YUZU...
MY VOICE ...
WAS THAT THE TRUTH?
I CAN'T SING ...
CAN MY SINGING ...

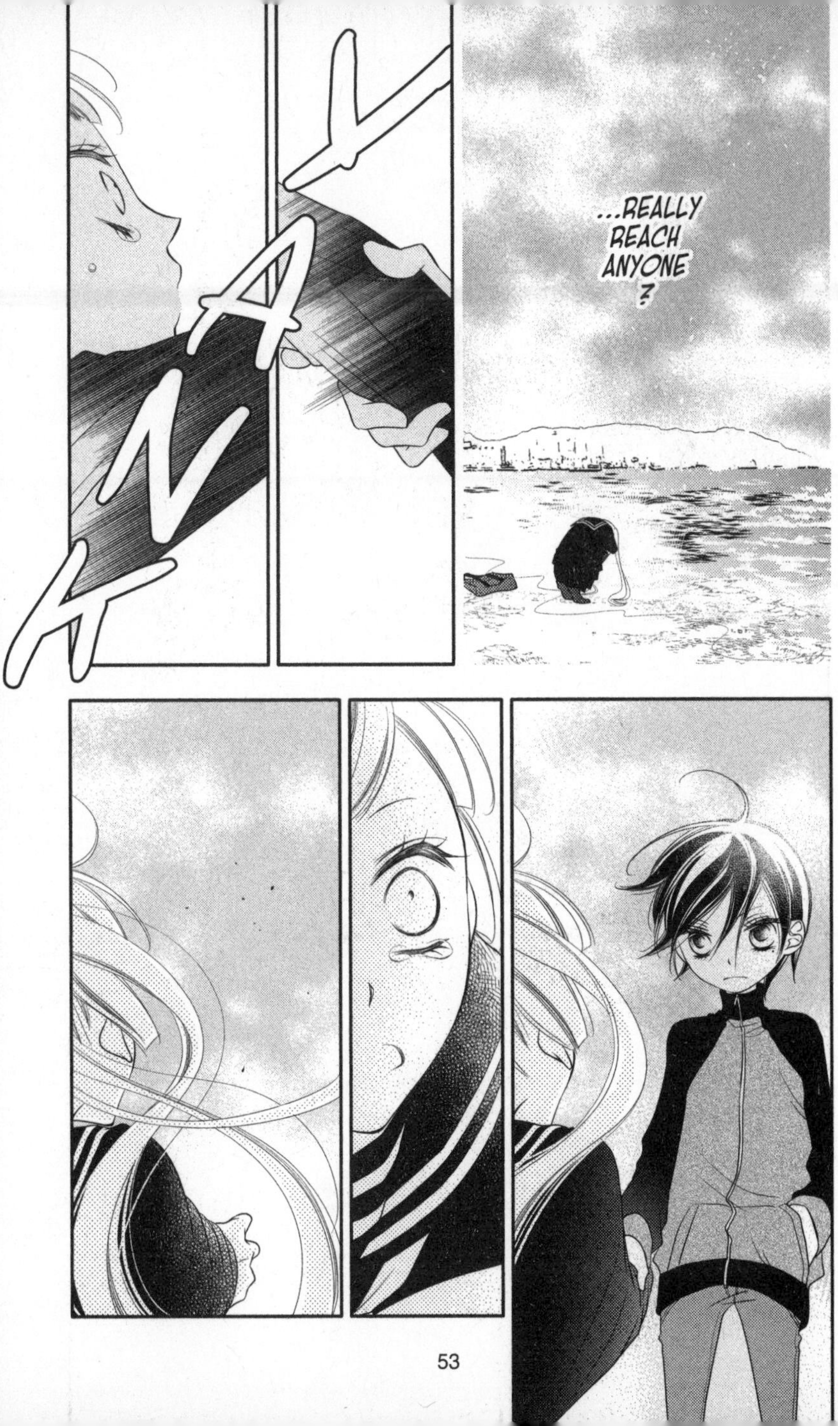
...REALLY REACH ANYONE?
YANK

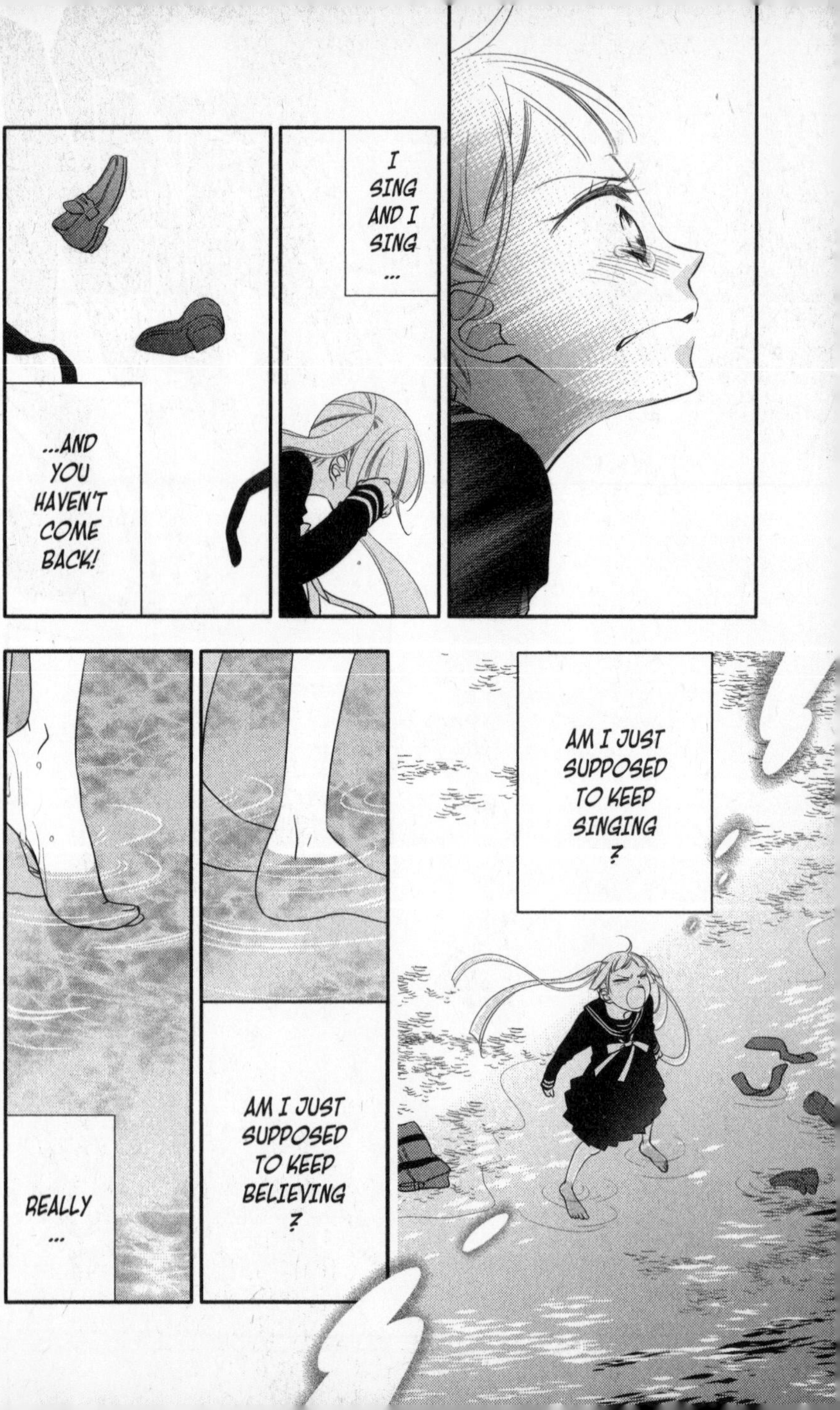
I SING AND I SING ...
...AND YOU HAVEN'T COME BACK!
AM I JUST SUPPOSED TO KEEP SINGING?
AM I JUST SUPPOSED TO KEEP BELIEVING?
REALLY ...

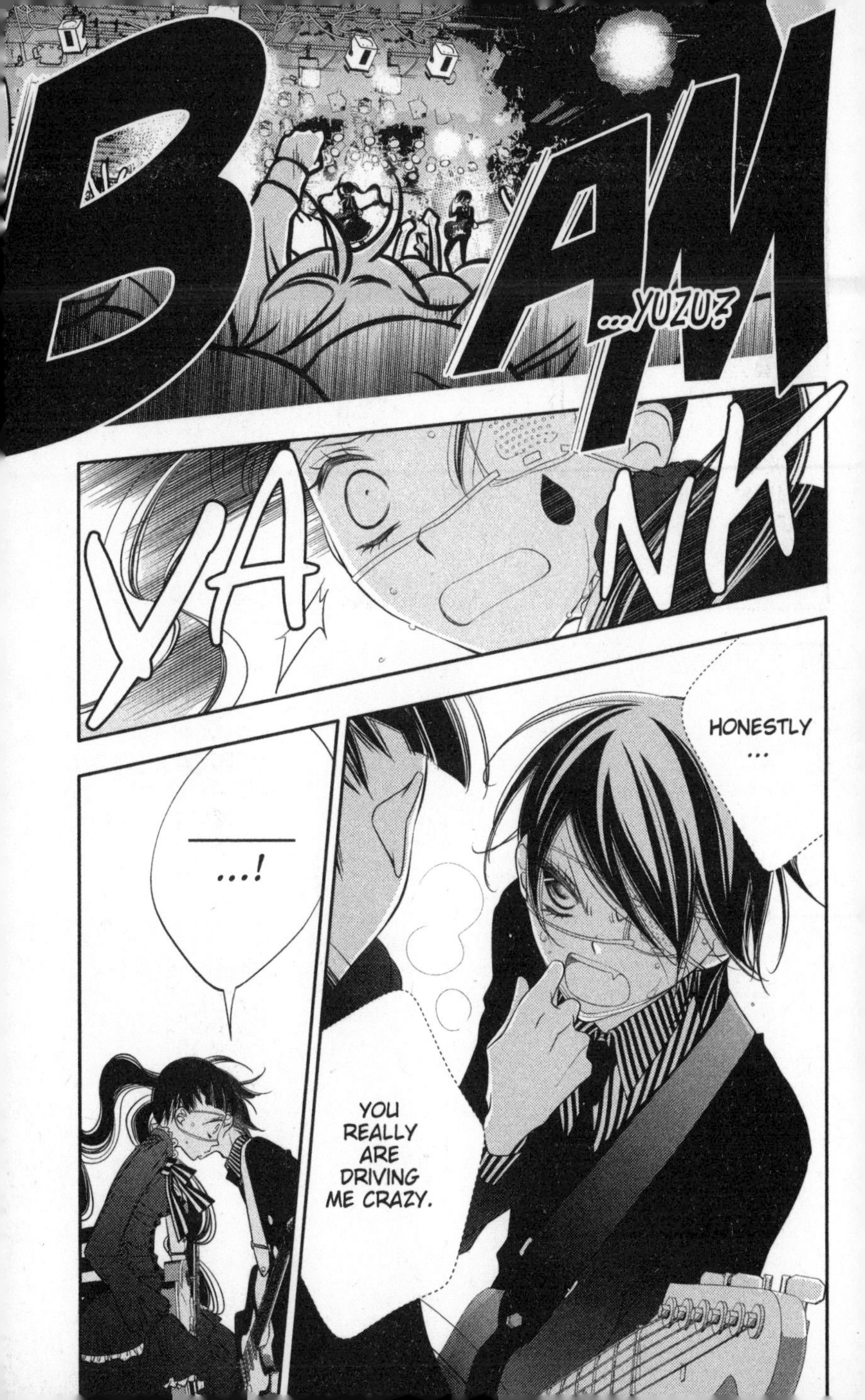
BAM
...YUZU?
YANK
HONESTLY ...
YOU REALLY ARE DRIVING ME CRAZY.
—...!

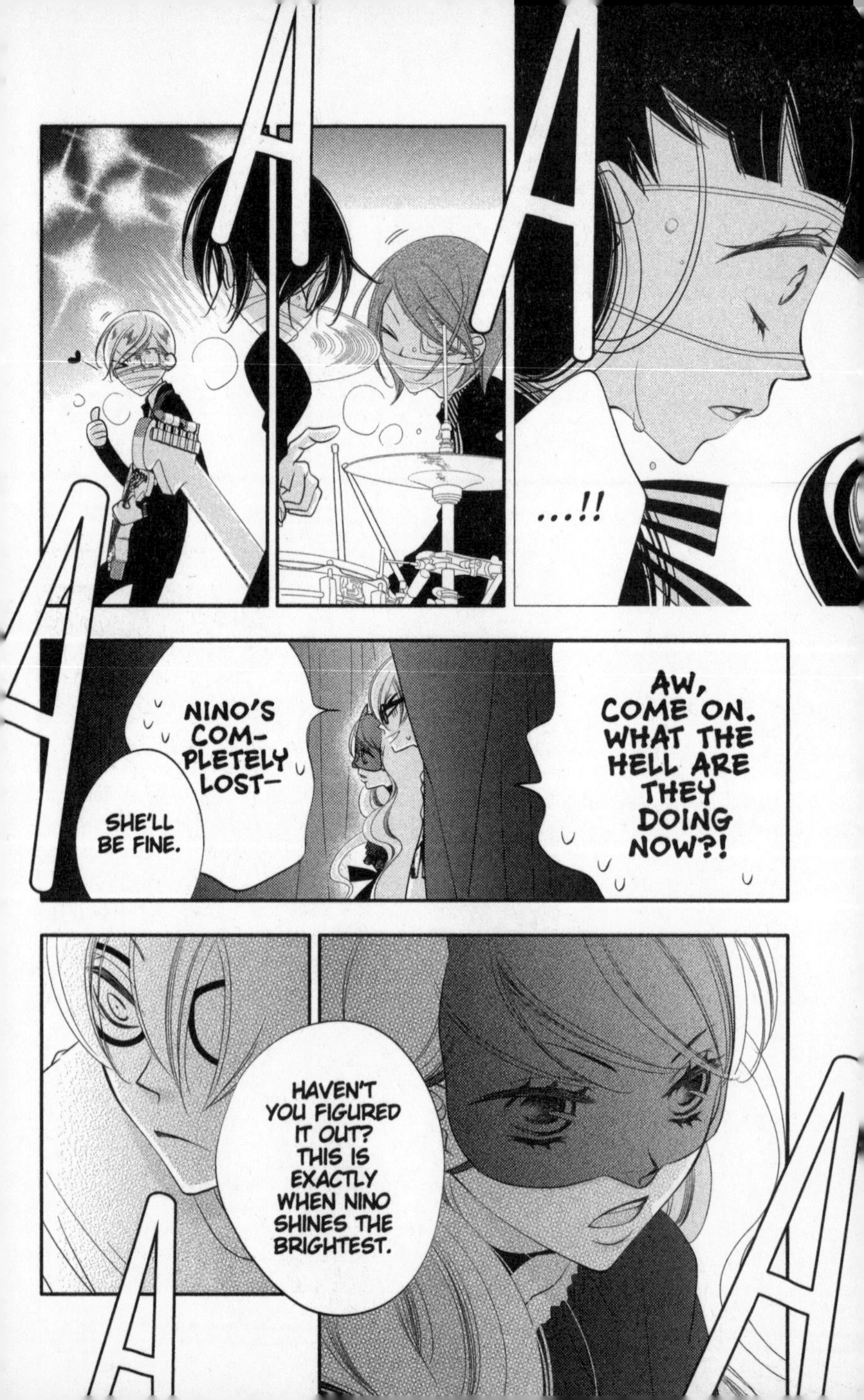
...!!
AW, COME ON. WHAT THE HELL ARE THEY DOING NOW?!
NINO'S COM-PLETELY LOST—
SHE'LL BE FINE.
HAVEN'T YOU FIGURED IT OUT? THIS IS EXACTLY WHEN NINO SHINES THE BRIGHTEST.

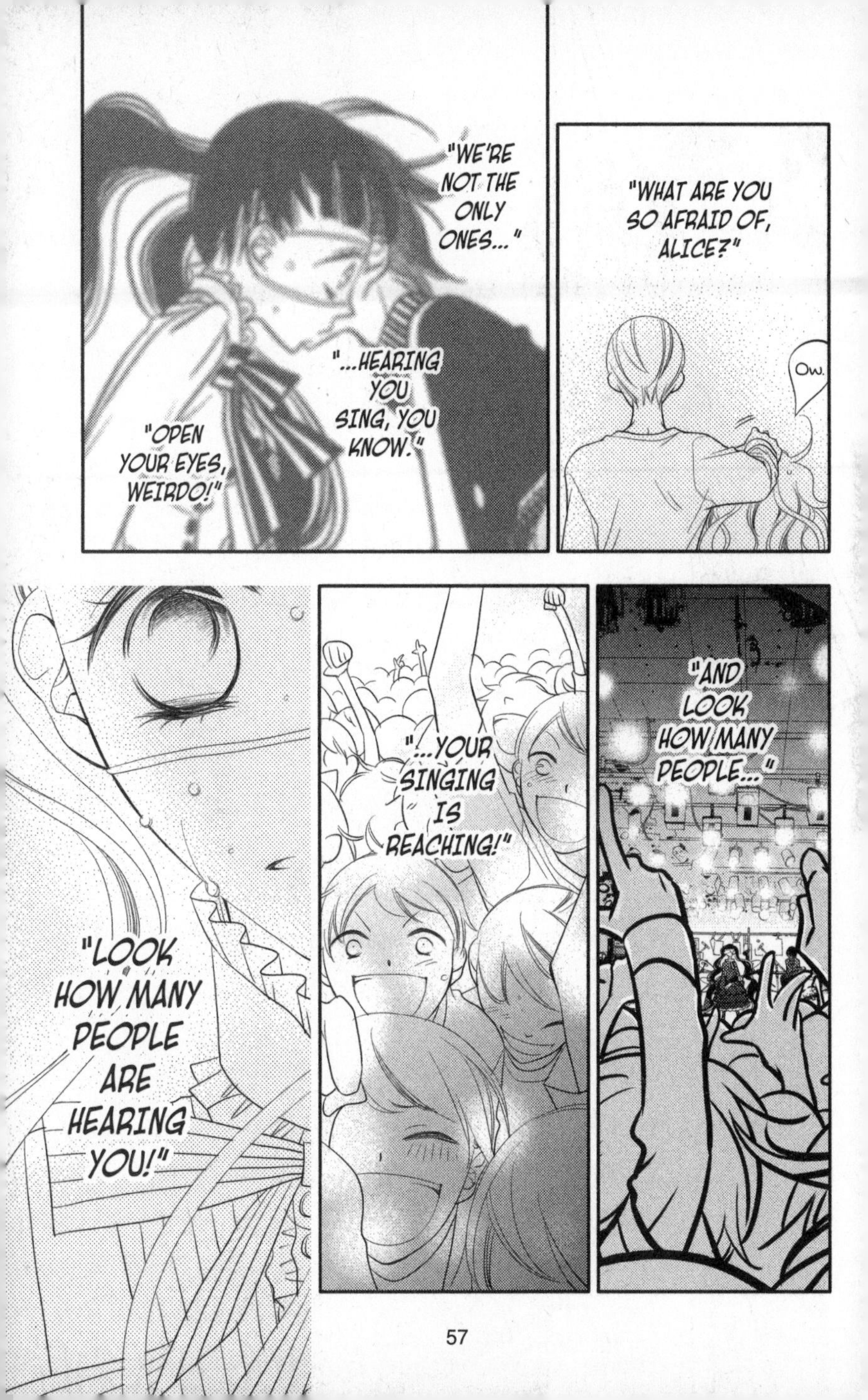
"WHAT ARE YOU SO AFRAID OF, ALICE?"
Ow.
"WE'RE NOT THE ONLY ONES..."
"...HEARING YOU SING, YOU KNOW."
"OPEN YOUR EYES, WEIRDO!"
"AND LOOK HOW MANY PEOPLE..."
"...YOUR SINGING IS REACHING!"
"LOOK HOW MANY PEOPLE ARE HEARING YOU!"

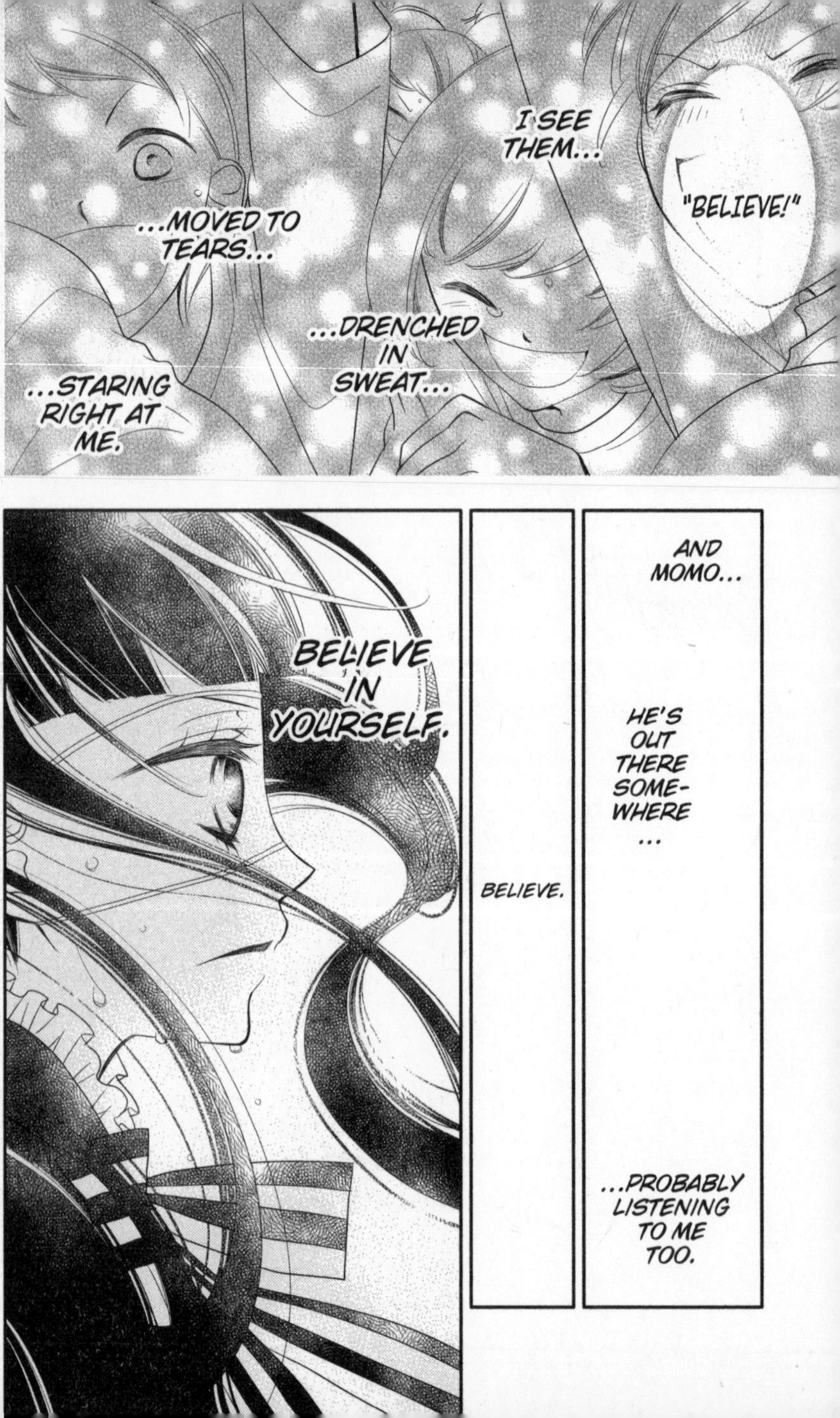
"BELIEVE!"
I SEE THEM...
...MOVED TO TEARS...
...DRENCHED IN SWEAT...
...STARING RIGHT AT ME.
AND MOMO...
HE'S OUT THERE SOMEWHERE...
...PROBABLY LISTENING TO ME TOO.
BELIEVE.
BELIEVE IN YOURSELF.

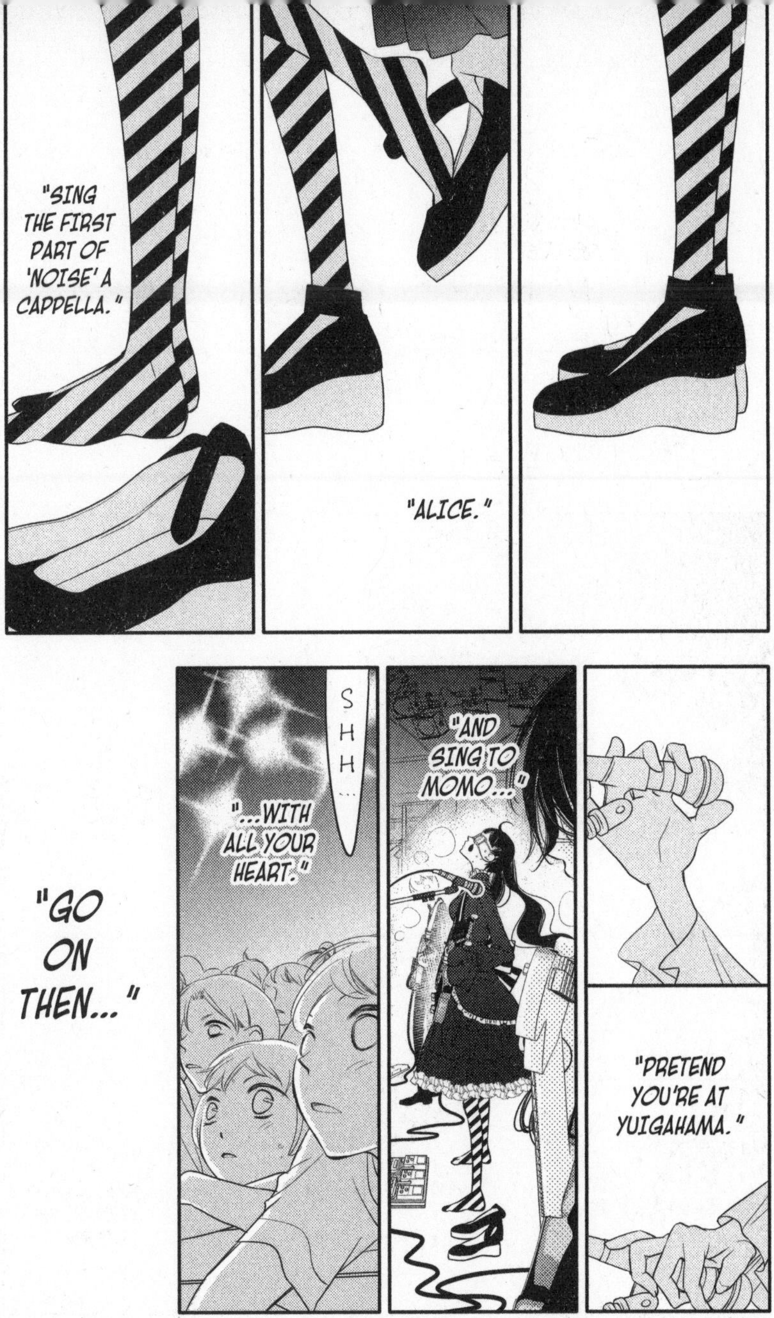

"ALICE."
"SING THE FIRST PART OF 'NOISE' A CAPPELLA."
"PRETEND YOU'RE AT YUIGAHAMA."
"AND SING TO MOMO..."
SHH...
"...WITH ALL YOUR HEART."
"GO ON THEN..."

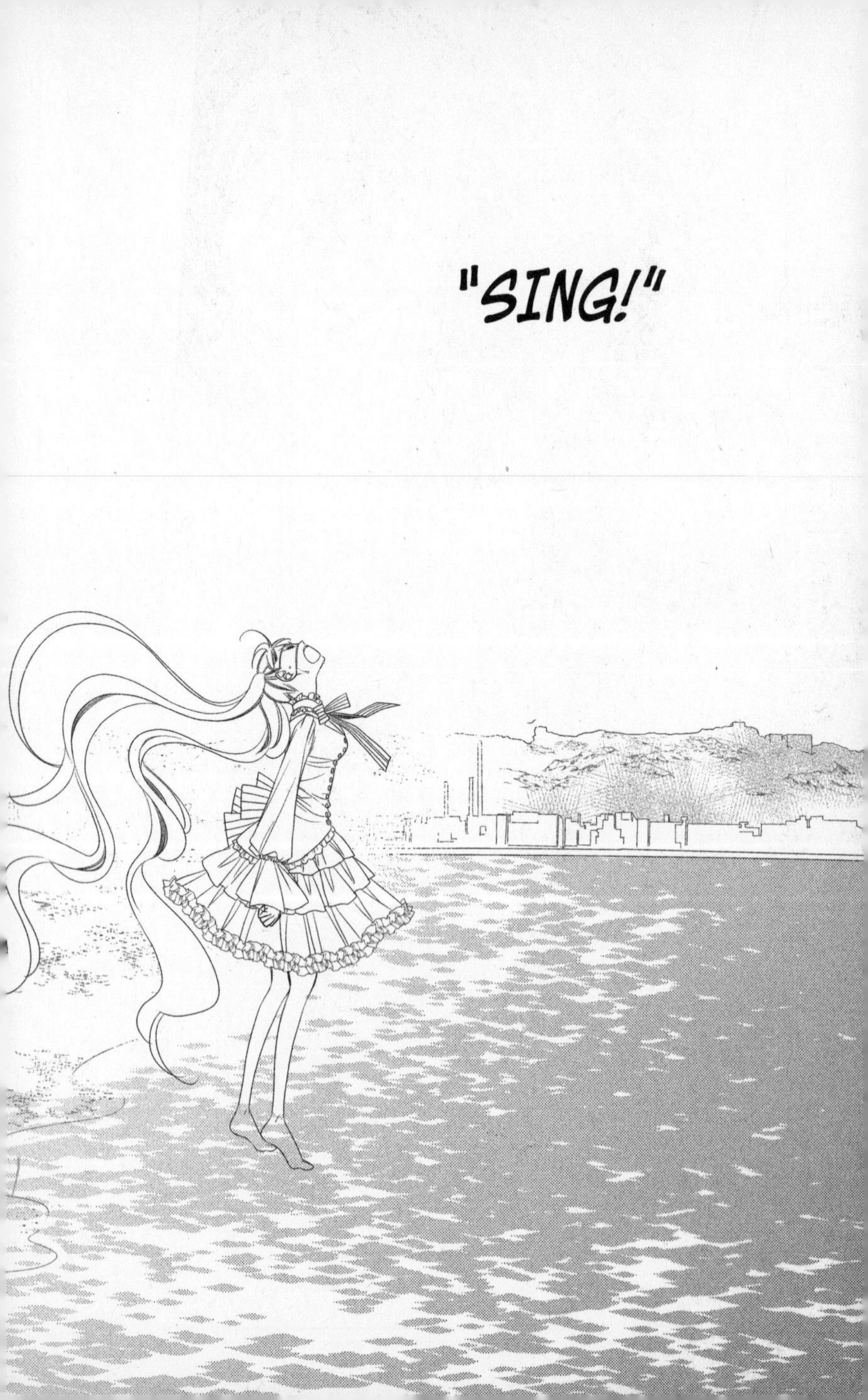
"SING!"

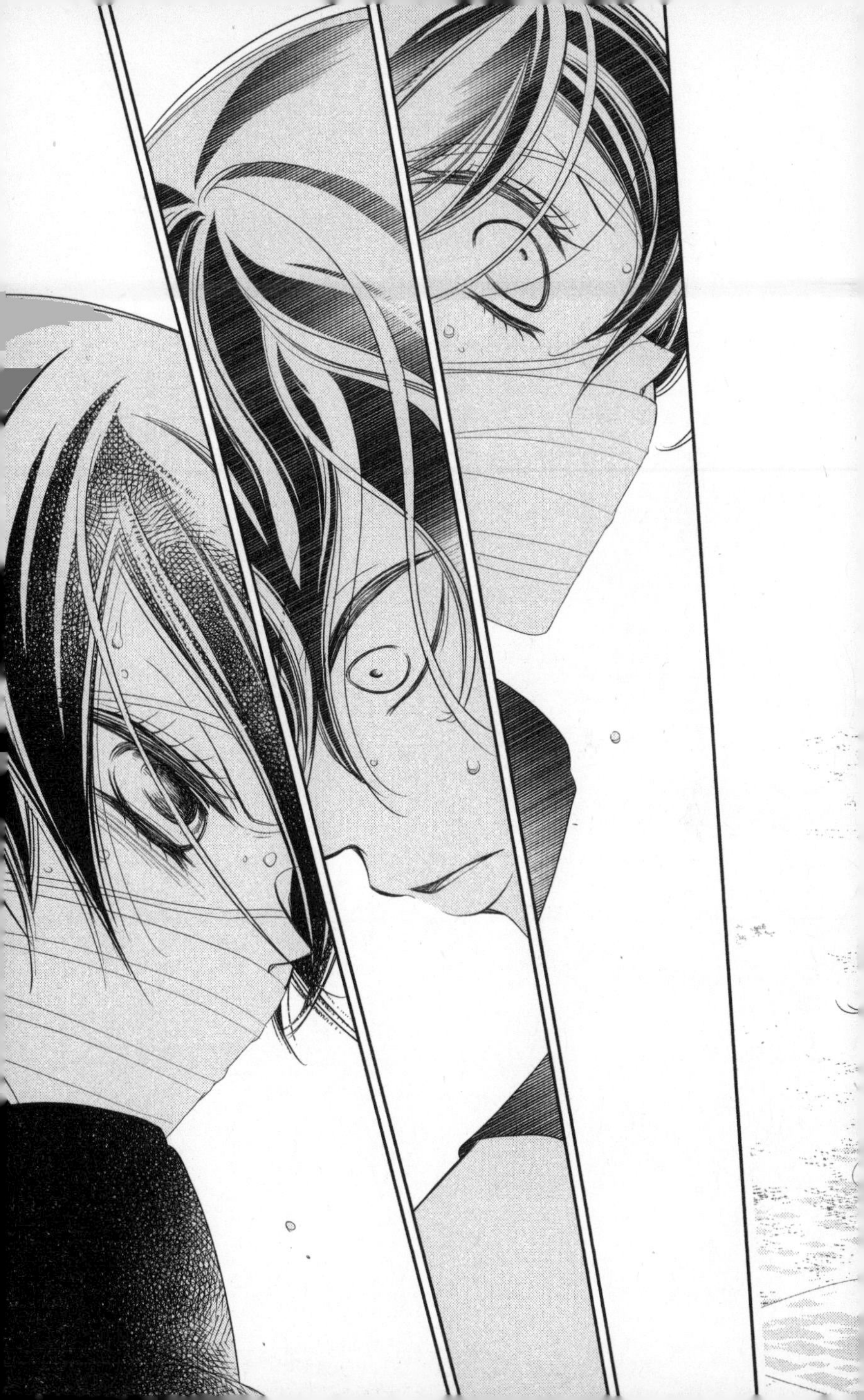

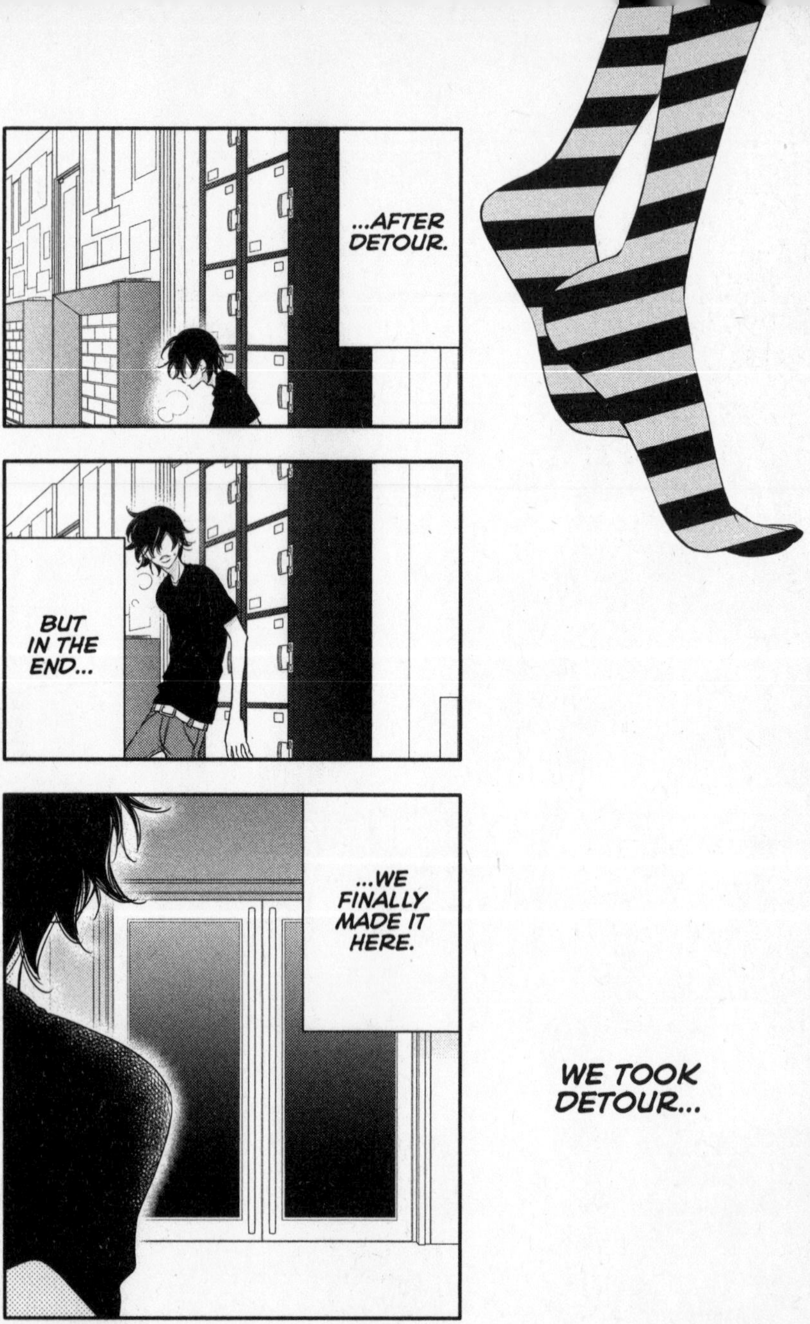
WE TOOK DETOUR...
...AFTER DETOUR.
BUT IN THE END...
...WE FINALLY MADE IT HERE.

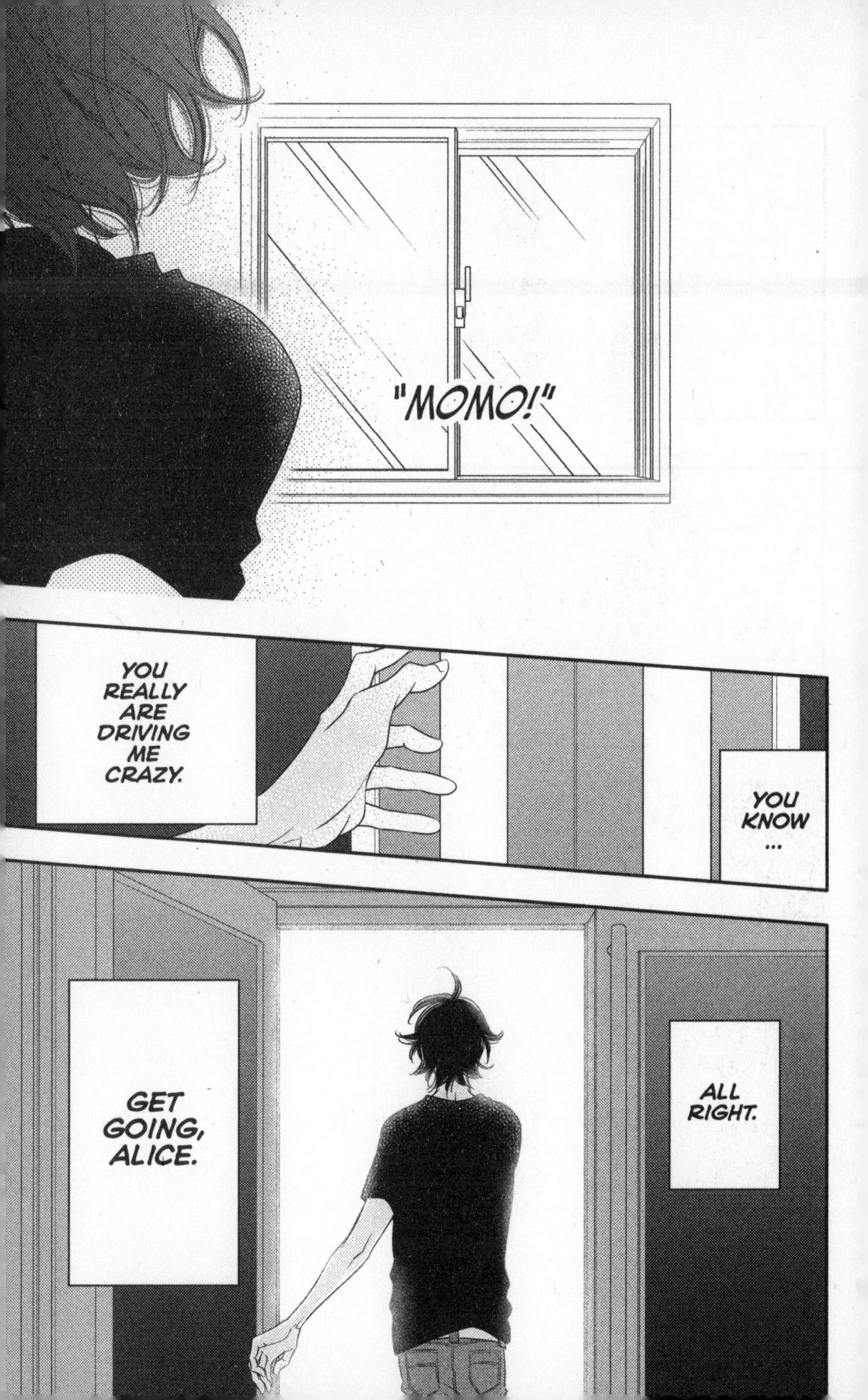
"MOMO!"
YOU KNOW ...
YOU REALLY ARE DRIVING ME CRAZY.
ALL RIGHT.
GET GOING, ALICE.

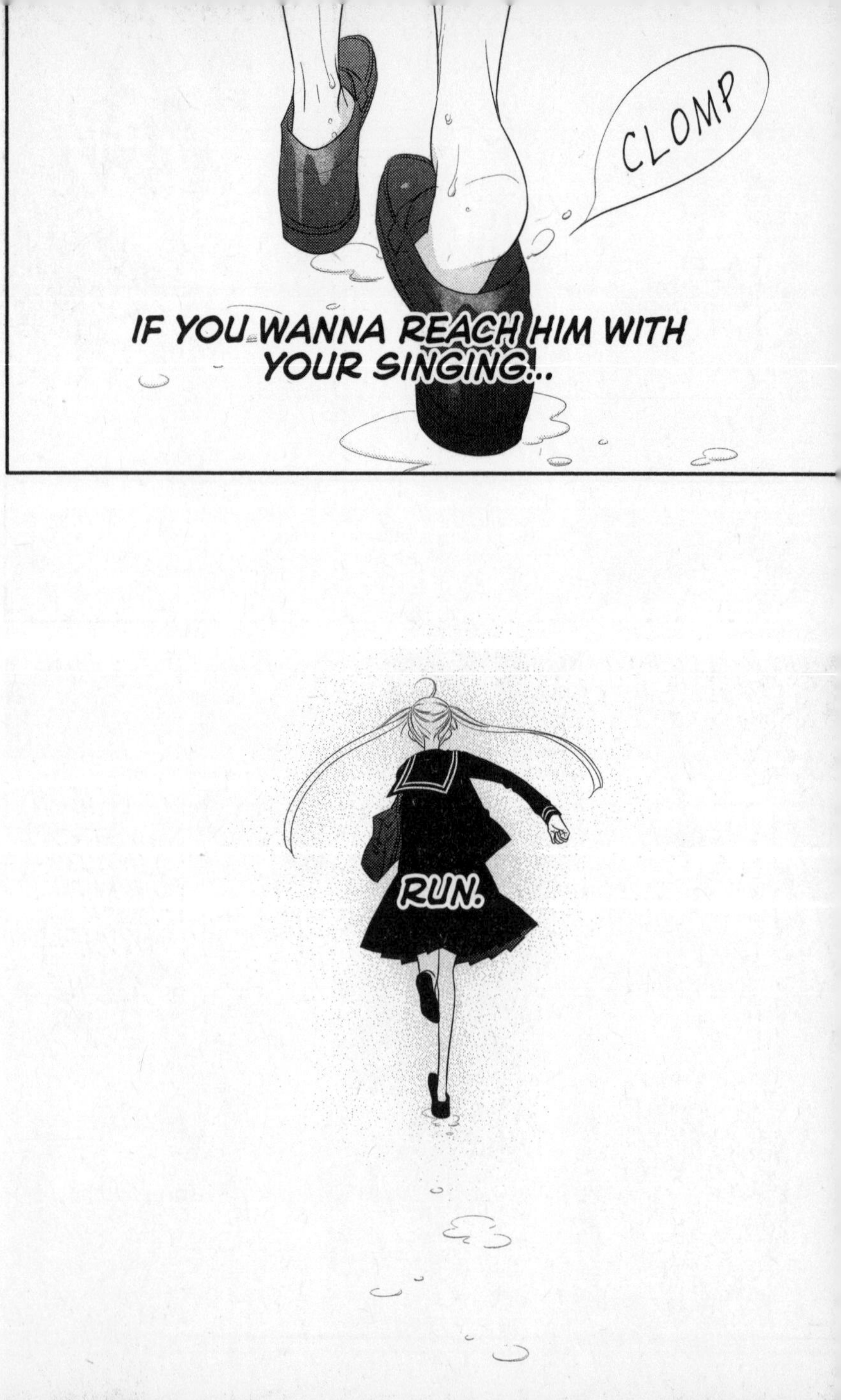
CLOMP
IF YOU WANNA REACH HIM WITH YOUR SINGING...
RUN.

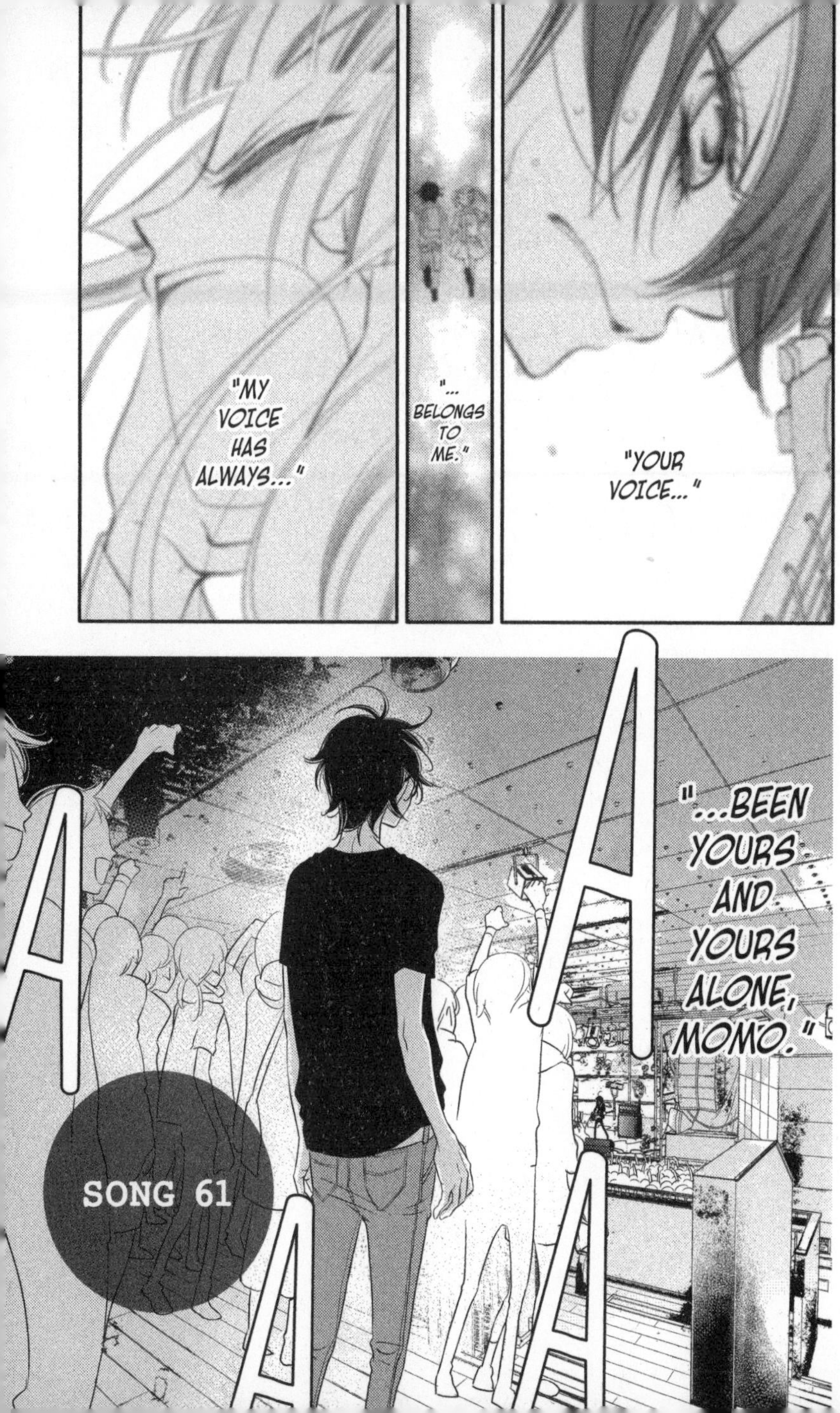
"YOUR VOICE..."
"...BELONGS TO ME."
"MY VOICE HAS ALWAYS..."
"...BEEN YOURS AND YOURS ALONE, MOMO."
AAAA
SONG 61

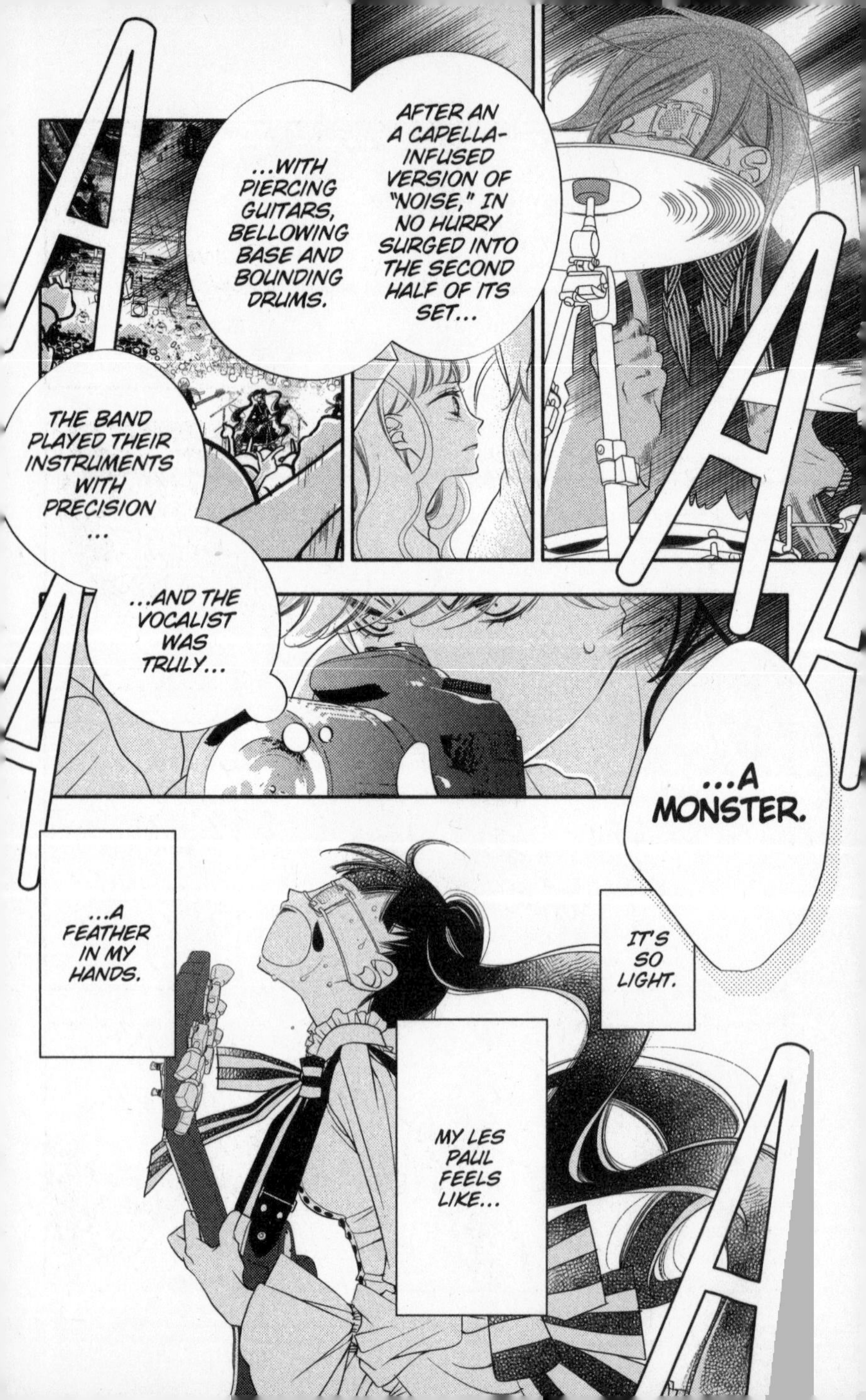
AFTER AN A CAPELLA-INFUSED VERSION OF "NOISE," IN NO HURRY SURGED INTO THE SECOND HALF OF ITS SET...
...WITH PIERCING GUITARS, BELLOWING BASE AND BOUNDING DRUMS.
THE BAND PLAYED THEIR INSTRUMENTS WITH PRECISION...
...AND THE VOCALIST WAS TRULY...
...A MONSTER.
IT'S SO LIGHT.
MY LES PAUL FEELS LIKE...
...A FEATHER IN MY HANDS.

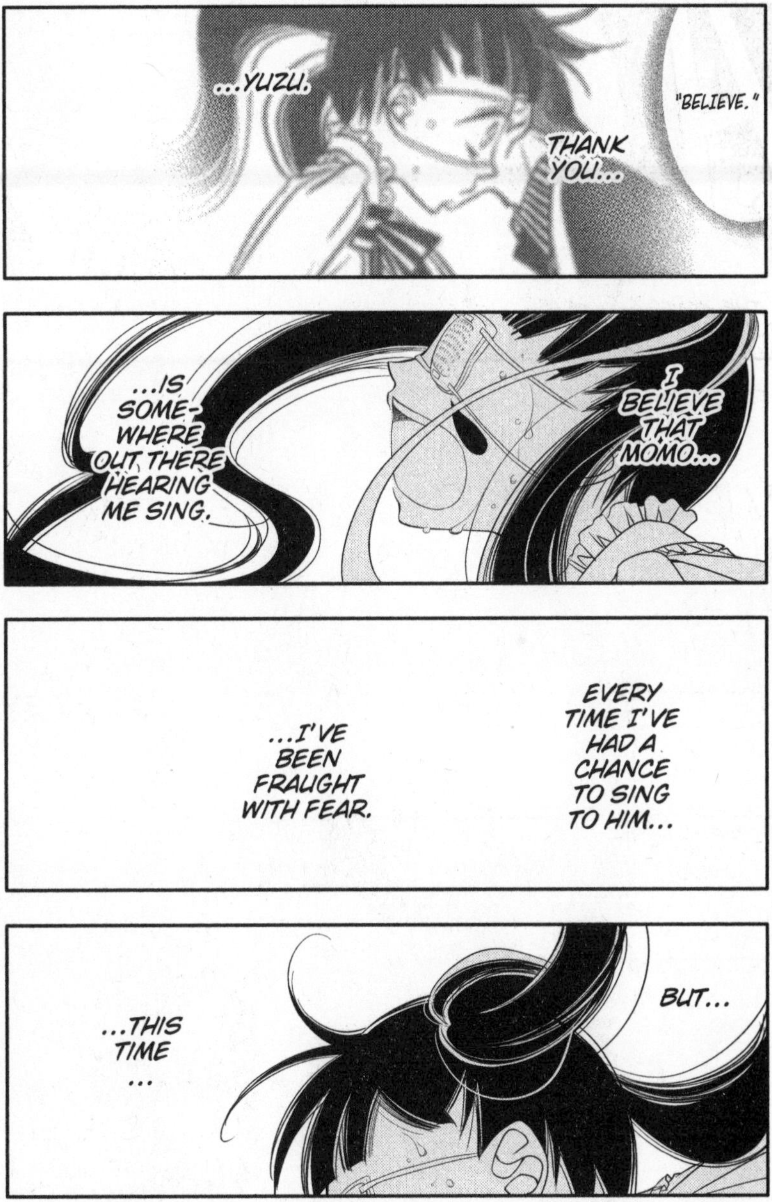
"BELIEVE."
THANK YOU...
...YUZU.
I BELIEVE THAT MOMO...
...IS SOME-WHERE OUT THERE HEARING ME SING.
EVERY TIME I'VE HAD A CHANCE TO SING TO HIM...
...I'VE BEEN FRAUGHT WITH FEAR.
BUT...
...THIS TIME ...

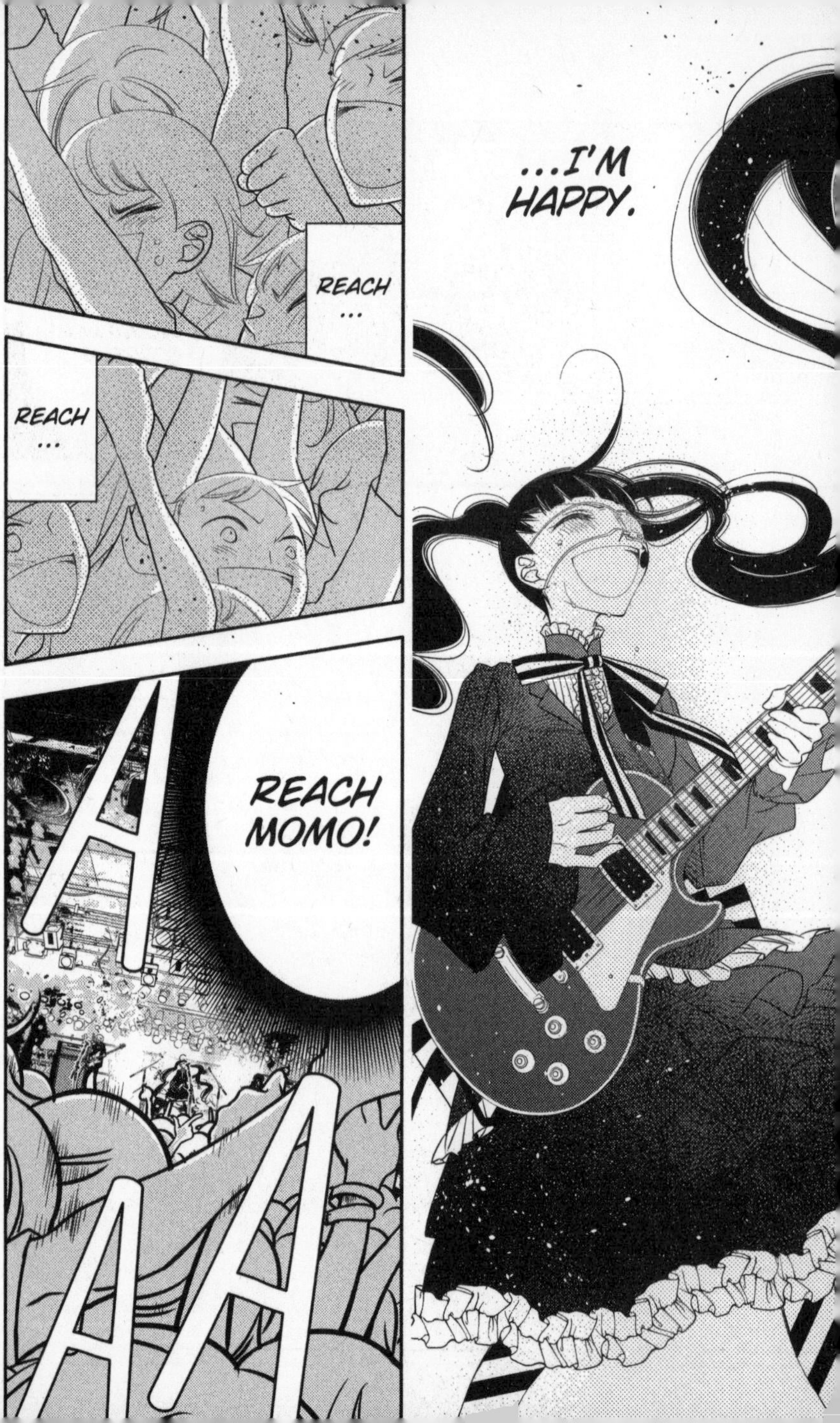
...I'M HAPPY.
REACH ...
REACH ...
REACH MOMO!
AAA

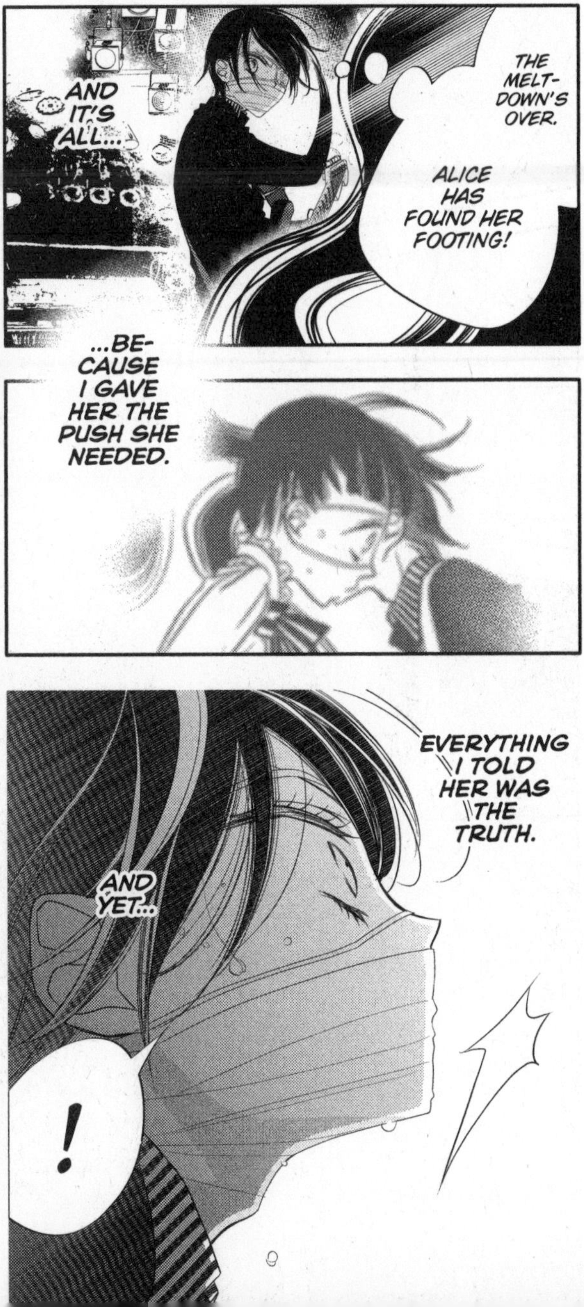
THE MELT-DOWN'S OVER.
ALICE HAS FOUND HER FOOTING!
AND IT'S ALL...
...BE-CAUSE I GAVE HER THE PUSH SHE NEEDED.
EVERYTHING I TOLD HER WAS THE TRUTH.
AND YET...
!

3

Yesterday, before the first day of shooting, we had a purification ceremony at a shrine. There, I met the cast for the first time, and...

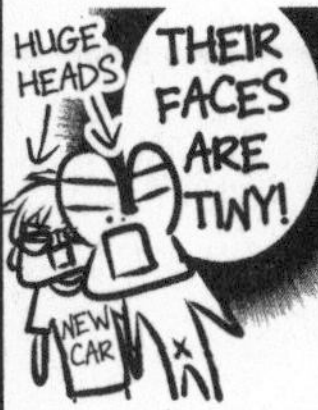
HUGE HEADS
THEIR FACES ARE TINY!
NEW CAR

I just couldn't get over how small their faces were!* What sort of wonderful things must they have done in their past lives to be rewarded with such tiny faces? How many of my past lives must I redo to get that small of a face myself?!

Incidentally, I haven't seen the movie Your Name yet.

I WONDER WHEN I'LL FINALLY HAVE A CHANCE...

*Having a small face is considered to be a beautiful trait in Japan.

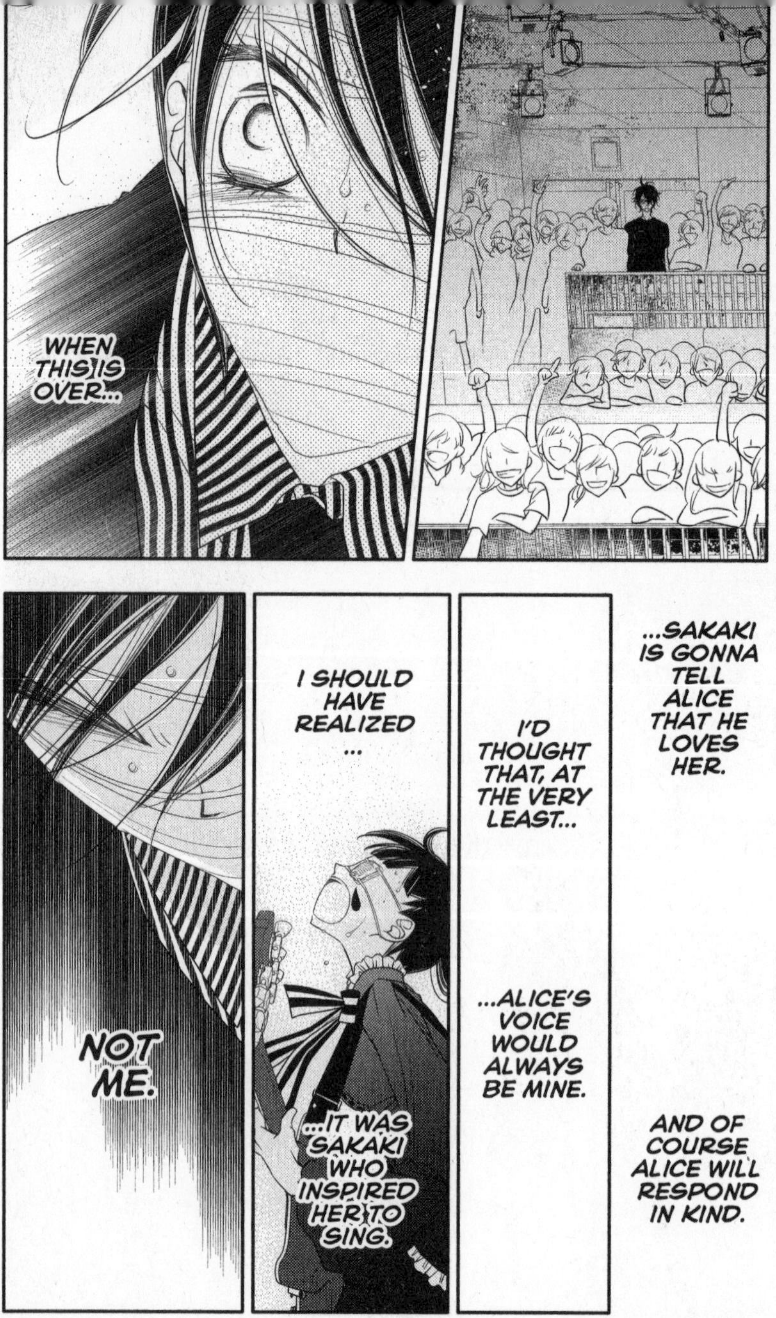
WHEN THIS IS OVER...
...SAKAKI IS GONNA TELL ALICE THAT HE LOVES HER.
AND OF COURSE ALICE WILL RESPOND IN KIND.
I'D THOUGHT THAT, AT THE VERY LEAST...
...ALICE'S VOICE WOULD ALWAYS BE MINE.
I SHOULD HAVE REALIZED...
...IT WAS SAKAKI WHO INSPIRED HER TO SING.
NOT ME.

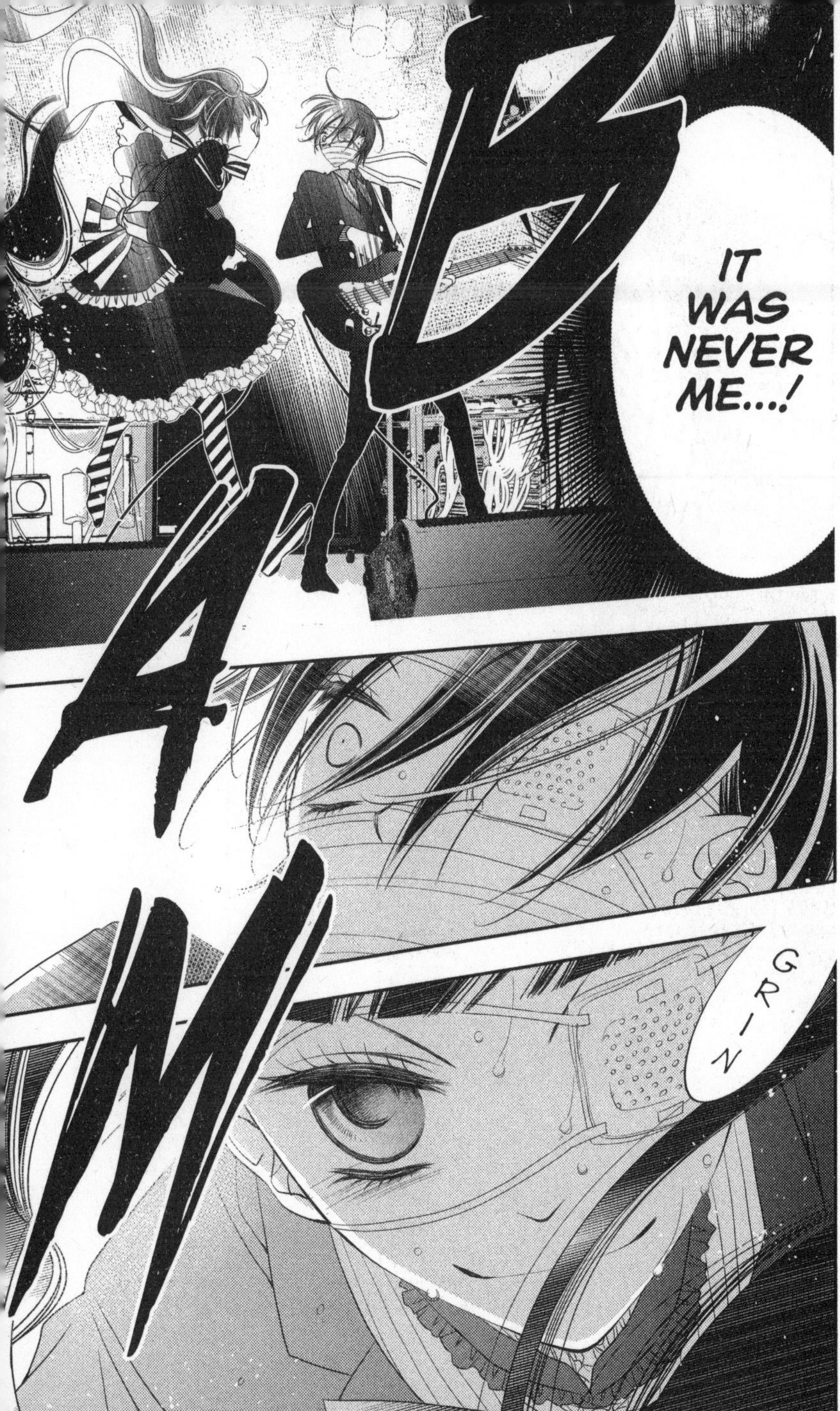
IT WAS NEVER ME...!
GRIN

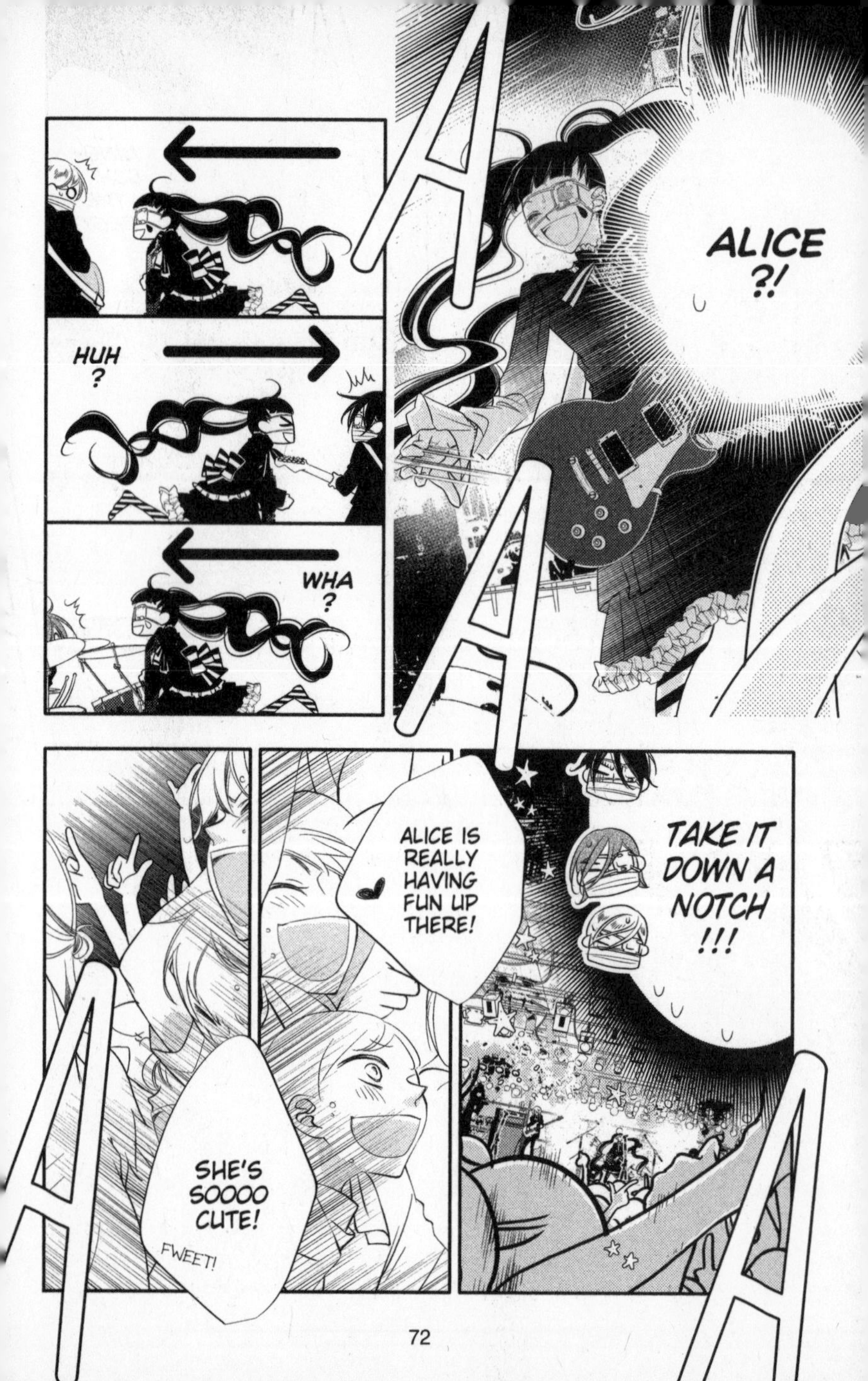
ALICE ?!
HUH ?
WHA ?
TAKE IT DOWN A NOTCH !!!
ALICE IS REALLY HAVING FUN UP THERE!
SHE'S SOOOO CUTE!
FWEET!

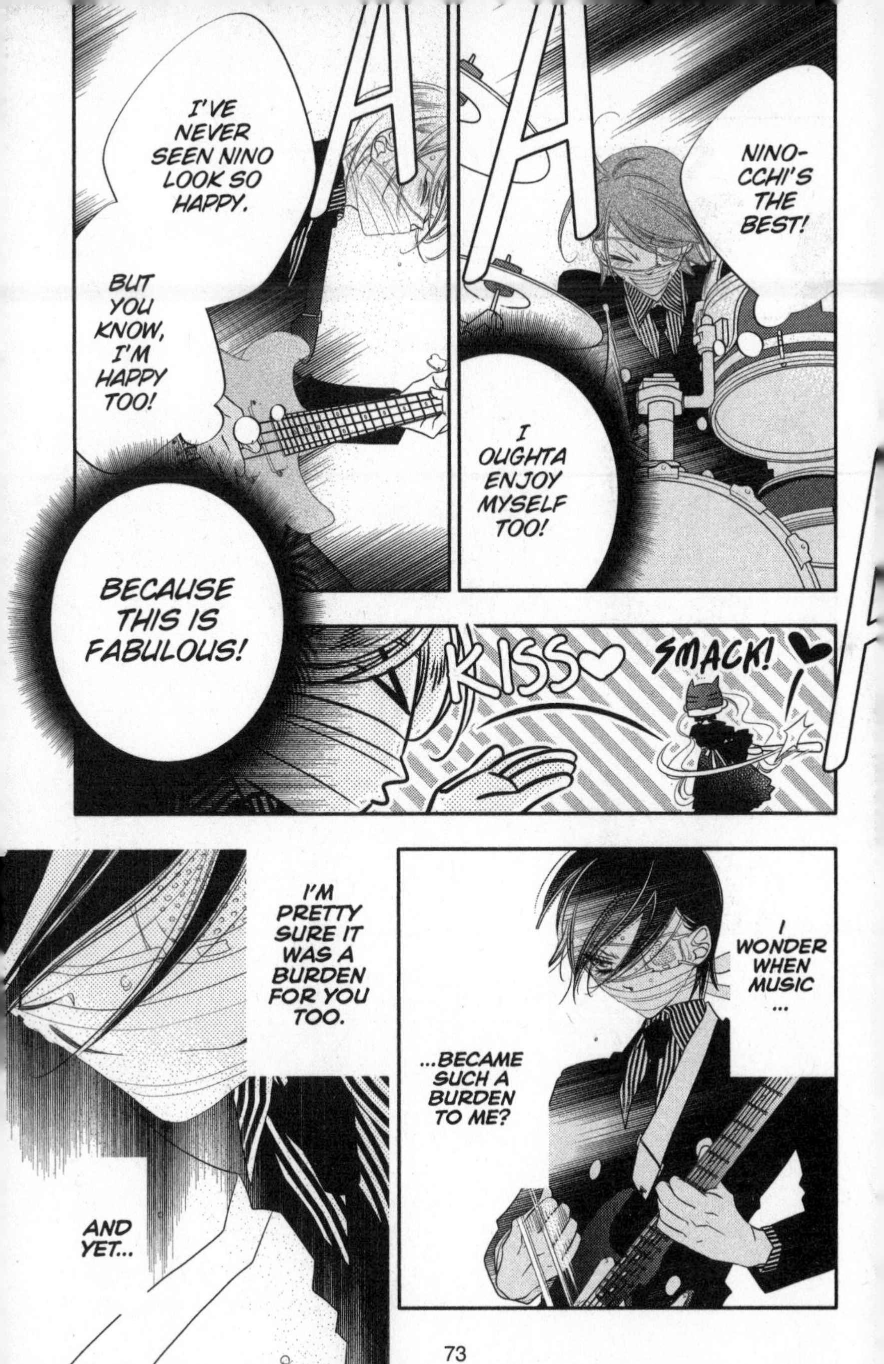
NINO-CCHI'S THE BEST!
I OUGHTA ENJOY MYSELF TOO!
I'VE NEVER SEEN NINO LOOK SO HAPPY.
BUT YOU KNOW, I'M HAPPY TOO!
BECAUSE THIS IS FABULOUS!
SMACK!
KISS
I WONDER WHEN MUSIC ...
...BECAME SUCH A BURDEN TO ME?
I'M PRETTY SURE IT WAS A BURDEN FOR YOU TOO.
AND YET...

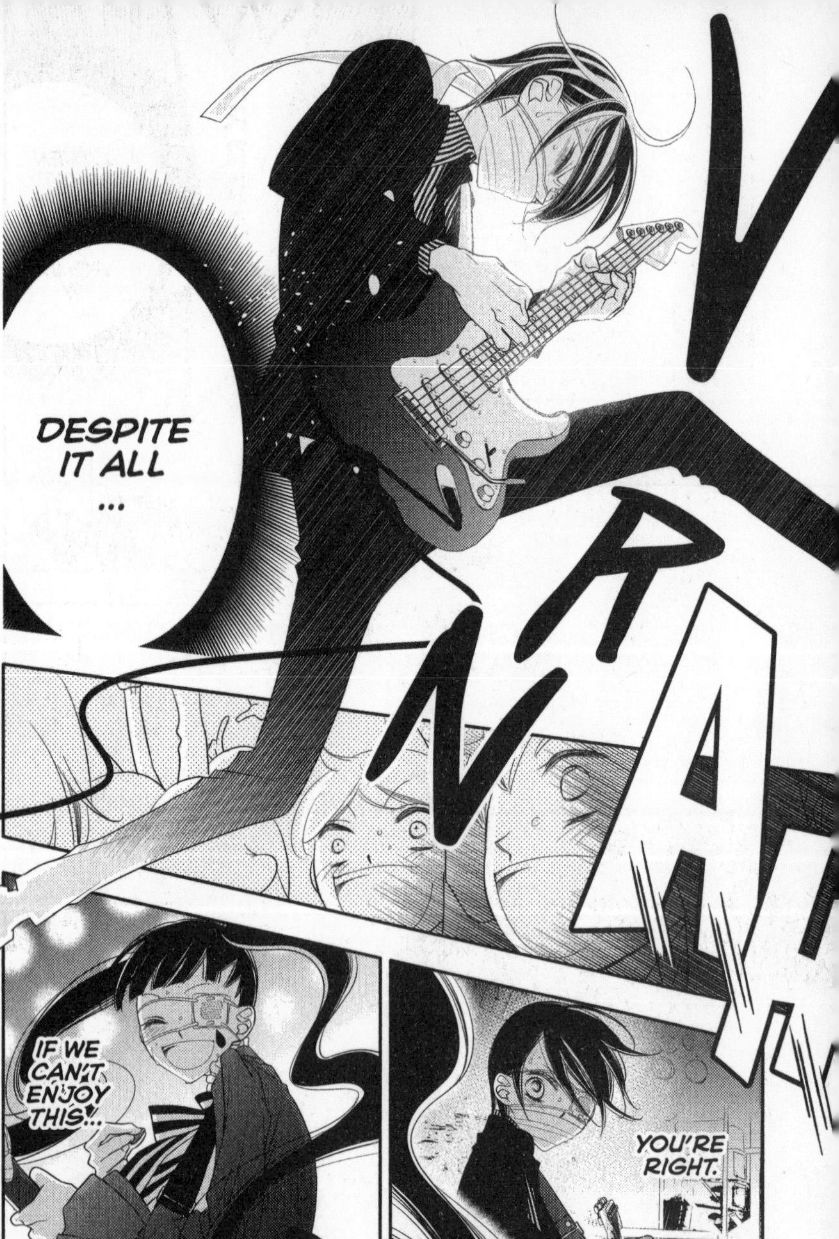
DESPITE IT ALL ...
YOU'RE RIGHT.
IF WE CAN'T ENJOY THIS...

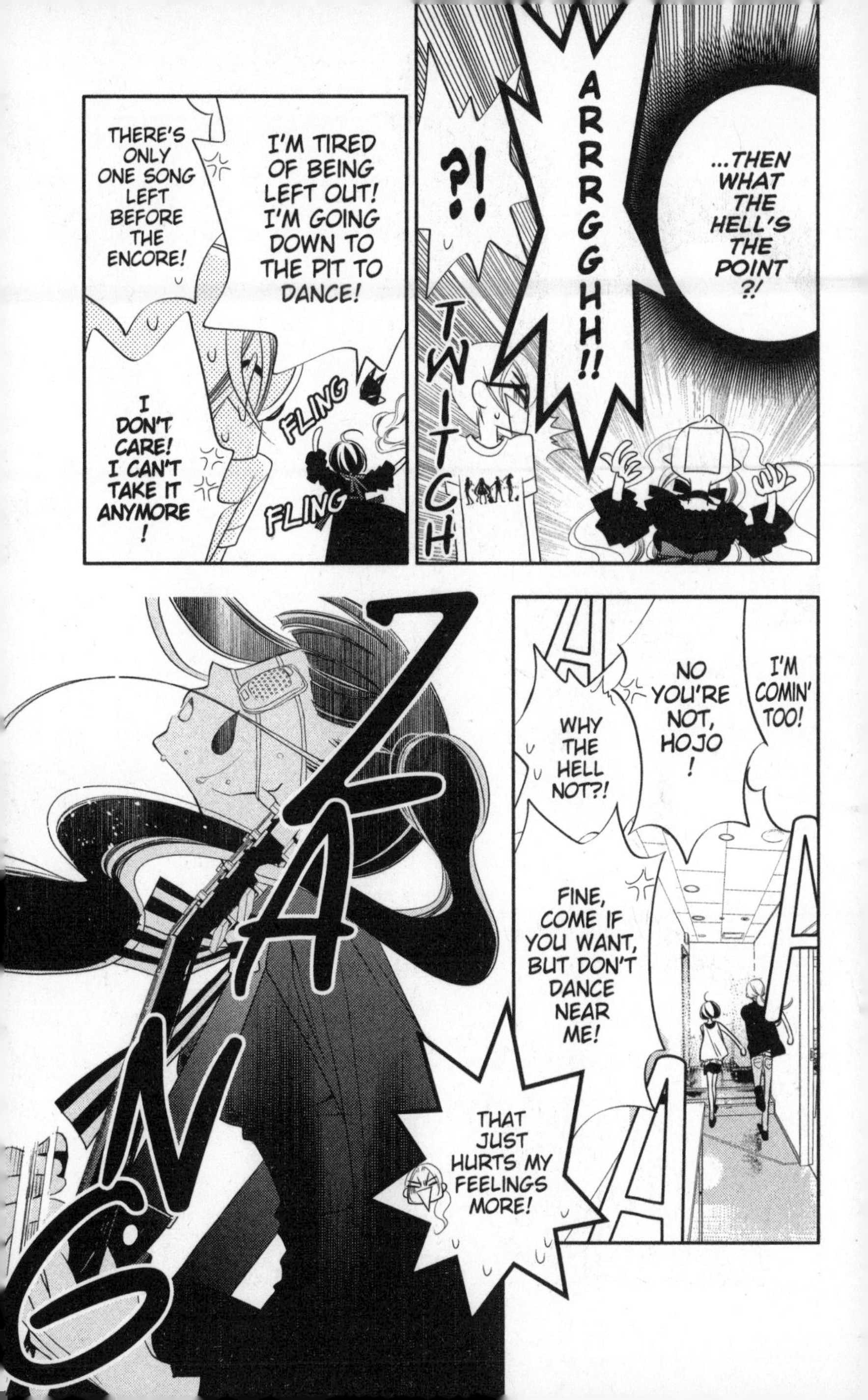
...THEN WHAT THE HELL'S THE POINT?!
ARRRGGHH!!
?!
TWITCH
I'M TIRED OF BEING LEFT OUT! I'M GOING DOWN TO THE PIT TO DANCE!
THERE'S ONLY ONE SONG LEFT BEFORE THE ENCORE!
FLING
FLING
I DON'T CARE! I CAN'T TAKE IT ANYMORE!
I'M COMIN' TOO!
NO YOU'RE NOT, HOJO!
WHY THE HELL NOT?!
FINE, COME IF YOU WANT, BUT DON'T DANCE NEAR ME!
THAT JUST HURTS MY FEELINGS MORE!

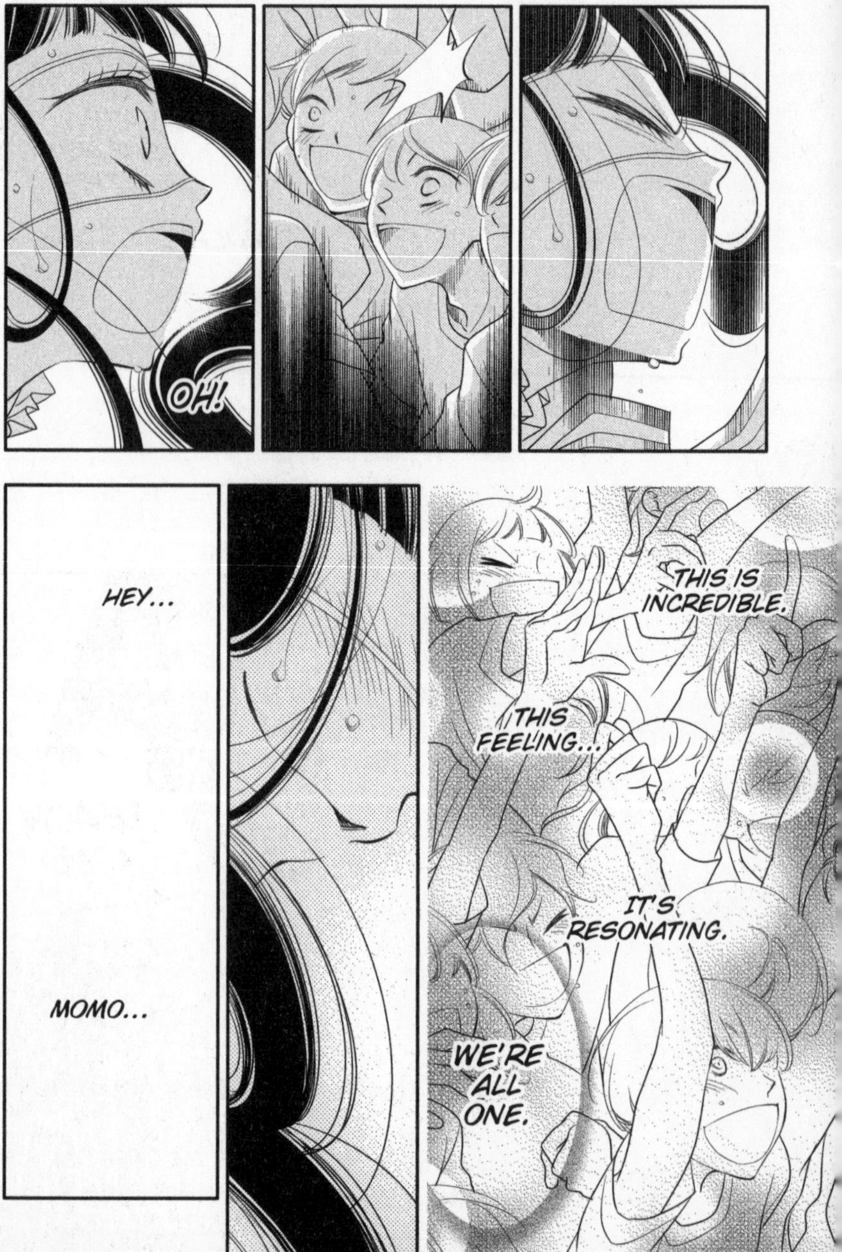
OH!
THIS IS INCREDIBLE.
THIS FEELING...
IT'S RESONATING.
WE'RE ALL ONE.
HEY...
MOMO...

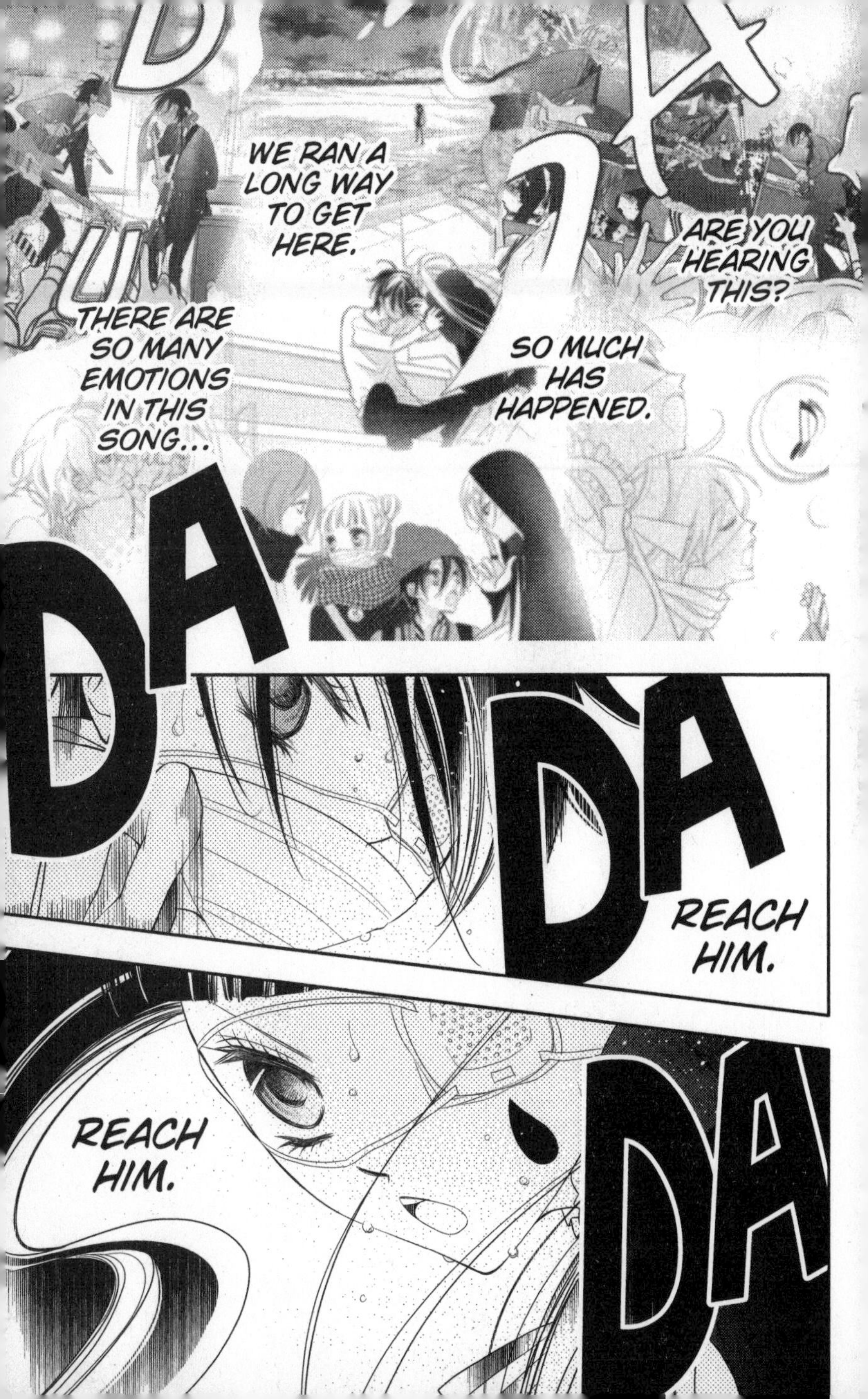
ARE YOU HEARING THIS?
WE RAN A LONG WAY TO GET HERE.
SO MUCH HAS HAPPENED.
THERE ARE SO MANY EMOTIONS IN THIS SONG...
DA
DA
REACH HIM.
DA
REACH HIM.

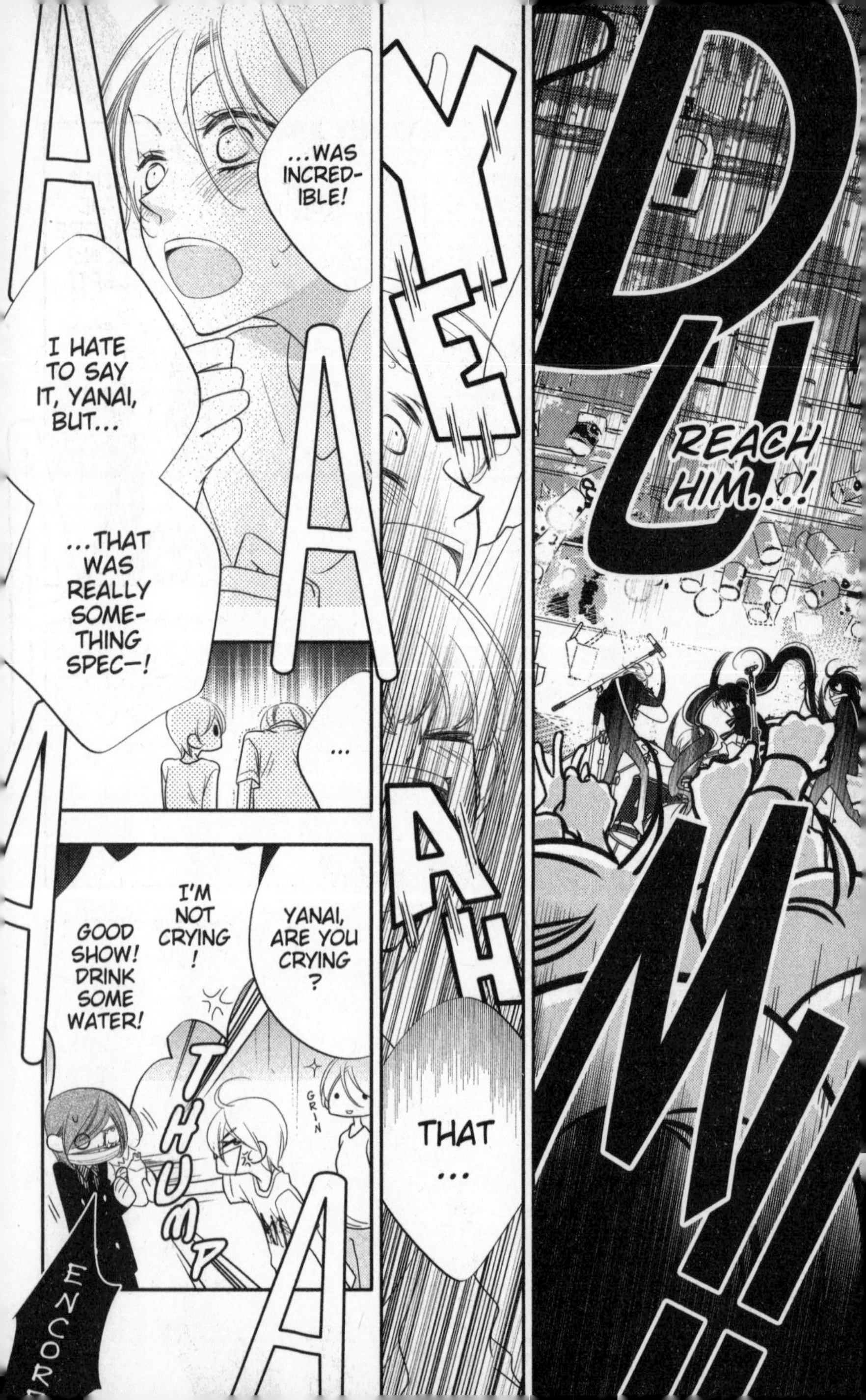
DUMM!!
REACH HIM..!!
YEAH
THAT...
...WAS INCREDIBLE!
I HATE TO SAY IT, YANAI, BUT...
...THAT WAS REALLY SOMETHING SPEC—!
AAAA
...
YANAI, ARE YOU CRYING?
I'M NOT CRYING!
GOOD SHOW! DRINK SOME WATER!
GRIN
THUMP
ENCOR

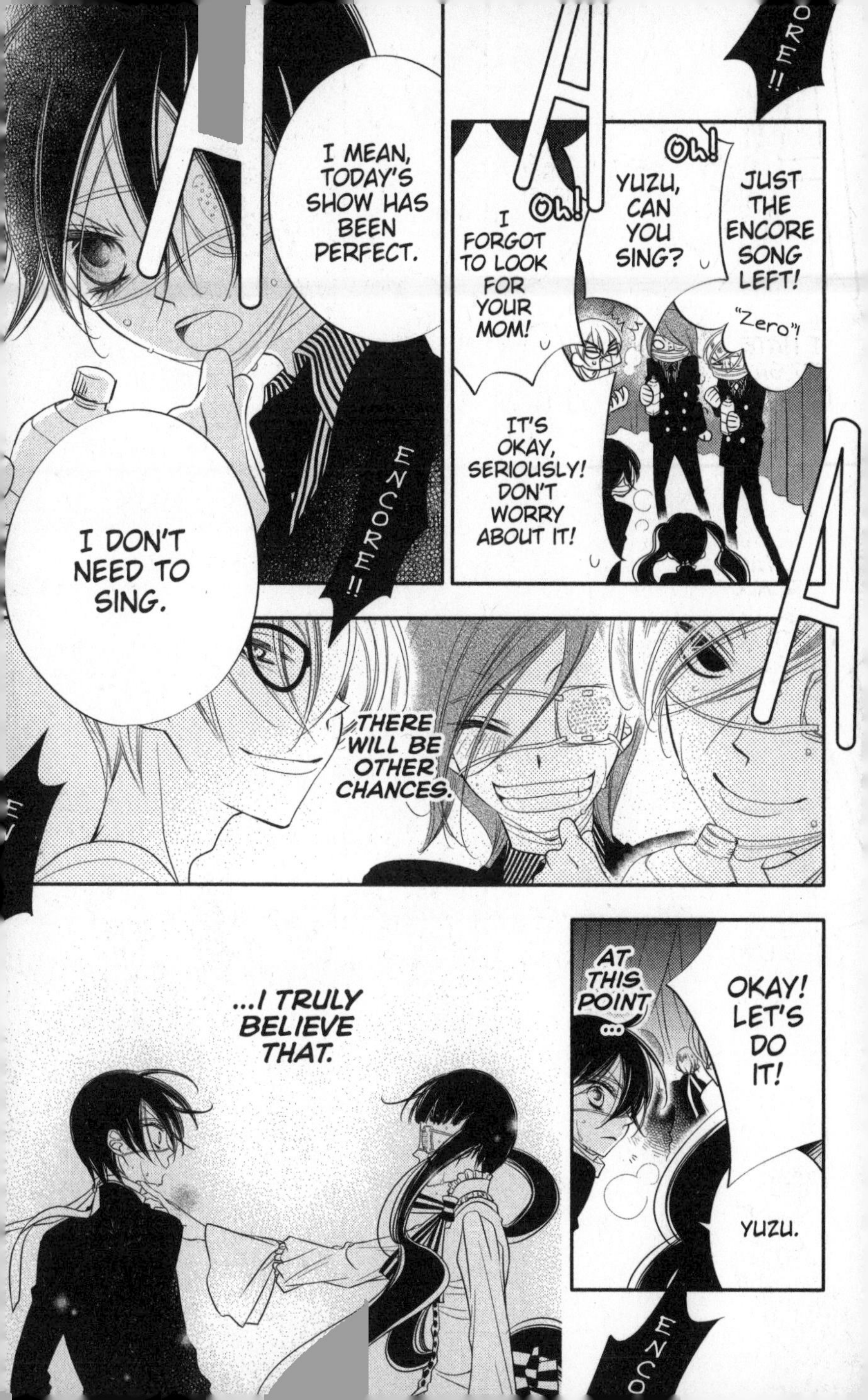

ENCORE!!
JUST THE ENCORE SONG LEFT!
Oh!
YUZU, CAN YOU SING?
"Zero"!
Oh!
I FORGOT TO LOOK FOR YOUR MOM!
IT'S OKAY, SERIOUSLY! DON'T WORRY ABOUT IT!
I MEAN, TODAY'S SHOW HAS BEEN PERFECT.
ENCORE!!
I DON'T NEED TO SING.
THERE WILL BE OTHER CHANCES.
OKAY! LET'S DO IT!
AT THIS POINT...
YUZU.
ENCO
...I TRULY BELIEVE THAT.

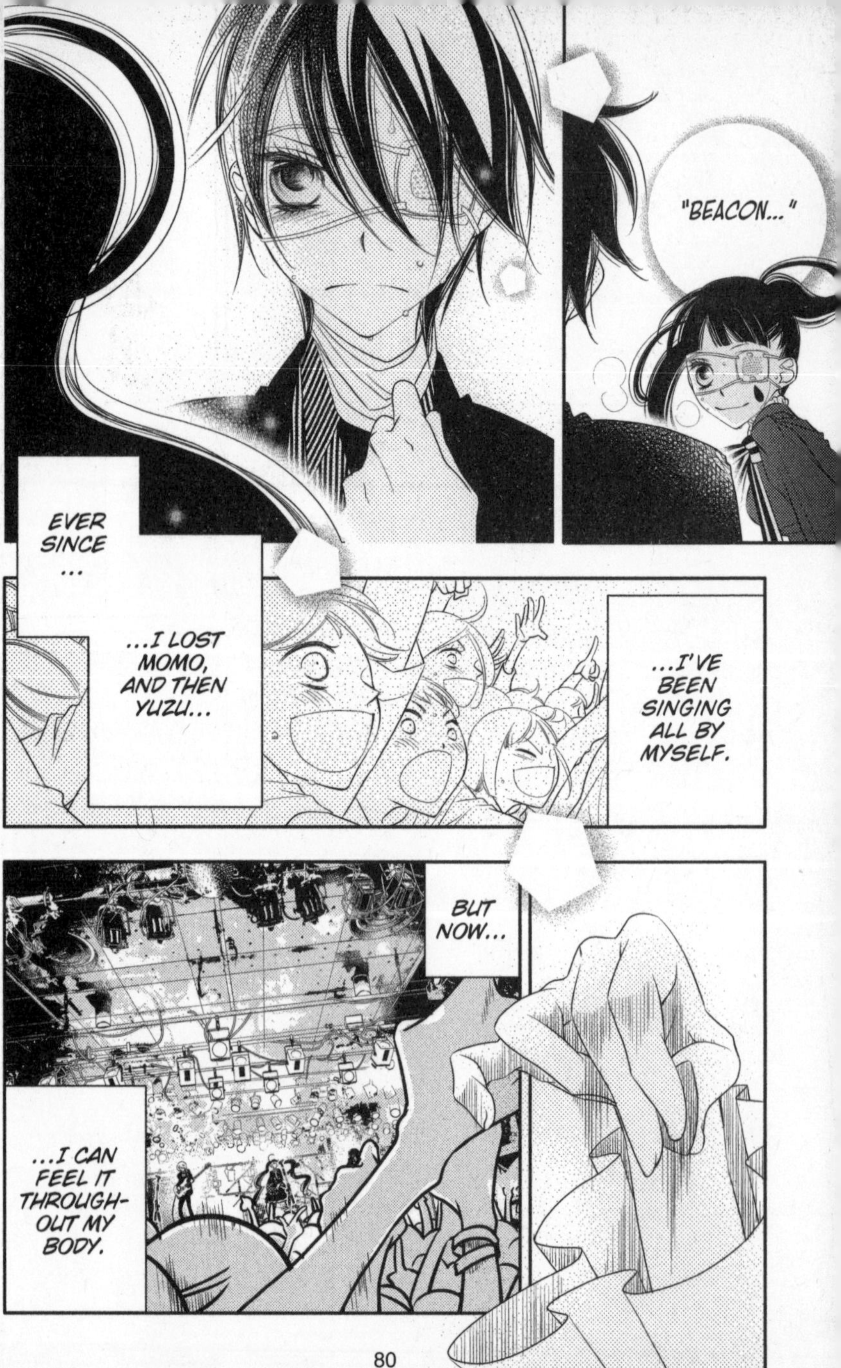
"BEACON..."
EVER SINCE...
...I LOST MOMO, AND THEN YUZU...
...I'VE BEEN SINGING ALL BY MYSELF.
BUT NOW...
...I CAN FEEL IT THROUGH-OUT MY BODY.

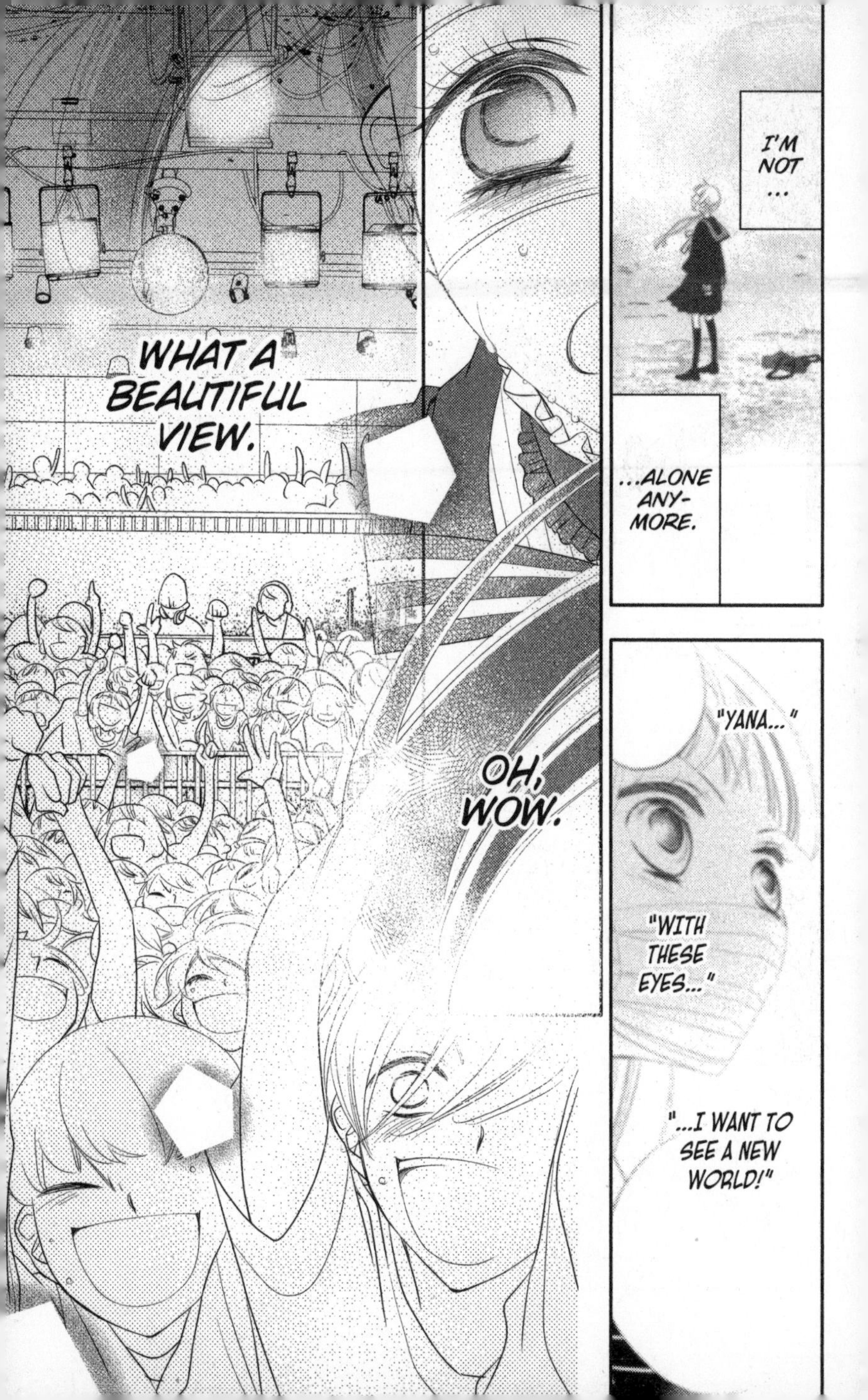
I'M NOT ...
...ALONE ANYMORE.
"YANA..."
"WITH THESE EYES..."
"...I WANT TO SEE A NEW WORLD!"
OH, WOW.
WHAT A BEAUTIFUL VIEW.

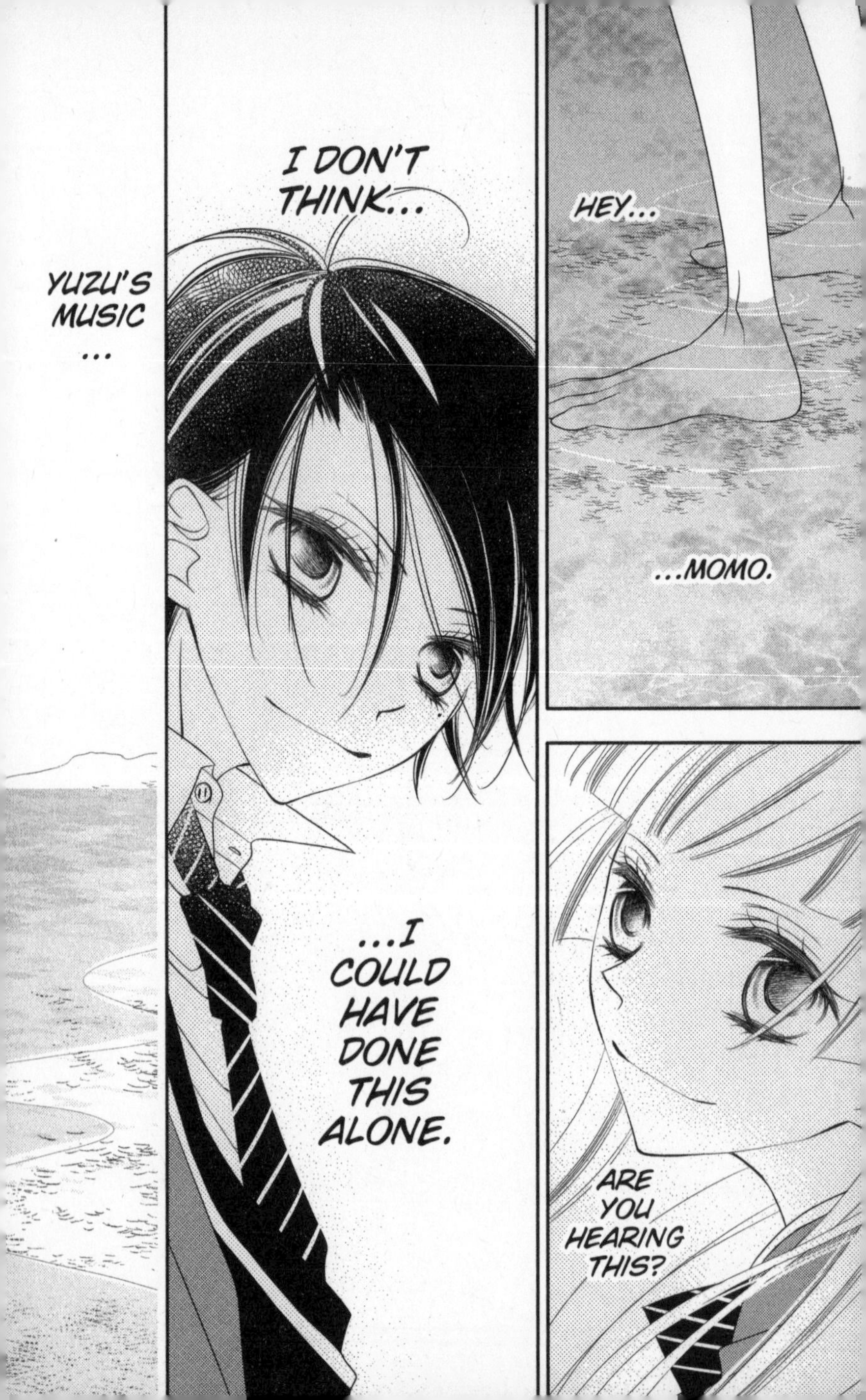
HEY...
...MOMO.
ARE YOU HEARING THIS?
I DON'T THINK...
...I COULD HAVE DONE THIS ALONE.
YUZU'S MUSIC ...

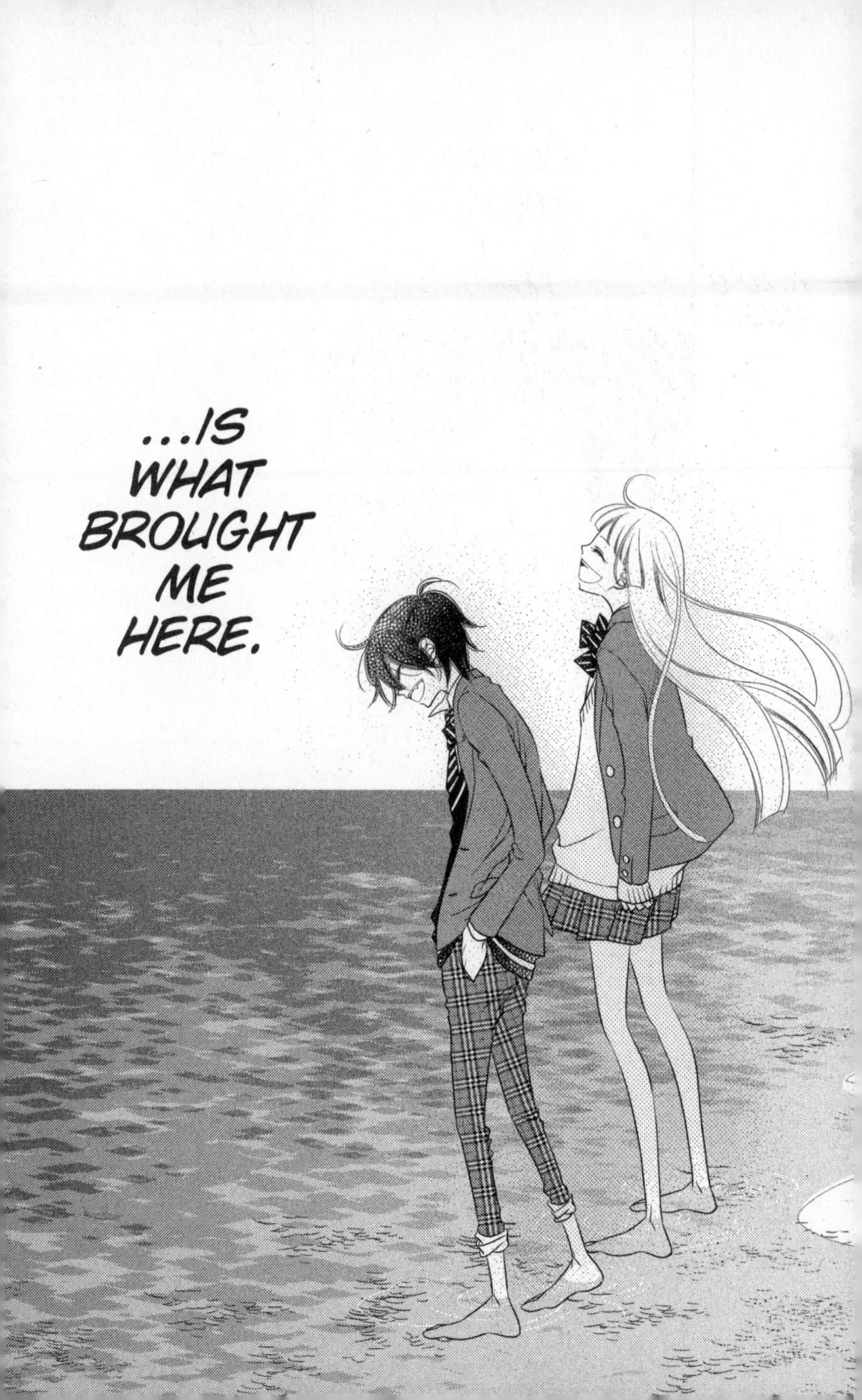
...IS WHAT BROUGHT ME HERE.

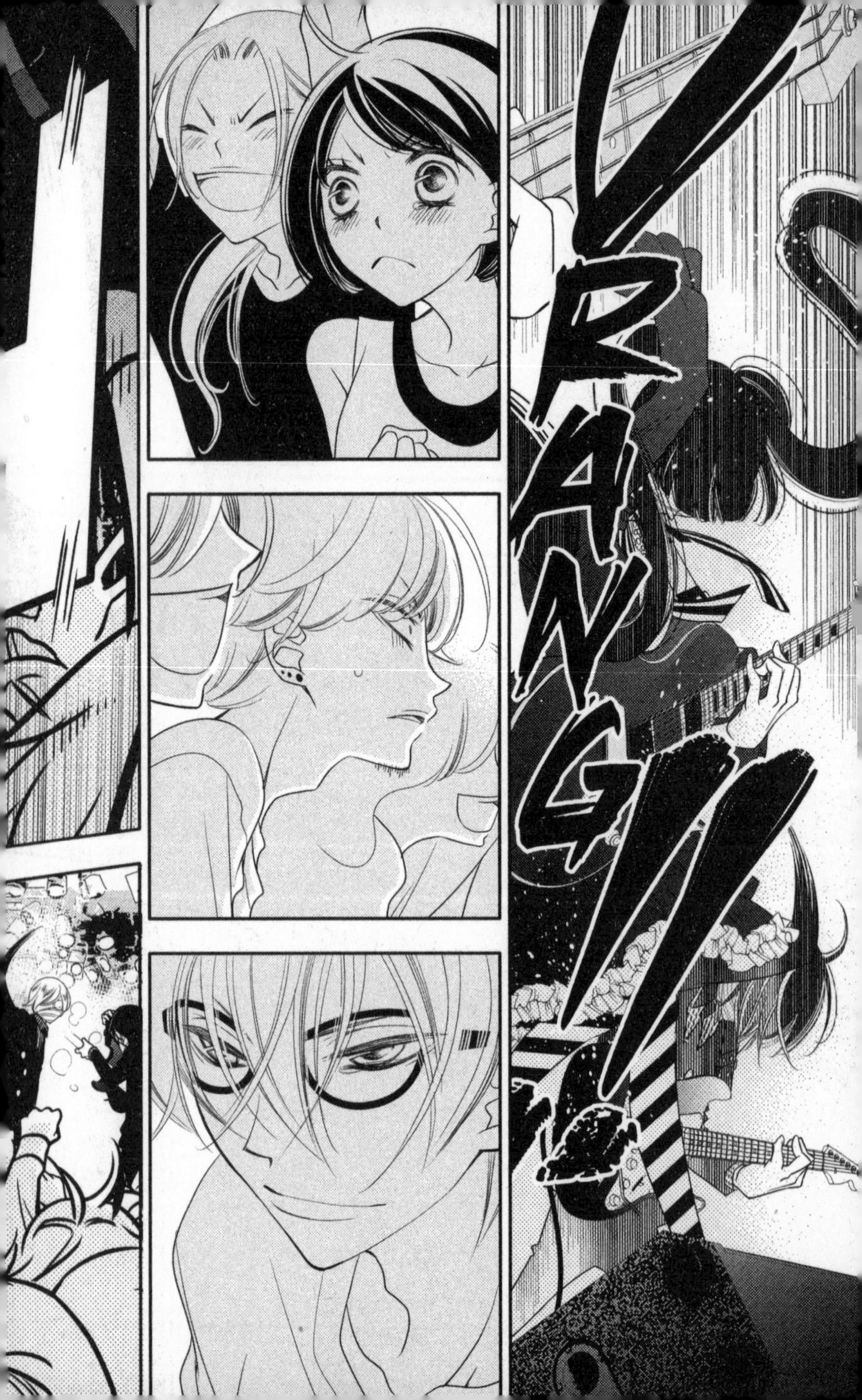
VRANG!!

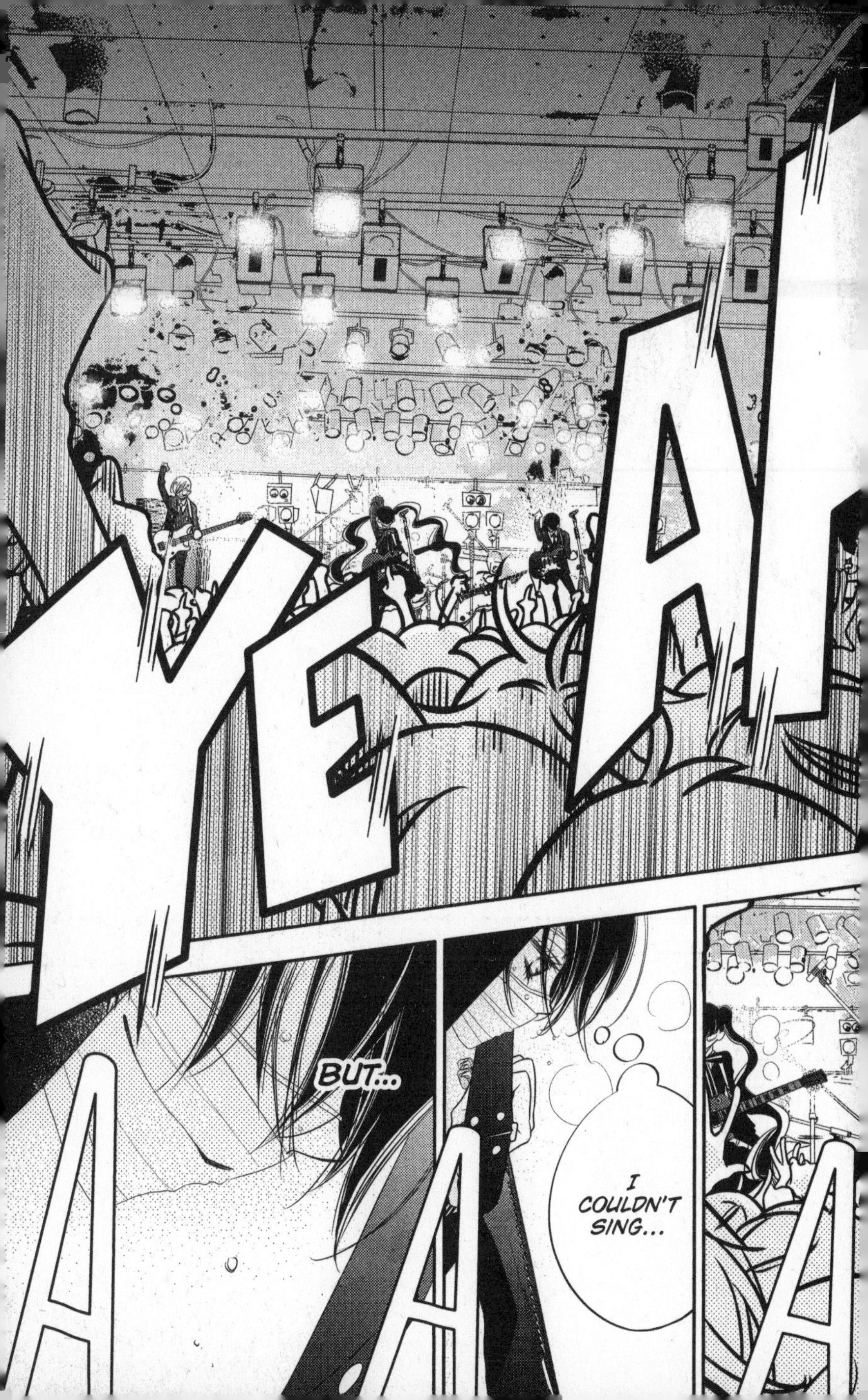
YEA
AAAA
I COULDN'T SING...
BUT...

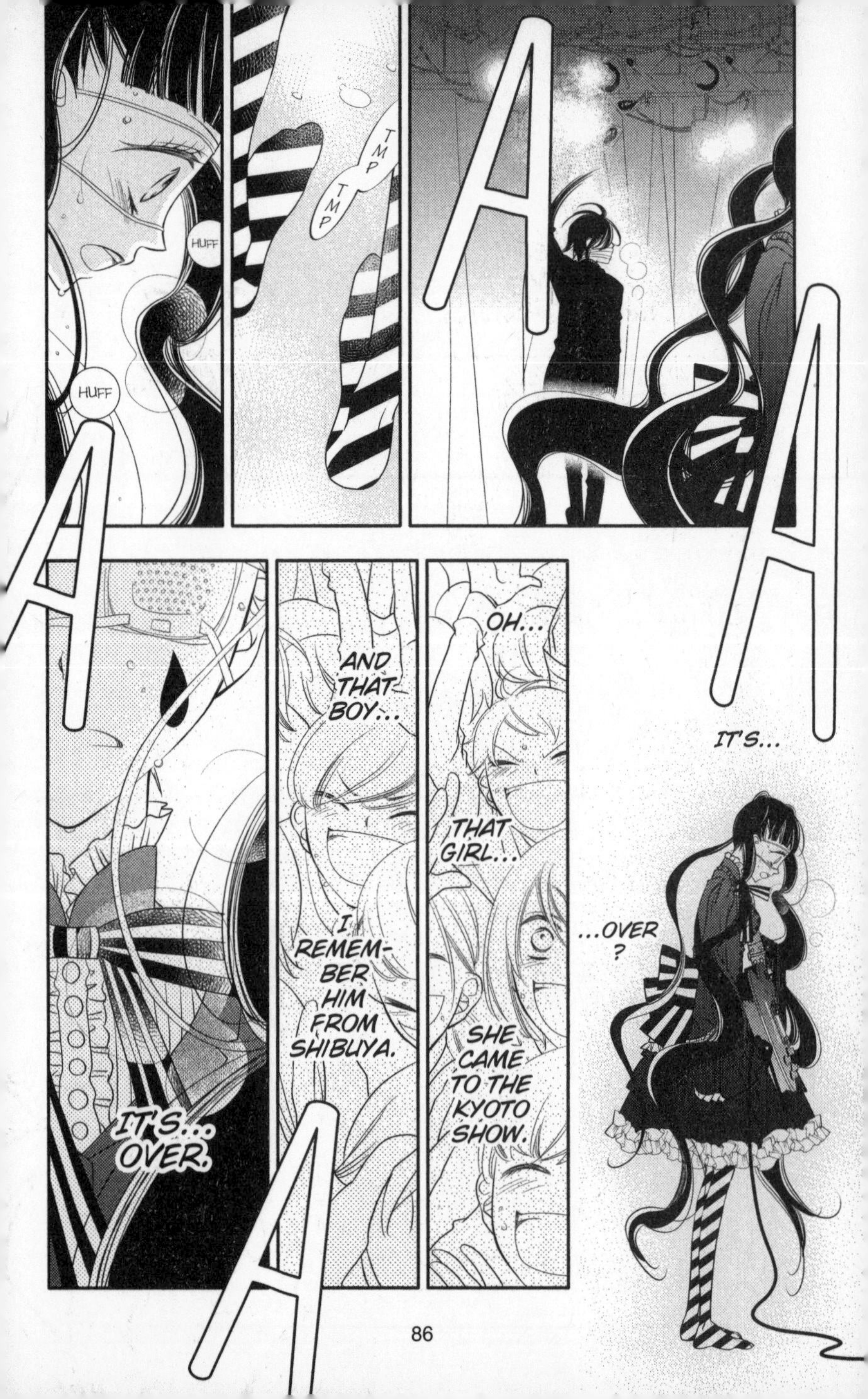
A
A
A
TMP TMP
HUFF
HUFF
A
IT'S...
...OVER?
OH...
THAT GIRL...
SHE CAME TO THE KYOTO SHOW.
AND THAT BOY...
I REMEMBER HIM FROM SHIBUYA.
A
IT'S... OVER.

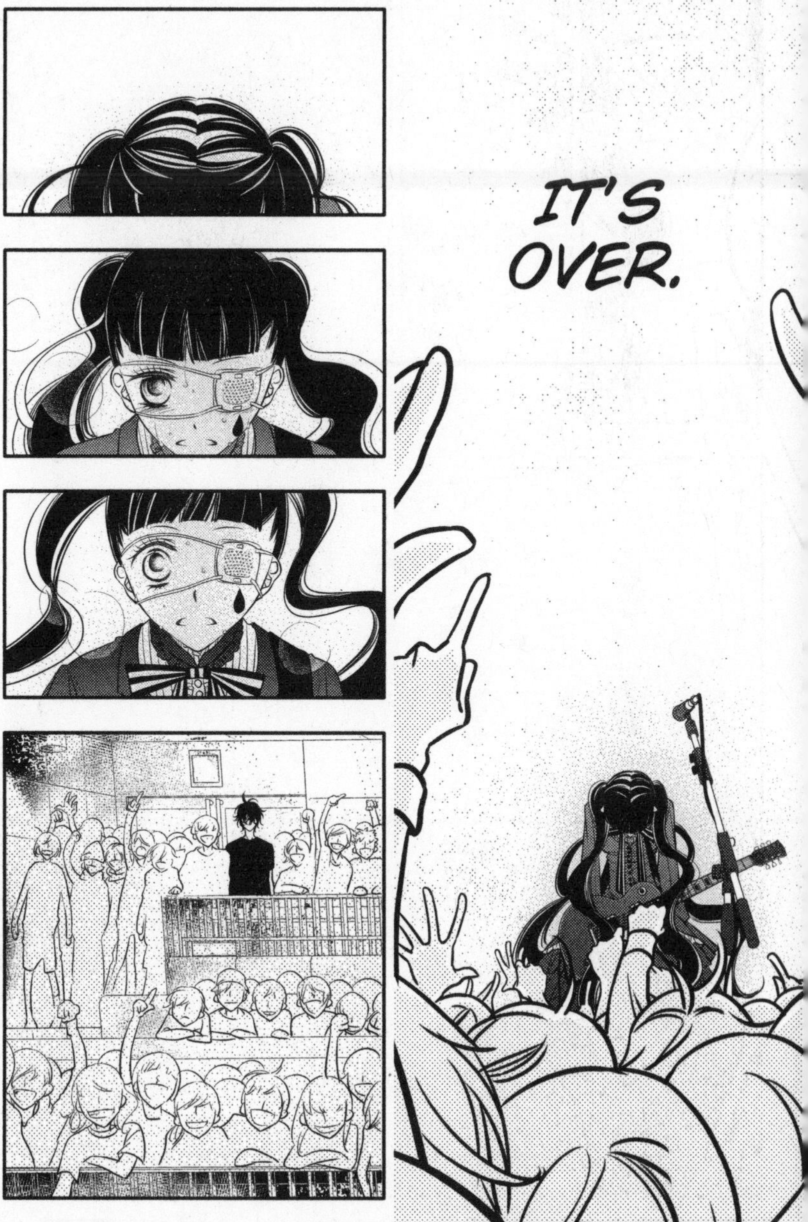
IT'S OVER.

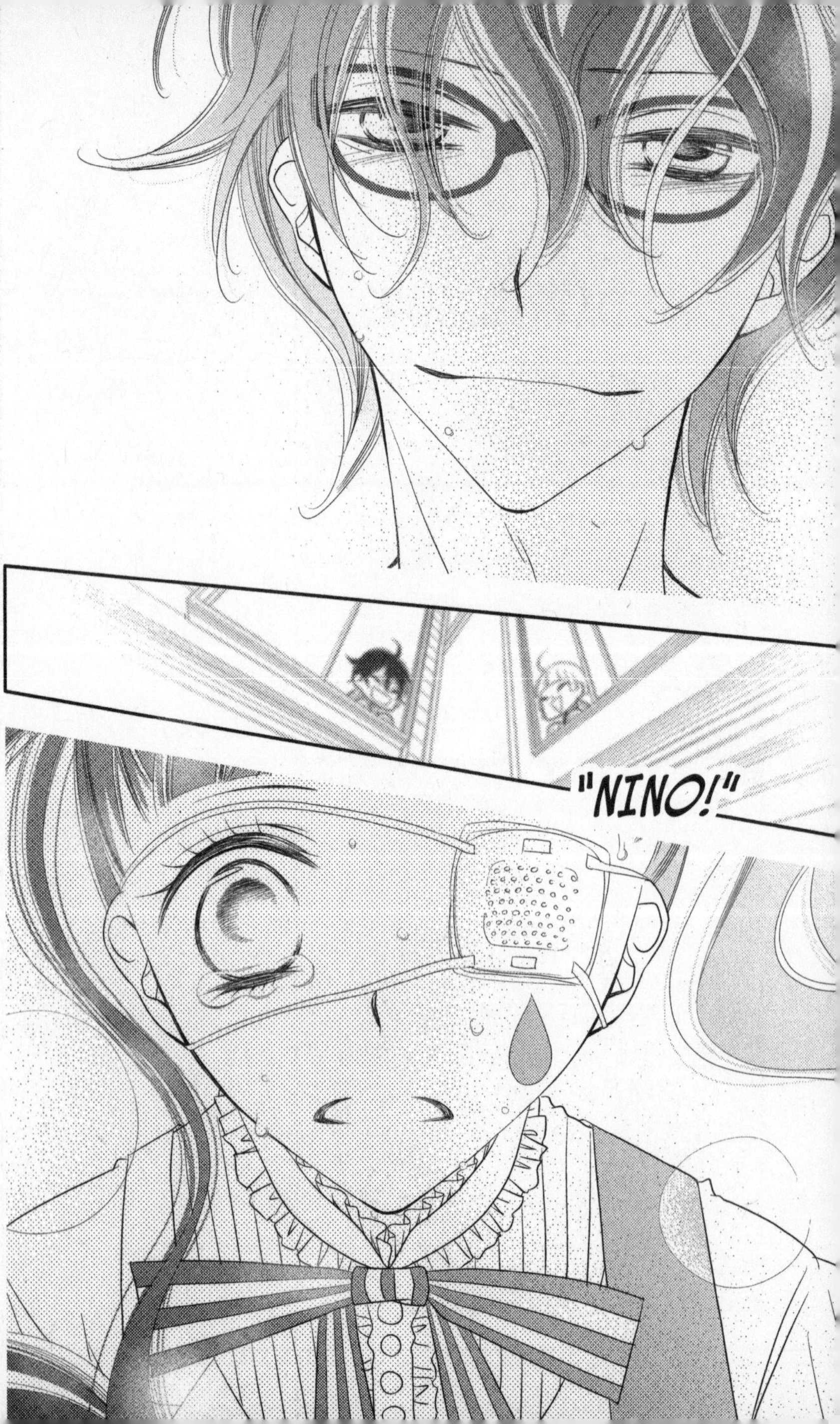
"NINO!"

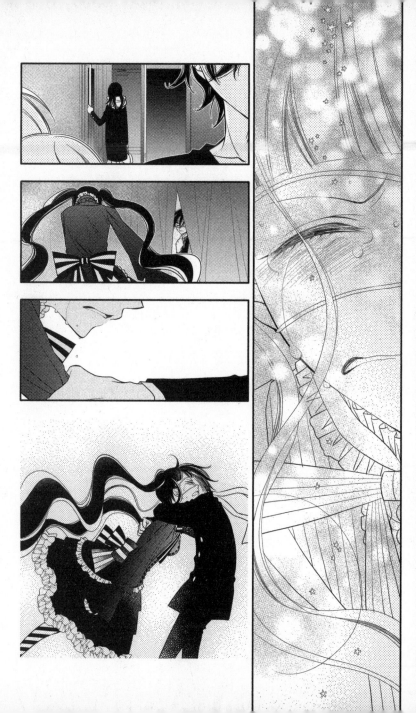

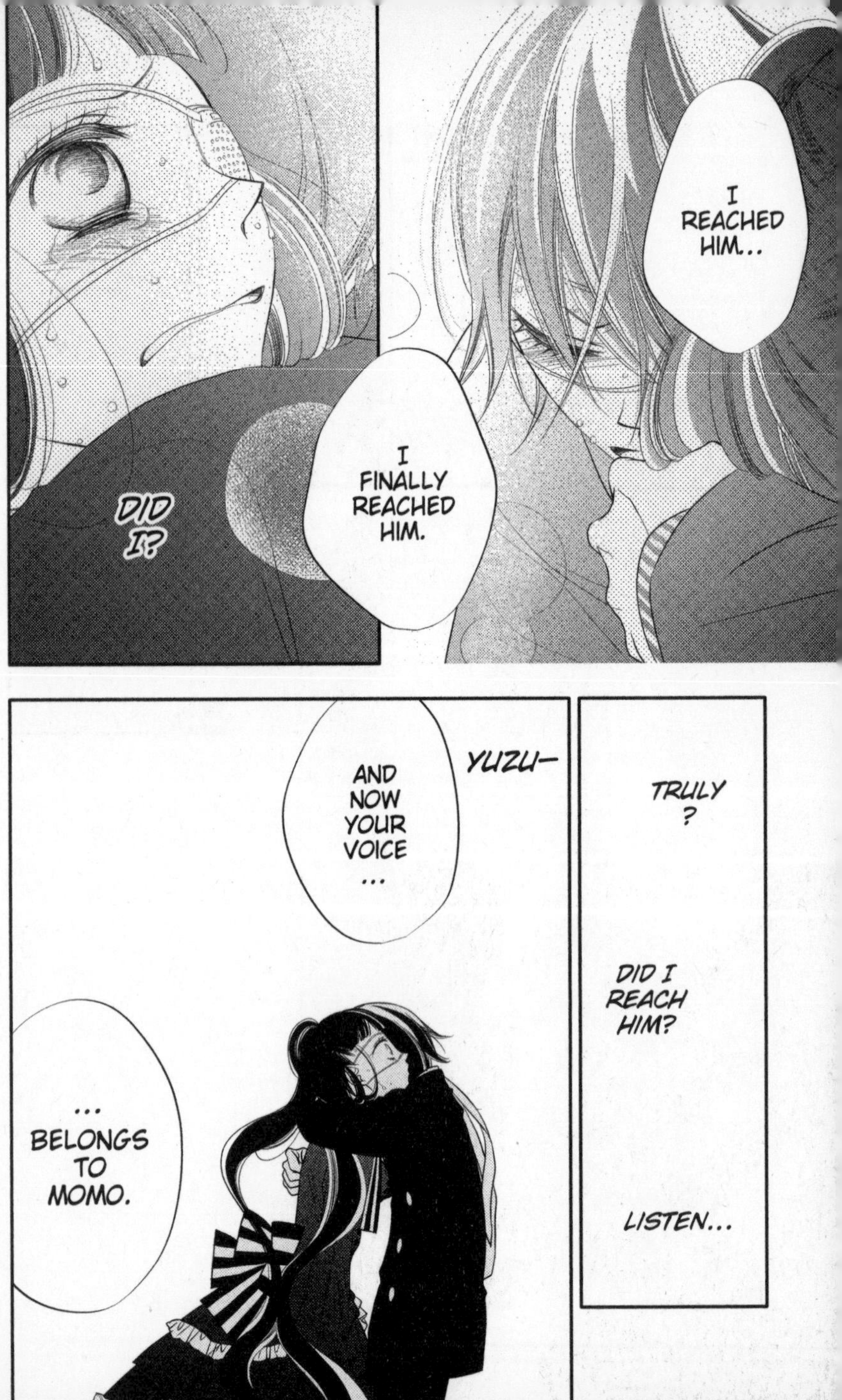
I REACHED HIM...
I FINALLY REACHED HIM.
DID I?
TRULY?
DID I REACH HIM?
LISTEN...
YUZU—
AND NOW YOUR VOICE...
...BELONGS TO MOMO.

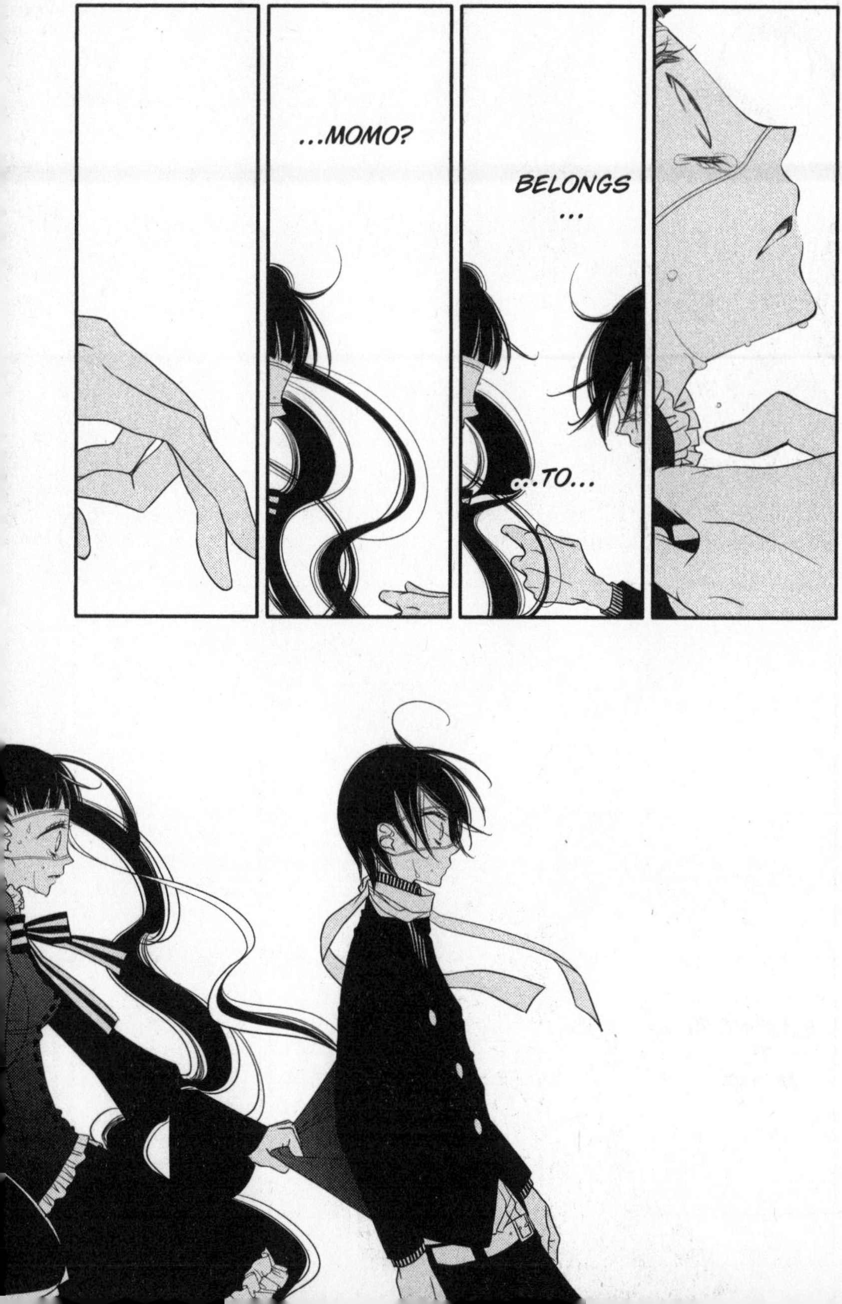
BELONGS ...
...TO...
...MOMO?

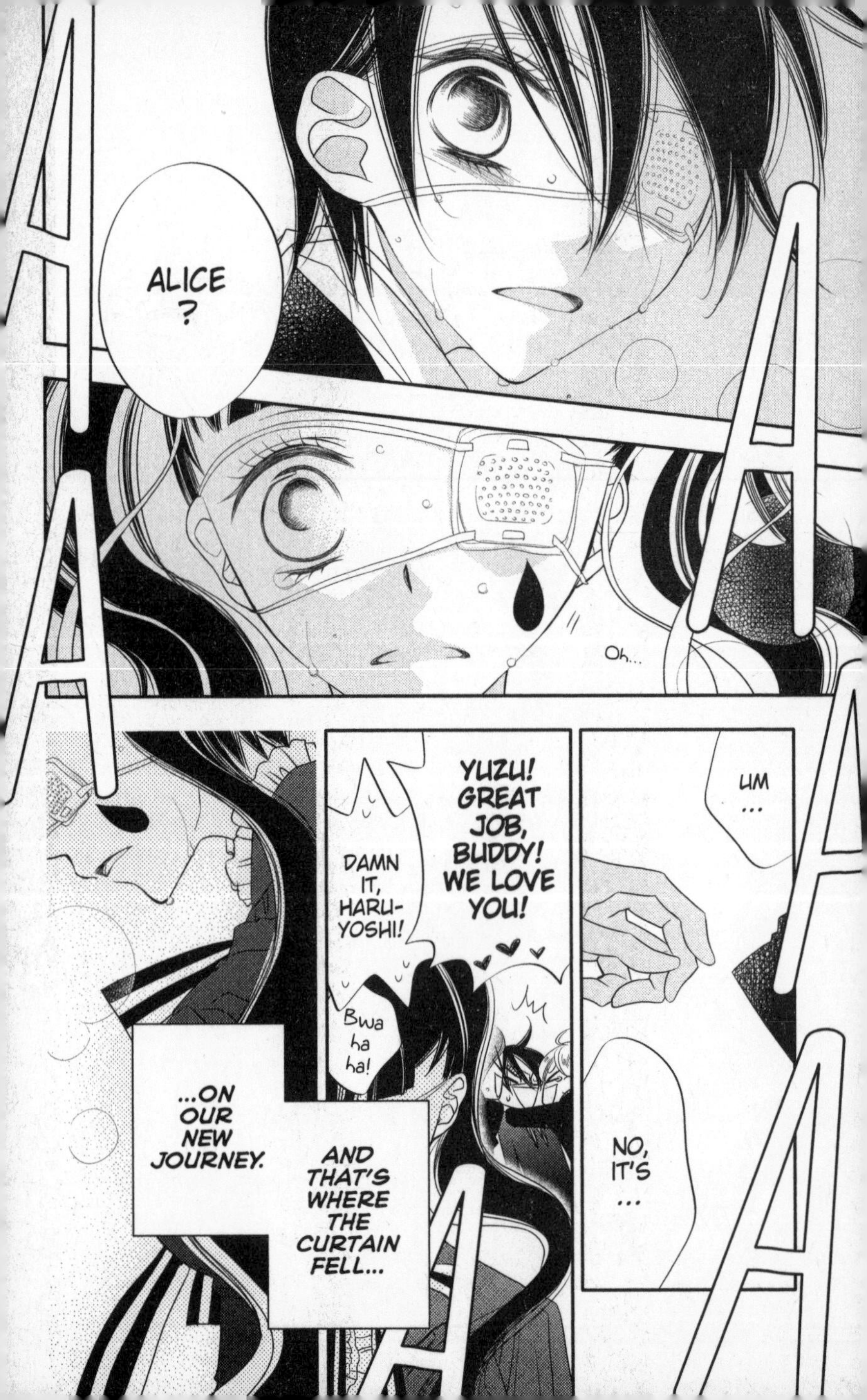
ALICE?
Oh...
UM...
NO, IT'S...
YUZU! GREAT JOB, BUDDY! WE LOVE YOU!
DAMN IT, HARUYOSHI!
Bwa ha ha!
AND THAT'S WHERE THE CURTAIN FELL...
...ON OUR NEW JOURNEY.

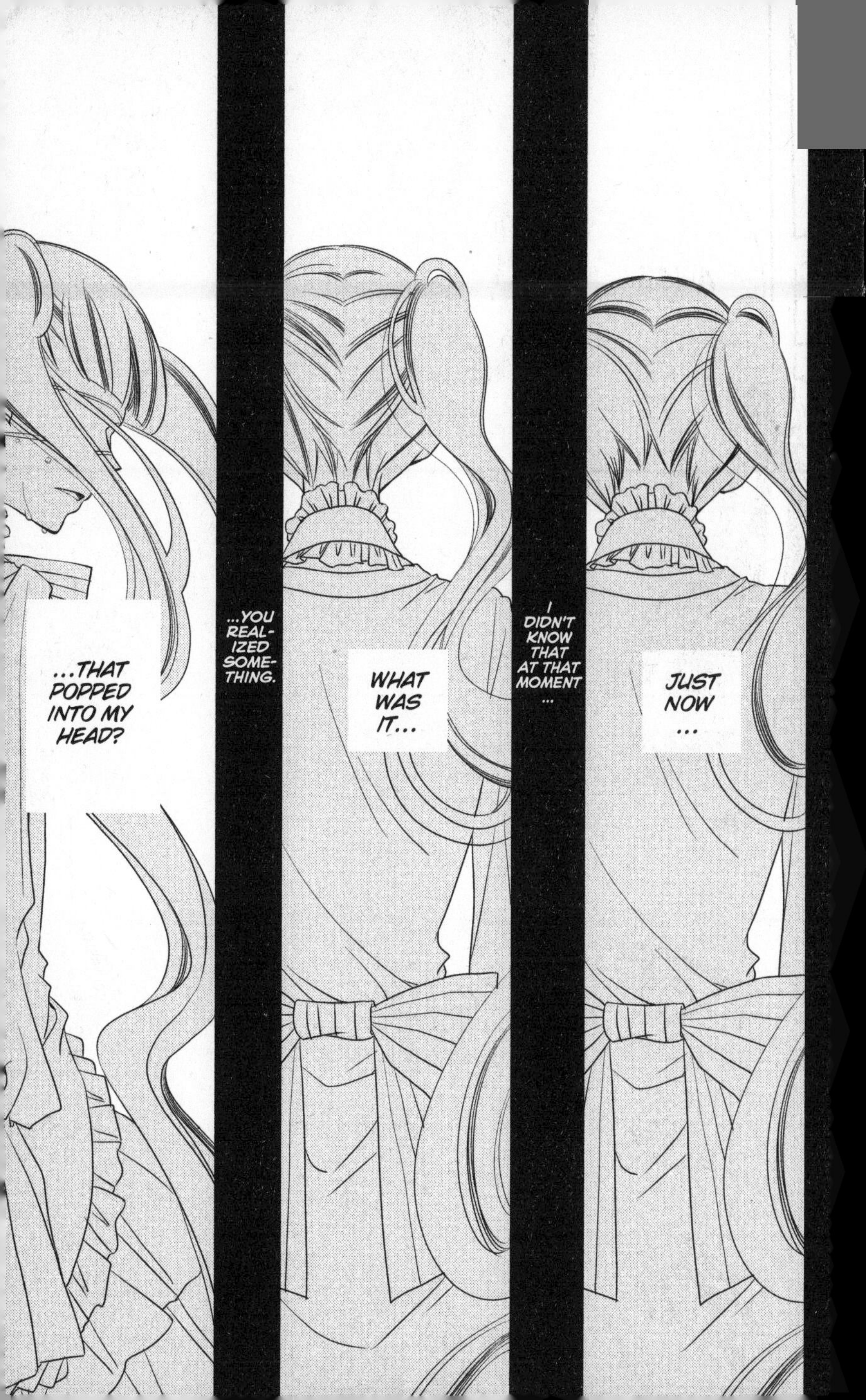
JUST NOW ...
I DIDN'T KNOW THAT AT THAT MOMENT ...
WHAT WAS IT...
...YOU REALIZED SOMETHING.
...THAT POPPED INTO MY HEAD?

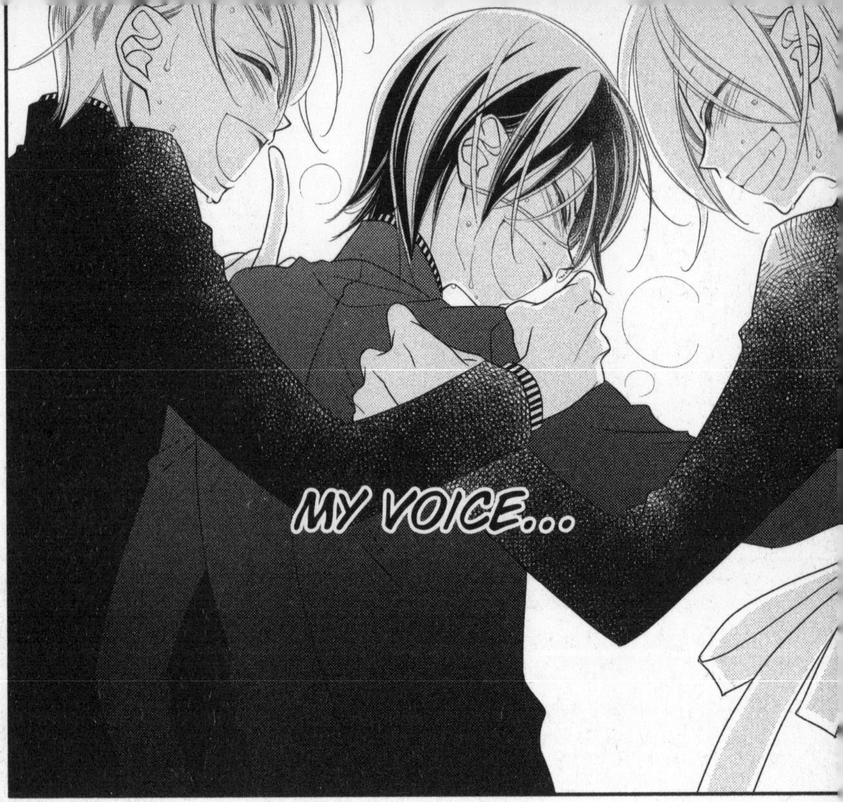
MY VOICE...

...BELONGS TO YOU, YUZU.

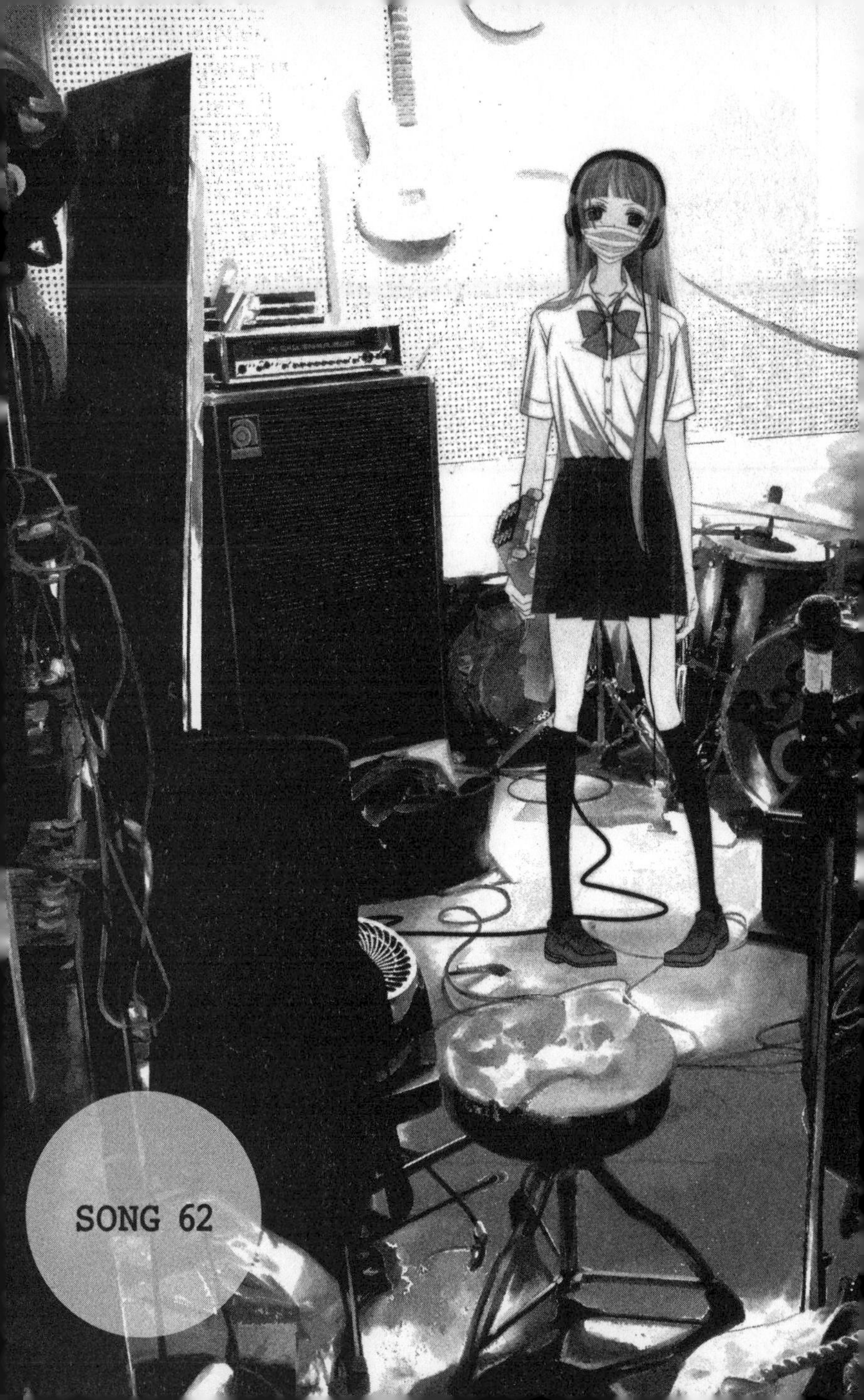
SONG 62

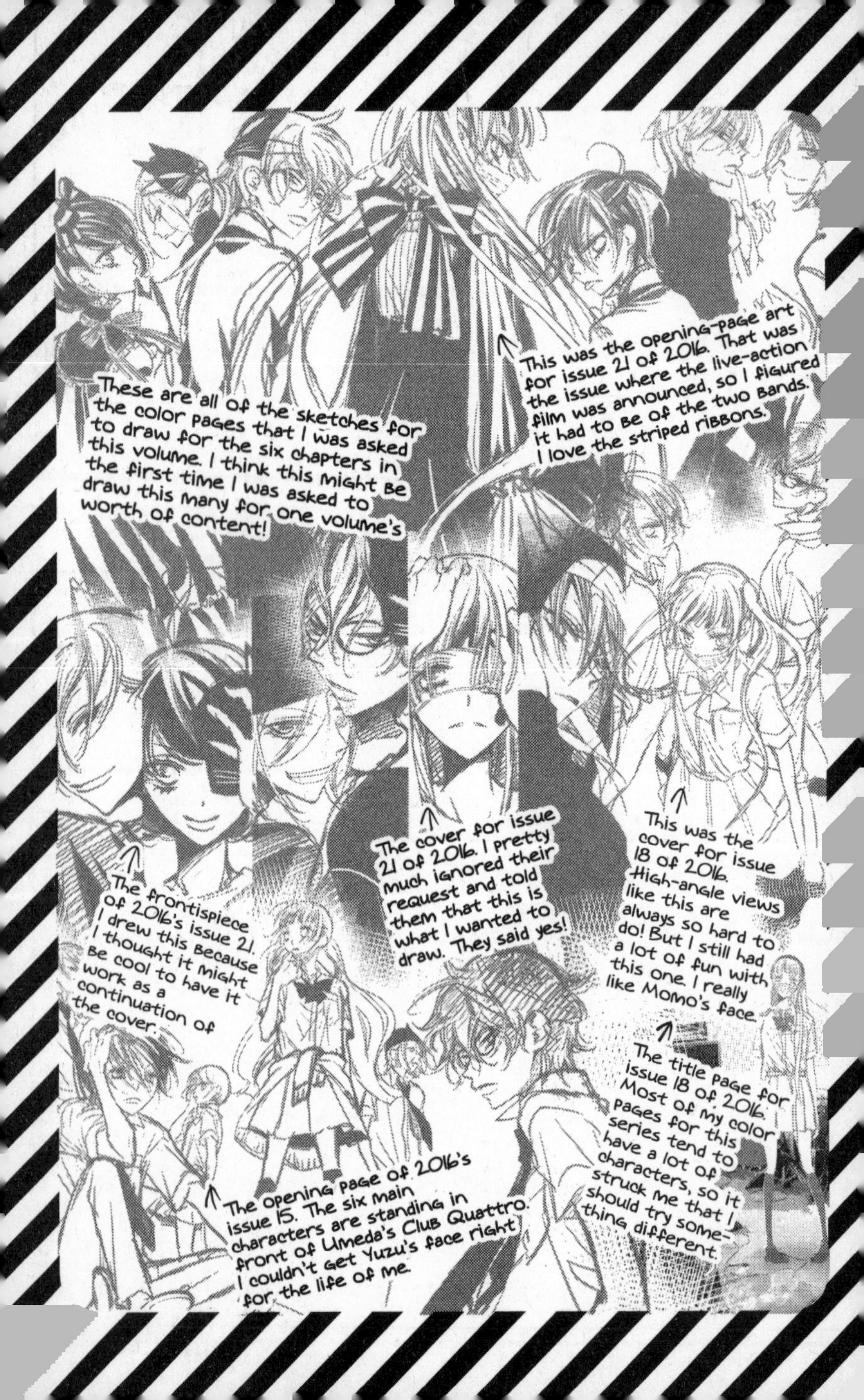
This was the opening-page art for issue 21 of 2016. That was the issue where the live-action film was announced, so I figured it had to be of the two bands. I love the striped ribbons.
These are all of the sketches for the color pages that I was asked to draw for the six chapters in this volume. I think this might be the first time I was asked to draw this many for one volume's worth of content!
This was the cover for issue 18 of 2016. High-angle views like this are always so hard to do! But I still had a lot of fun with this one. I really like Momo's face.
The cover for issue 21 of 2016. I pretty much ignored their request and told them that this is what I wanted to draw. They said yes!
The frontispiece of 2016's issue 21. I drew this because I thought it might be cool to have it work as a continuation of the cover.
The title page for issue 18 of 2016. Most of my color pages for this series tend to have a lot of characters, so it struck me that I should try something different.
The opening page of 2016's issue 15. The six main characters are standing in front of Umeda's Club Quattro. I couldn't get Yuzu's face right for the life of me.

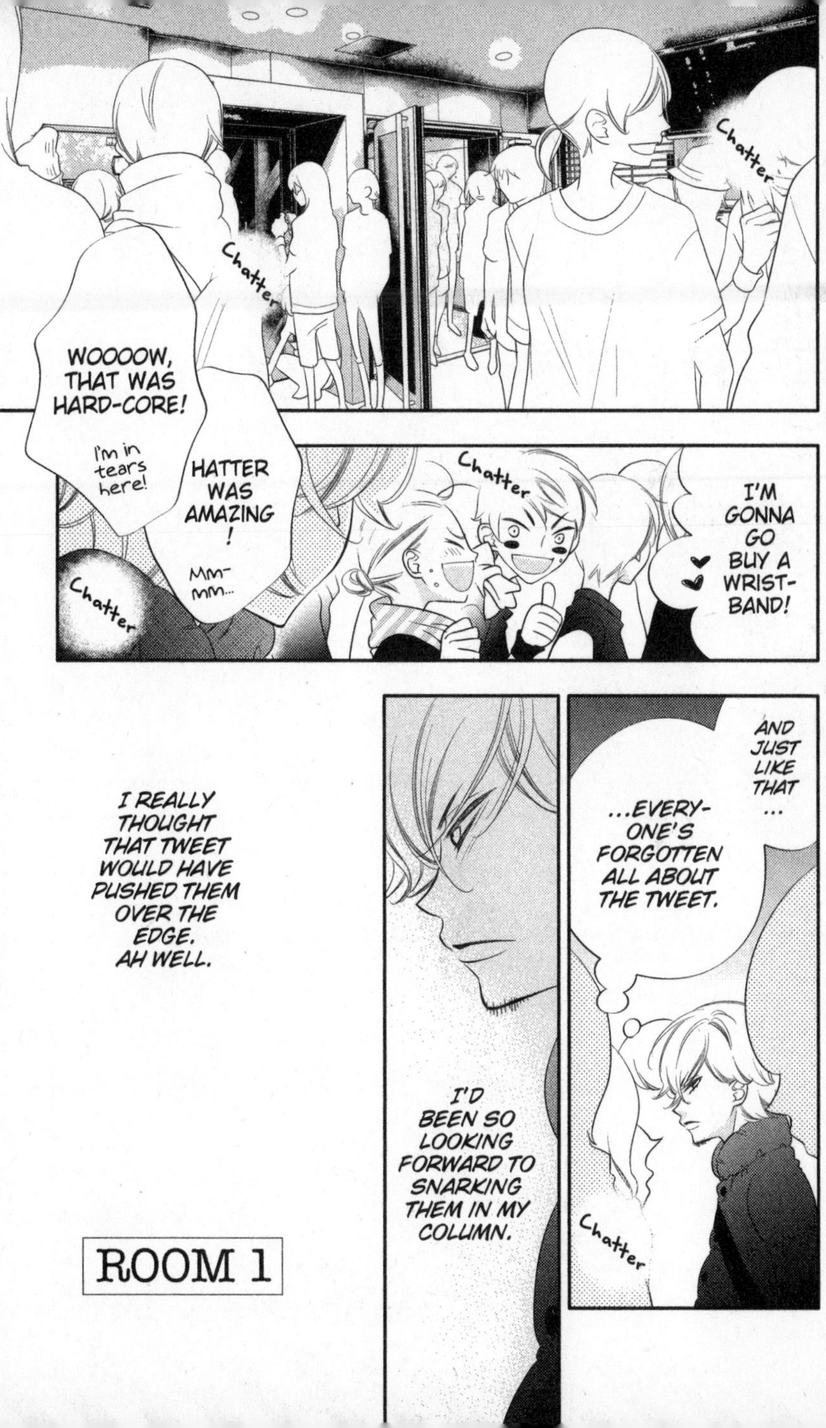
Chatter
Chatter
WOOOOW, THAT WAS HARD-CORE!
I'M GONNA GO BUY A WRIST-BAND!
Chatter
HATTER WAS AMAZING!
Mm-mm...
I'm in tears here!
Chatter
AND JUST LIKE THAT...
...EVERY-ONE'S FORGOTTEN ALL ABOUT THE TWEET.
Chatter
I'D BEEN SO LOOKING FORWARD TO SNARKING THEM IN MY COLUMN.
I REALLY THOUGHT THAT TWEET WOULD HAVE PUSHED THEM OVER THE EDGE. AH WELL.
ROOM 1

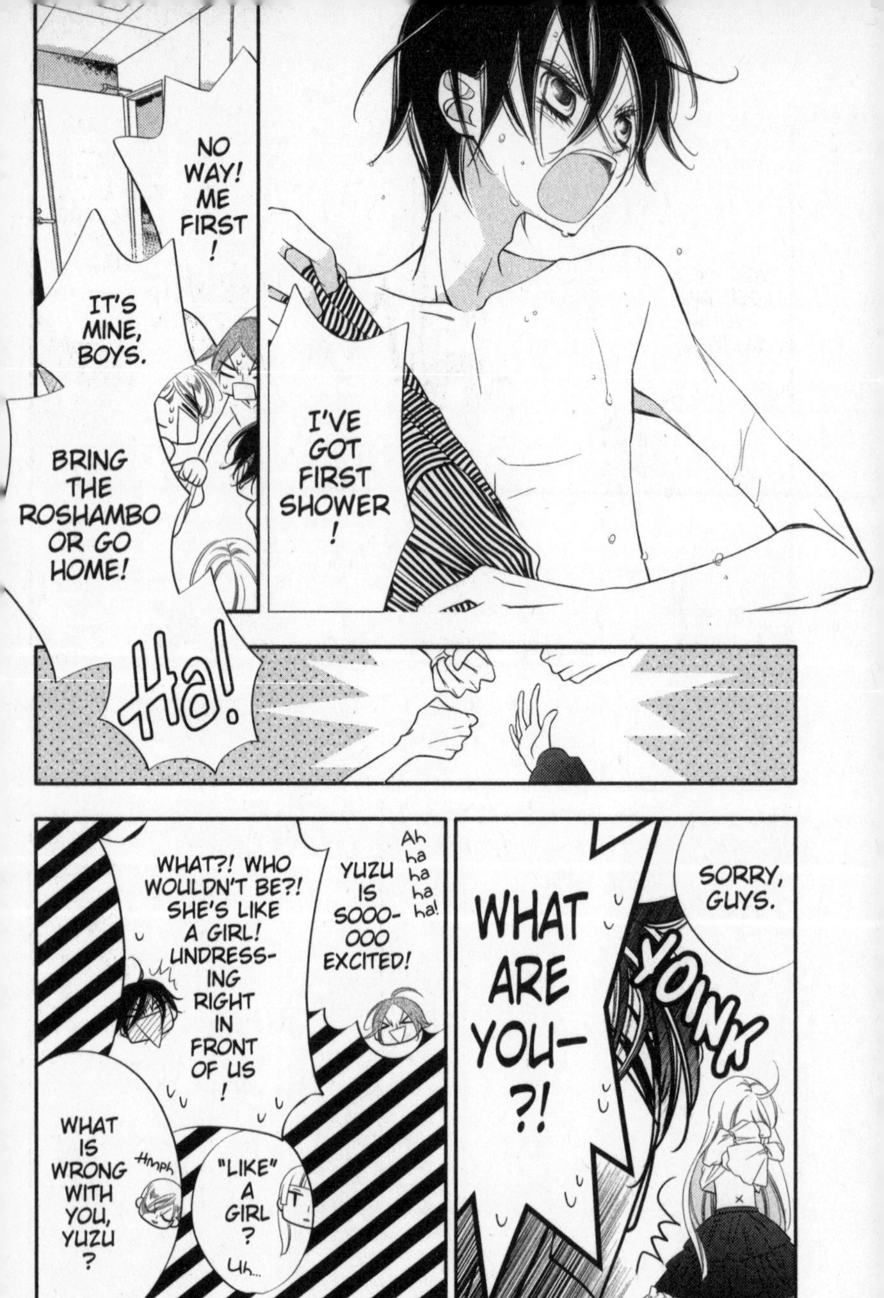
I'VE GOT FIRST SHOWER!
NO WAY! ME FIRST!
IT'S MINE, BOYS.
BRING THE ROSHAMBO OR GO HOME!
Ha!
SORRY, GUYS.
YOINK
WHAT ARE YOU—?!
Ah ha ha ha ha!
YUZU IS SOOOOOO EXCITED!
WHAT?! WHO WOULDN'T BE?! SHE'S LIKE A GIRL! UNDRESSING RIGHT IN FRONT OF US!
"LIKE" A GIRL?
Uh...
Hmph
WHAT IS WRONG WITH YOU, YUZU?

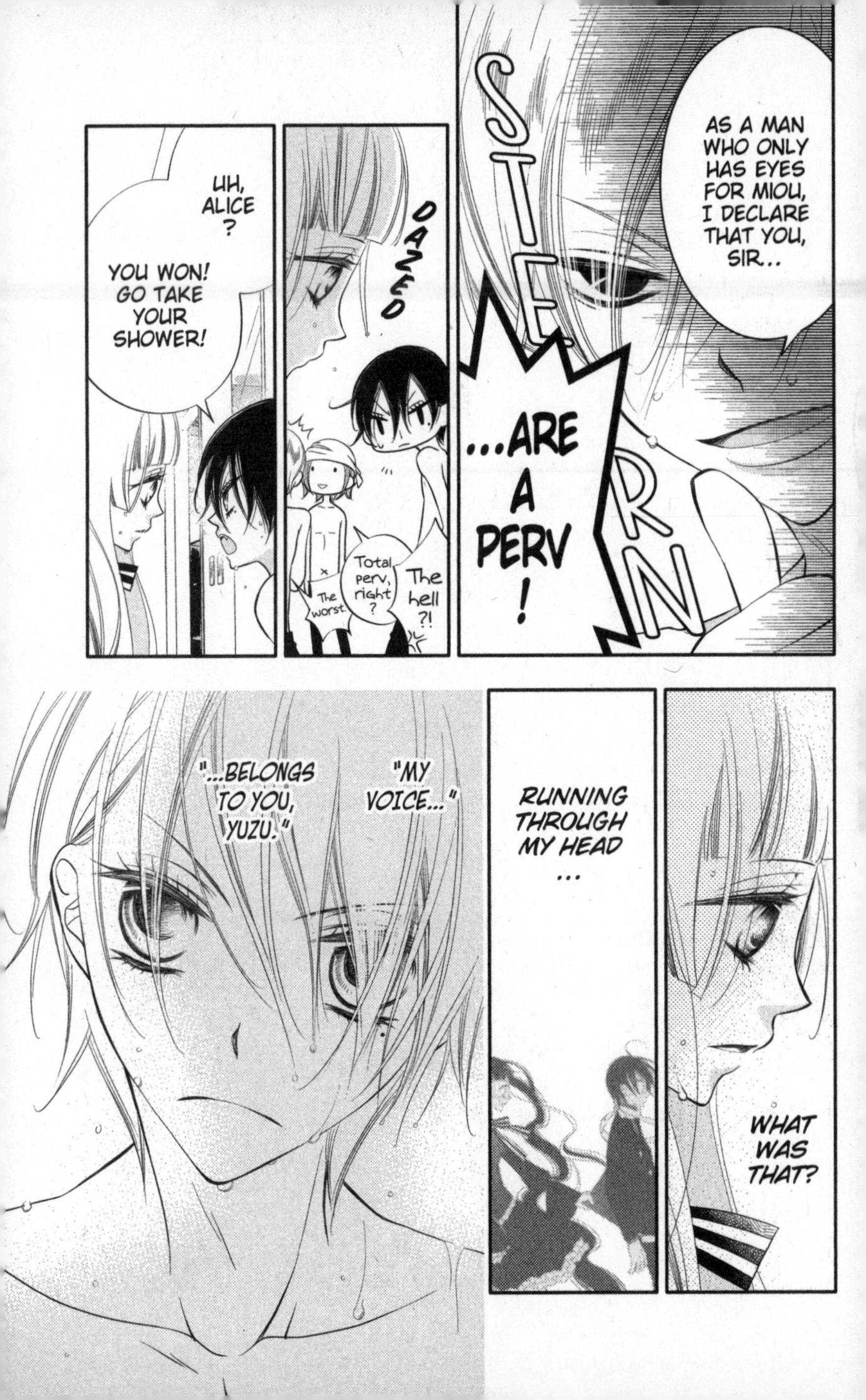
AS A MAN WHO ONLY HAS EYES FOR MIOU, I DECLARE THAT YOU, SIR...
STERN
...ARE A PERV!
DAZED
The hell?!
Total perv, right?
The worst.
UH, ALICE?
YOU WON! GO TAKE YOUR SHOWER!
WHAT WAS THAT?
RUNNING THROUGH MY HEAD...
"MY VOICE..."
"...BELONGS TO YOU, YUZU."

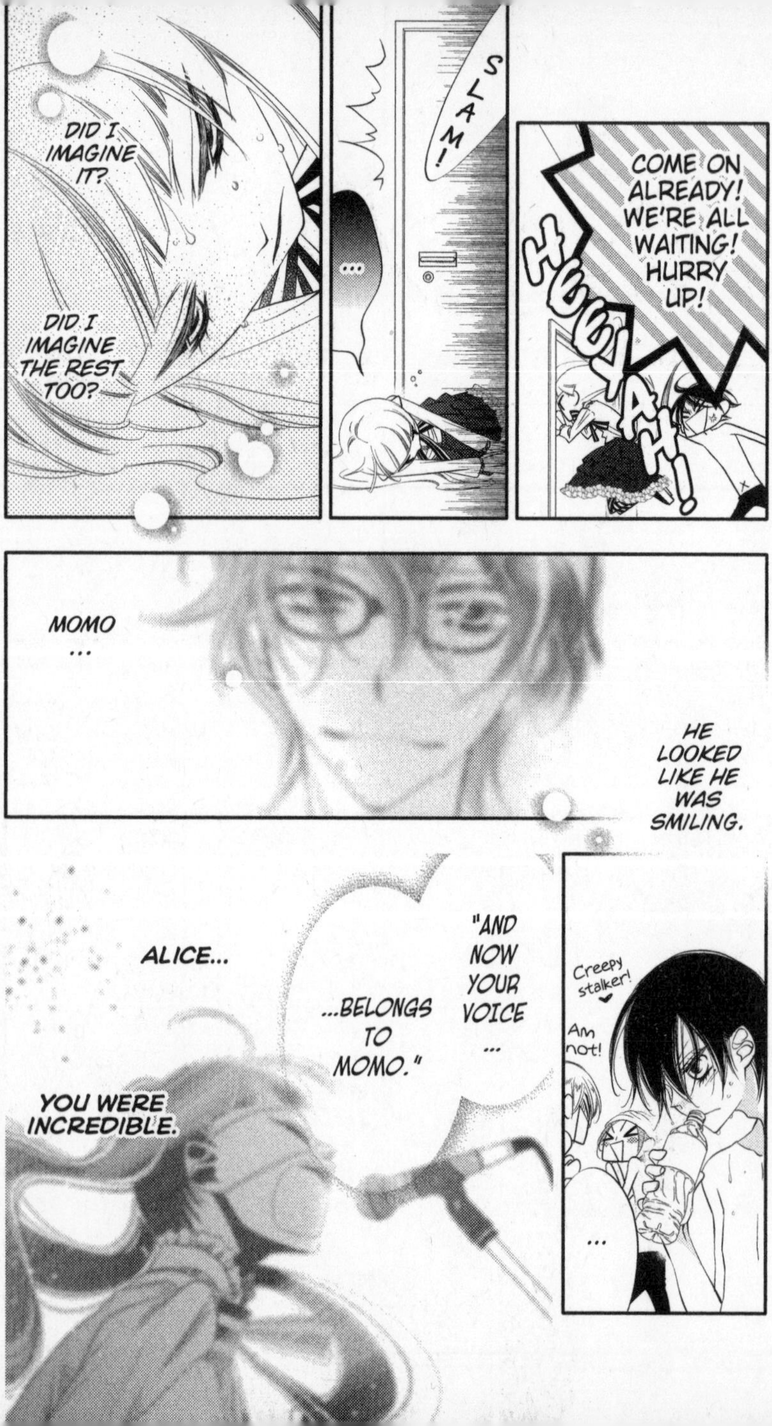
COME ON ALREADY! WE'RE ALL WAITING! HURRY UP!
HEEYAH!
SLAM!
...
DID I IMAGINE IT?
DID I IMAGINE THE REST TOO?
MOMO...
HE LOOKED LIKE HE WAS SMILING.
Creepy stalker!
Am not!
...
"AND NOW YOUR VOICE...
...BELONGS TO MOMO."
ALICE...
YOU WERE INCREDIBLE.

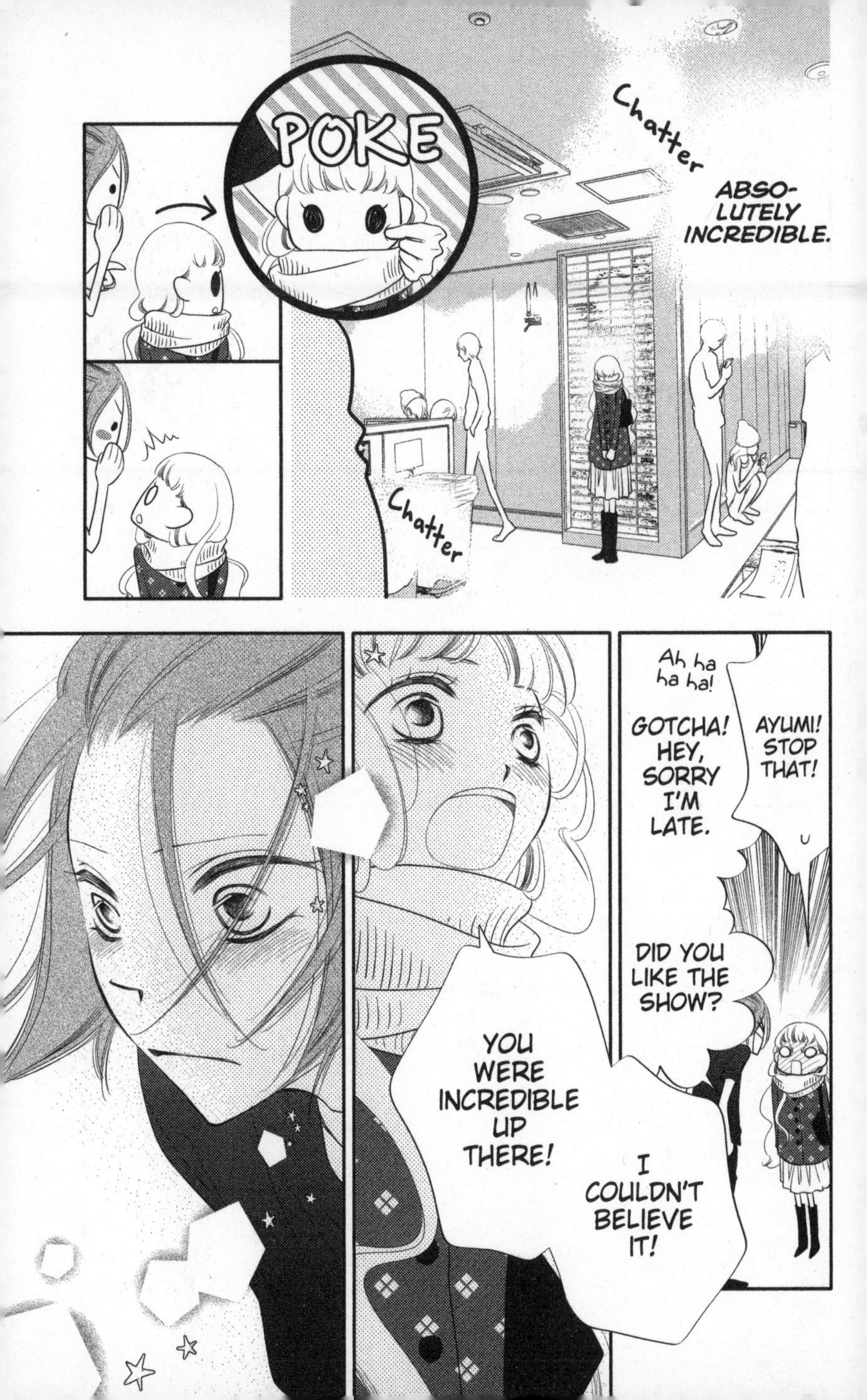
Chatter
ABSO-LUTELY INCREDIBLE.
Chatter
POKE
AYUMI! STOP THAT!
Ah ha ha ha!
GOTCHA! HEY, SORRY I'M LATE.
DID YOU LIKE THE SHOW?
YOU WERE INCREDIBLE UP THERE!
I COULDN'T BELIEVE IT!

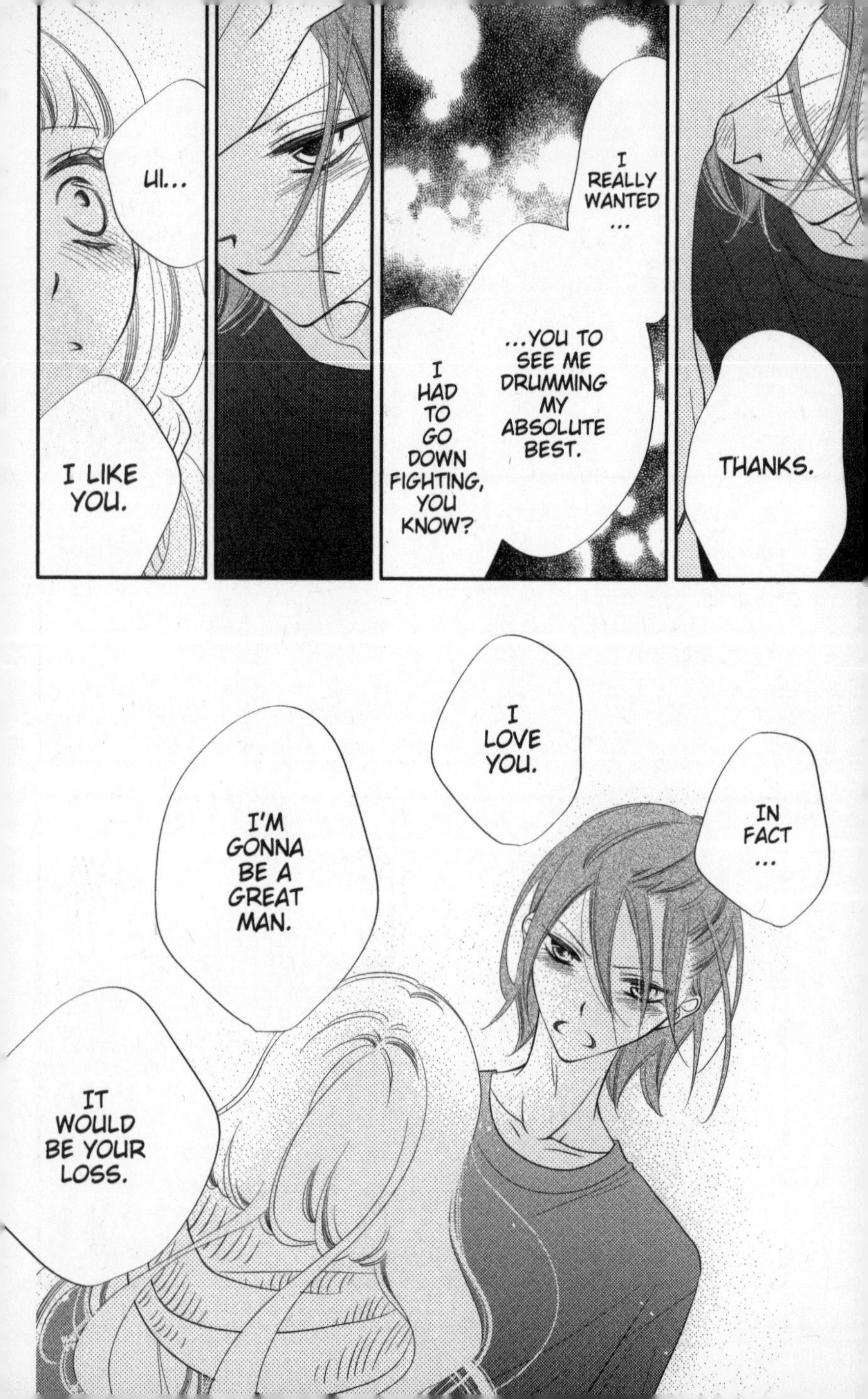
THANKS.
I REALLY WANTED...
...YOU TO SEE ME DRUMMING MY ABSOLUTE BEST.
I HAD TO GO DOWN FIGHTING, YOU KNOW?
UI...
I LIKE YOU.
IN FACT...
I LOVE YOU.
I'M GONNA BE A GREAT MAN.
IT WOULD BE YOUR LOSS.

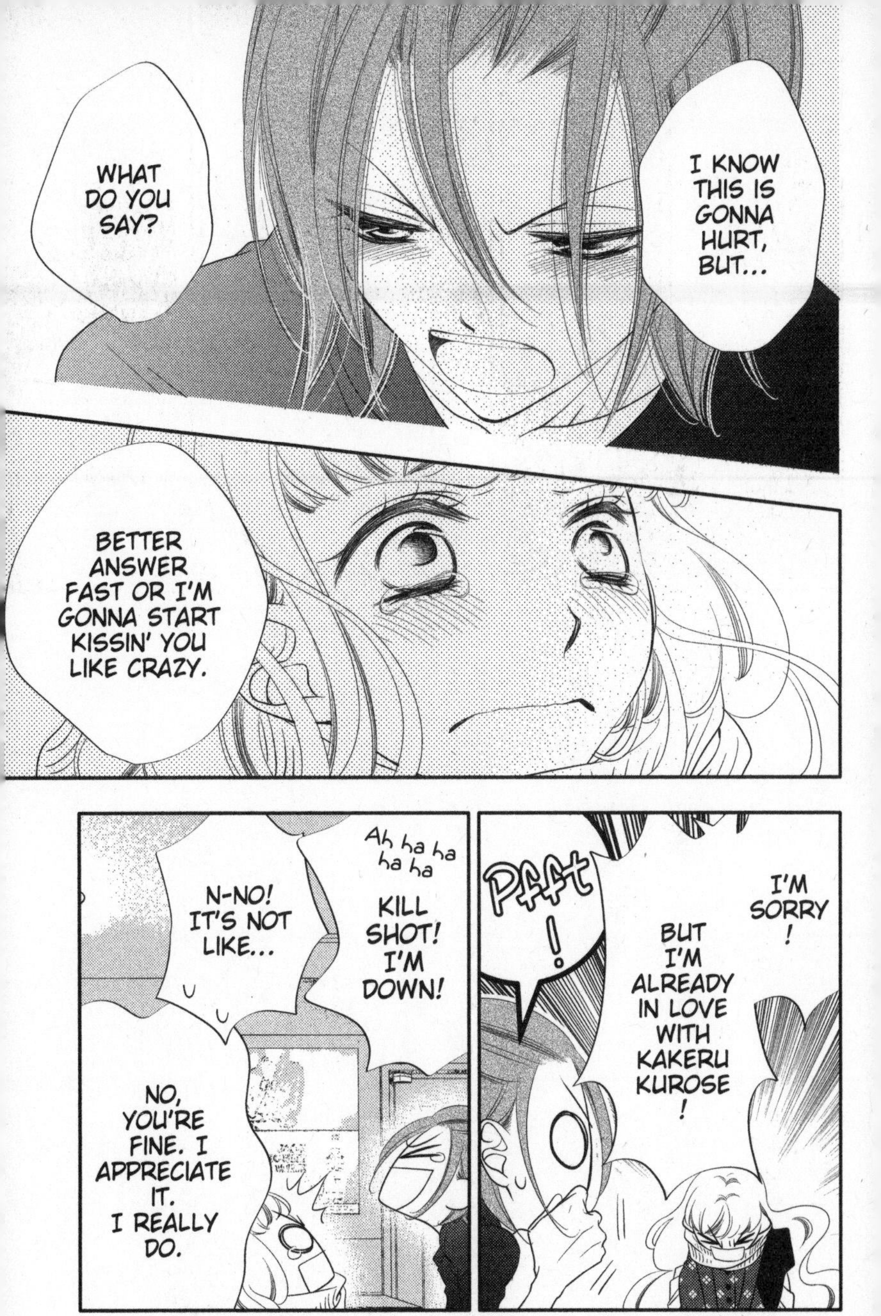
I KNOW THIS IS GONNA HURT, BUT...
WHAT DO YOU SAY?
BETTER ANSWER FAST OR I'M GONNA START KISSIN' YOU LIKE CRAZY.
I'M SORRY!
BUT I'M ALREADY IN LOVE WITH KAKERU KUROSE!
Pfft!
Ah ha ha ha ha
KILL SHOT! I'M DOWN!
N-NO! IT'S NOT LIKE...
NO, YOU'RE FINE. I APPRECIATE IT. I REALLY DO.

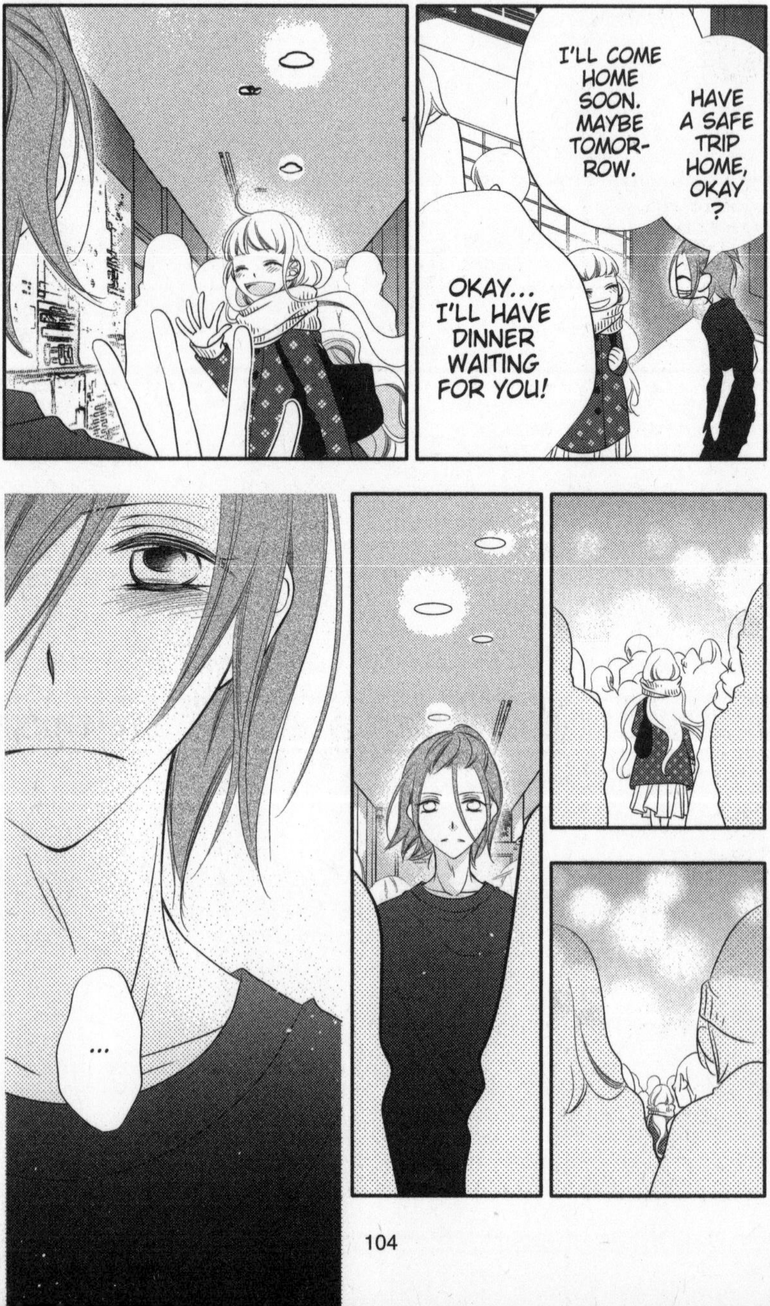
I'LL COME HOME SOON. MAYBE TOMOR-ROW.
HAVE A SAFE TRIP HOME, OKAY?
OKAY... I'LL HAVE DINNER WAITING FOR YOU!
...

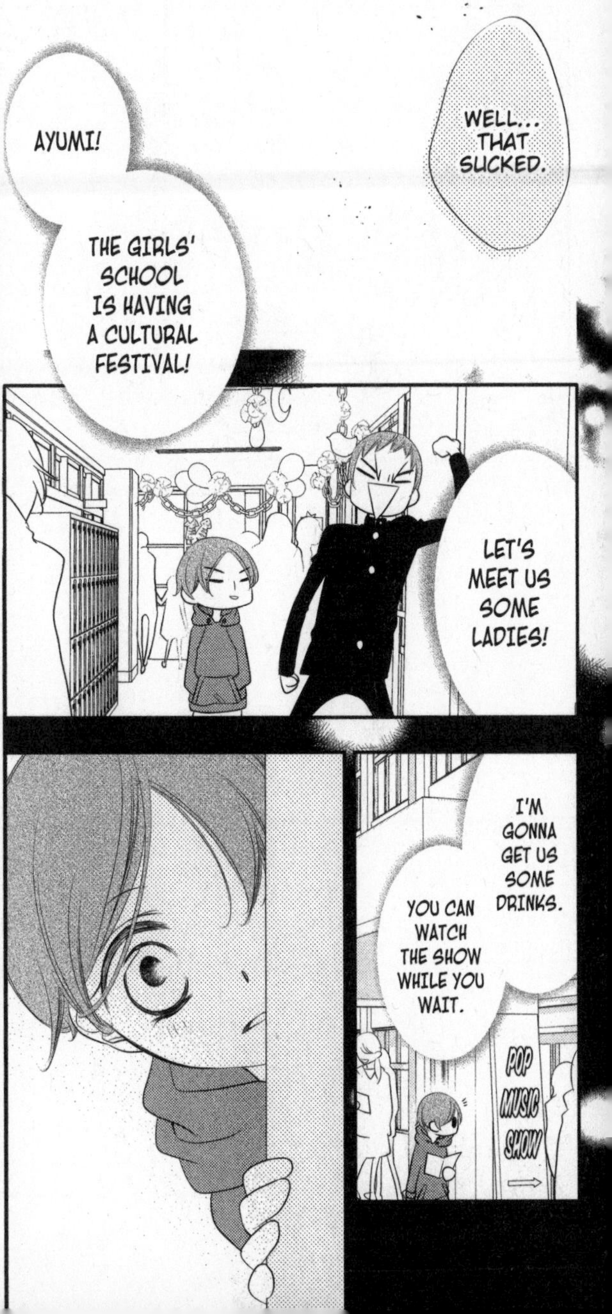
WELL... THAT SUCKED.
AYUMI!
THE GIRLS' SCHOOL IS HAVING A CULTURAL FESTIVAL!
LET'S MEET US SOME LADIES!
I'M GONNA GET US SOME DRINKS.
YOU CAN WATCH THE SHOW WHILE YOU WAIT.
POP MUSIC SHOW

4

The next day, I got to attend the read-through. Seeing the cast moving around and reading dialogue as their Anonymous Noise characters was a shockingly powerful experience. It didn't put all of my fears to rest, of course, but for the first time, it made me think, "This is something I really want my readers to experience." Between the stress and the anxiety and the excitement, I nearly burst into tears. I do hope that you'll join me in following along as the film and anime come together.

This wouldn't have been possible without you!

WEEE!

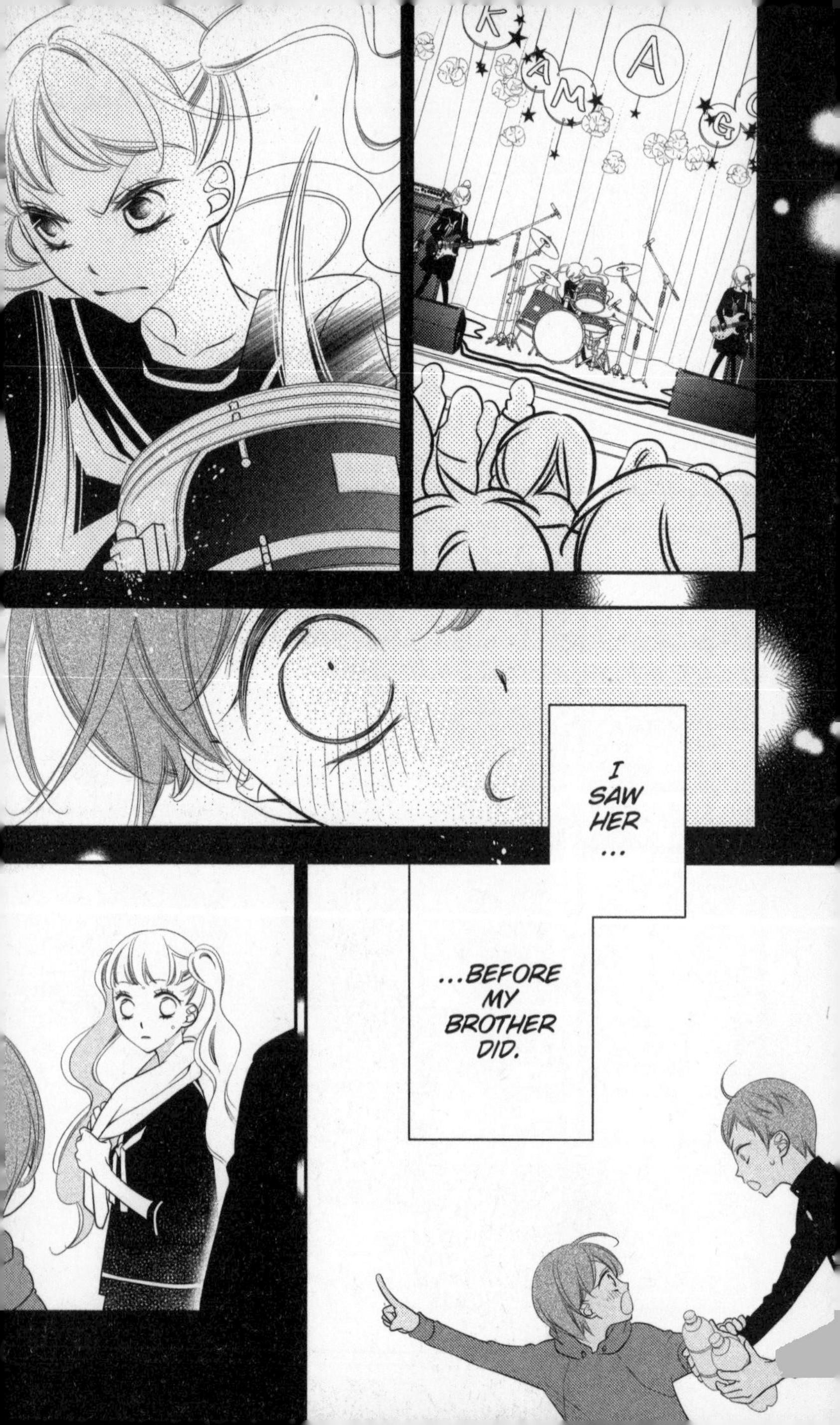
I SAW HER...
...BEFORE MY BROTHER DID.

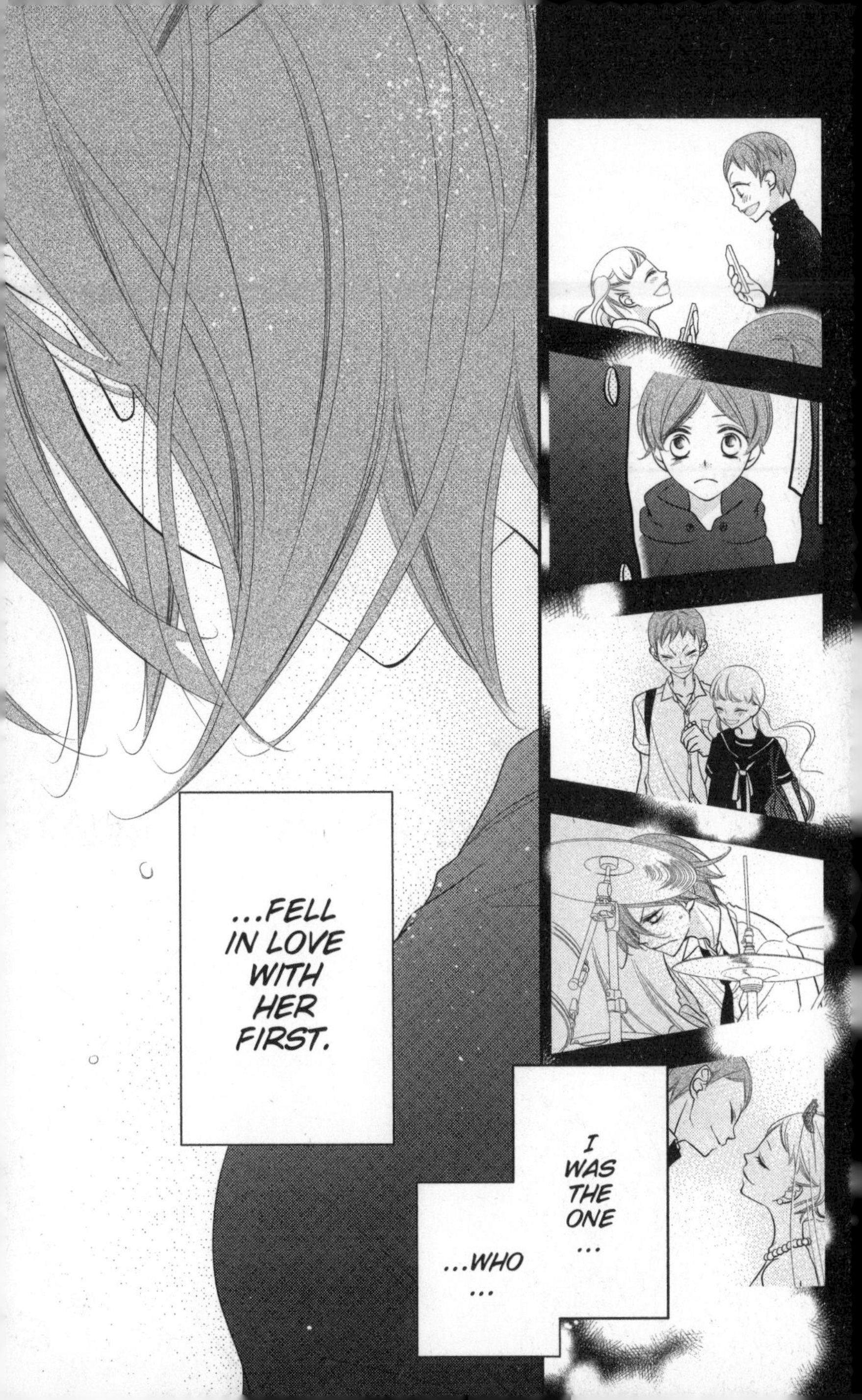
I WAS THE ONE ...
...WHO ...
...FELL IN LOVE WITH HER FIRST.

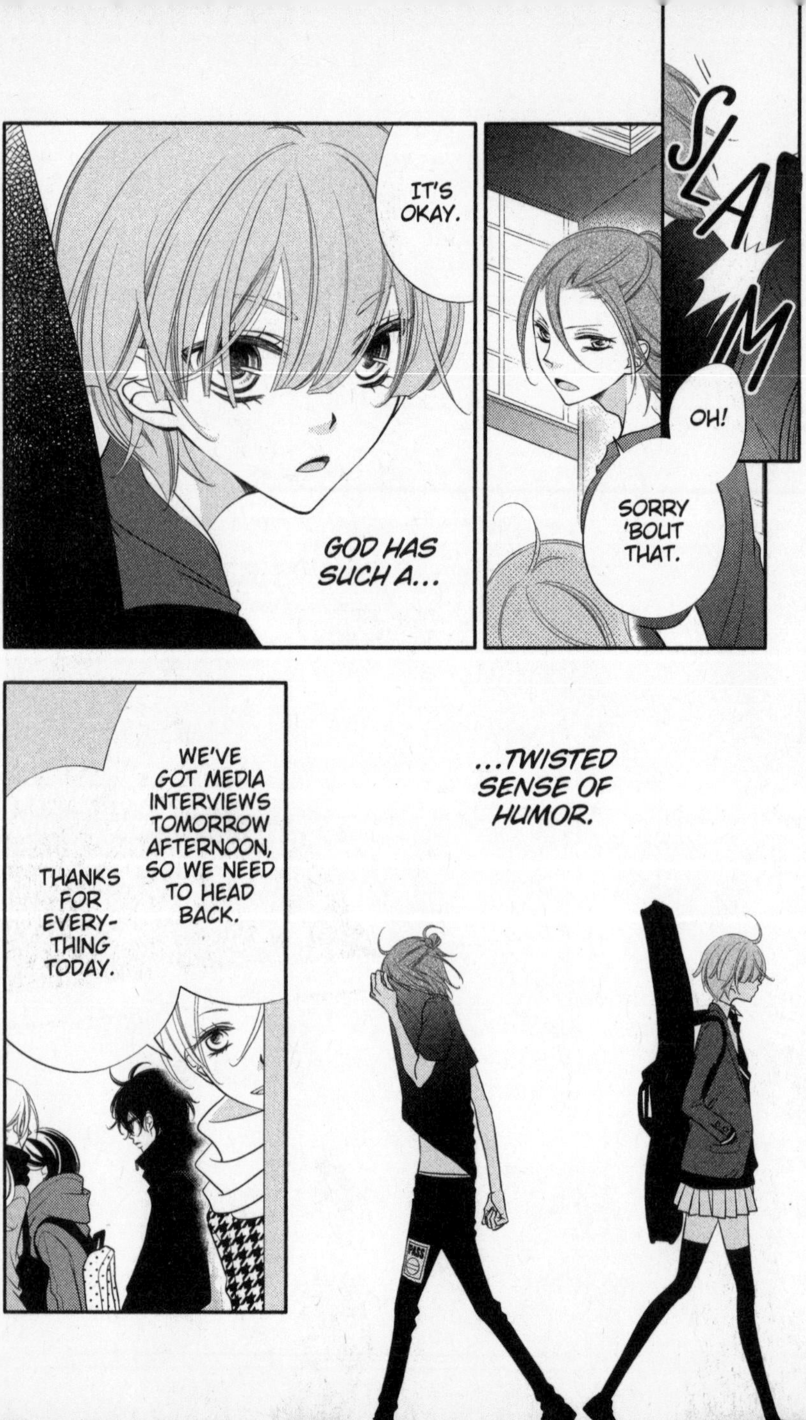
SLAM
OH!
SORRY 'BOUT THAT.
IT'S OKAY.
GOD HAS SUCH A...
...TWISTED SENSE OF HUMOR.
WE'VE GOT MEDIA INTERVIEWS TOMORROW AFTERNOON, SO WE NEED TO HEAD BACK.
THANKS FOR EVERY-THING TODAY.

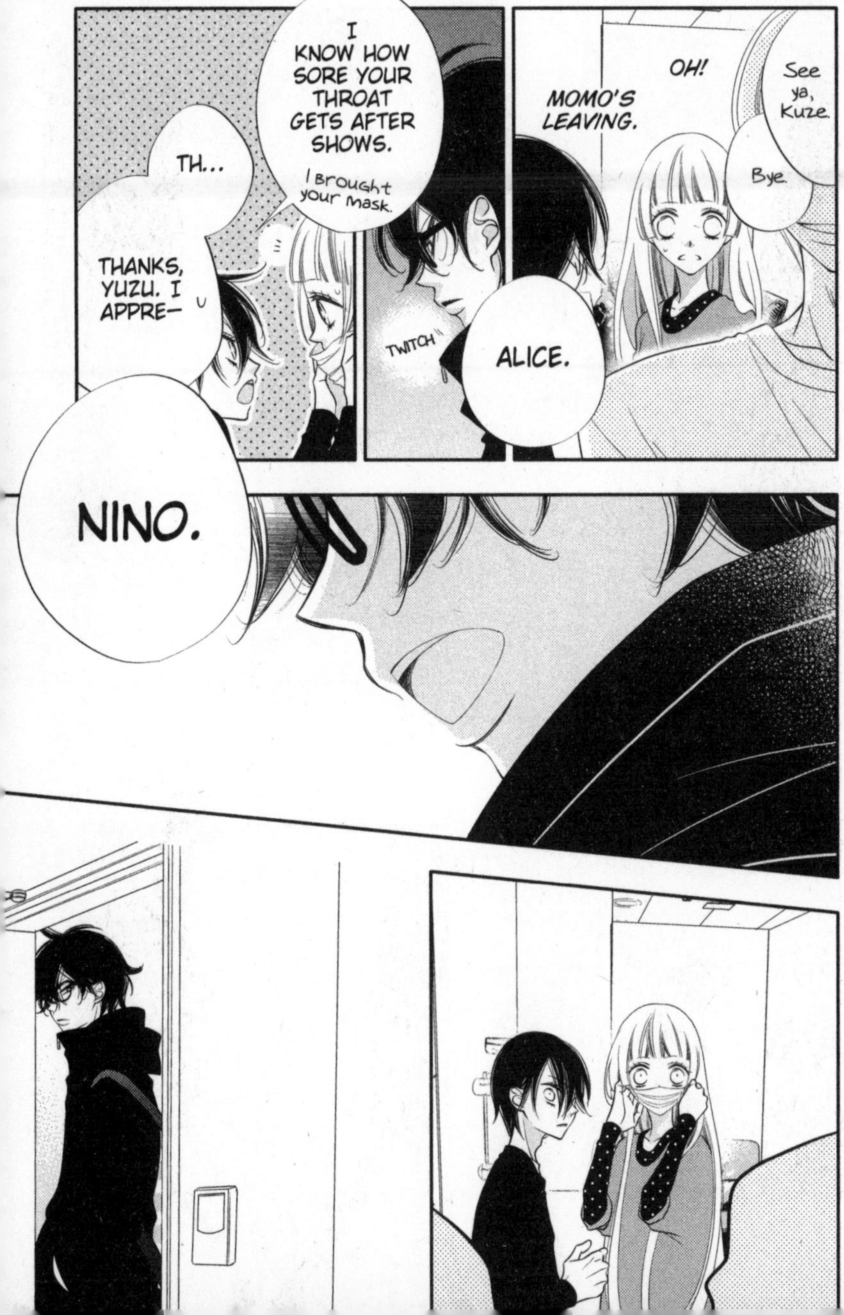
See ya, Kuze.
Bye.
OH!
MOMO'S LEAVING.
ALICE.
I KNOW HOW SORE YOUR THROAT GETS AFTER SHOWS.
I brought your mask.
TWITCH
TH...
THANKS, YUZU. I APPRE—
NINO.

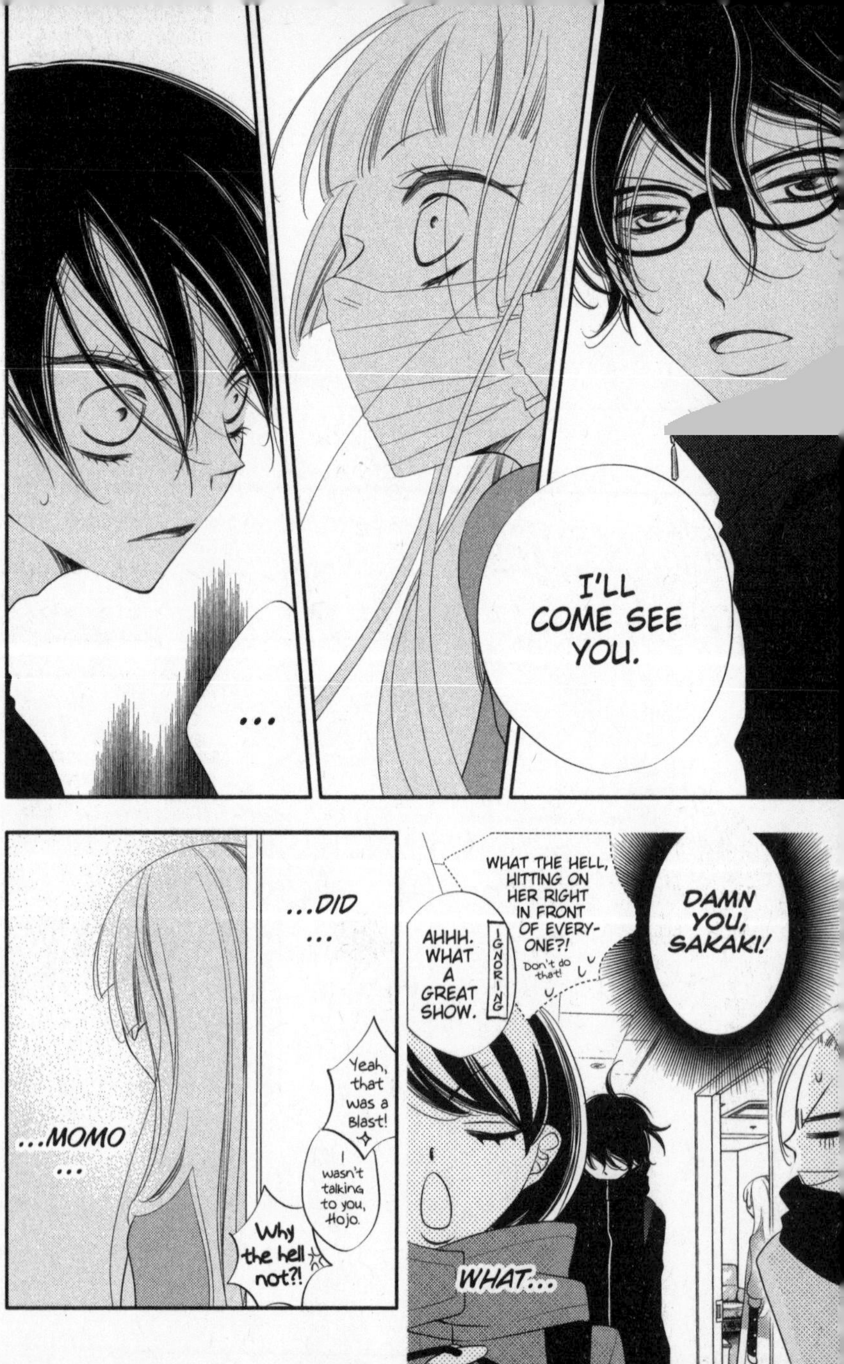
I'LL COME SEE YOU.
...
DAMN YOU, SAKAKI!
WHAT THE HELL, HITTING ON HER RIGHT IN FRONT OF EVERY-ONE?!
Don't do that!
IGNORING
AHHH. WHAT A GREAT SHOW.
WHAT...
...DID ...
Yeah, that was a Blast!
I wasn't talking to you, Hojo.
Why the hell not?!
...MOMO ...

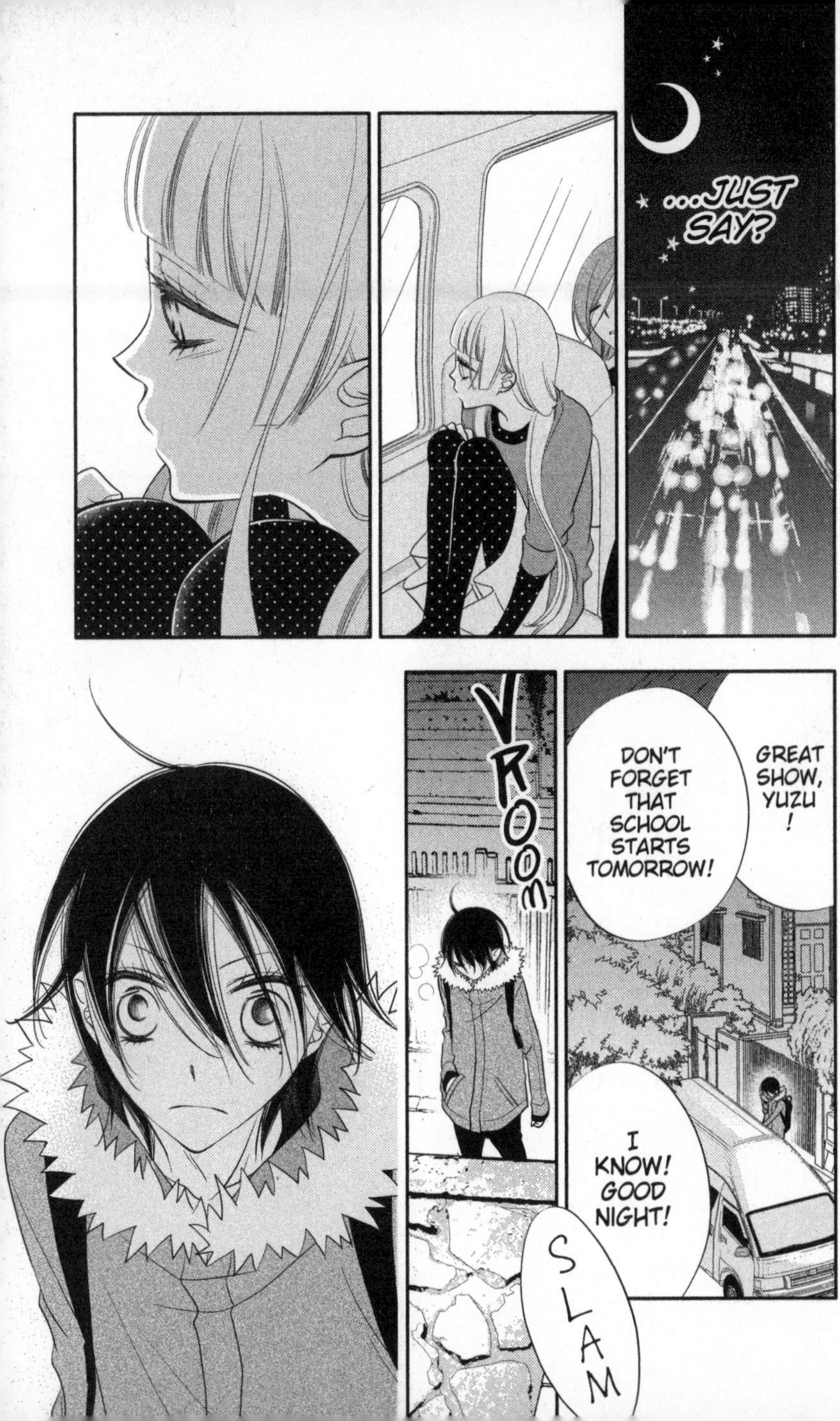
...JUST SAY?
GREAT SHOW, YUZU!
DON'T FORGET THAT SCHOOL STARTS TOMORROW!
I KNOW! GOOD NIGHT!
SLAM
VROOM

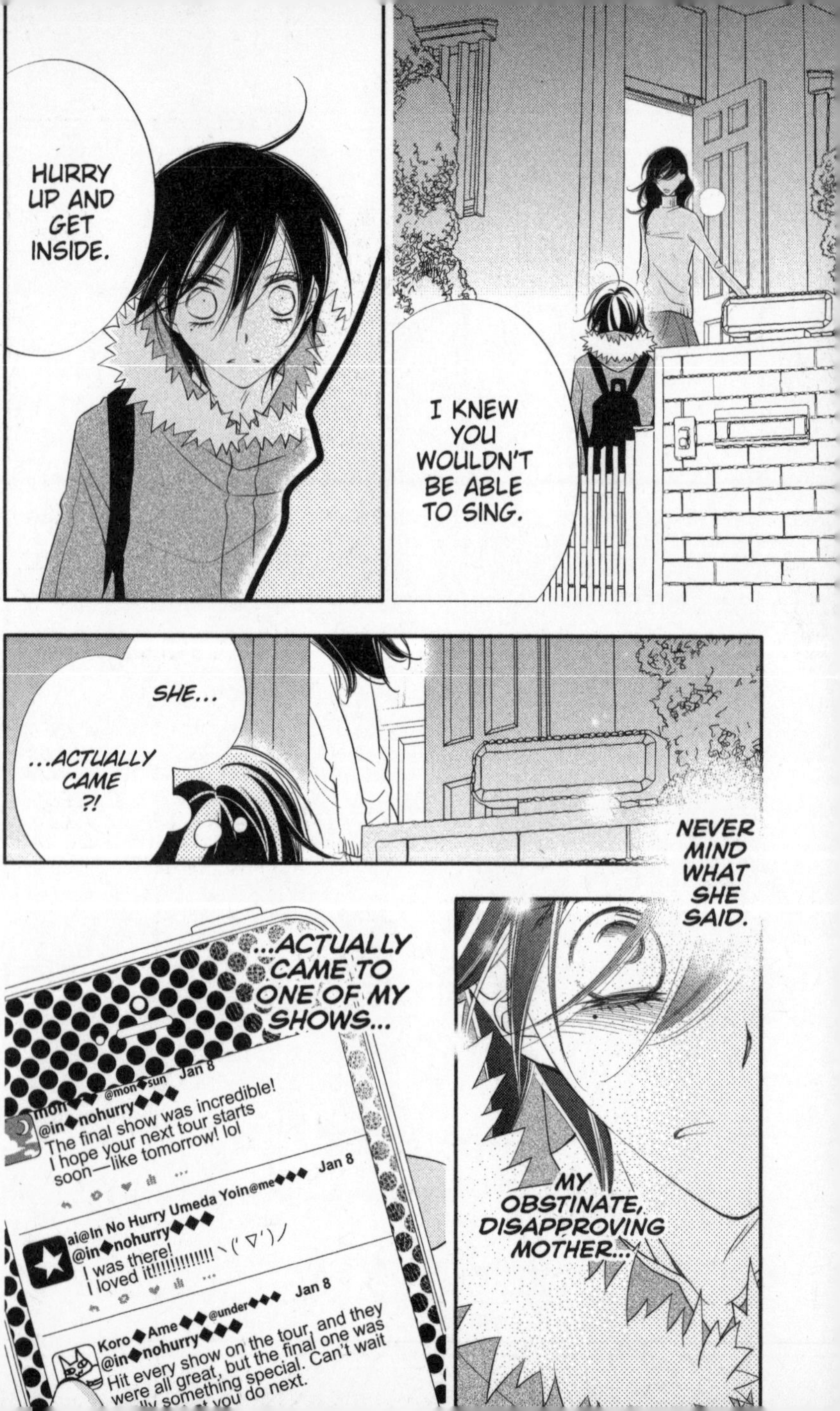
I KNEW YOU WOULDN'T BE ABLE TO SING.
HURRY UP AND GET INSIDE.
SHE...
...ACTUALLY CAME ?!
NEVER MIND WHAT SHE SAID.
MY OBSTINATE, DISAPPROVING MOTHER...
...ACTUALLY CAME TO ONE OF MY SHOWS...
mon◆◆ @mon◆sun Jan 8
@in◆nohurry◆◆◆
The final show was incredible!
I hope your next tour starts soon—like tomorrow! lol
ai@In No Hurry Umeda Yoin@me◆◆◆ Jan 8
@in◆nohurry◆◆◆
I was there!
I loved it!!!!!!!!!!!!!!!ヽ(´▽`)ノ
Koro◆Ame◆◆ @under◆◆◆ Jan 8
@in◆nohurry◆◆◆
Hit every show on the tour, and they were all great, but the final one was

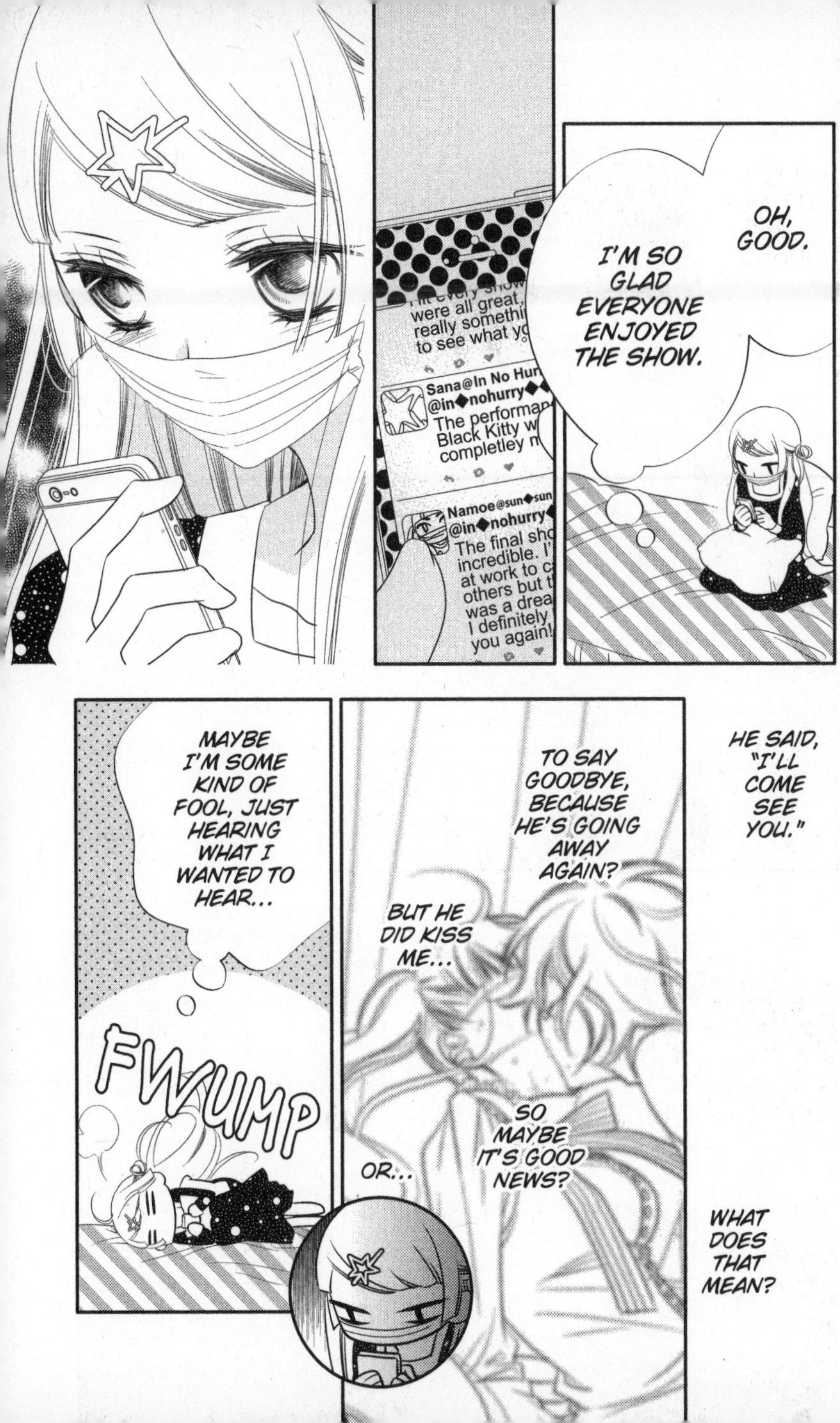
OH, GOOD.
I'M SO GLAD EVERYONE ENJOYED THE SHOW.
HE SAID, "I'LL COME SEE YOU."
WHAT DOES THAT MEAN?
TO SAY GOODBYE, BECAUSE HE'S GOING AWAY AGAIN?
BUT HE DID KISS ME...
SO MAYBE IT'S GOOD NEWS?
OR...
MAYBE I'M SOME KIND OF FOOL, JUST HEARING WHAT I WANTED TO HEAR...
FWUMP

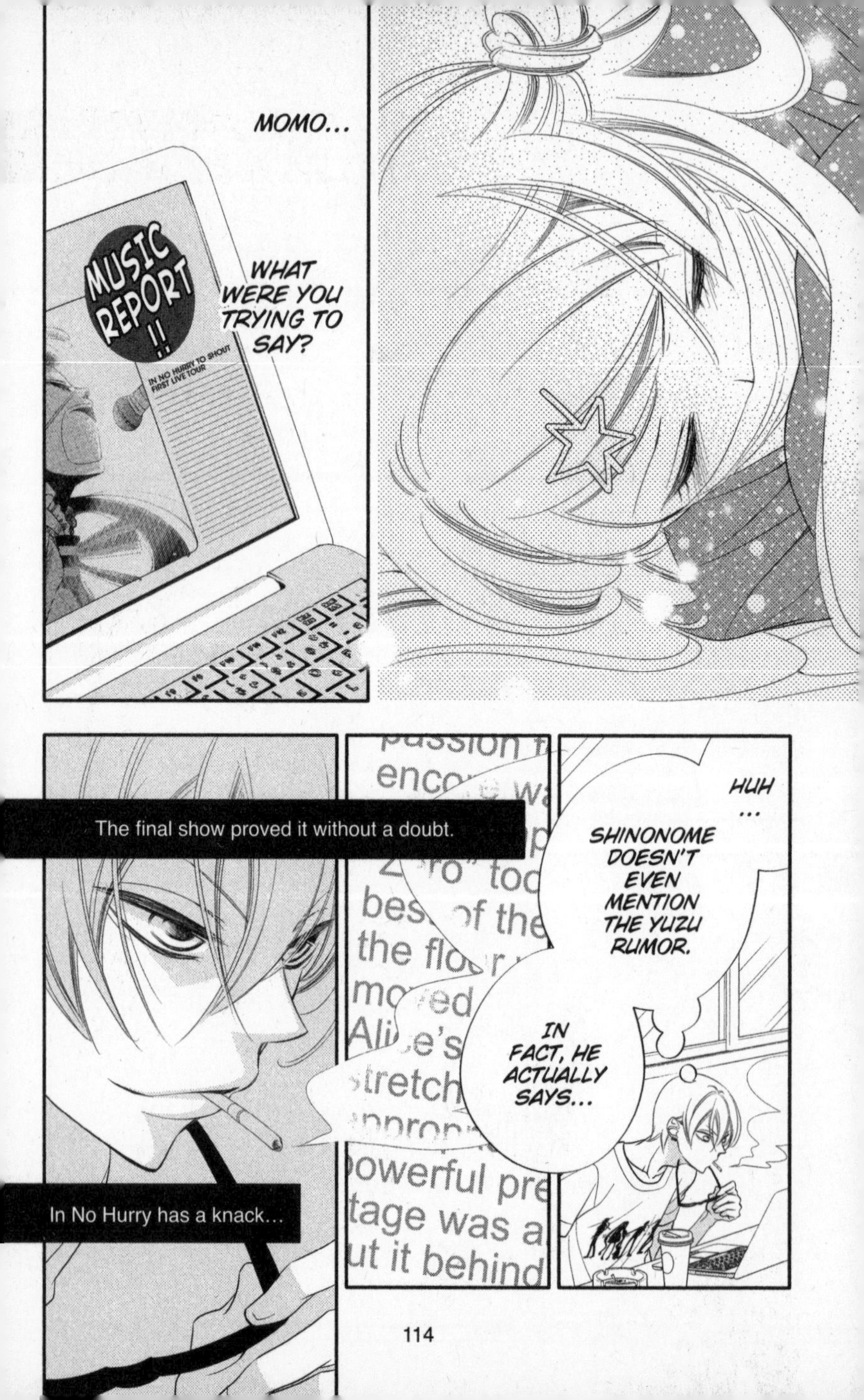
MOMO...
MUSIC REPORT !!
IN NO HURRY TO SHOUT FIRST LIVE TOUR
WHAT WERE YOU TRYING TO SAY?
HUH ...
SHINONOME DOESN'T EVEN MENTION THE YUZU RUMOR.
IN FACT, HE ACTUALLY SAYS...
The final show proved it without a doubt.
In No Hurry has a knack...

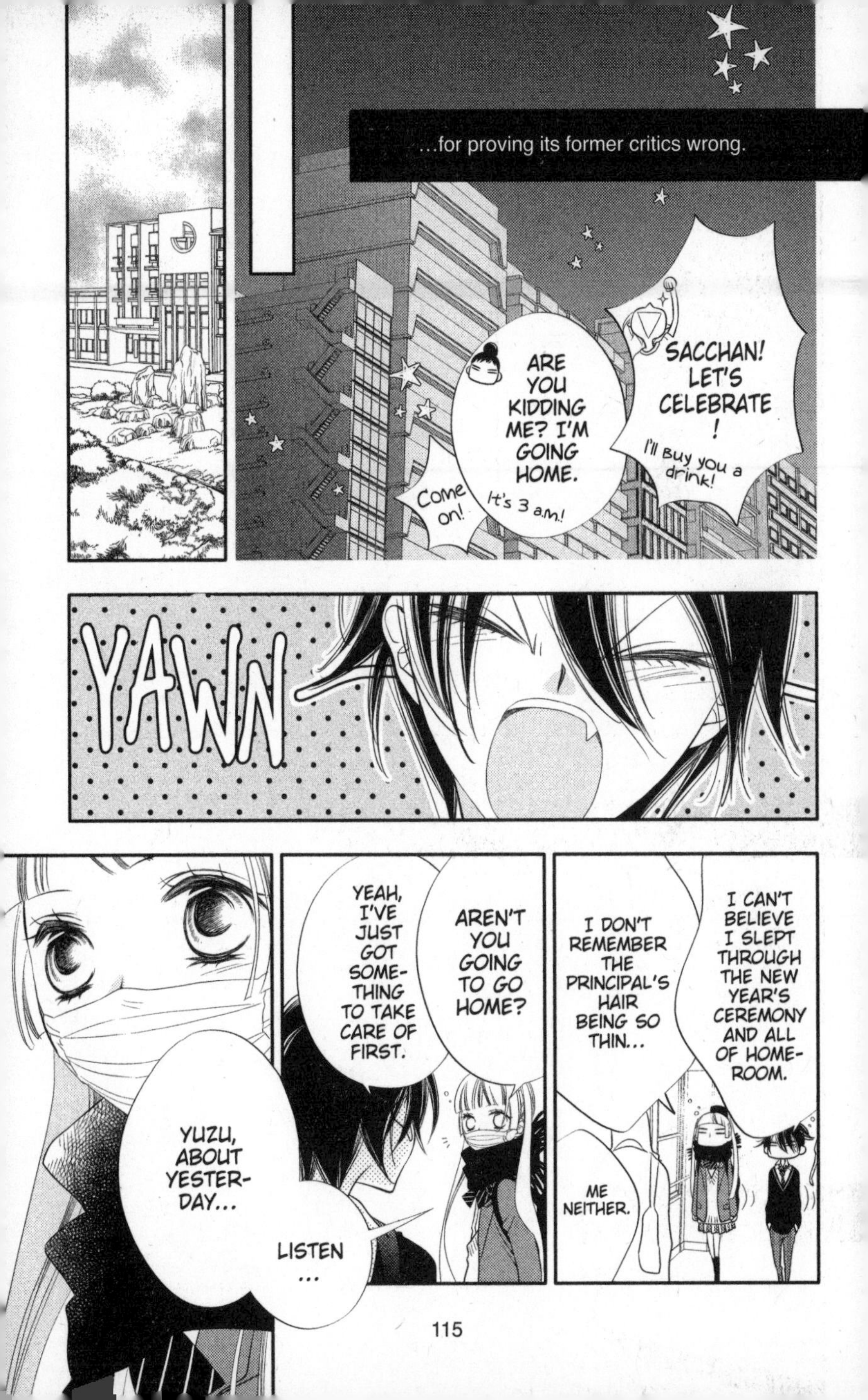
…for proving its former critics wrong.
SACCHAN! LET'S CELEBRATE!
I'll buy you a drink!
ARE YOU KIDDING ME? I'M GOING HOME.
It's 3 a.m.!
Come on!
YAWN
I CAN'T BELIEVE I SLEPT THROUGH THE NEW YEAR'S CEREMONY AND ALL OF HOMEROOM.
I DON'T REMEMBER THE PRINCIPAL'S HAIR BEING SO THIN…
ME NEITHER.
AREN'T YOU GOING TO GO HOME?
YEAH, I'VE JUST GOT SOMETHING TO TAKE CARE OF FIRST.
LISTEN…
YUZU, ABOUT YESTERDAY…

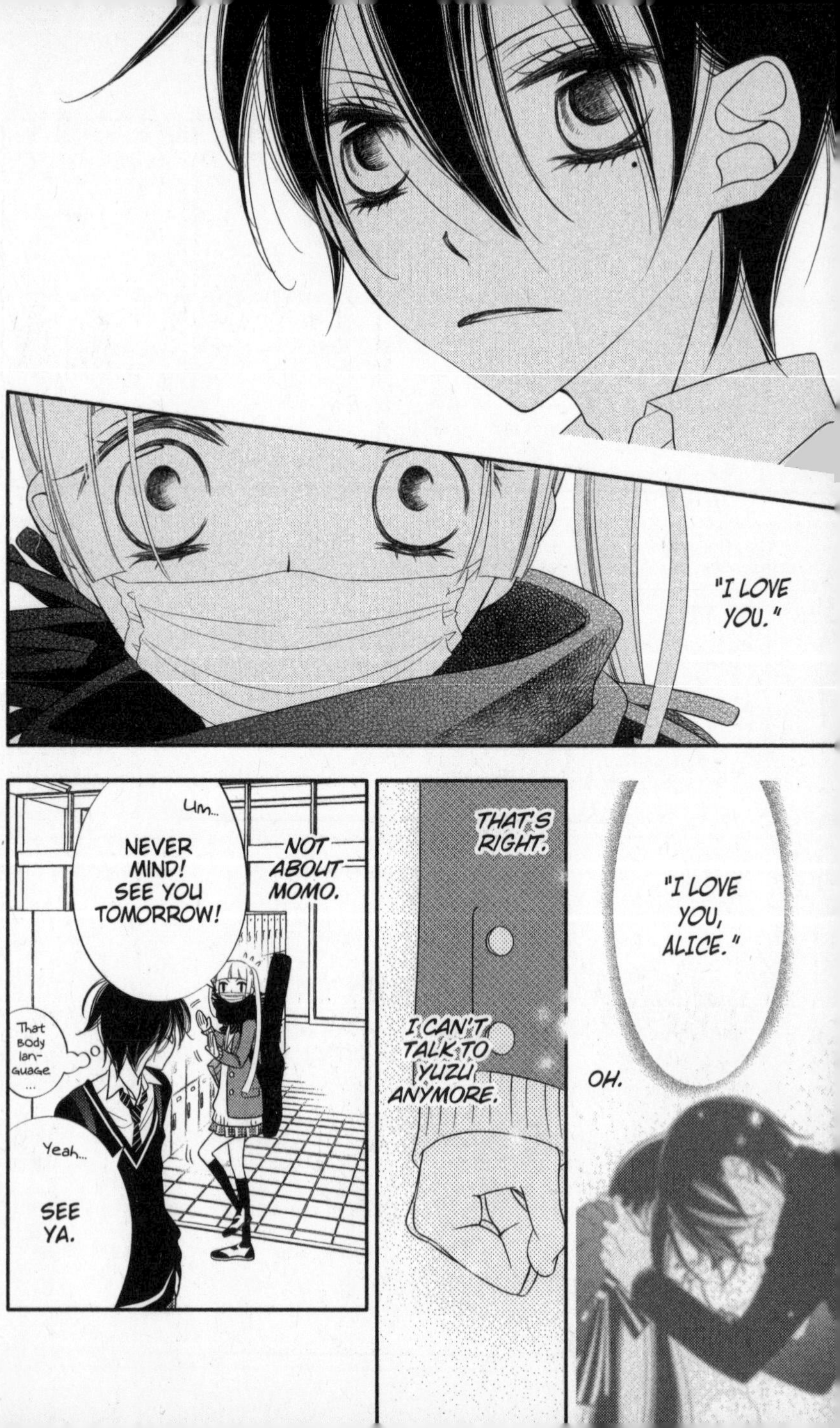
"I LOVE YOU."
"I LOVE YOU, ALICE."
OH.
THAT'S RIGHT.
I CAN'T TALK TO YUZU ANYMORE.
Um... NEVER MIND! SEE YOU TOMORROW!
NOT ABOUT MOMO.
That body language...
Yeah... SEE YA.

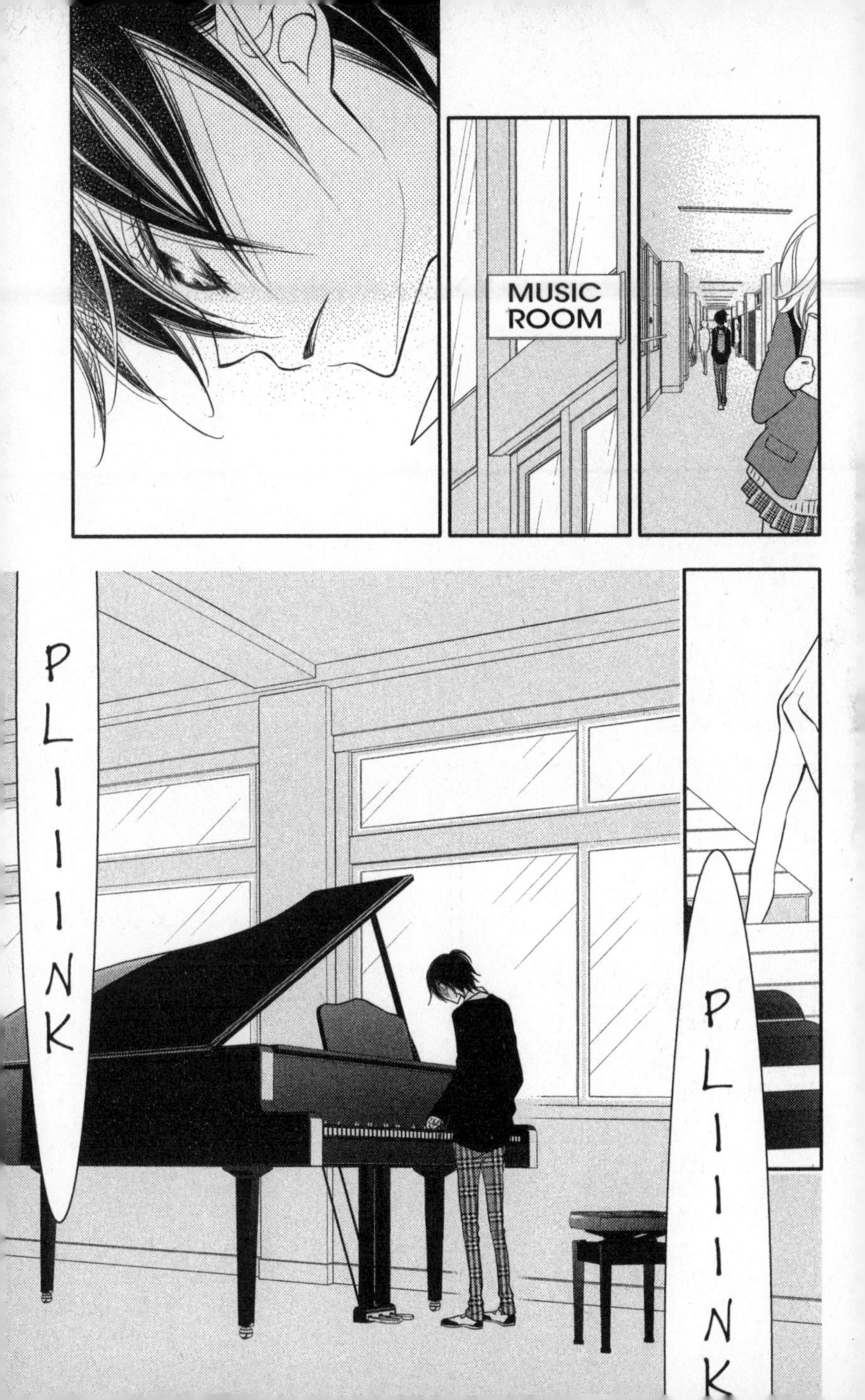
MUSIC ROOM
PLIIINK
PLIIINK

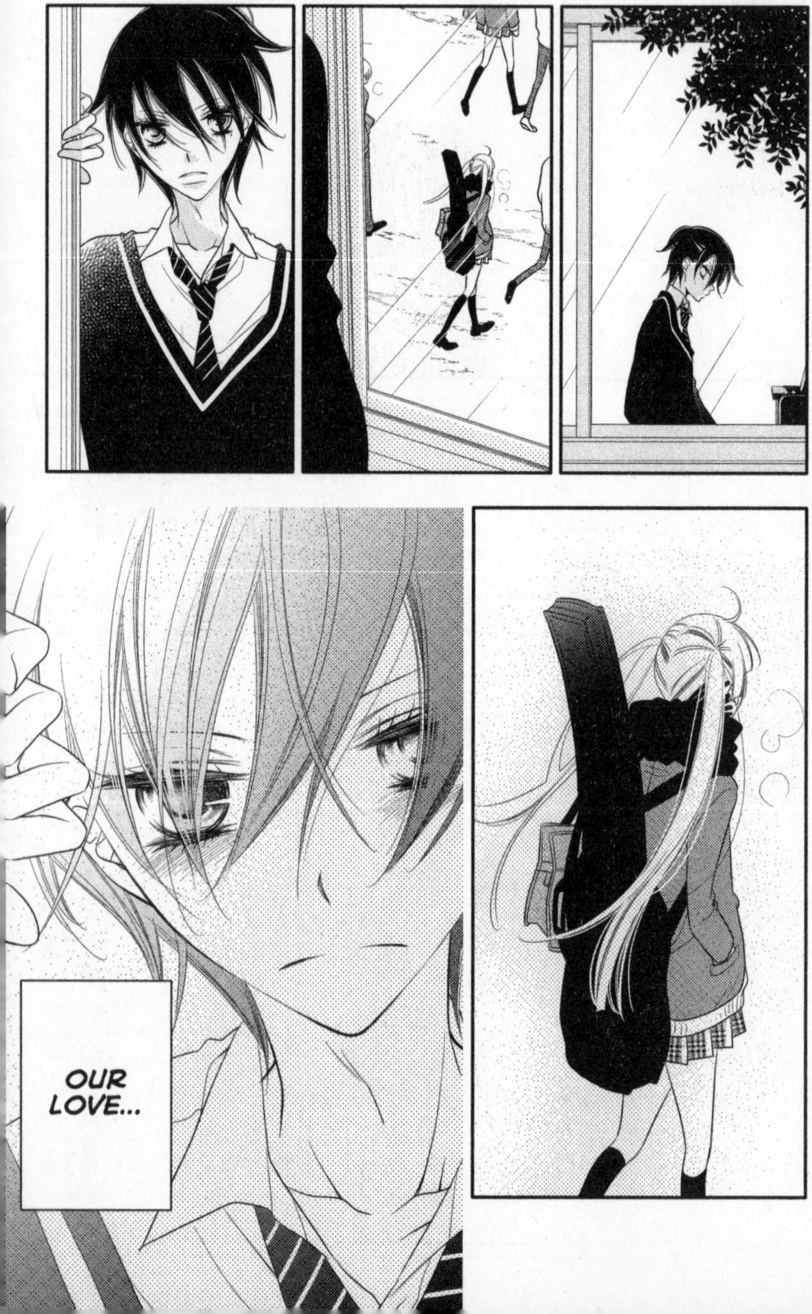
OUR LOVE...

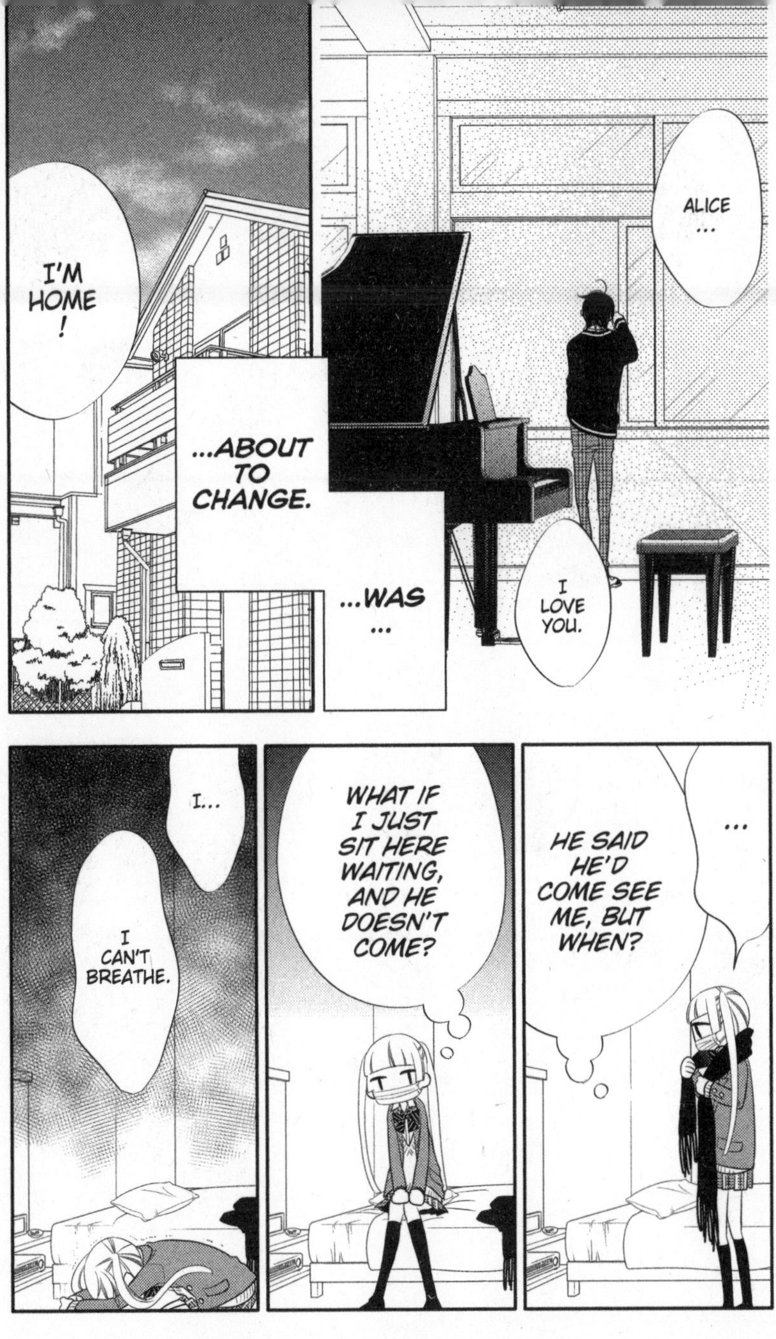
ALICE ...
I LOVE YOU.
...WAS ...
...ABOUT TO CHANGE.
I'M HOME !
...
HE SAID HE'D COME SEE ME, BUT WHEN?
WHAT IF I JUST SIT HERE WAITING, AND HE DOESN'T COME?
I...
I CAN'T BREATHE.

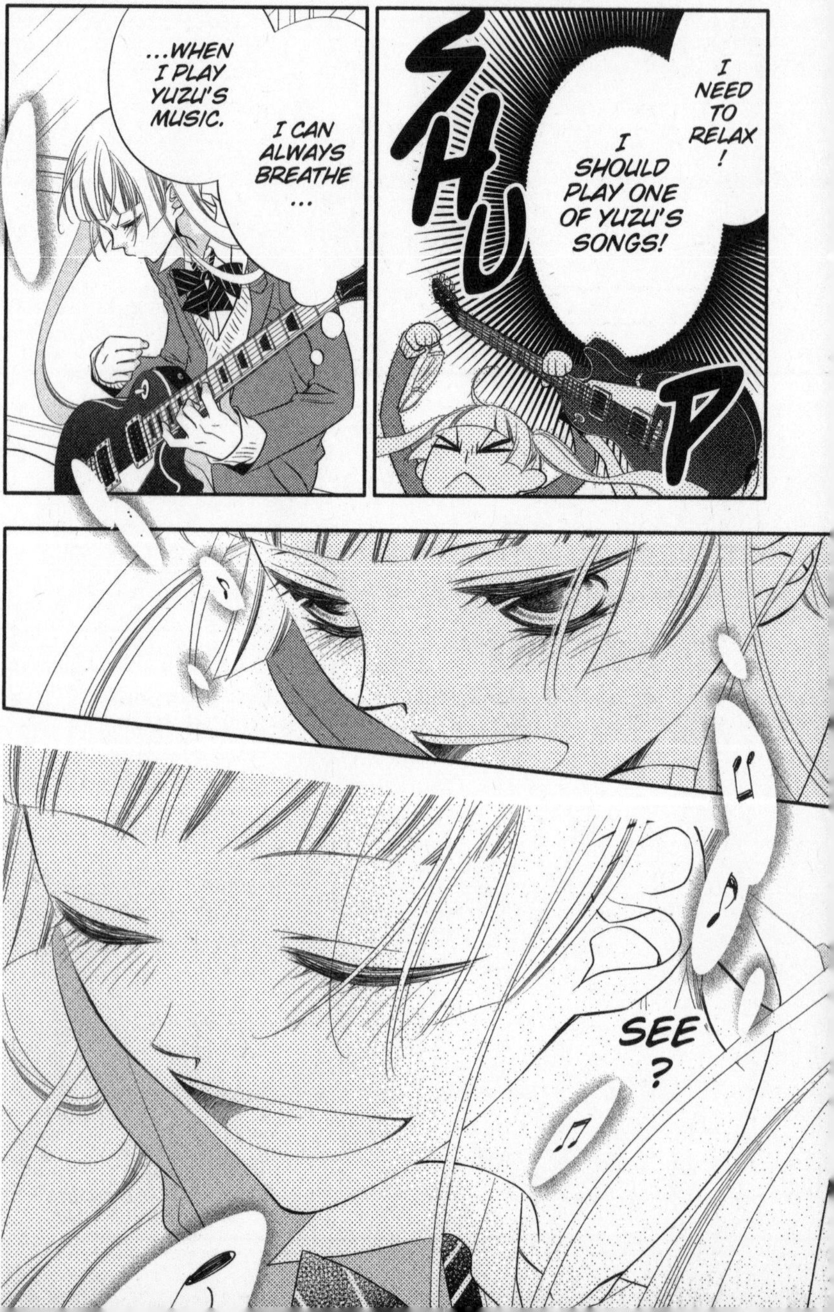
SHUP
I NEED TO RELAX!
I SHOULD PLAY ONE OF YUZU'S SONGS!
I CAN ALWAYS BREATHE...
...WHEN I PLAY YUZU'S MUSIC.
SEE?

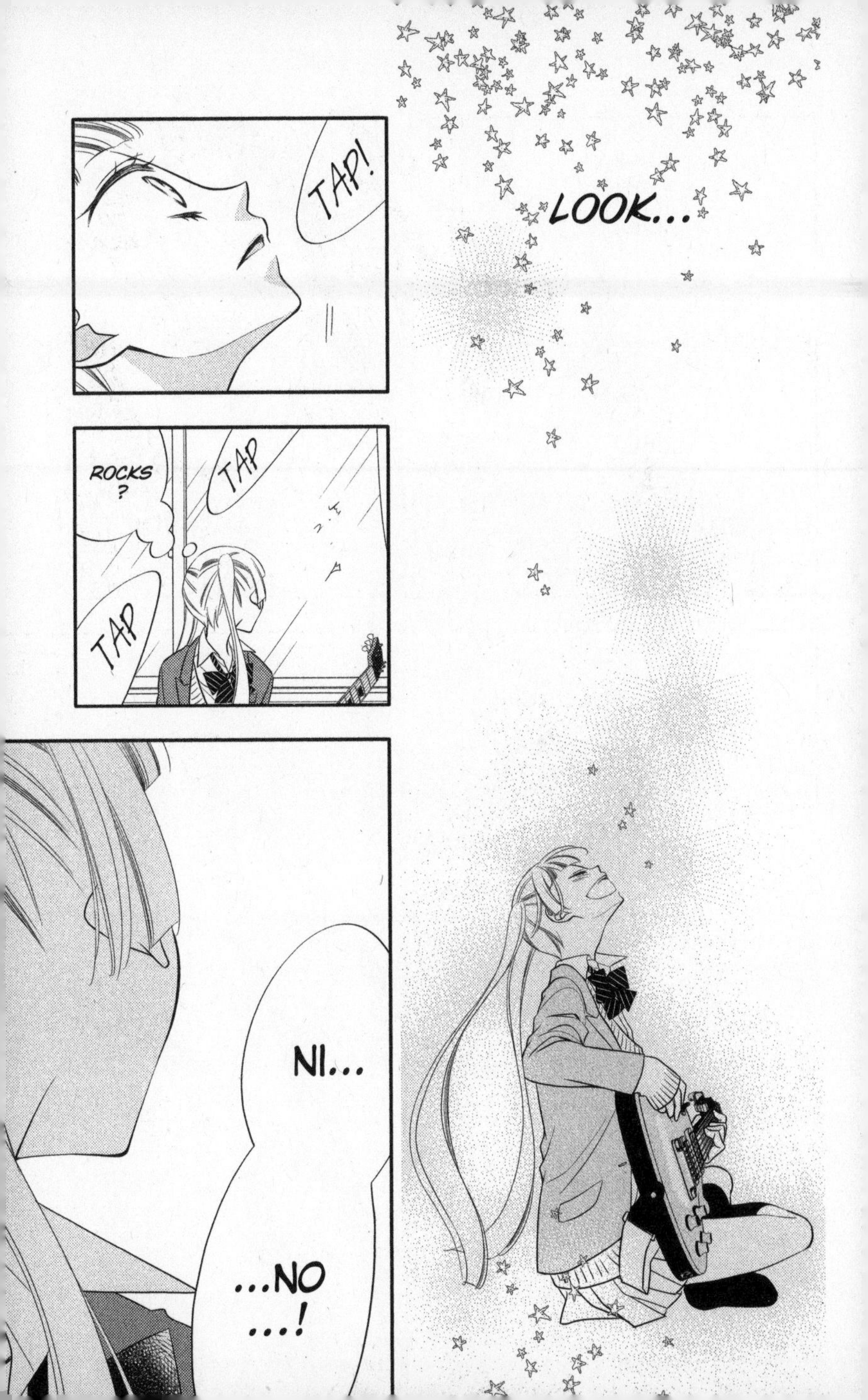
LOOK...
TAP!
TAP
ROCKS ?
TAP
NI...
...NO ...!

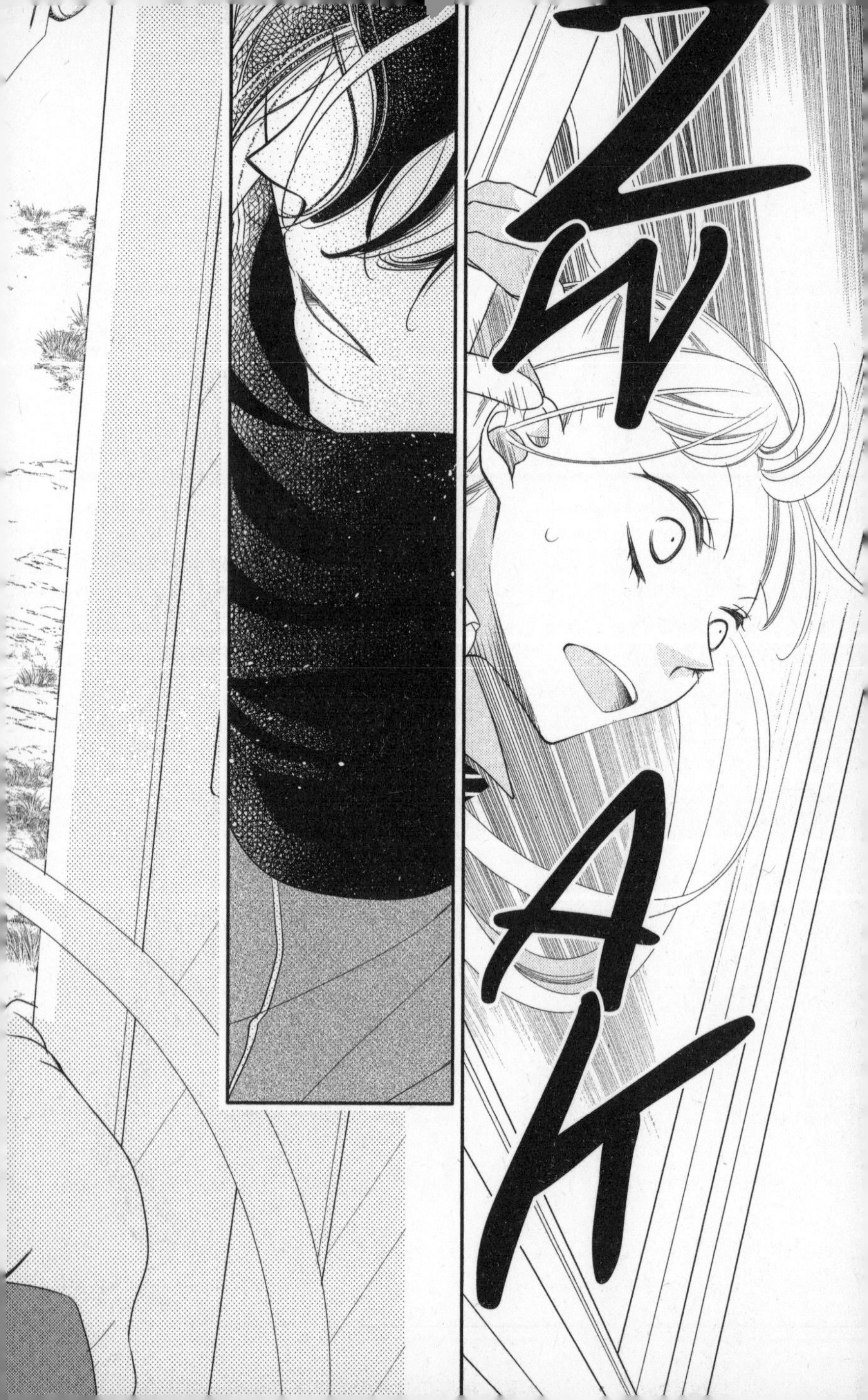

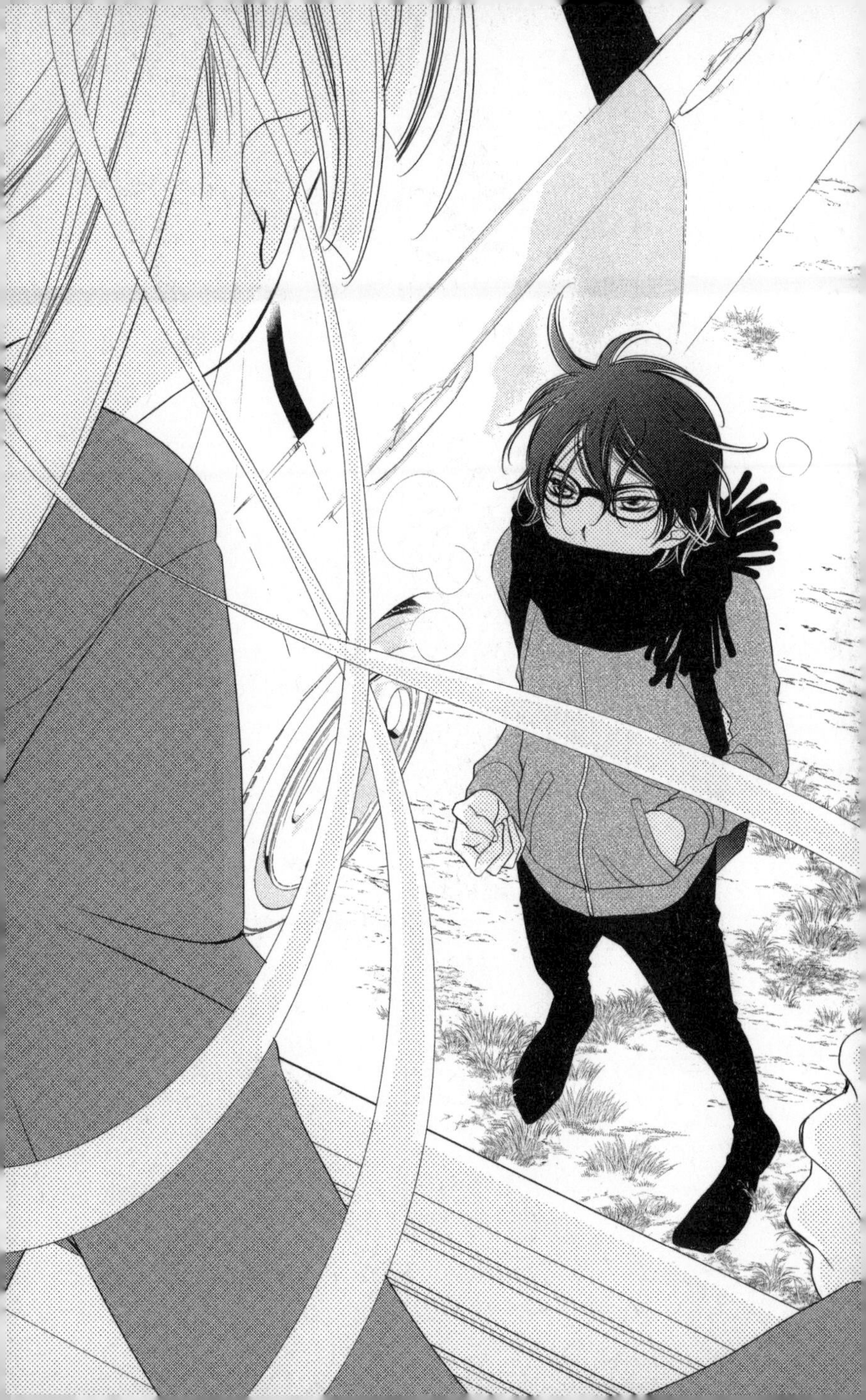

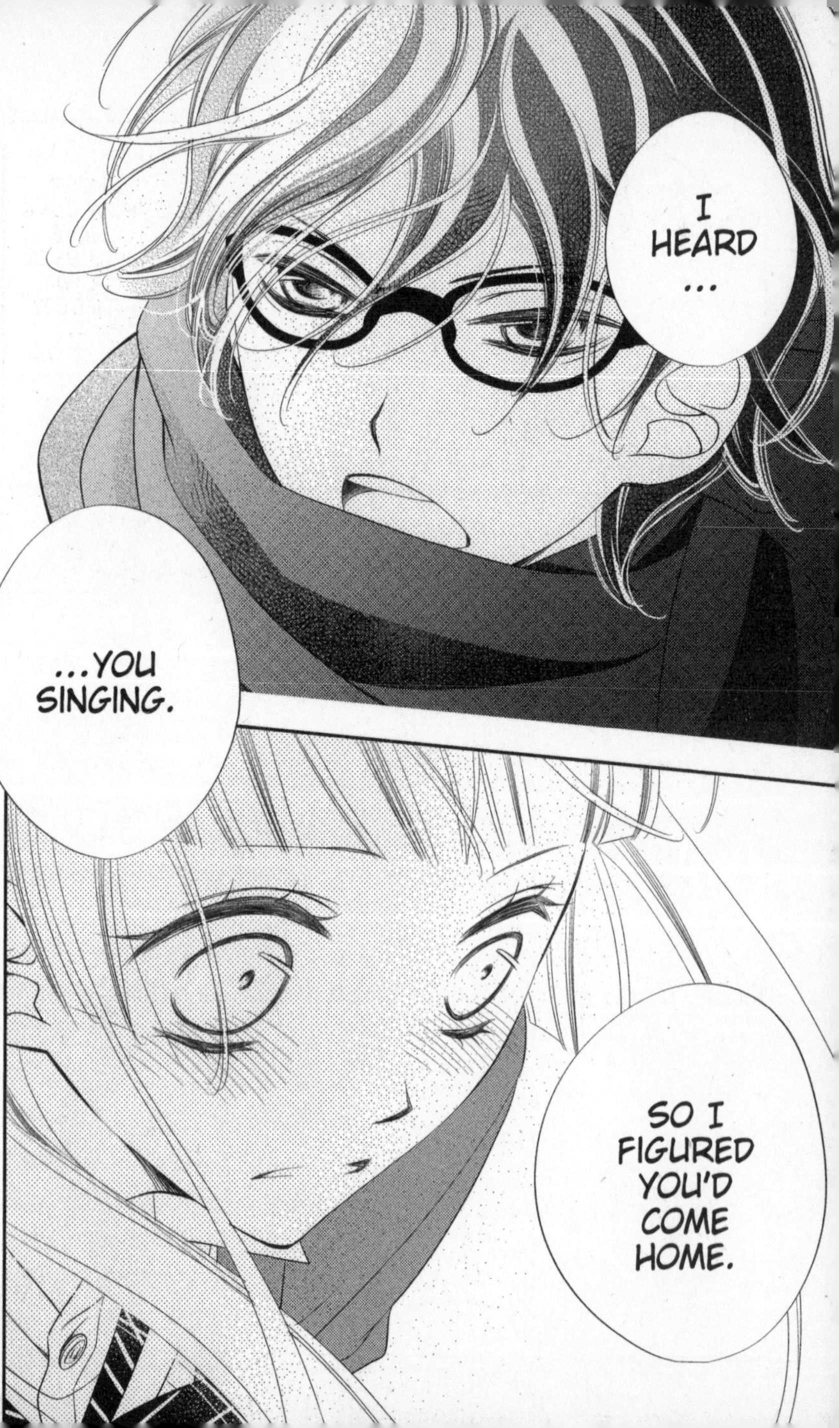
I HEARD ...
...YOU SINGING.
SO I FIGURED YOU'D COME HOME.

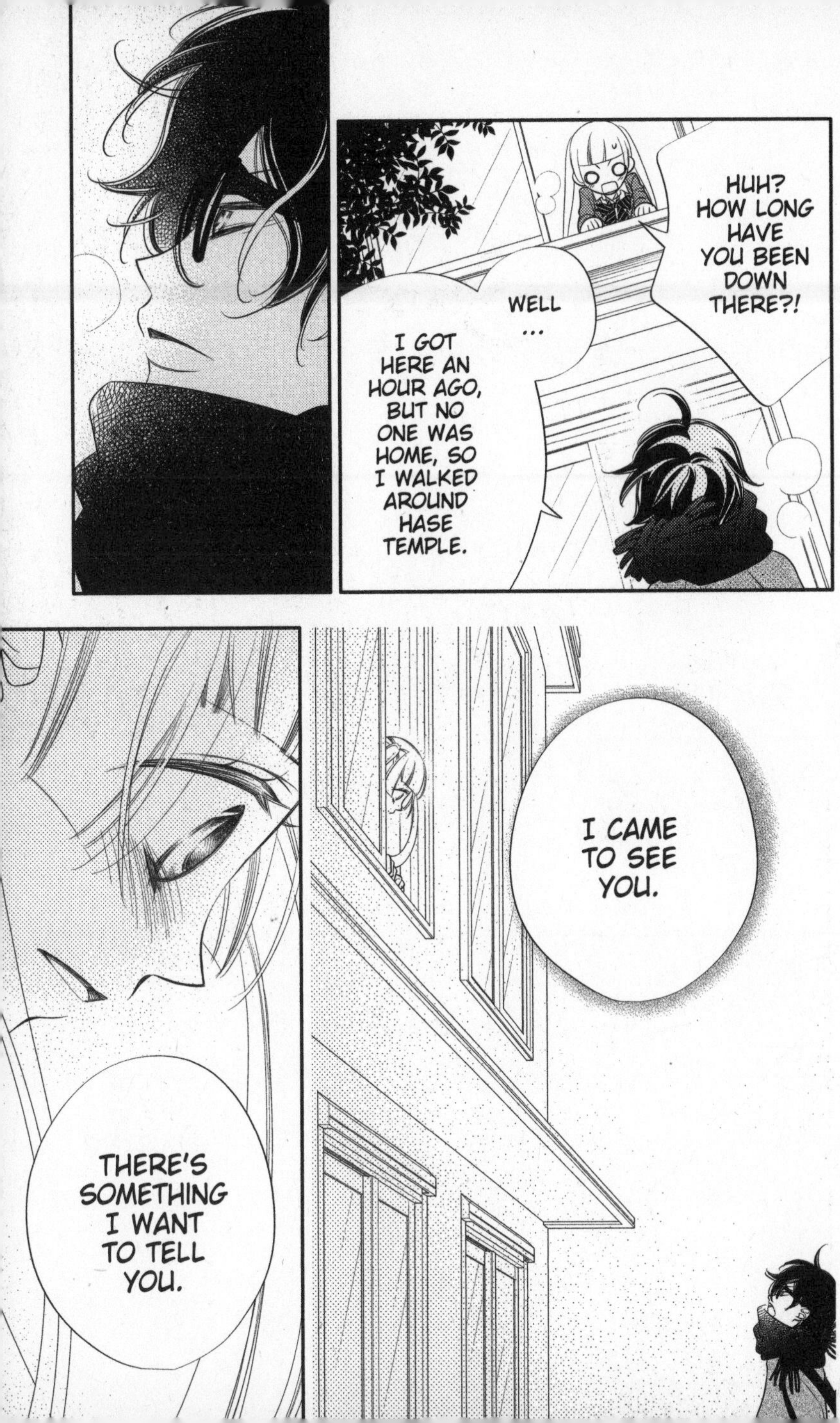

HUH? HOW LONG HAVE YOU BEEN DOWN THERE?!
WELL ...
I GOT HERE AN HOUR AGO, BUT NO ONE WAS HOME, SO I WALKED AROUND HASE TEMPLE.
I CAME TO SEE YOU.
THERE'S SOMETHING I WANT TO TELL YOU.

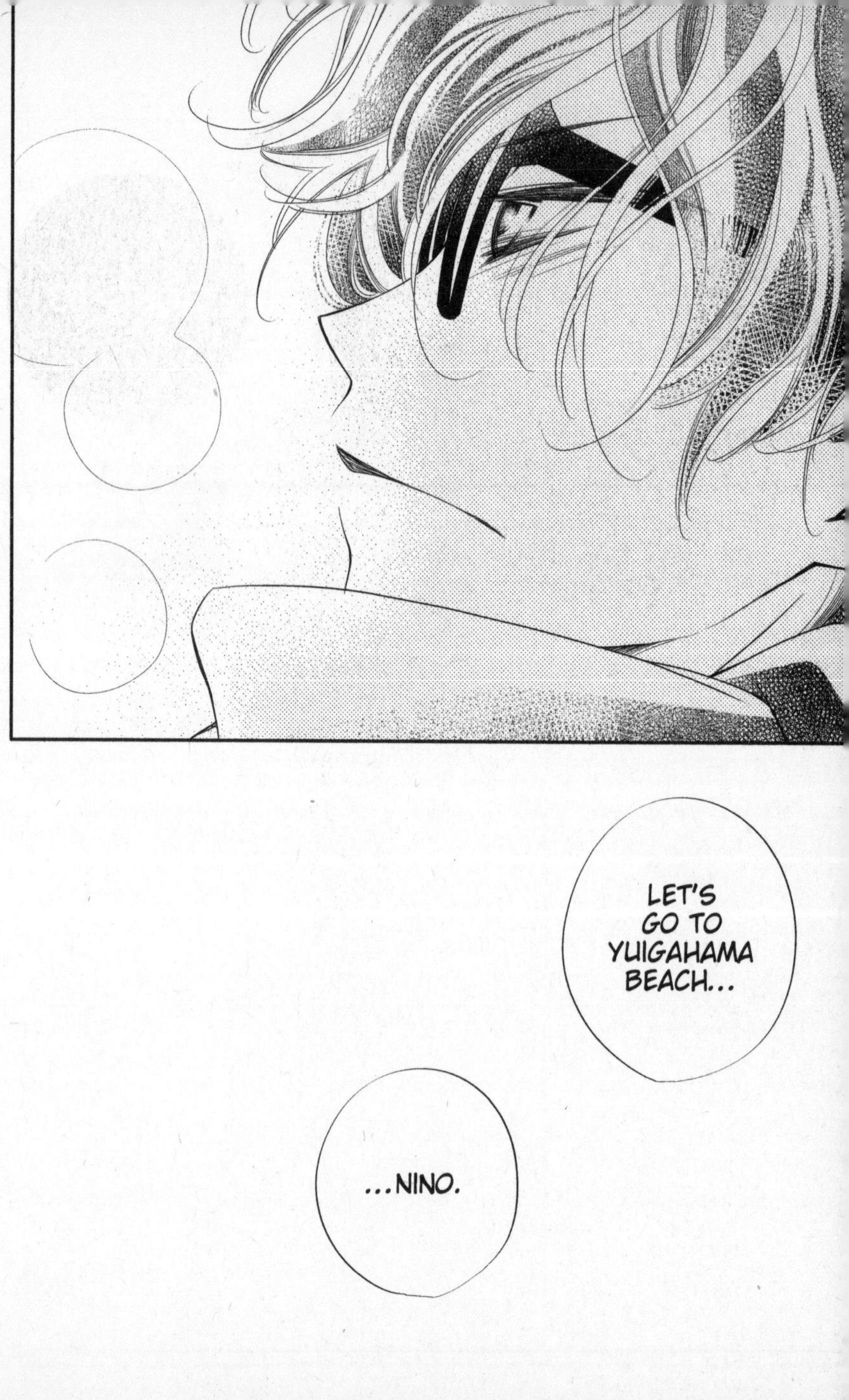
LET'S GO TO YUIGAHAMA BEACH...
...NINO.

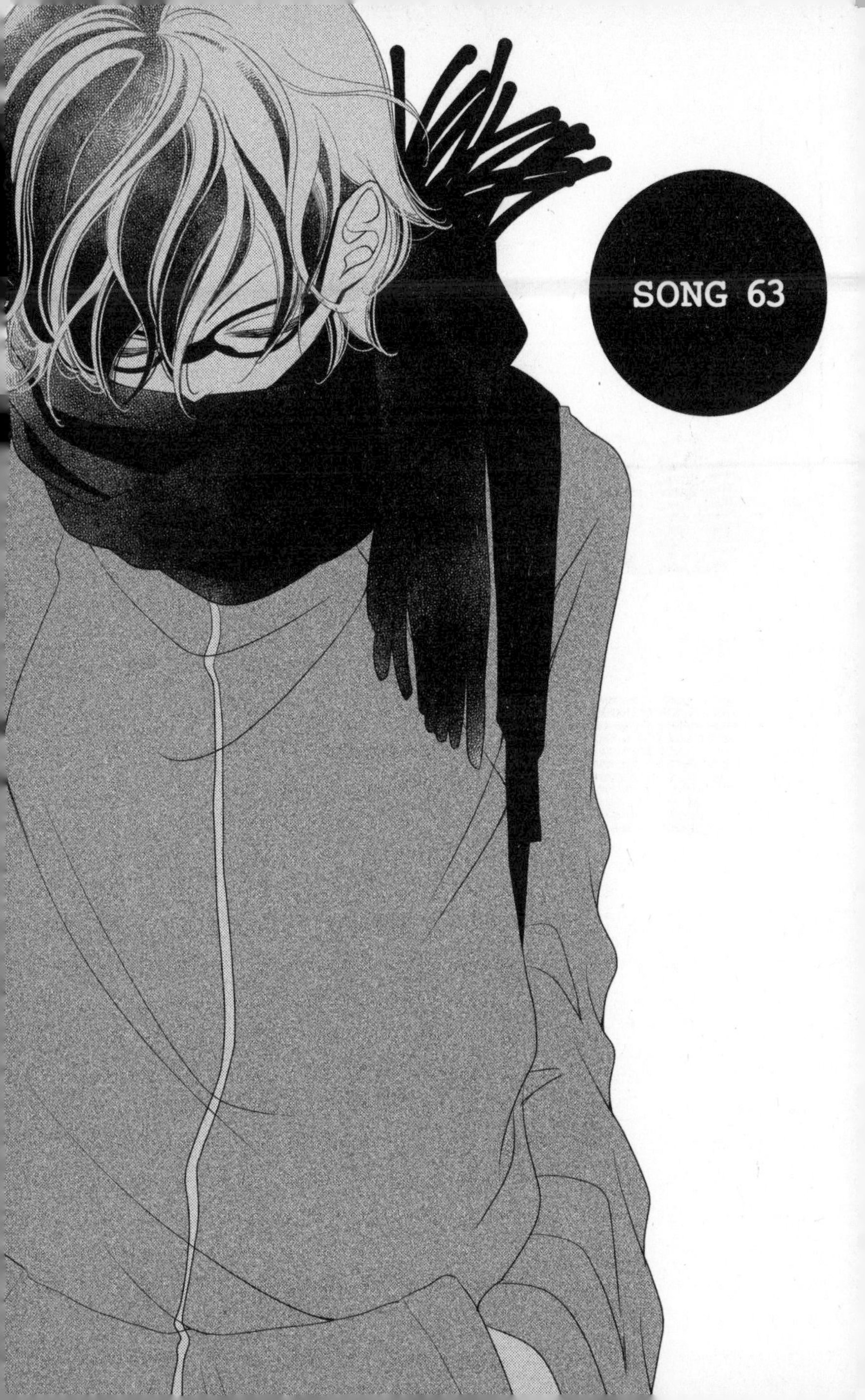
SONG 63

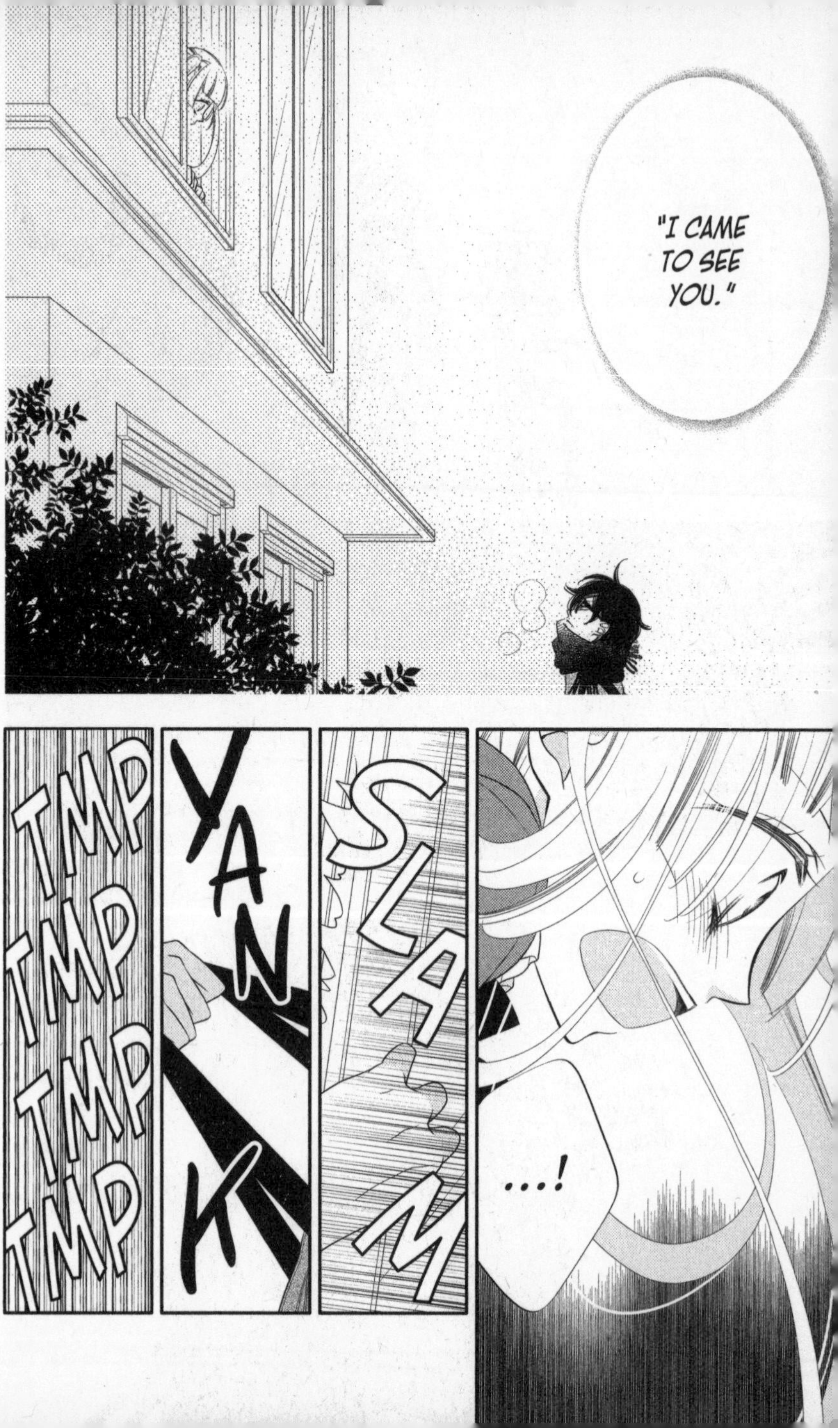
"I CAME TO SEE YOU."
...!
SLAM
YANK
TMP TMP TMP TMP

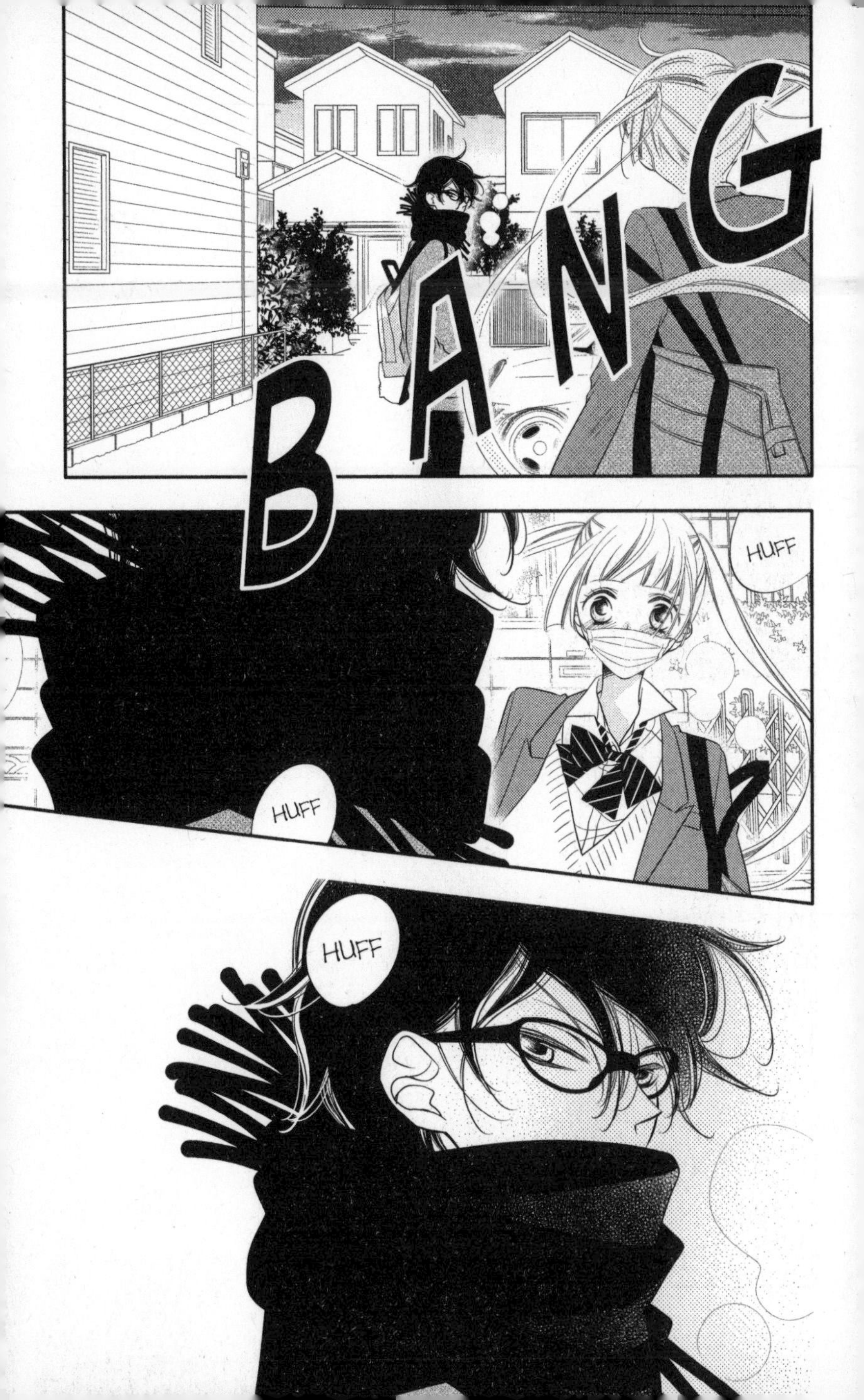
BANG
HUFF
HUFF
HUFF

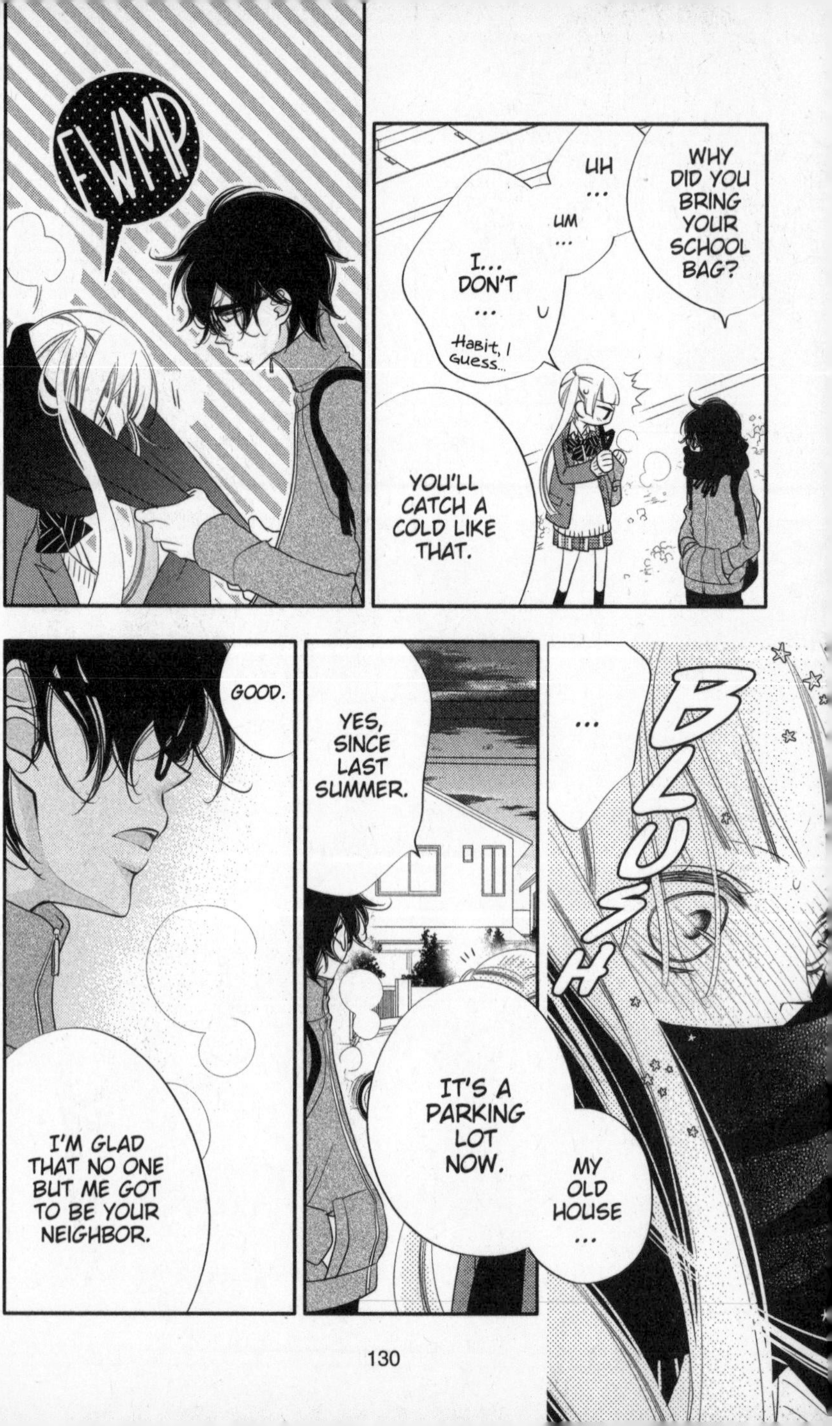
WHY DID YOU BRING YOUR SCHOOL BAG?
UH ...
UM ...
I... DON'T ...
Habit, I guess...
YOU'LL CATCH A COLD LIKE THAT.
FWMP
...
BLUSH
MY OLD HOUSE ...
IT'S A PARKING LOT NOW.
YES, SINCE LAST SUMMER.
GOOD.
I'M GLAD THAT NO ONE BUT ME GOT TO BE YOUR NEIGHBOR.

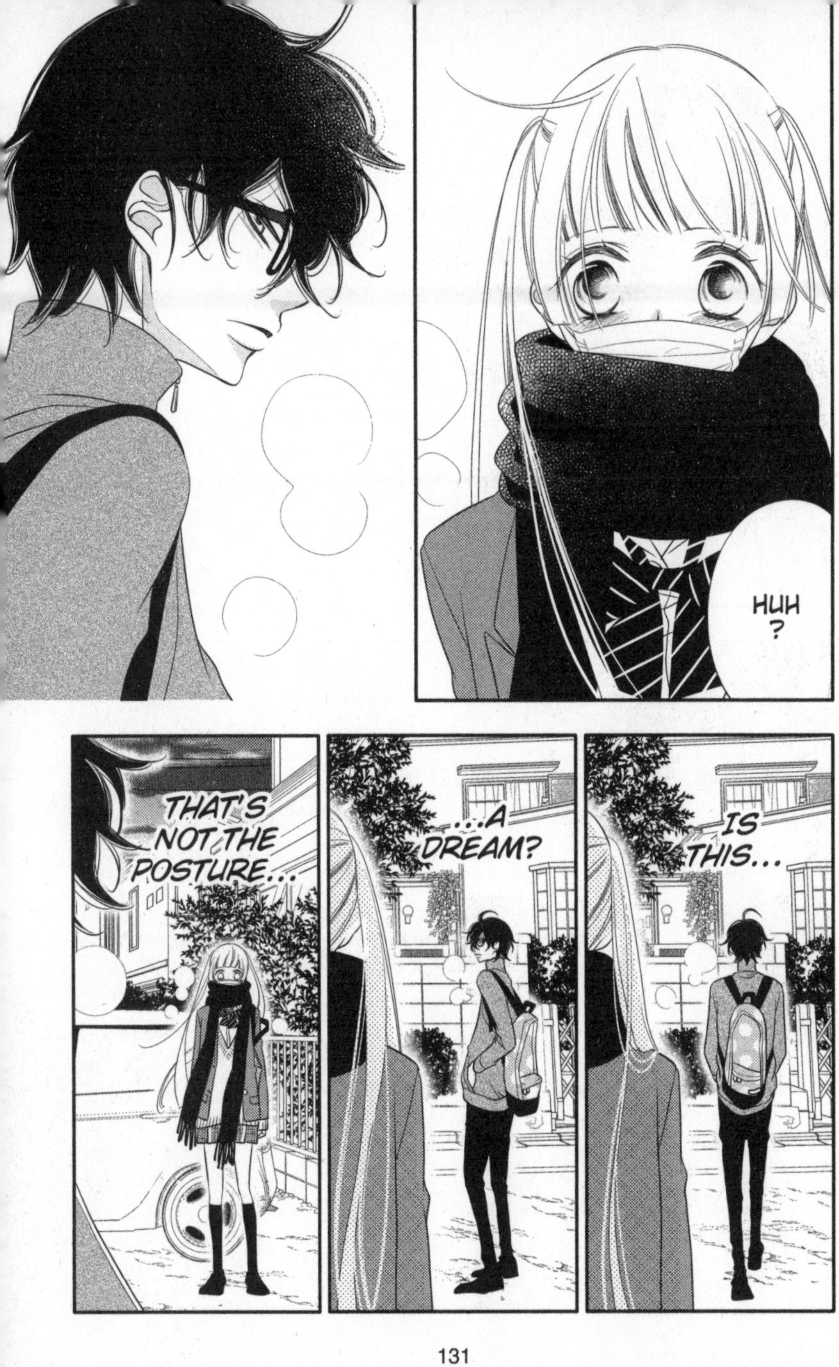
HUH?
IS THIS...
...A DREAM?
THAT'S NOT THE POSTURE...

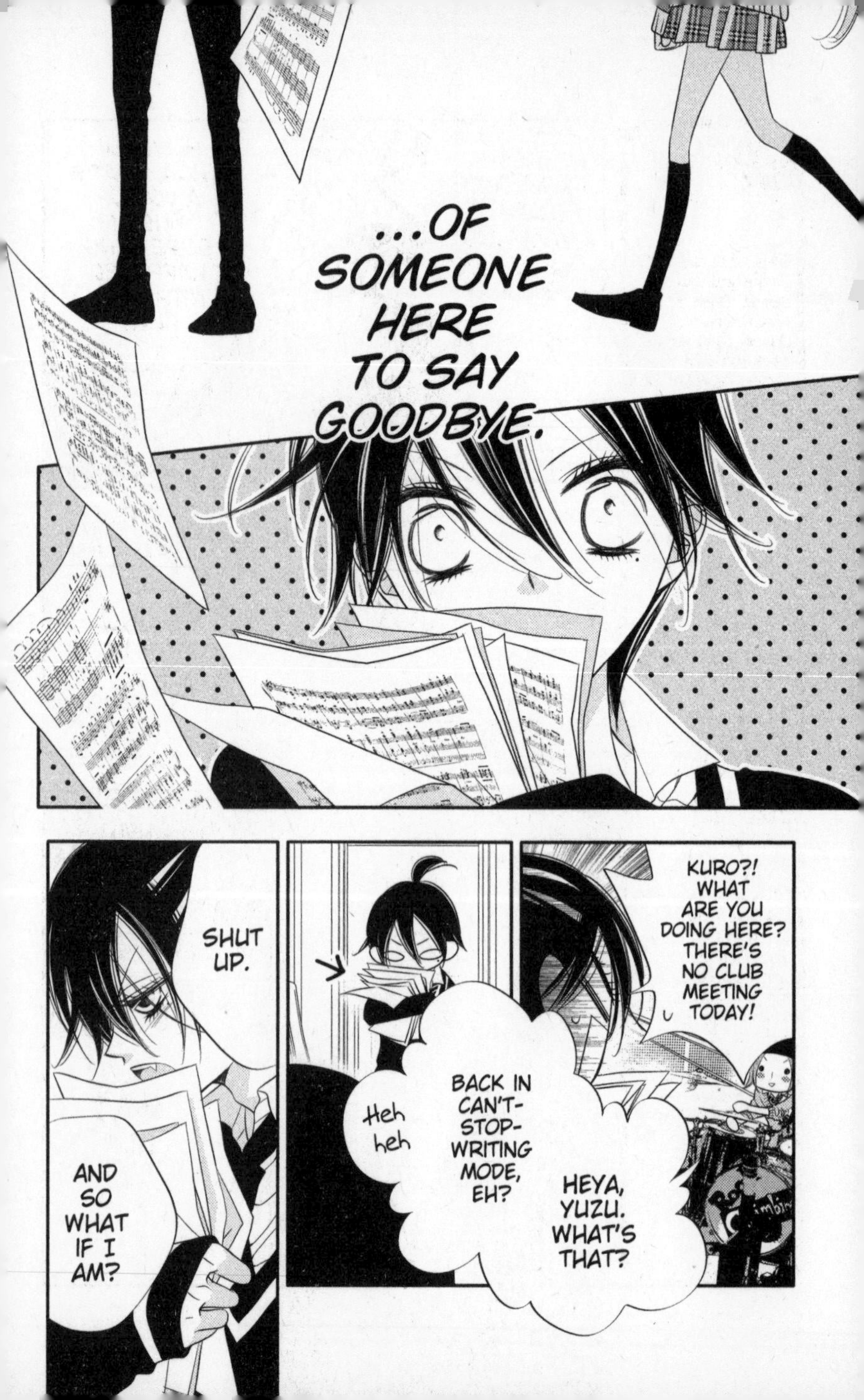
...OF SOMEONE HERE TO SAY GOODBYE.
KURO?! WHAT ARE YOU DOING HERE? THERE'S NO CLUB MEETING TODAY!
HEYA, YUZU. WHAT'S THAT?
BACK IN CAN'T-STOP-WRITING MODE, EH?
Heh heh
SHUT UP.
AND SO WHAT IF I AM?

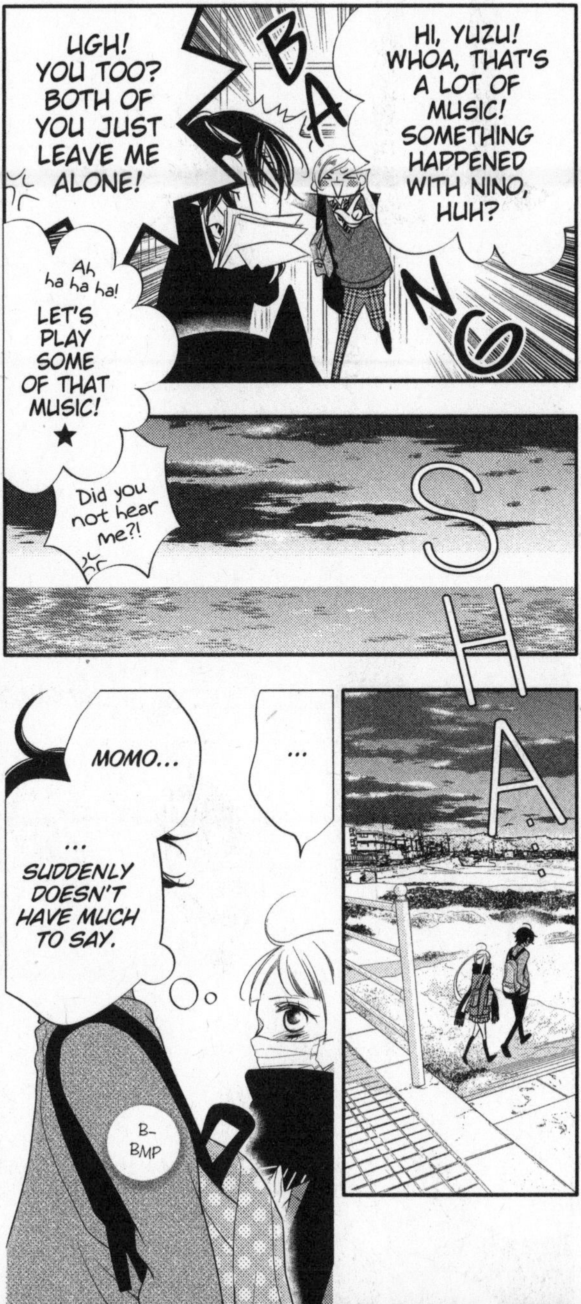
HI, YUZU! WHOA, THAT'S A LOT OF MUSIC! SOMETHING HAPPENED WITH NINO, HUH?
BANG
UGH! YOU TOO? BOTH OF YOU JUST LEAVE ME ALONE!
Ah ha ha ha! LET'S PLAY SOME OF THAT MUSIC! ★
SHAA
Did you not hear me?!
...
MOMO...
... SUDDENLY DOESN'T HAVE MUCH TO SAY.
B-BMP

5

This actually happened quite some time ago, but Rock in Japan allowed me back to get more reference photos! Once again, I took a ton of pictures—nearly 5,000 of them. And this time, I managed to get lots of shots of drummers.

It was my third time doing it, so I wasn't as nervous, and for the first time I figured it would be okay to eat something besides rice. The whelk and abalone were delicious!

This year, some of the staff from the anime joined me on-site, so it was a lot of fun! Is there anything better than listening to live music under a bright blue sky? I love Rock in Japan!! Thank you so much for having me!!

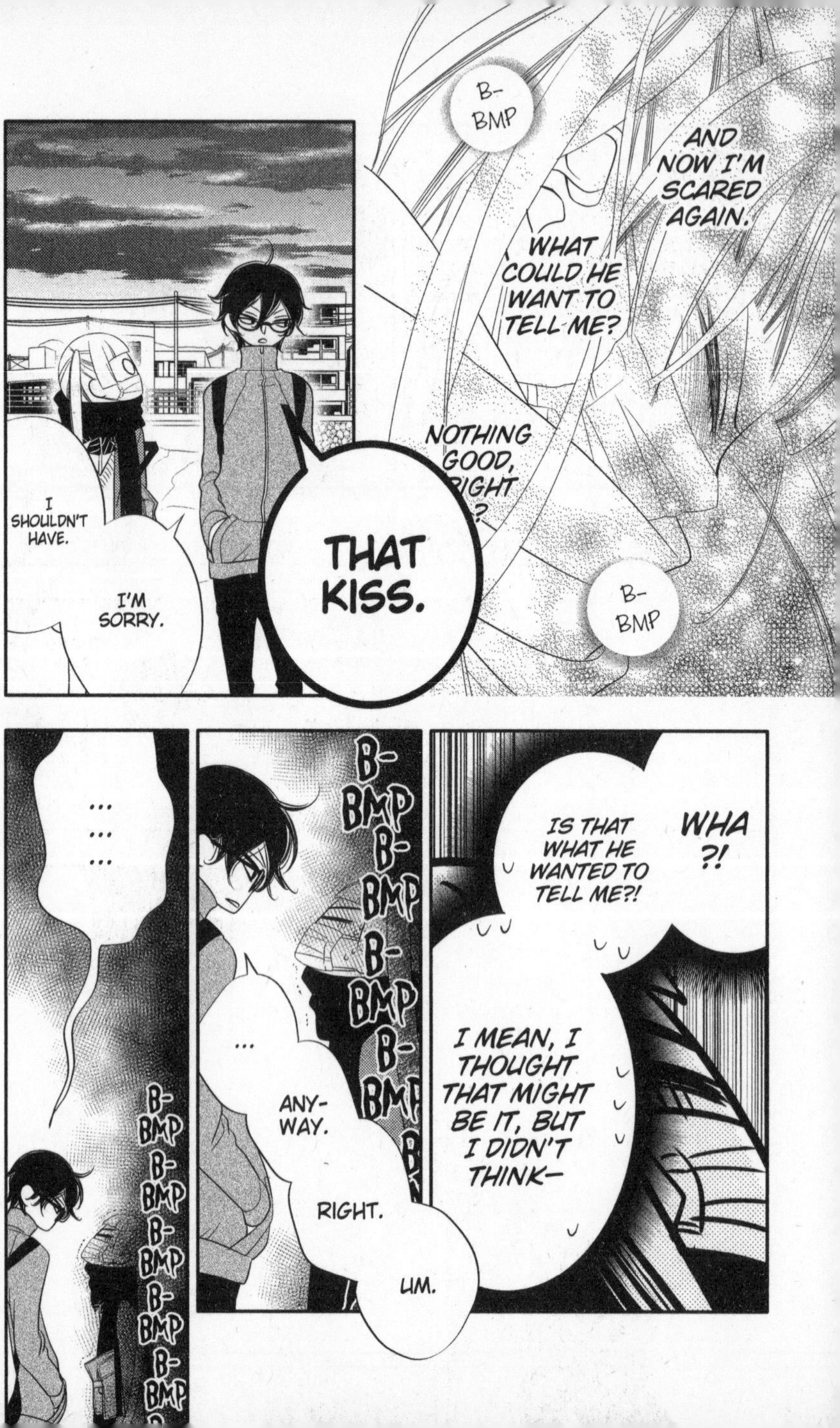
B-BMP
AND NOW I'M SCARED AGAIN.
WHAT COULD HE WANT TO TELL ME?
NOTHING GOOD, RIGHT?
B-BMP
THAT KISS.
I SHOULDN'T HAVE.
I'M SORRY.
WHA?!
IS THAT WHAT HE WANTED TO TELL ME?!
I MEAN, I THOUGHT THAT MIGHT BE IT, BUT I DIDN'T THINK—
B-BMP B-BMP B-BMP B-BMP
...
ANY-WAY.
RIGHT.
UM.
... ... ...
B-BMP B-BMP B-BMP B-BMP B-BMP

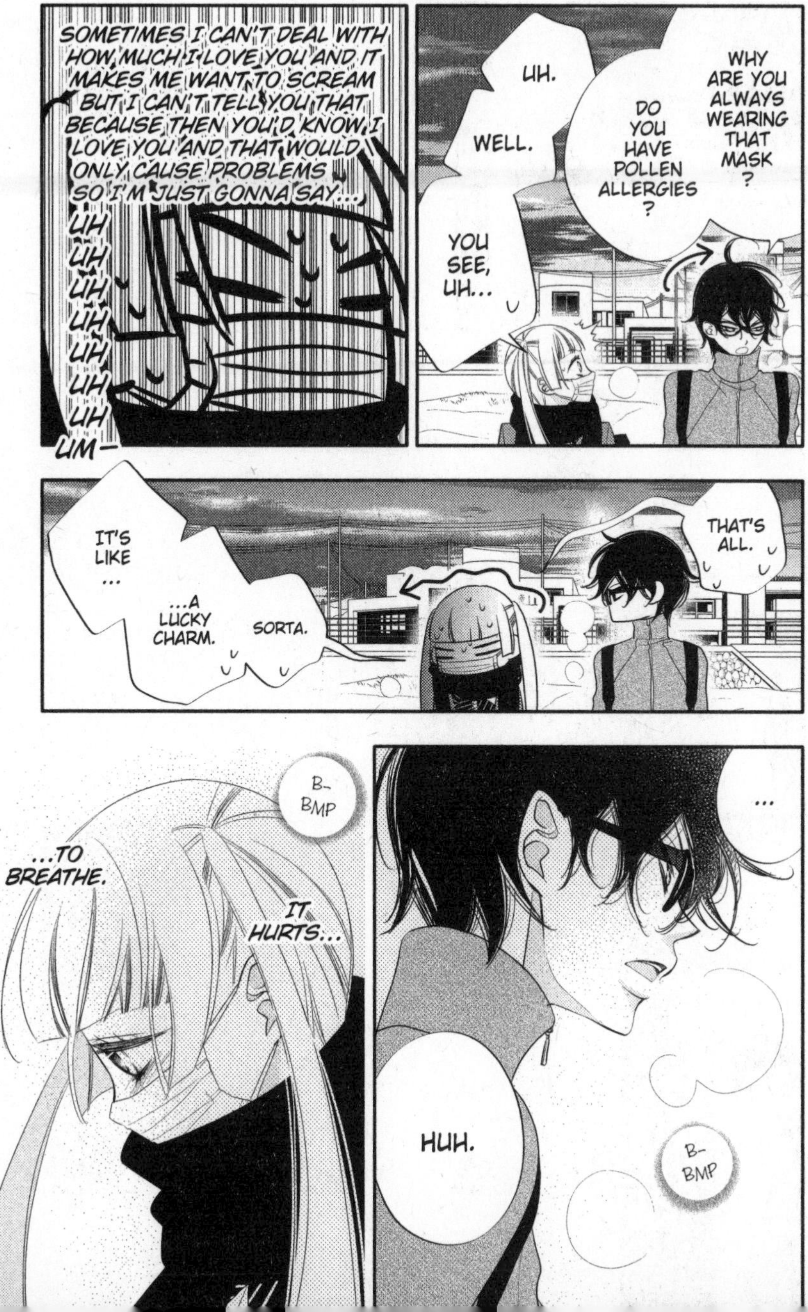
WHY ARE YOU ALWAYS WEARING THAT MASK?
DO YOU HAVE POLLEN ALLERGIES?
UH.
WELL.
YOU SEE, UH...
SOMETIMES I CAN'T DEAL WITH HOW MUCH I LOVE YOU AND IT MAKES ME WANT TO SCREAM BUT I CAN'T TELL YOU THAT BECAUSE THEN YOU'D KNOW I LOVE YOU AND THAT WOULD ONLY CAUSE PROBLEMS SO I'M JUST GONNA SAY...
UH UH UH UH UH UH UH UM—
THAT'S ALL.
IT'S LIKE...
...A LUCKY CHARM.
SORTA.
...
HUH.
B-BMP
B-BMP
...TO BREATHE.
IT HURTS...

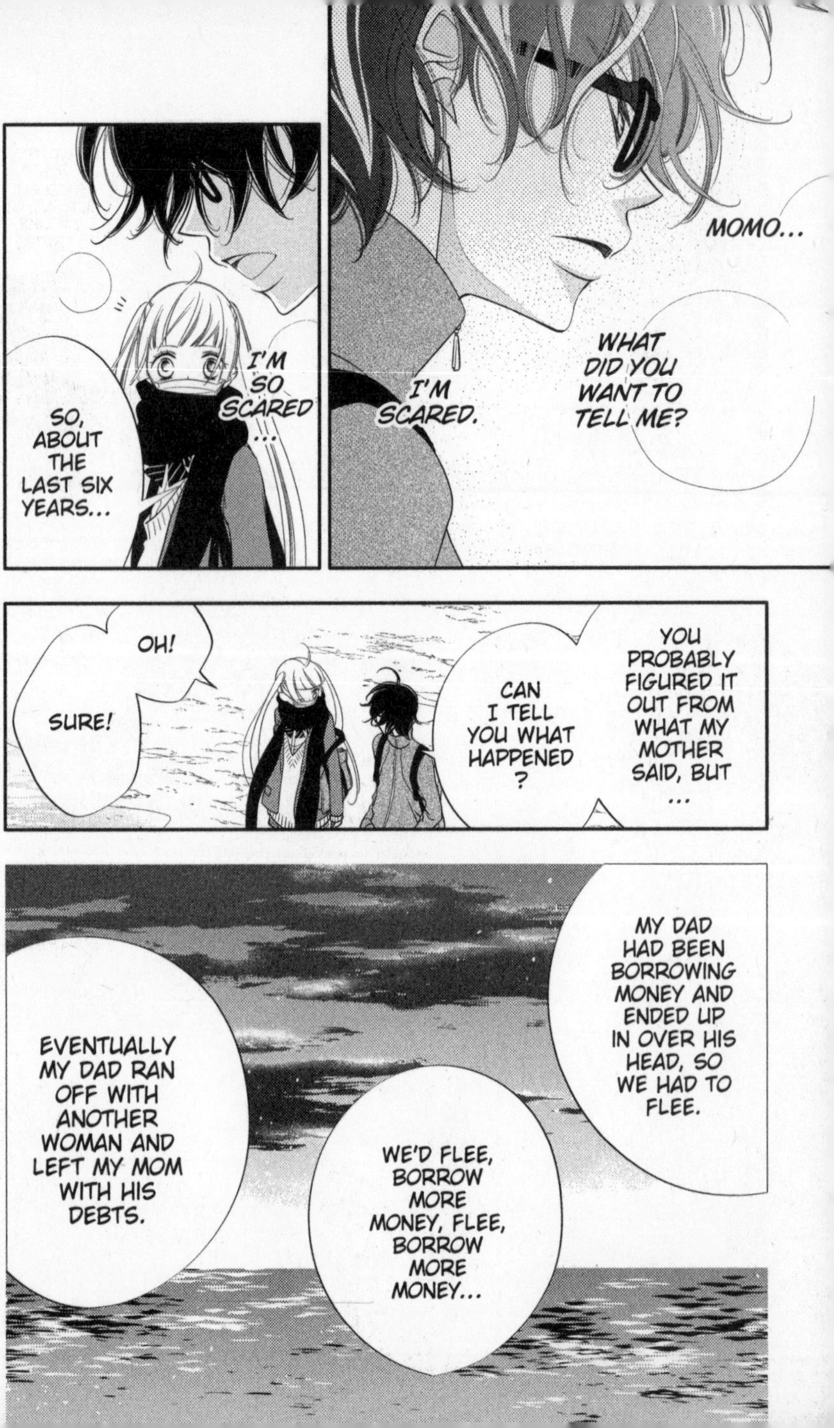
MOMO...
WHAT DID YOU WANT TO TELL ME?
I'M SCARED.
I'M SO SCARED...
SO, ABOUT THE LAST SIX YEARS...
YOU PROBABLY FIGURED IT OUT FROM WHAT MY MOTHER SAID, BUT...
CAN I TELL YOU WHAT HAPPENED?
OH!
SURE!
MY DAD HAD BEEN BORROWING MONEY AND ENDED UP IN OVER HIS HEAD, SO WE HAD TO FLEE.
WE'D FLEE, BORROW MORE MONEY, FLEE, BORROW MORE MONEY...
EVENTUALLY MY DAD RAN OFF WITH ANOTHER WOMAN AND LEFT MY MOM WITH HIS DEBTS.

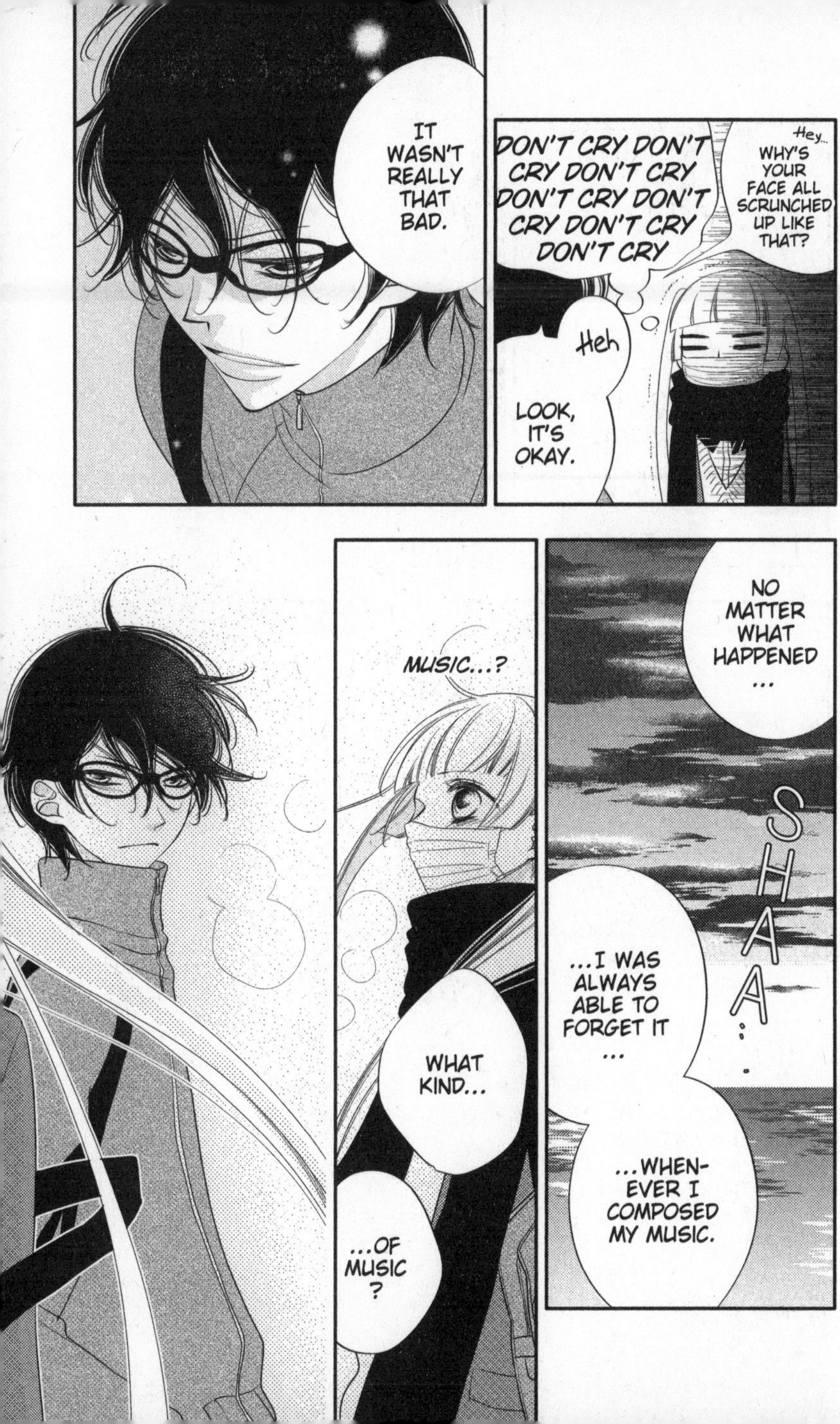
Hey... WHY'S YOUR FACE ALL SCRUNCHED UP LIKE THAT?
DON'T CRY DON'T CRY DON'T CRY DON'T CRY DON'T CRY DON'T CRY DON'T CRY DON'T CRY
Heh
LOOK, IT'S OKAY.
IT WASN'T REALLY THAT BAD.
NO MATTER WHAT HAPPENED...
SHAA...
...I WAS ALWAYS ABLE TO FORGET IT...
...WHEN-EVER I COMPOSED MY MUSIC.
MUSIC...?
WHAT KIND...
...OF MUSIC?

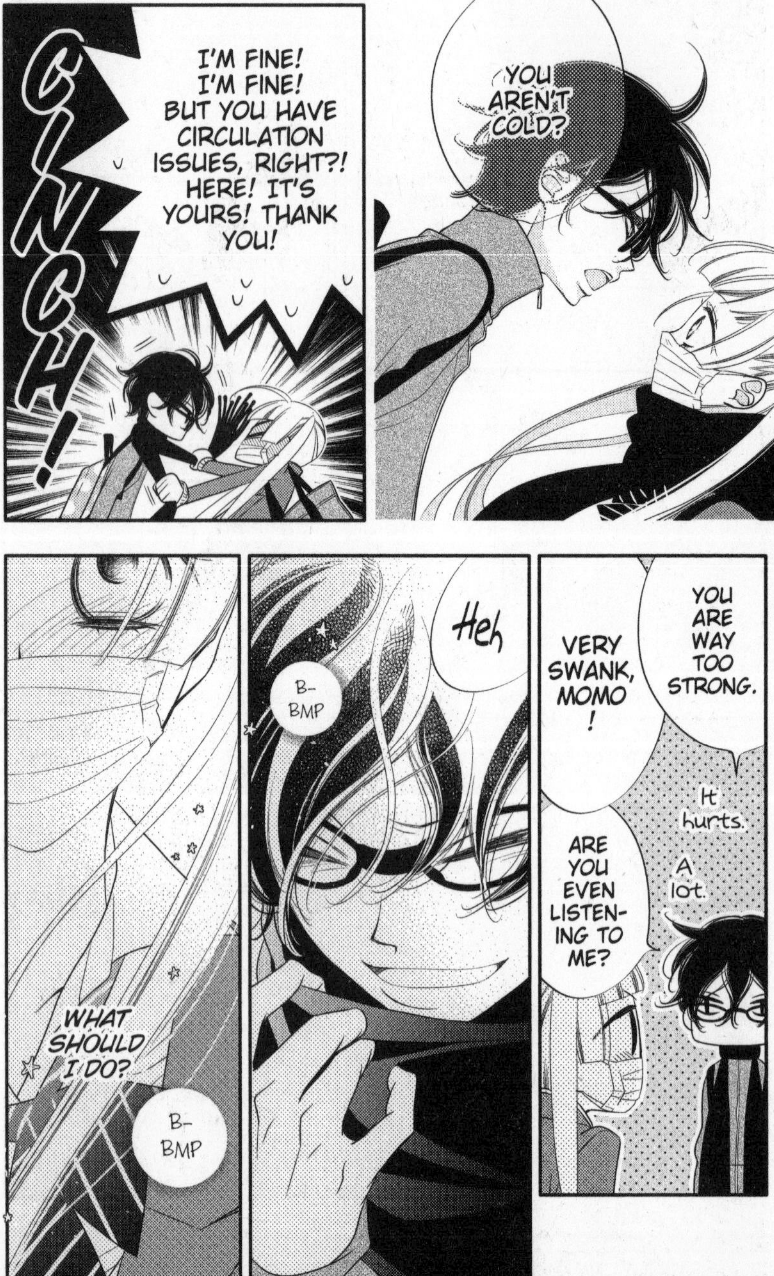
YOU AREN'T COLD?
I'M FINE! I'M FINE! BUT YOU HAVE CIRCULATION ISSUES, RIGHT?! HERE! IT'S YOURS! THANK YOU!
CINCH!
YOU ARE WAY TOO STRONG.
VERY SWANK, MOMO!
It hurts.
A lot.
ARE YOU EVEN LISTENING TO ME?
Heh
B-BMP
WHAT SHOULD I DO?
B-BMP

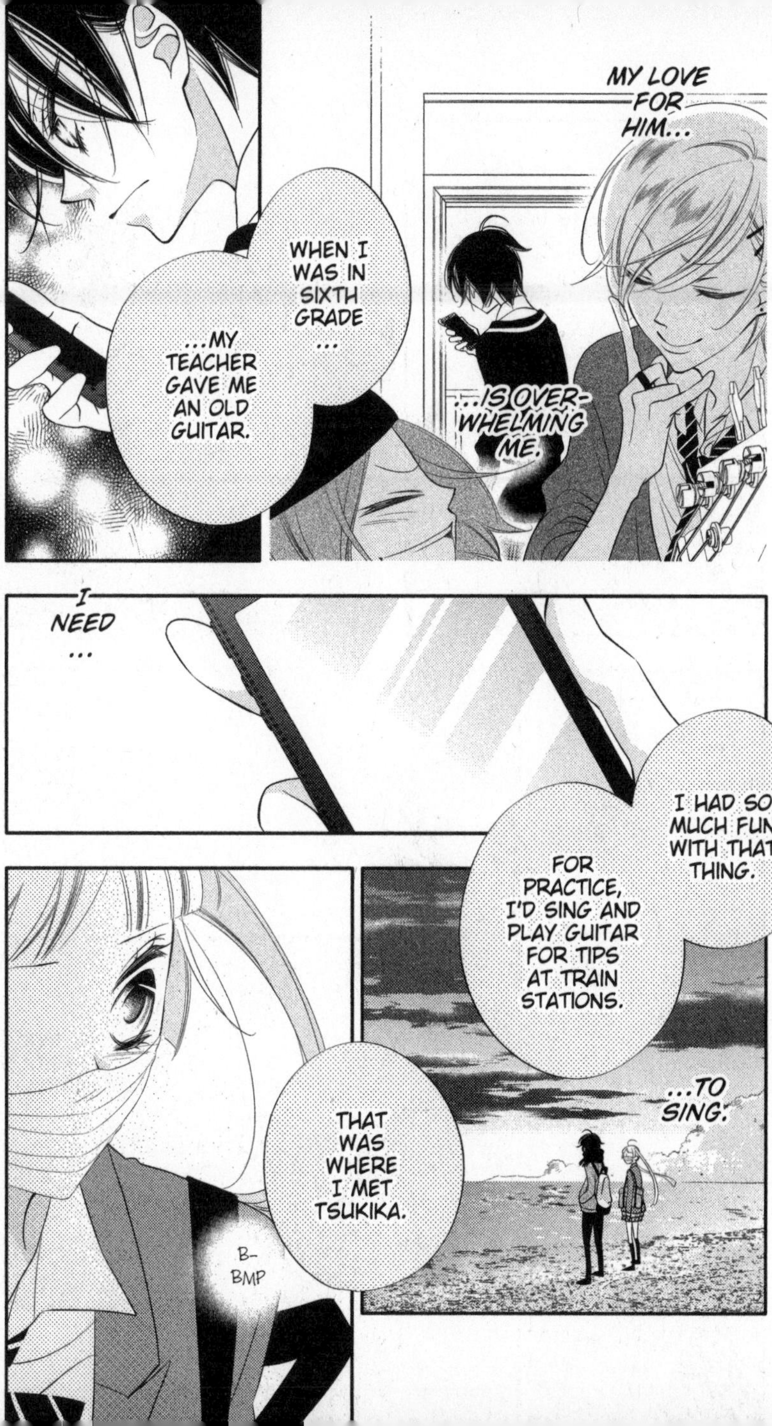
MY LOVE FOR HIM...
...IS OVER-WHELMING ME.
WHEN I WAS IN SIXTH GRADE...
...MY TEACHER GAVE ME AN OLD GUITAR.
I NEED...
I HAD SO MUCH FUN WITH THAT THING.
FOR PRACTICE, I'D SING AND PLAY GUITAR FOR TIPS AT TRAIN STATIONS.
...TO SING.
THAT WAS WHERE I MET TSUKIKA.
B-BMP

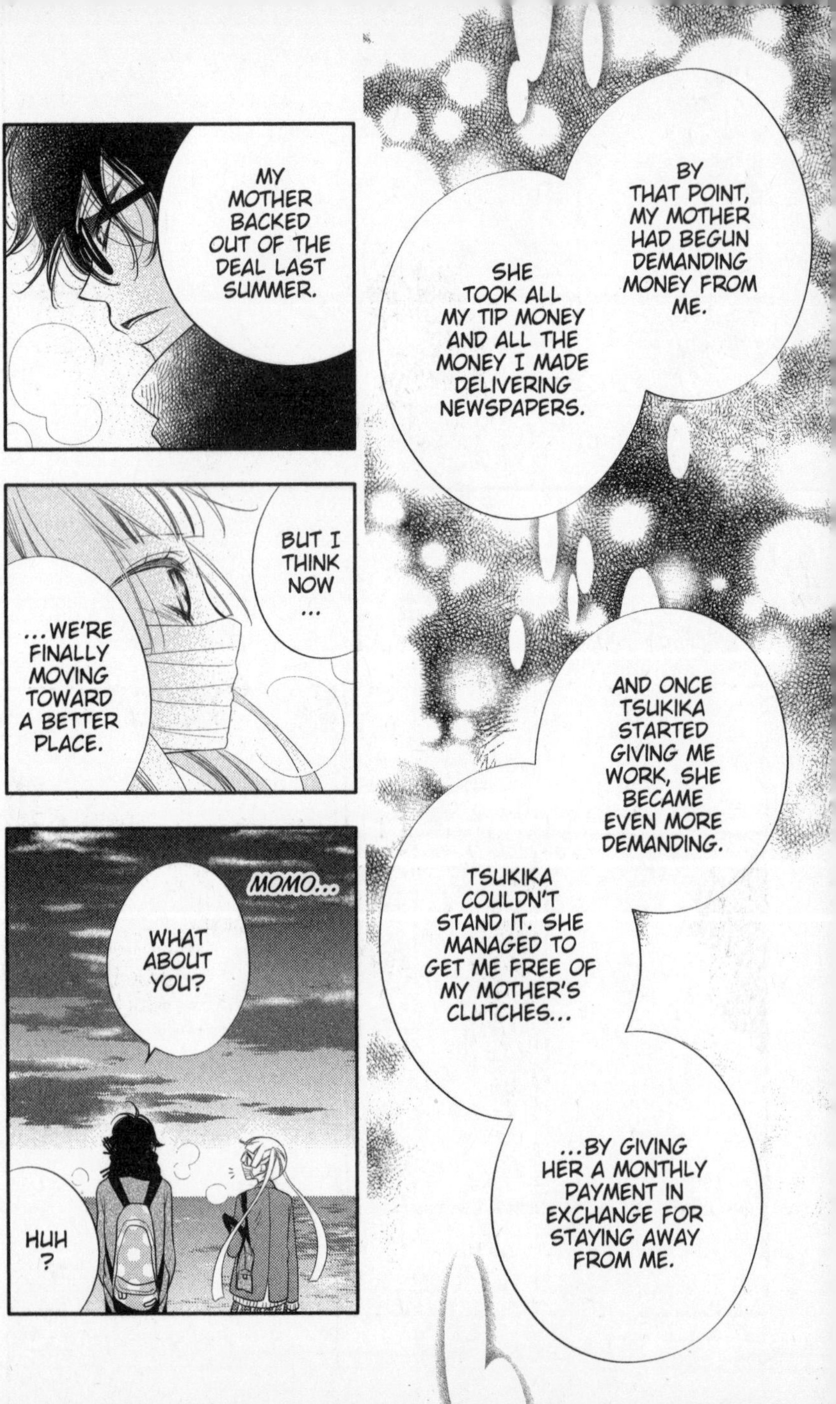
BY THAT POINT, MY MOTHER HAD BEGUN DEMANDING MONEY FROM ME.
SHE TOOK ALL MY TIP MONEY AND ALL THE MONEY I MADE DELIVERING NEWSPAPERS.
AND ONCE TSUKIKA STARTED GIVING ME WORK, SHE BECAME EVEN MORE DEMANDING.
TSUKIKA COULDN'T STAND IT. SHE MANAGED TO GET ME FREE OF MY MOTHER'S CLUTCHES...
...BY GIVING HER A MONTHLY PAYMENT IN EXCHANGE FOR STAYING AWAY FROM ME.
MY MOTHER BACKED OUT OF THE DEAL LAST SUMMER.
BUT I THINK NOW ...
...WE'RE FINALLY MOVING TOWARD A BETTER PLACE.
MOMO...
WHAT ABOUT YOU?
HUH ?

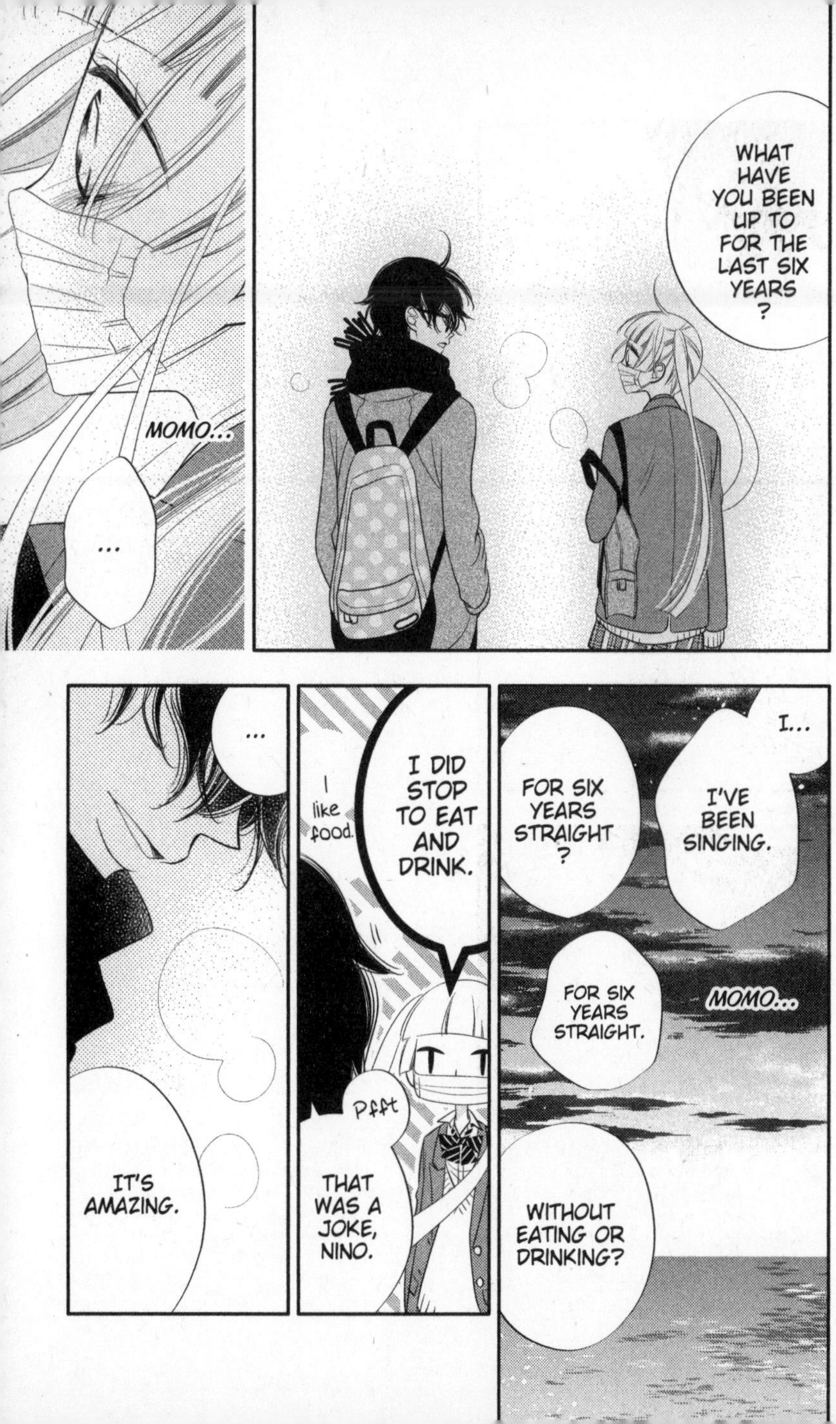
WHAT HAVE YOU BEEN UP TO FOR THE LAST SIX YEARS?
MOMO...
...
I...
I'VE BEEN SINGING.
FOR SIX YEARS STRAIGHT?
MOMO...
FOR SIX YEARS STRAIGHT.
WITHOUT EATING OR DRINKING?
I DID STOP TO EAT AND DRINK.
I like food.
Pfft
THAT WAS A JOKE, NINO.
...
IT'S AMAZING.

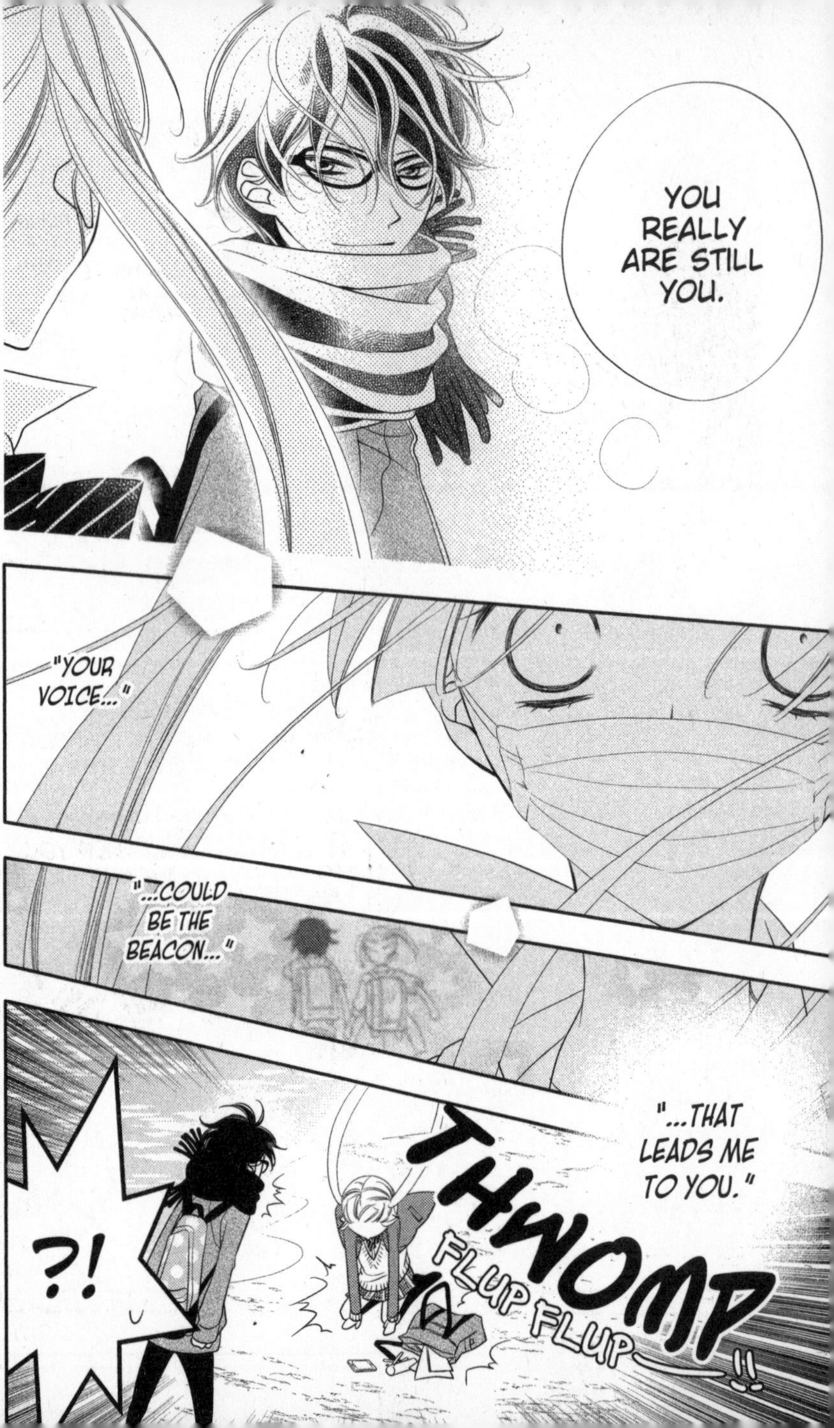
YOU REALLY ARE STILL YOU.
"YOUR VOICE..."
"...COULD BE THE BEACON..."
"...THAT LEADS ME TO YOU."
THWOMP
FLUP FLUP FLUP—!!
?!

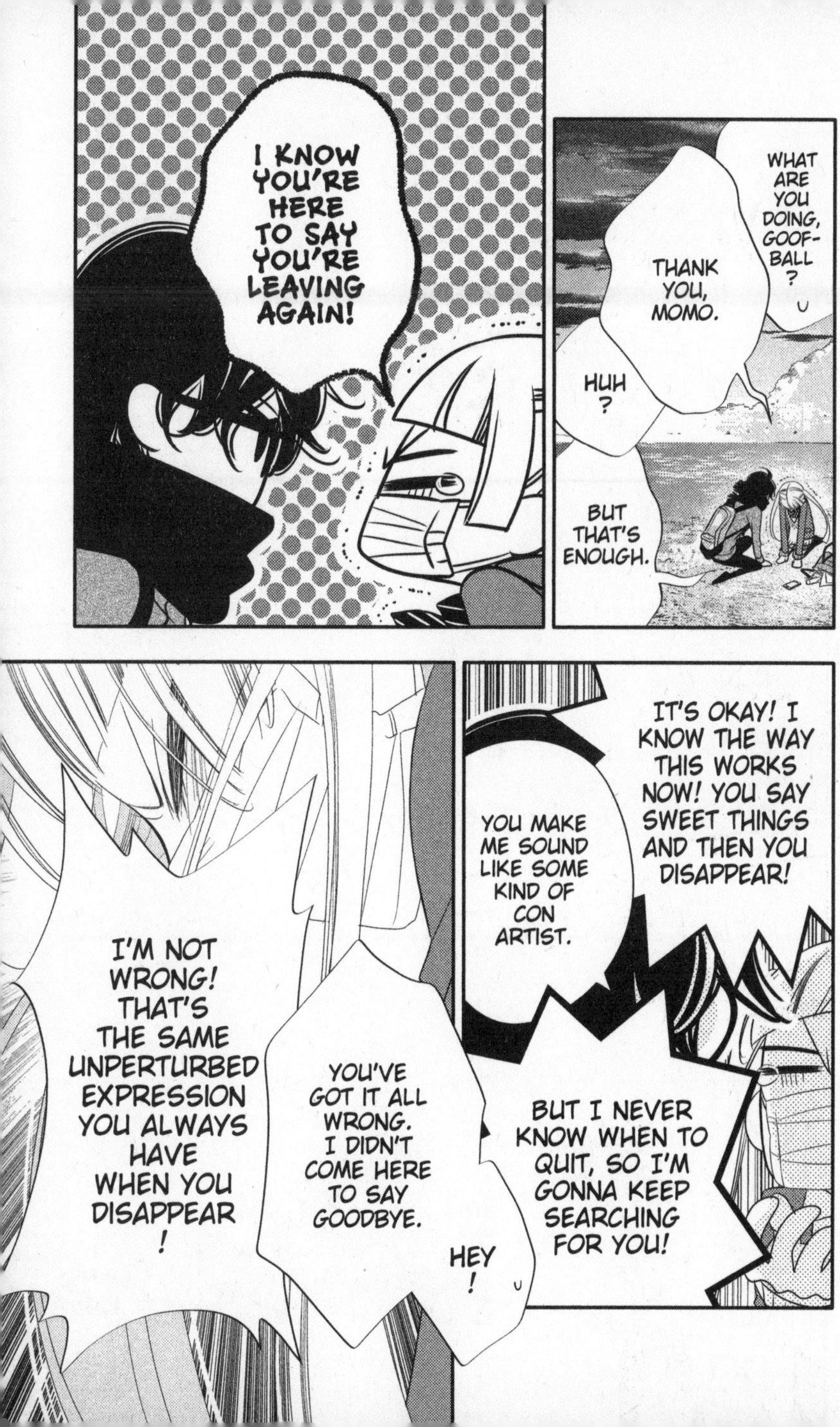
WHAT ARE YOU DOING, GOOF-BALL?
THANK YOU, MOMO.
HUH?
BUT THAT'S ENOUGH.
I KNOW YOU'RE HERE TO SAY YOU'RE LEAVING AGAIN!
......
IT'S OKAY! I KNOW THE WAY THIS WORKS NOW! YOU SAY SWEET THINGS AND THEN YOU DISAPPEAR!
YOU MAKE ME SOUND LIKE SOME KIND OF CON ARTIST.
BUT I NEVER KNOW WHEN TO QUIT, SO I'M GONNA KEEP SEARCHING FOR YOU!
I'M NOT WRONG! THAT'S THE SAME UNPERTURBED EXPRESSION YOU ALWAYS HAVE WHEN YOU DISAPPEAR!
YOU'VE GOT IT ALL WRONG. I DIDN'T COME HERE TO SAY GOODBYE.
HEY!

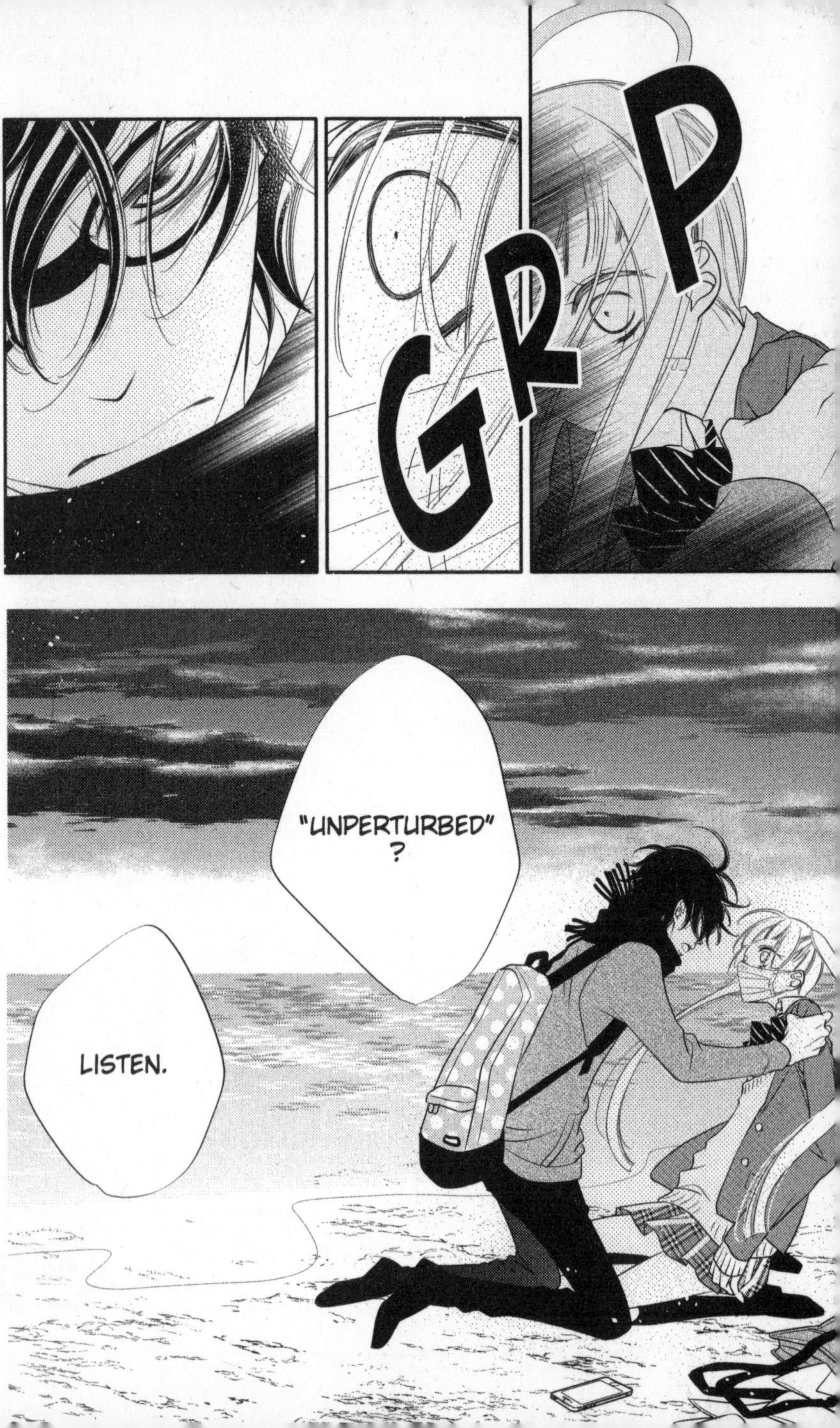
GRIP
"UNPERTURBED" ?
LISTEN.

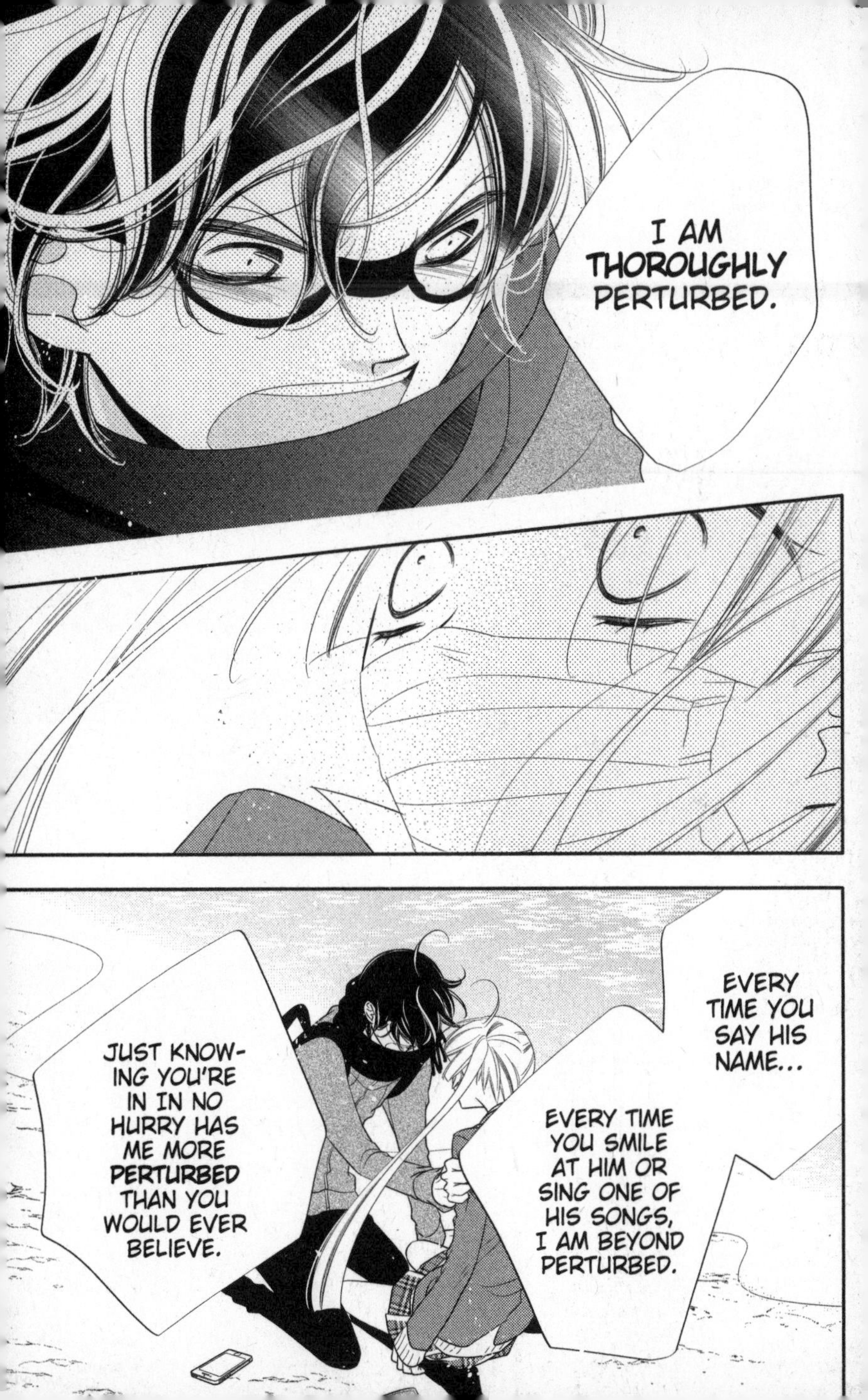
I AM THOROUGHLY PERTURBED.
EVERY TIME YOU SAY HIS NAME...
EVERY TIME YOU SMILE AT HIM OR SING ONE OF HIS SONGS, I AM BEYOND PERTURBED.
JUST KNOWING YOU'RE IN IN NO HURRY HAS ME MORE PERTURBED THAN YOU WOULD EVER BELIEVE.

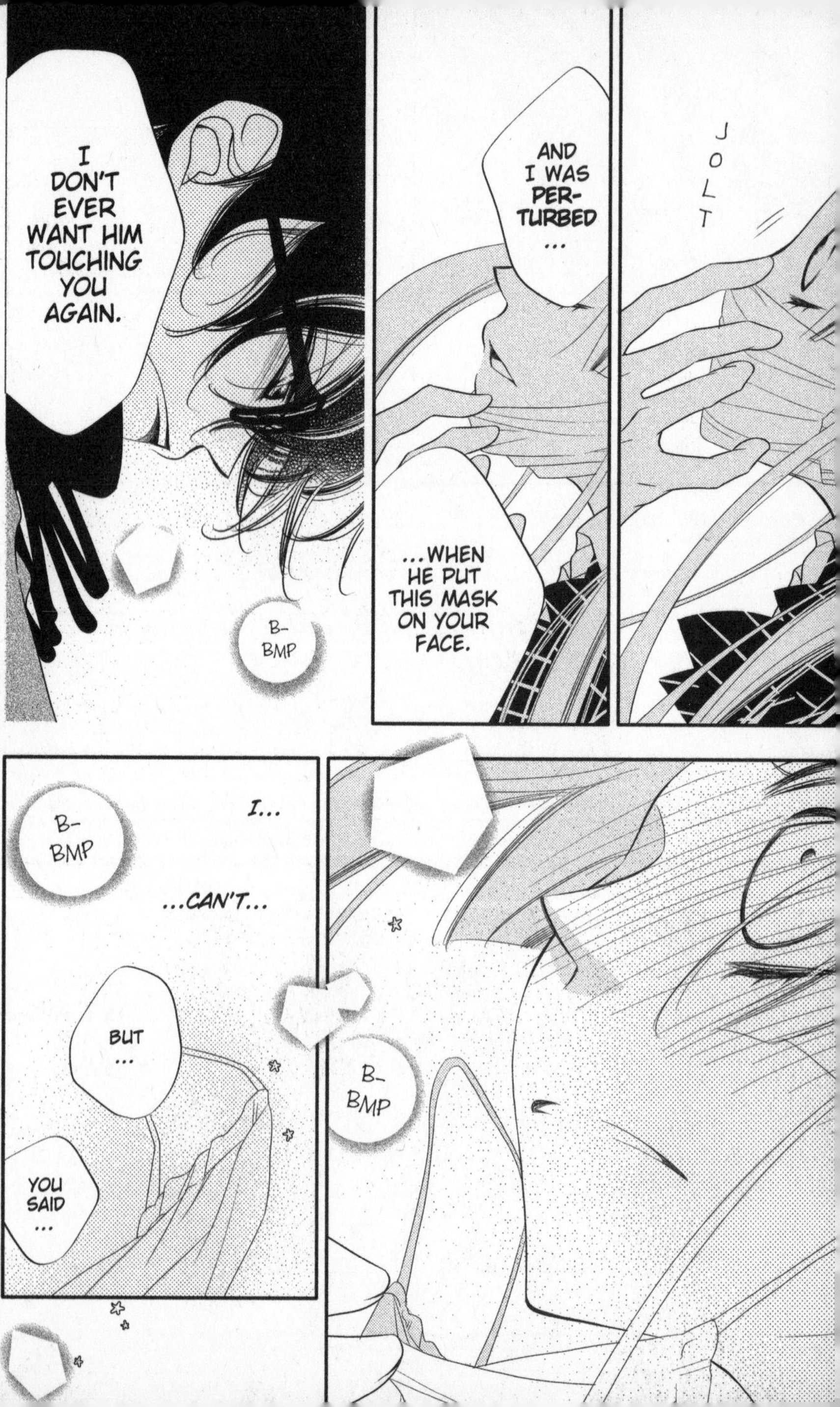
JOLT
AND I WAS PER-TURBED ...
...WHEN HE PUT THIS MASK ON YOUR FACE.
I DON'T EVER WANT HIM TOUCHING YOU AGAIN.
B-BMP
B-BMP
I...
B-BMP
...CAN'T...
BUT ...
YOU SAID ...

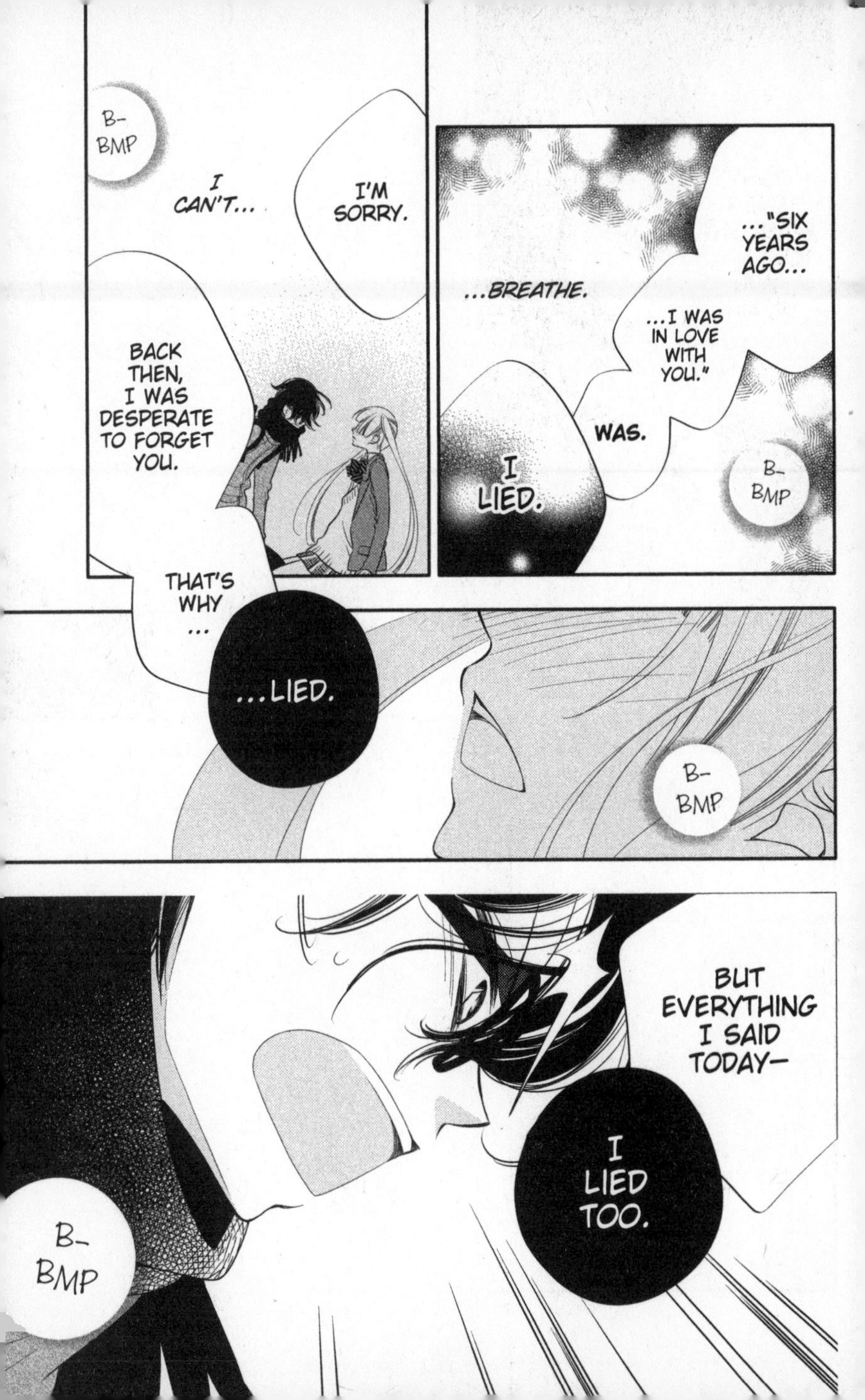
..."SIX YEARS AGO...
...I WAS IN LOVE WITH YOU."
...BREATHE.
WAS.
B-BMP
I LIED.
I'M SORRY.
I CAN'T...
B-BMP
BACK THEN, I WAS DESPERATE TO FORGET YOU.
THAT'S WHY ...
...LIED.
B-BMP
BUT EVERYTHING I SAID TODAY—
I LIED TOO.
B-BMP

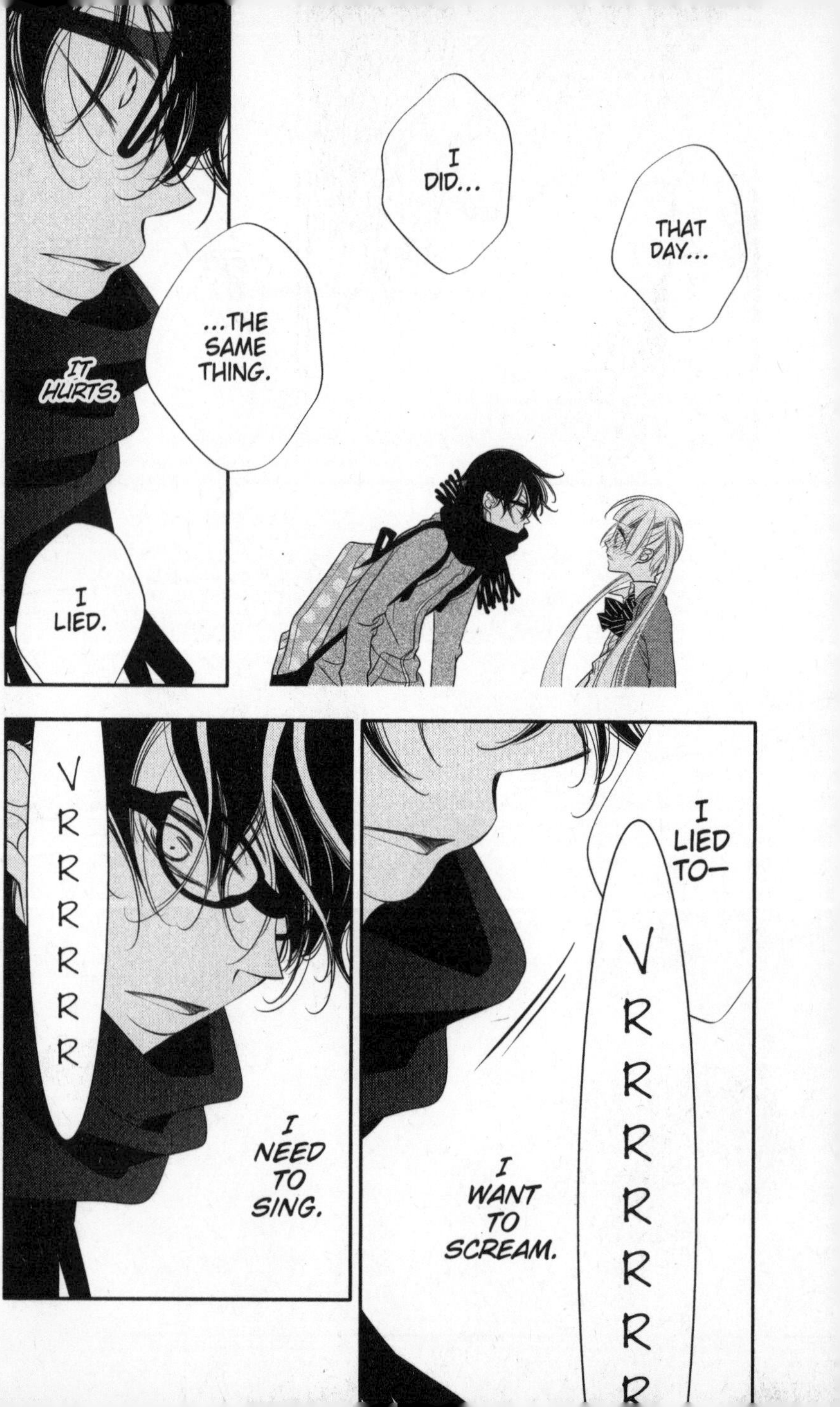
THAT DAY...
I DID...
...THE SAME THING.
IT HURTS.
I LIED.
I LIED TO—
VRRRRRRR
I WANT TO SCREAM.
VRRRRRR
I NEED TO SING.

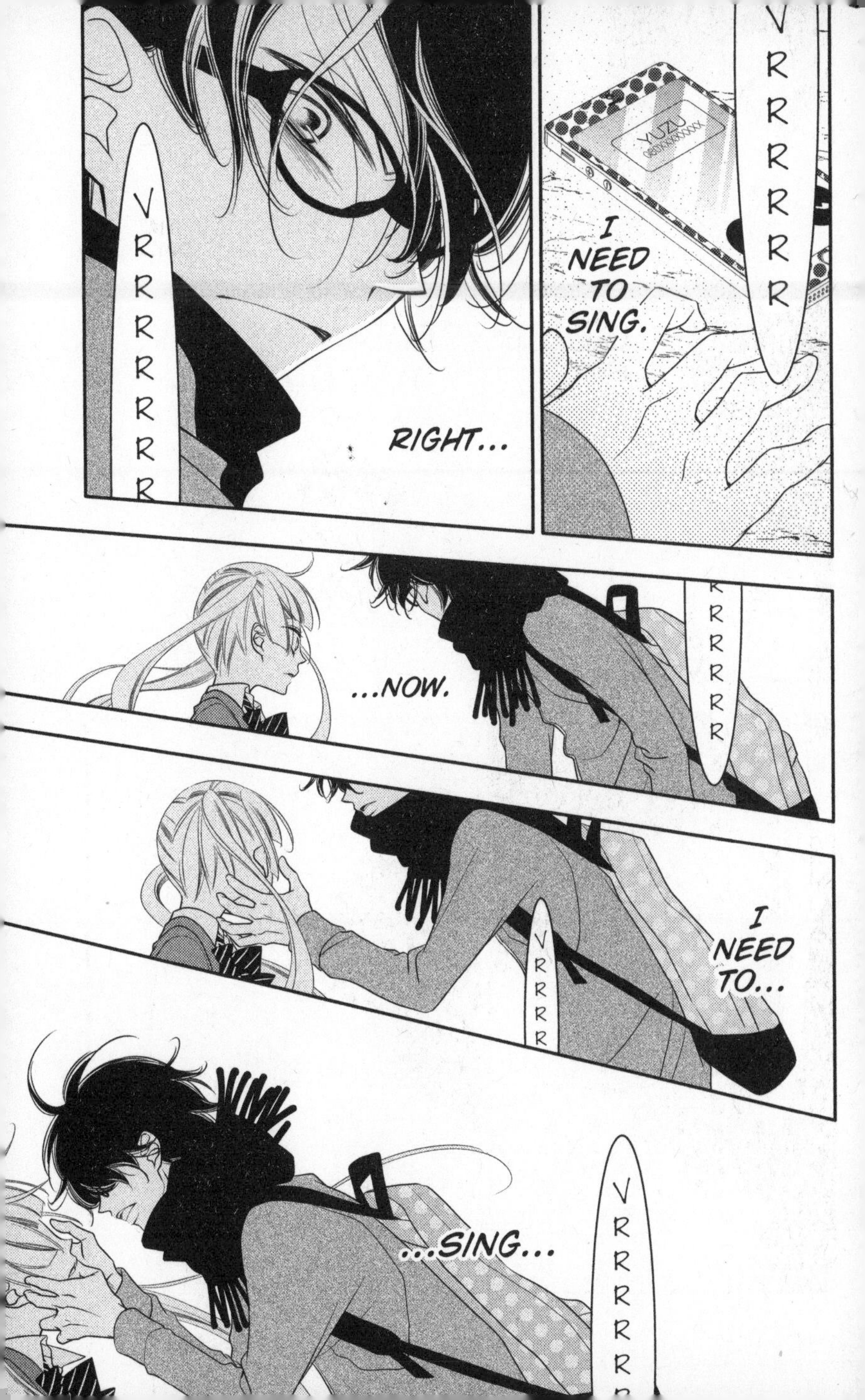
VRRRRRRR
YUZU
I NEED TO SING.
VRRRRRRR
RIGHT...
RRRRRRR
...NOW.
I NEED TO...
VRRRR
...SING...
VRRRRRRR

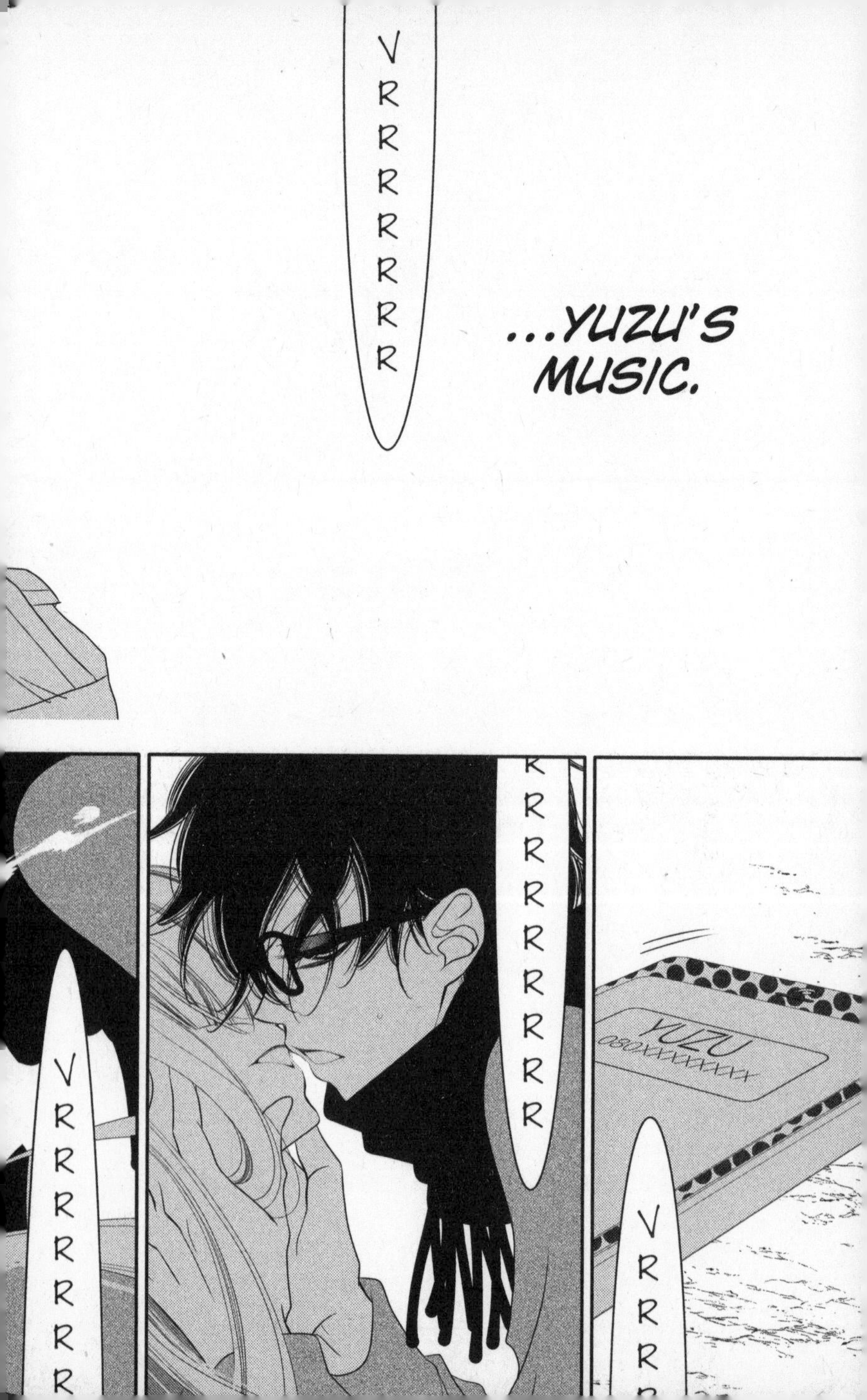

VRRRRRRR
...YUZU'S MUSIC.
YUZU
080XXXXXXXX
VRRR
RRRRRRRRR
VRRRRRRR

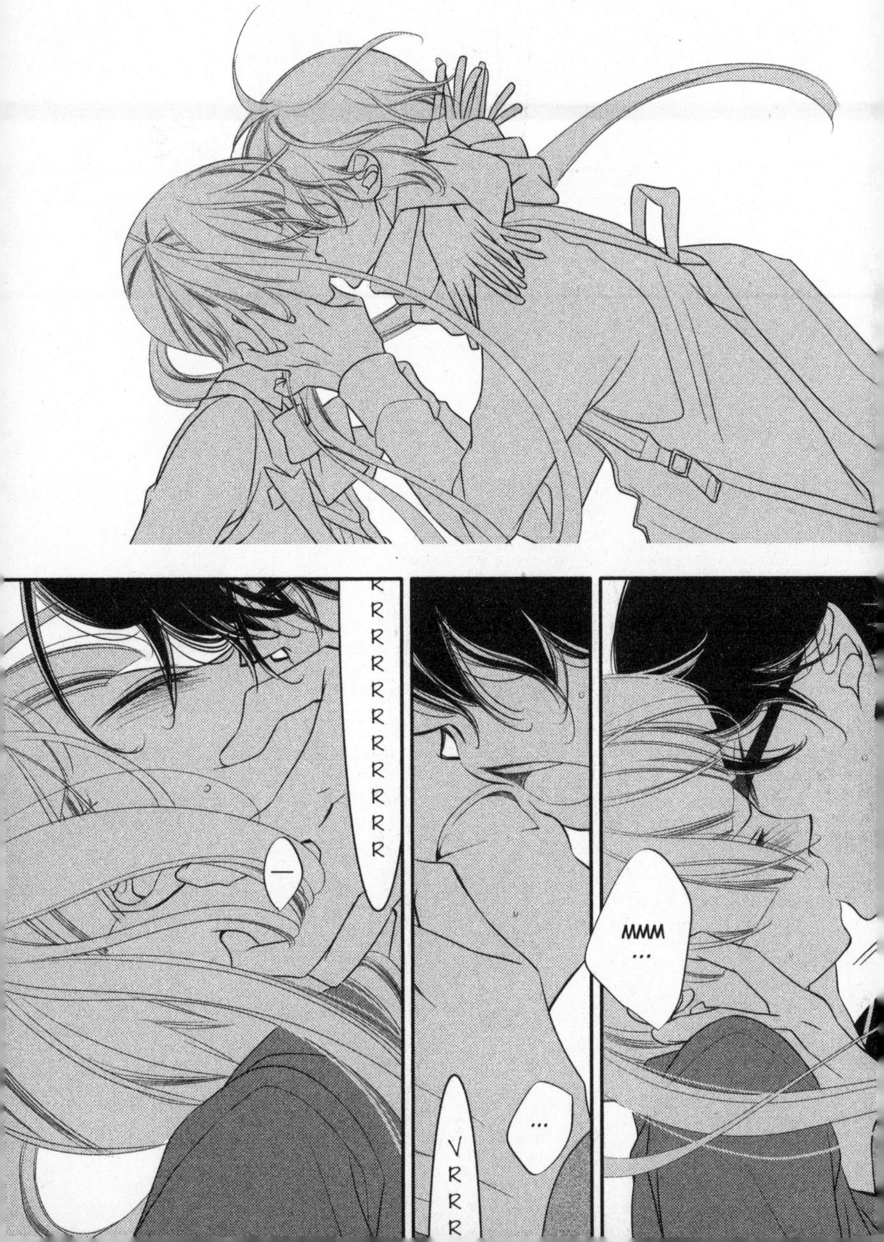
MMM
...
...
VRRR
RRRRRRRRRRRRR
—

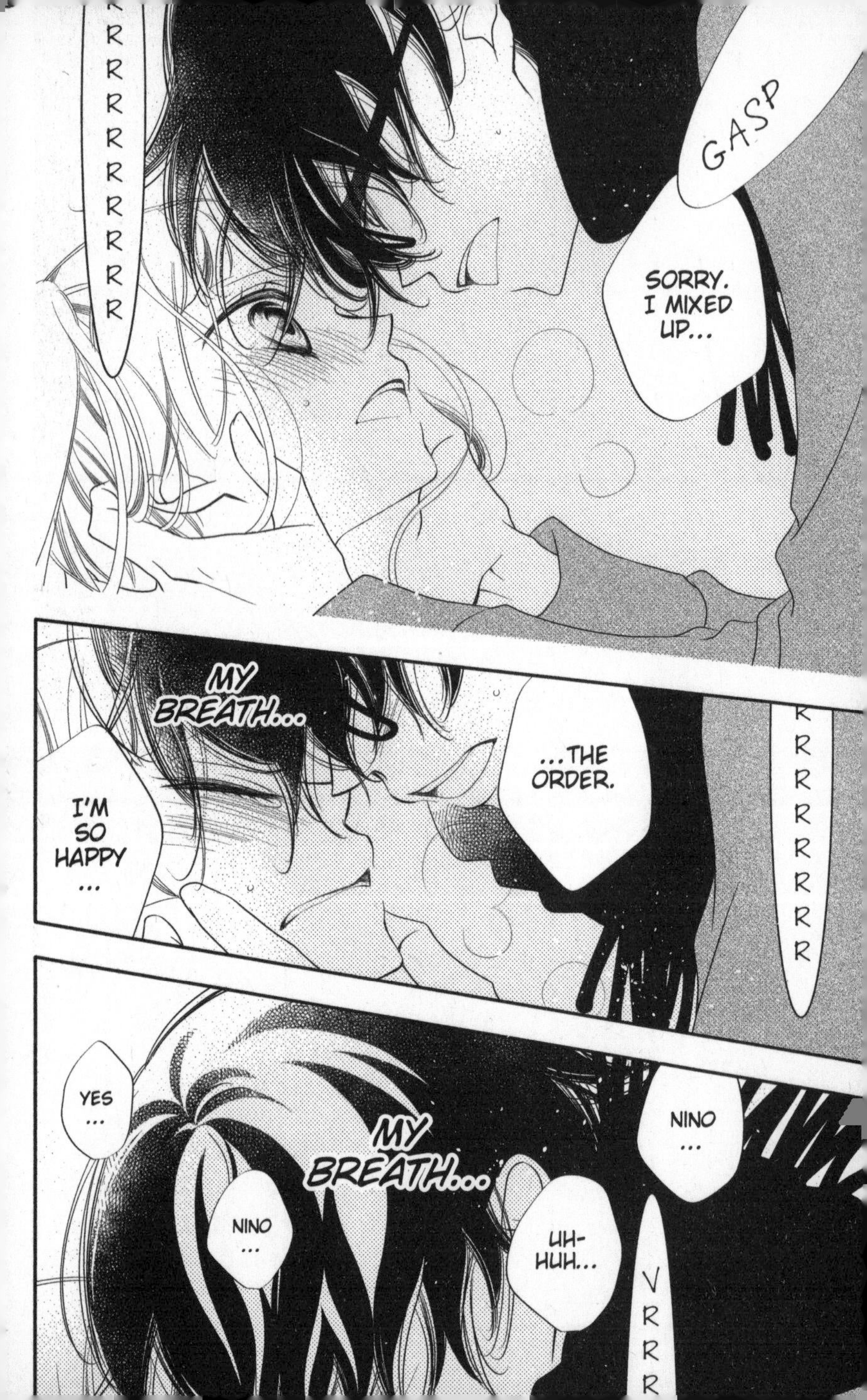
GASP
SORRY. I MIXED UP...
RRRRRRRRR
RRRRRRR
...THE ORDER.
MY BREATH...
I'M SO HAPPY...
NINO...
VRRR
UH-HUH...
MY BREATH...
NINO...
YES...

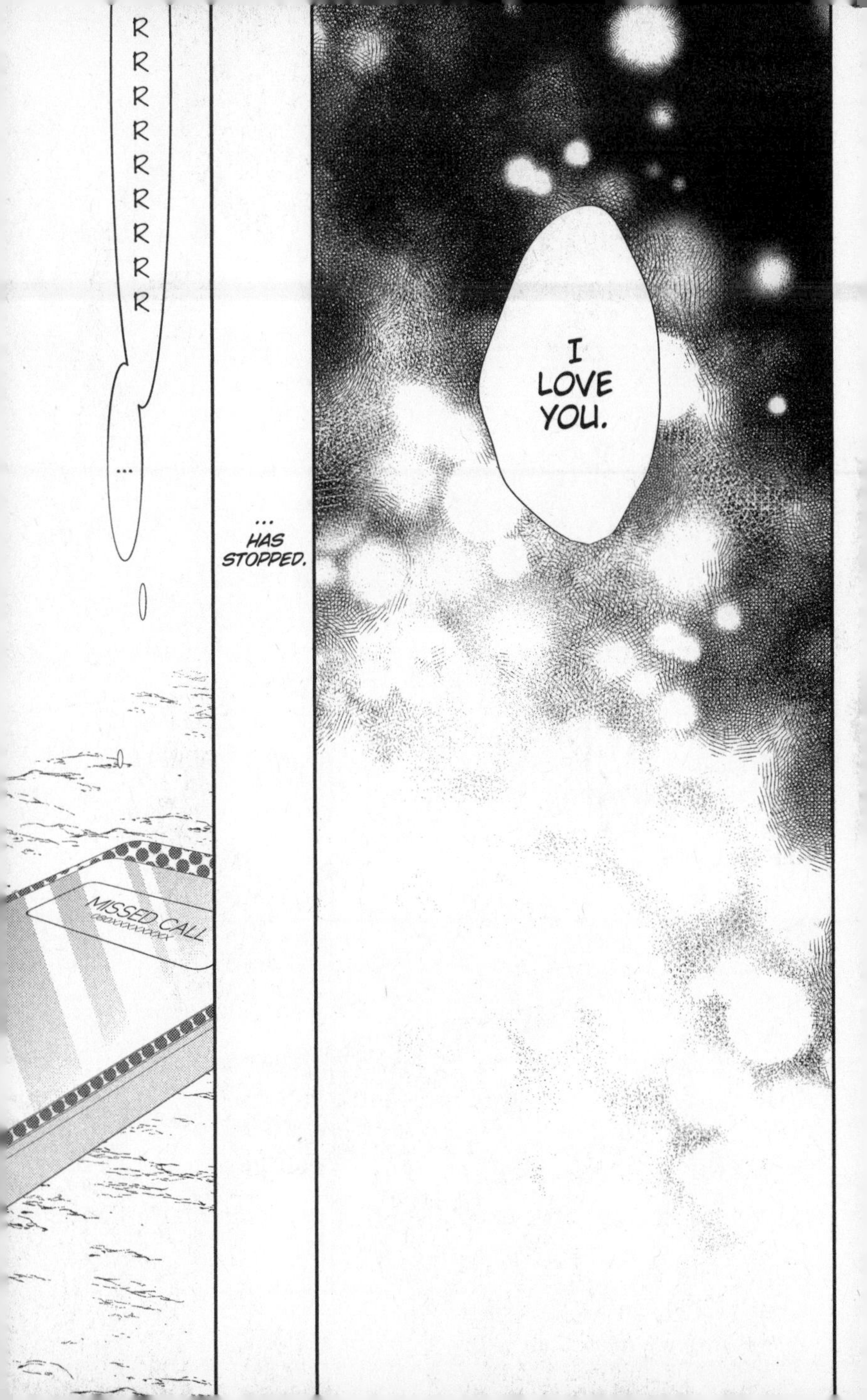
I LOVE YOU.
... HAS STOPPED.
RRRRRRRRR
...
MISSED CALL

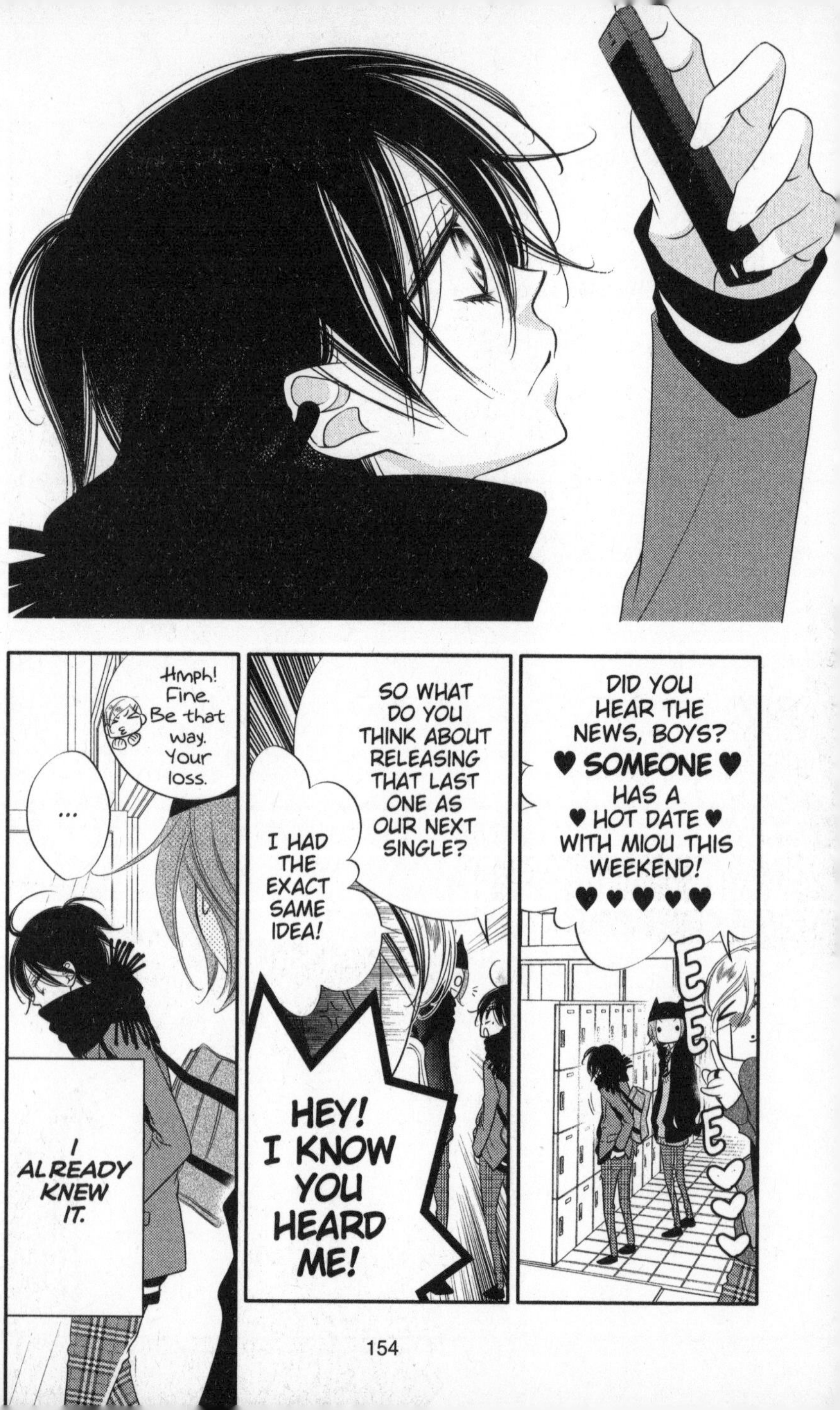
DID YOU HEAR THE NEWS, BOYS? ♥ SOMEONE ♥ HAS A ♥ HOT DATE ♥ WITH MIOU THIS WEEKEND! ♥ ♥ ♥ ♥ ♥
EEEE♥♥♥
SO WHAT DO YOU THINK ABOUT RELEASING THAT LAST ONE AS OUR NEXT SINGLE?
I HAD THE EXACT SAME IDEA!
HEY! I KNOW YOU HEARD ME!
Hmph! Fine. Be that way. Your loss.
...
I ALREADY KNEW IT.

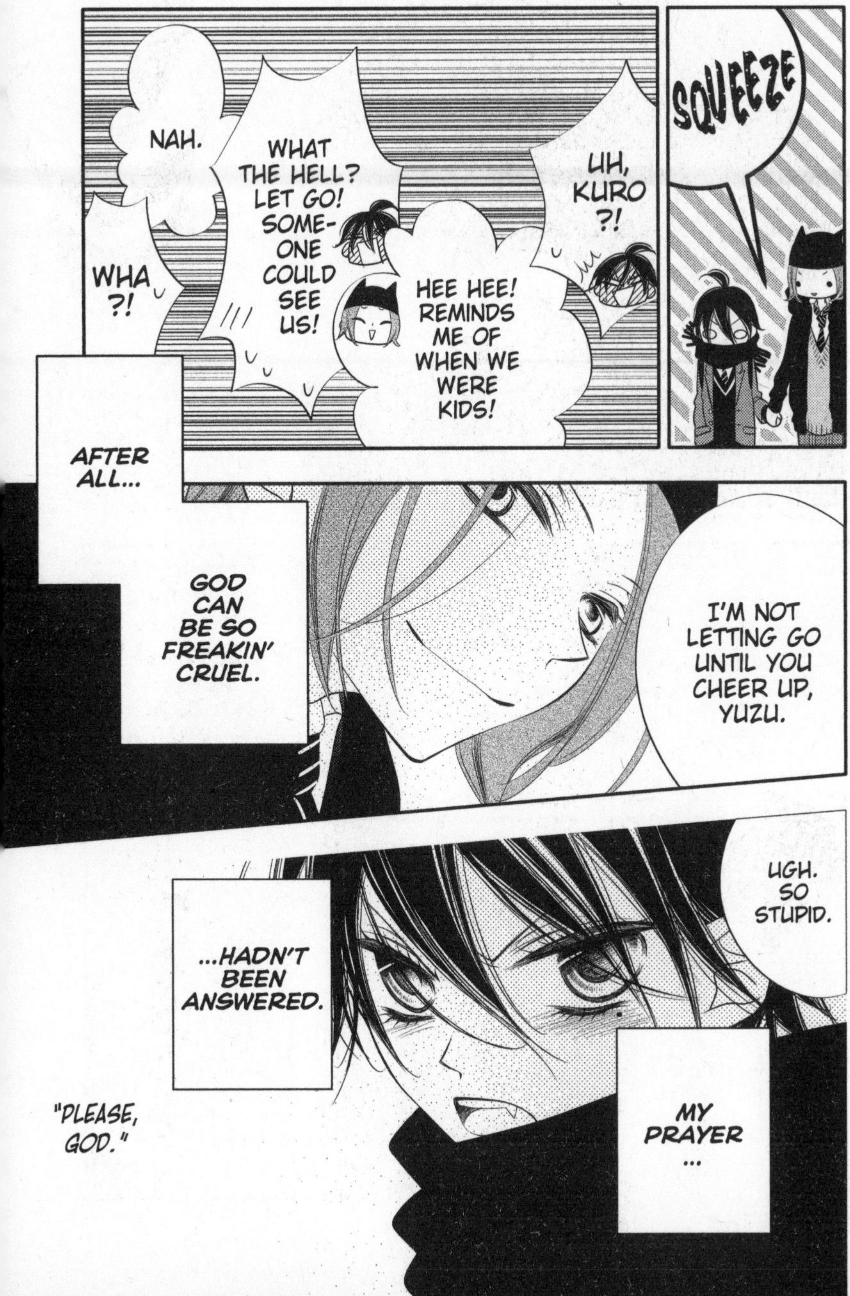
SQUEEZE
UH, KURO?!
HEE HEE! REMINDS ME OF WHEN WE WERE KIDS!
WHAT THE HELL? LET GO! SOME-ONE COULD SEE US!
NAH.
WHA?!
I'M NOT LETTING GO UNTIL YOU CHEER UP, YUZU.
AFTER ALL...
GOD CAN BE SO FREAKIN' CRUEL.
UGH. SO STUPID.
MY PRAYER...
...HADN'T BEEN ANSWERED.
"PLEASE, GOD."

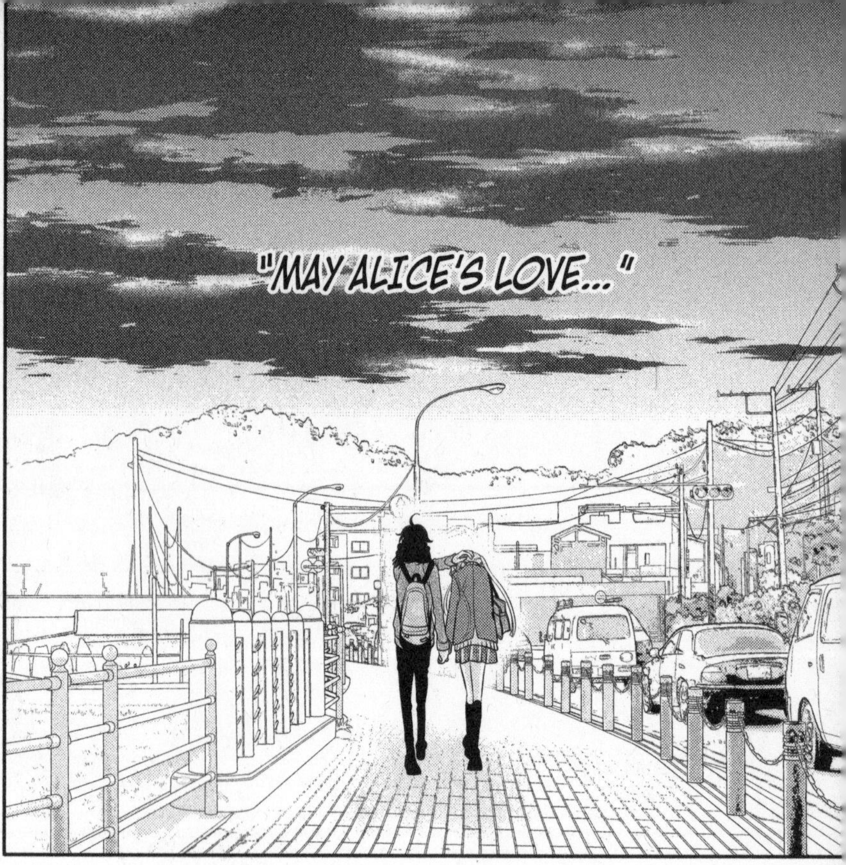
"MAY ALICE'S LOVE..."

"...NEVER COME TRUE."

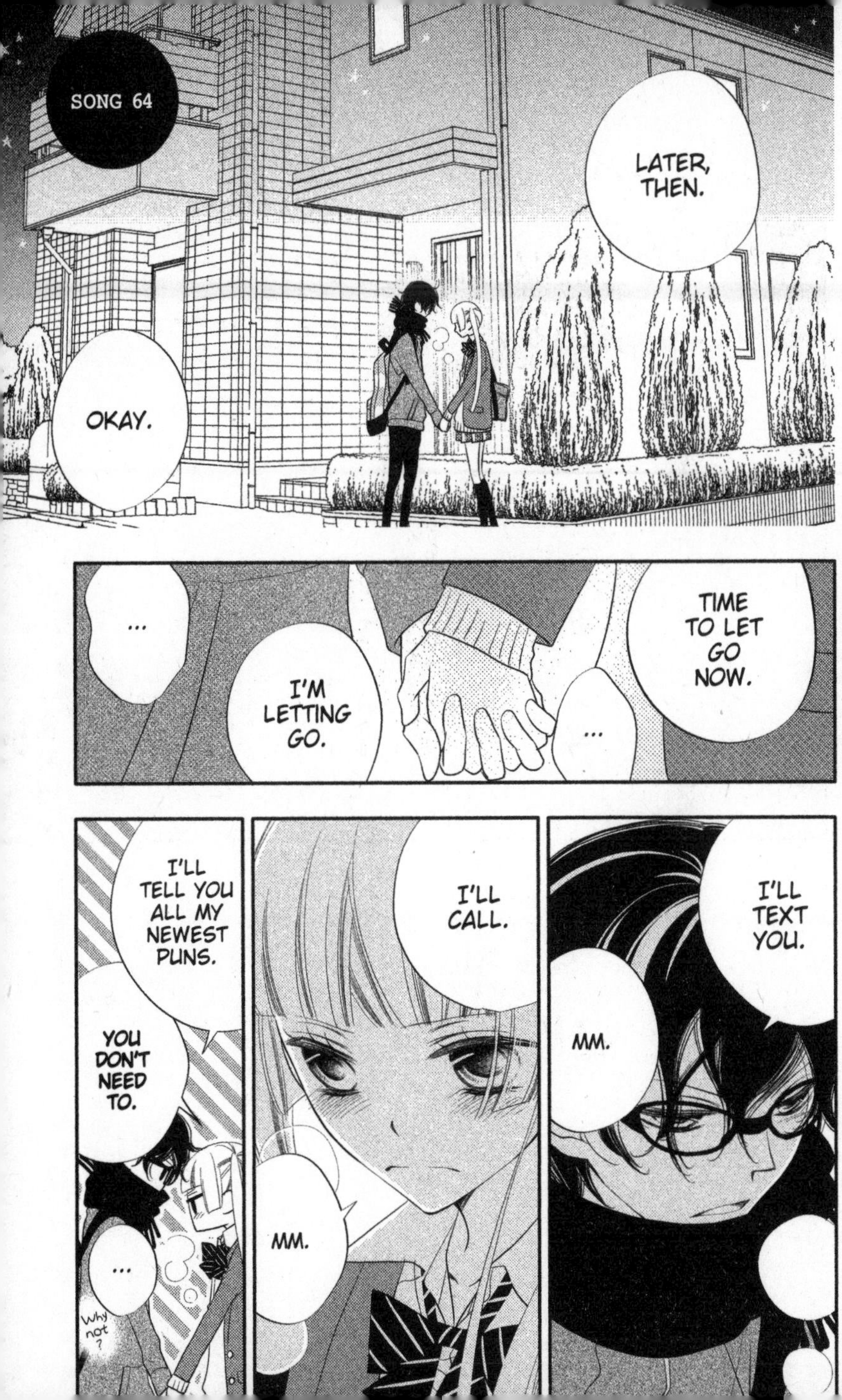
SONG 64
LATER, THEN.
OKAY.
TIME TO LET GO NOW.
...
I'M LETTING GO.
...
I'LL TEXT YOU.
MM.
I'LL CALL.
MM.
I'LL TELL YOU ALL MY NEWEST PUNS.
YOU DON'T NEED TO.
...
Why not?

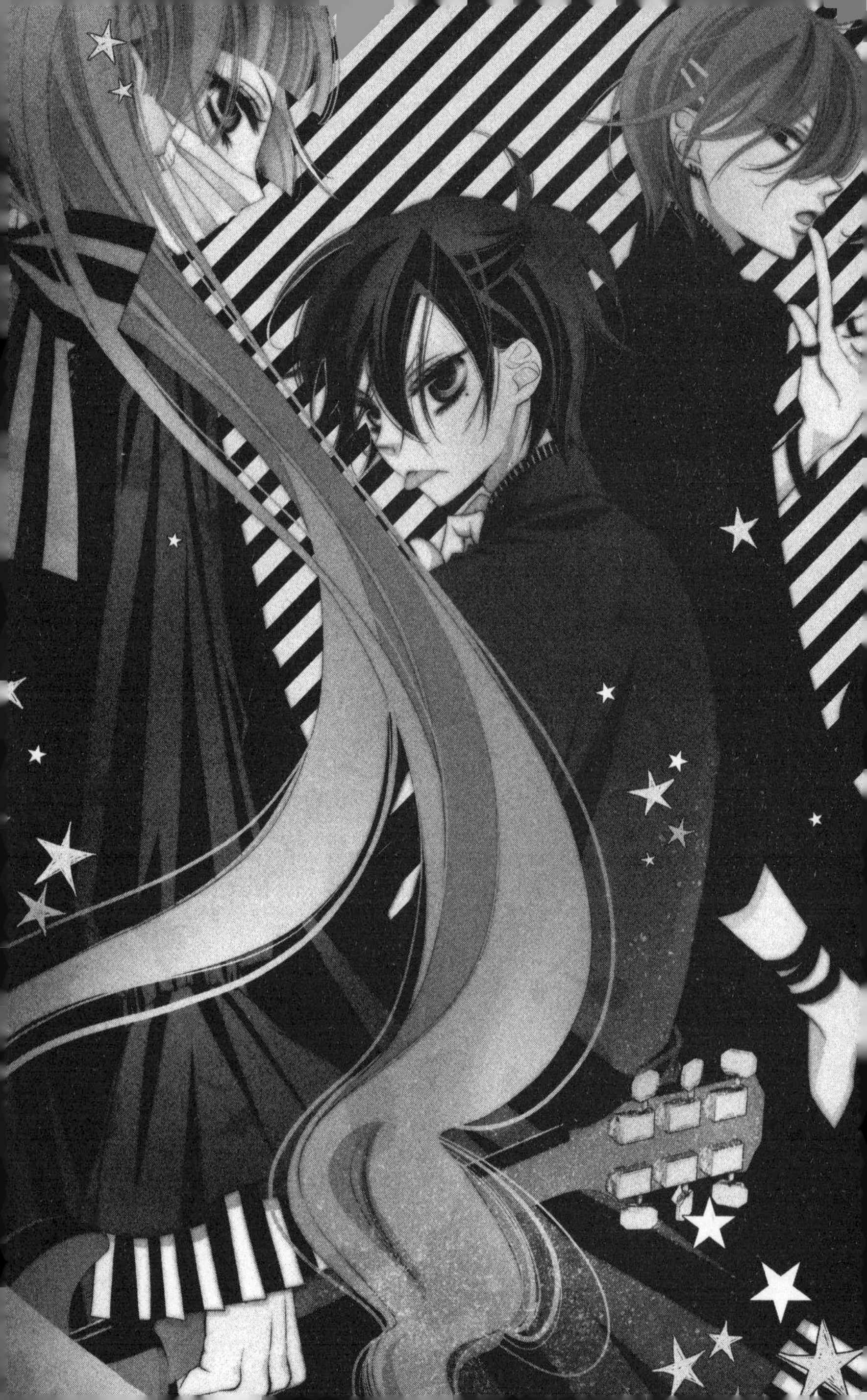

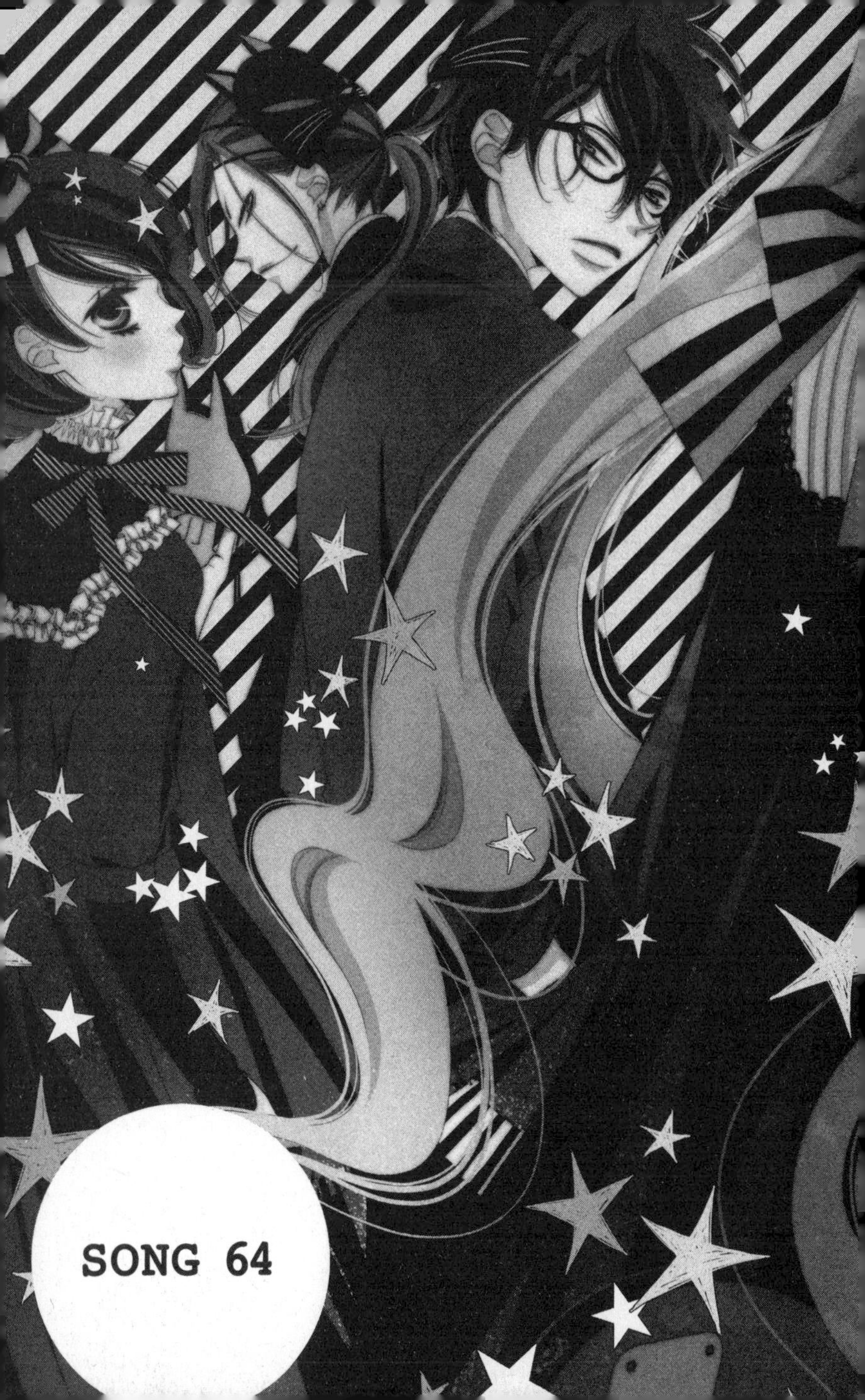
SONG 64

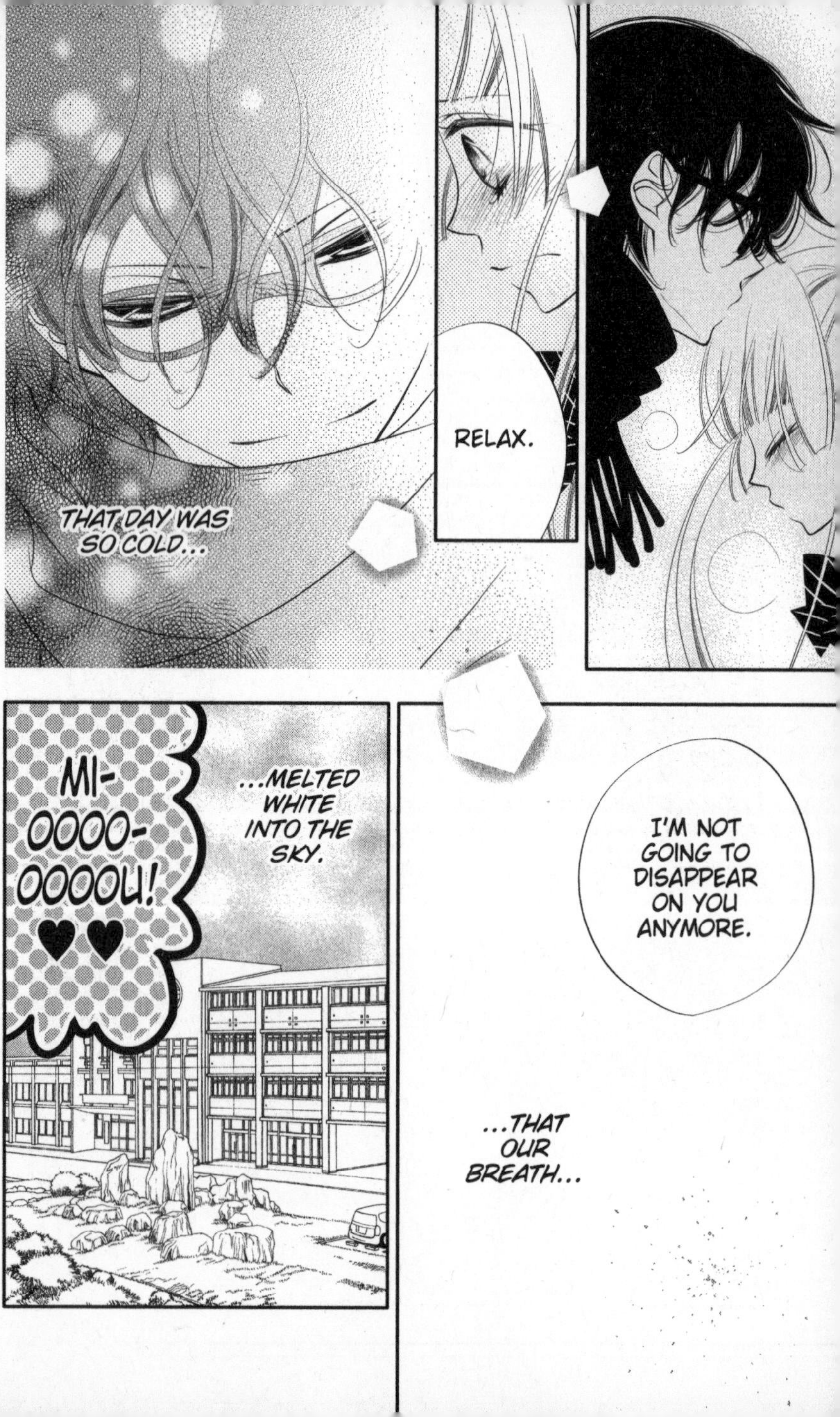
RELAX.
THAT DAY WAS SO COLD...
I'M NOT GOING TO DISAPPEAR ON YOU ANYMORE.
...THAT OUR BREATH...
...MELTED WHITE INTO THE SKY.
MI-OOOO-OOOOU! ♥♥

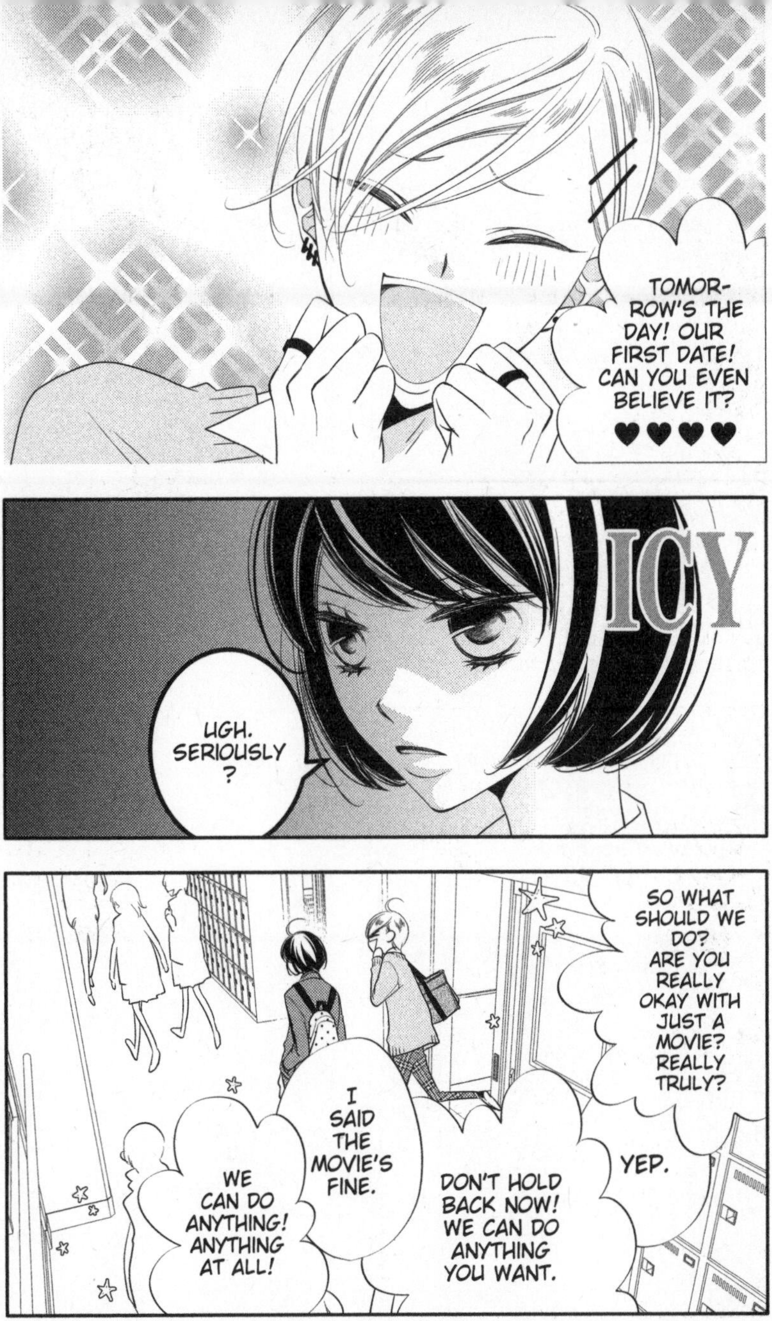
TOMORROW'S THE DAY! OUR FIRST DATE! CAN YOU EVEN BELIEVE IT? ♥♥♥♥
ICY
UGH. SERIOUSLY?
SO WHAT SHOULD WE DO? ARE YOU REALLY OKAY WITH JUST A MOVIE? REALLY TRULY?
YEP.
DON'T HOLD BACK NOW! WE CAN DO ANYTHING YOU WANT.
I SAID THE MOVIE'S FINE.
WE CAN DO ANYTHING! ANYTHING AT ALL!

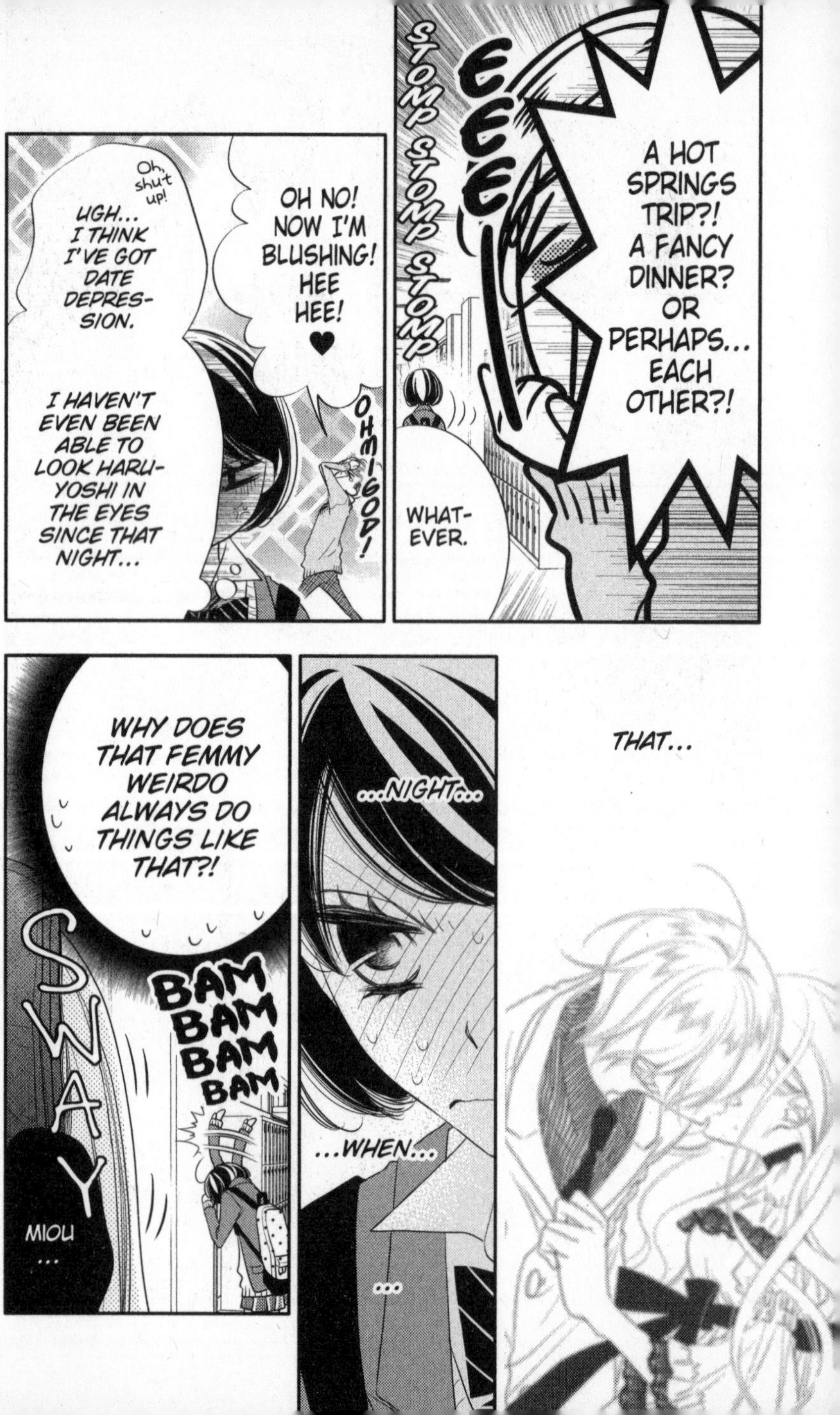
A HOT SPRINGS TRIP?! A FANCY DINNER? OR PERHAPS... EACH OTHER?!
EEE
STOMP STOMP STOMP STOMP
WHAT-EVER.
OH NO! NOW I'M BLUSHING! HEE HEE! ♥
Oh, shut up!
UGH... I THINK I'VE GOT DATE DEPRES-SION.
OHMIGOD!
I HAVEN'T EVEN BEEN ABLE TO LOOK HARU-YOSHI IN THE EYES SINCE THAT NIGHT...
THAT...
...NIGHT...
...WHEN...
...
WHY DOES THAT FEMMY WEIRDO ALWAYS DO THINGS LIKE THAT?!
SWAY
BAM BAM BAM BAM
MIOU ...

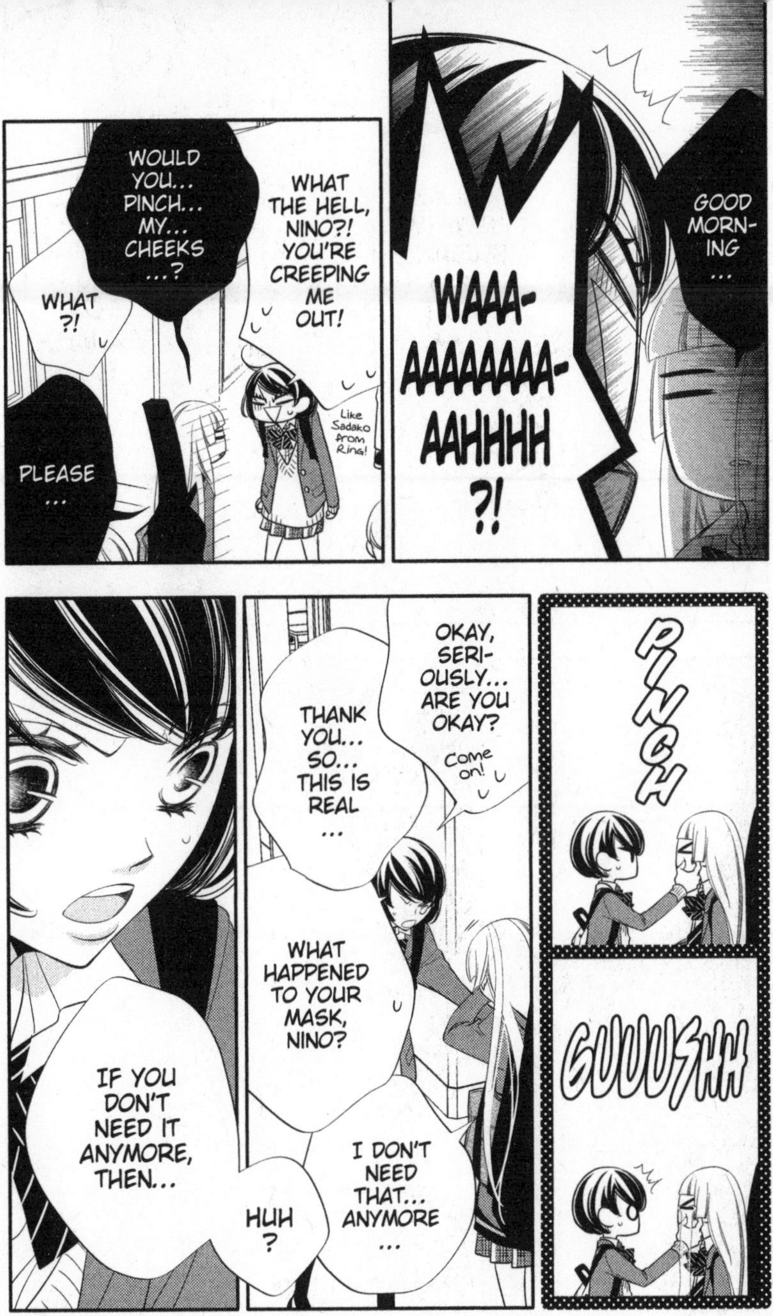

GOOD MORNING...
WAAAAAAAAAAAHHHHH?!
WHAT THE HELL, NINO?! YOU'RE CREEPING ME OUT!
Like Sadako from Ring!
WOULD YOU... PINCH... MY... CHEEKS...?
WHAT?!
PLEASE...
PINCH
GUUUSHH
OKAY, SERIOUSLY... ARE YOU OKAY?
Come on!
THANK YOU... SO... THIS IS REAL...
WHAT HAPPENED TO YOUR MASK, NINO?
I DON'T NEED THAT... ANYMORE...
HUH?
IF YOU DON'T NEED IT ANYMORE, THEN...

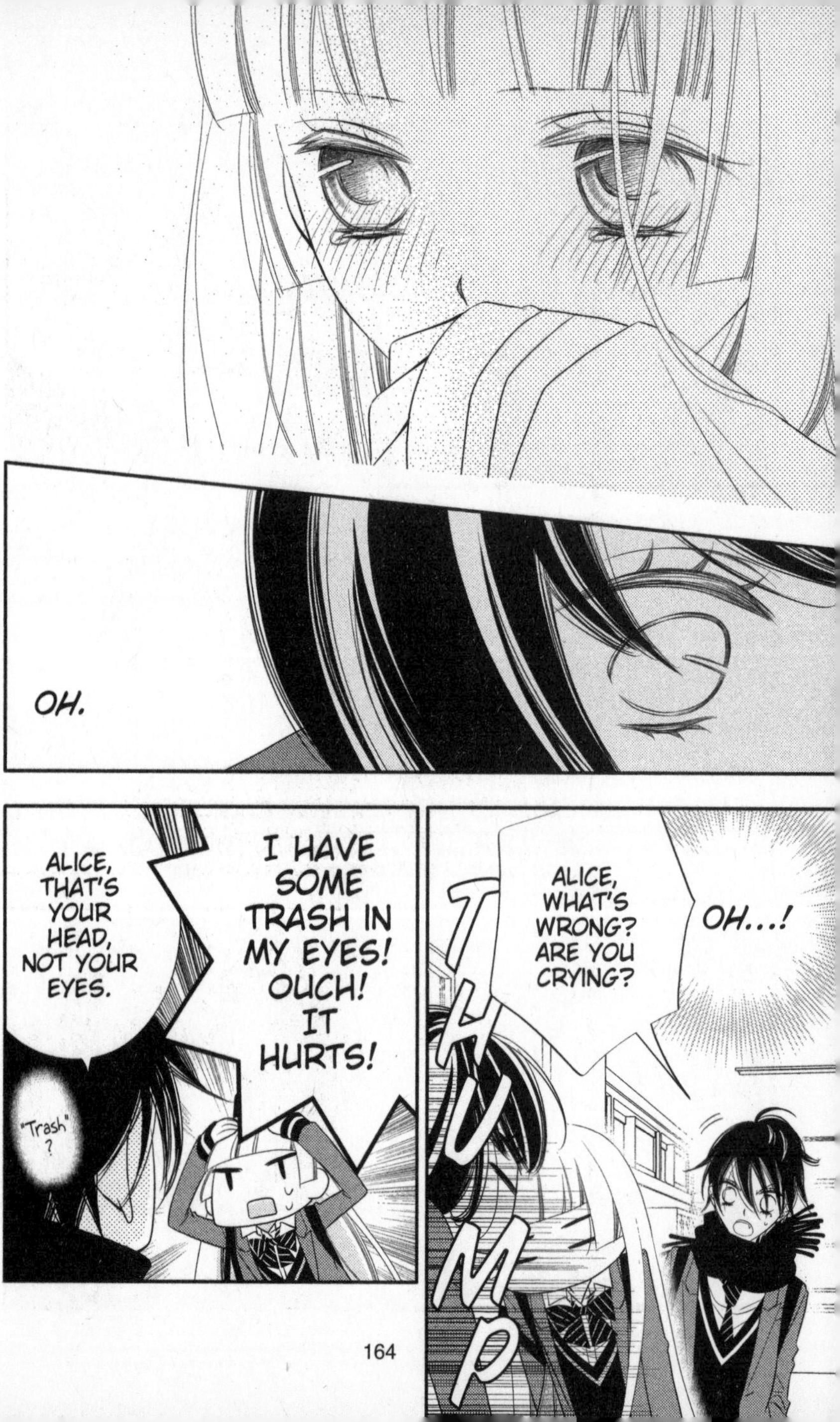
OH.
OH...!
ALICE, WHAT'S WRONG? ARE YOU CRYING?
THUMP
I HAVE SOME TRASH IN MY EYES! OUCH! IT HURTS!
ALICE, THAT'S YOUR HEAD, NOT YOUR EYES.
"Trash"?

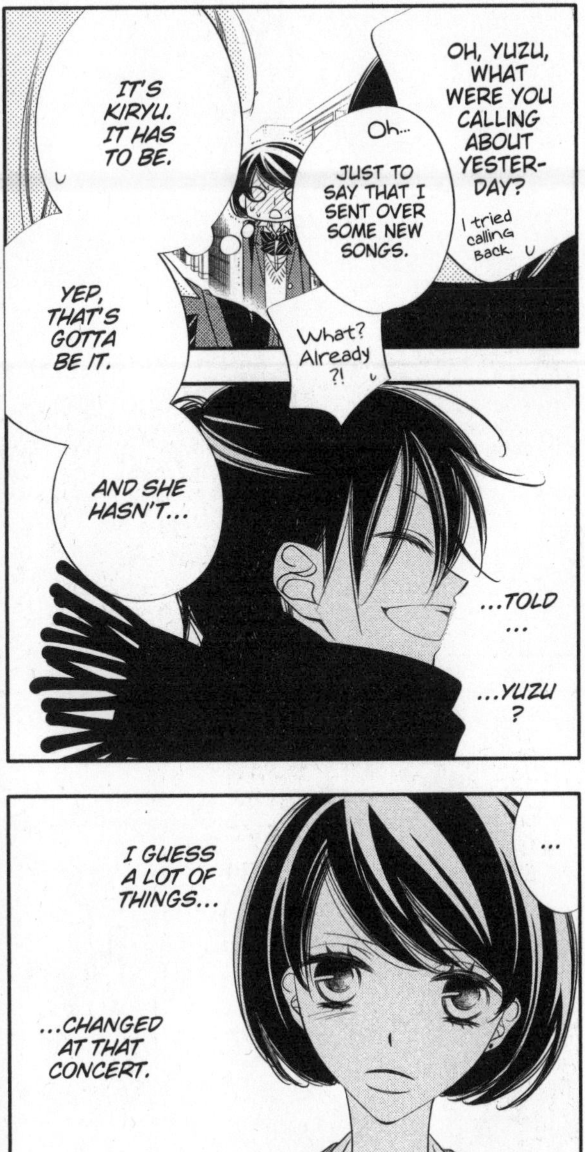
OH, YUZU, WHAT WERE YOU CALLING ABOUT YESTERDAY?
I tried calling back.
Oh...
JUST TO SAY THAT I SENT OVER SOME NEW SONGS.
What? Already ?!
IT'S KIRYU. IT HAS TO BE.
YEP, THAT'S GOTTA BE IT.
AND SHE HASN'T...
...TOLD ...
...YUZU ?
...
I GUESS A LOT OF THINGS...
...CHANGED AT THAT CONCERT.

6

Well, what did you think of volume 11?

Let me know your thoughts so that I may weep, dance and ultimately soar.

I truly hope to see you again in volume 12! Until then!

Ryoko Fukuyama

12/20/2016

[SPECIAL THANKS]
MOSAGE
TAKAYUKI NAGASHIMA
KENJU NORO
MY FAMILY
MY FRIENDS
AND YOU!!

Ryoko Fukuyama
c/o Anonymous Noise Editor
VIZ Media
P.O. Box 77010
San Francisco, CA 94107

HP http://ryoconet/
@ryocoryocoryoco
http://facebook.com/ryocoryocoryoco/

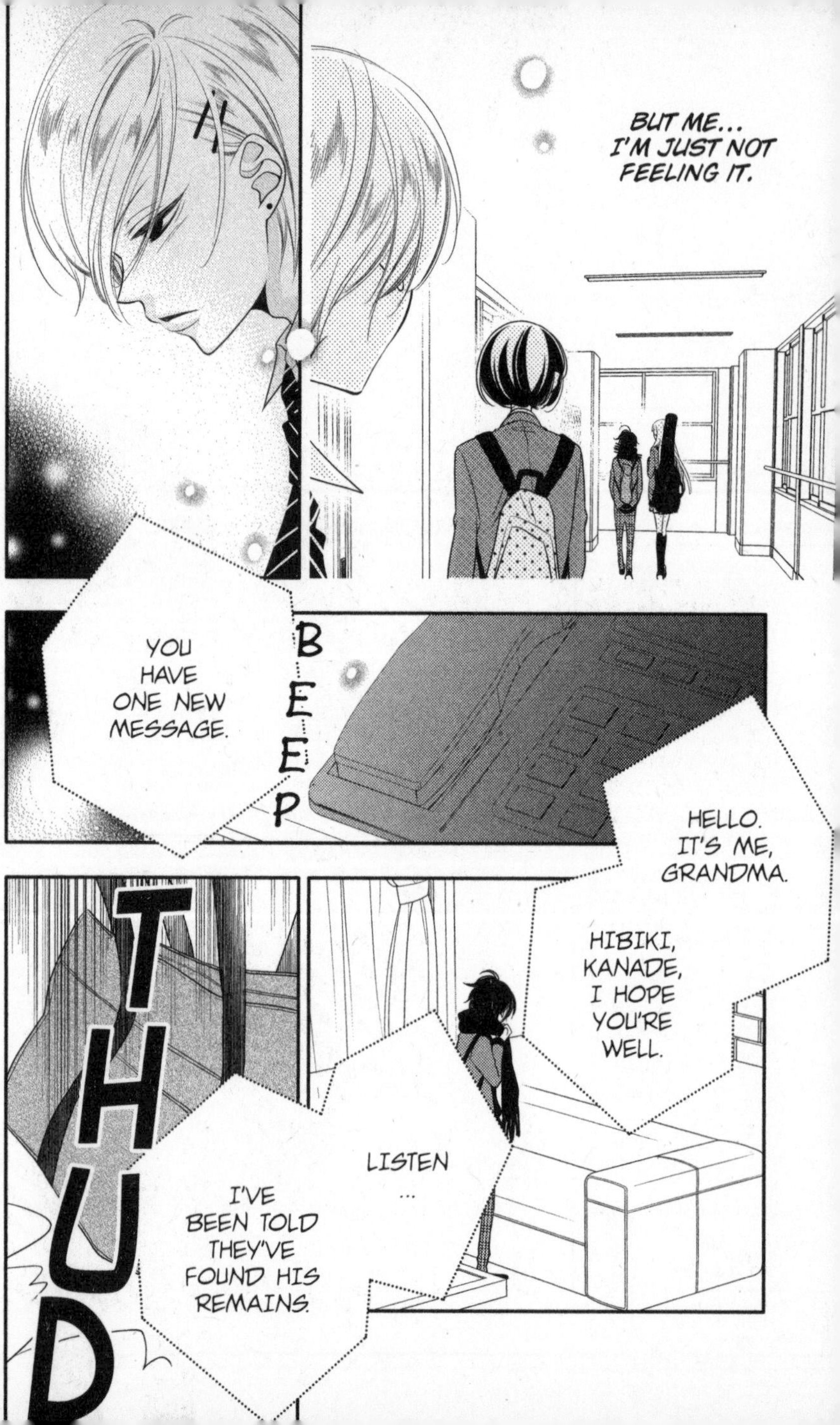
BUT ME... I'M JUST NOT FEELING IT.
YOU HAVE ONE NEW MESSAGE.
BEEP
HELLO. IT'S ME, GRANDMA.
HIBIKI, KANADE, I HOPE YOU'RE WELL.
LISTEN ...
I'VE BEEN TOLD THEY'VE FOUND HIS REMAINS.
THUD

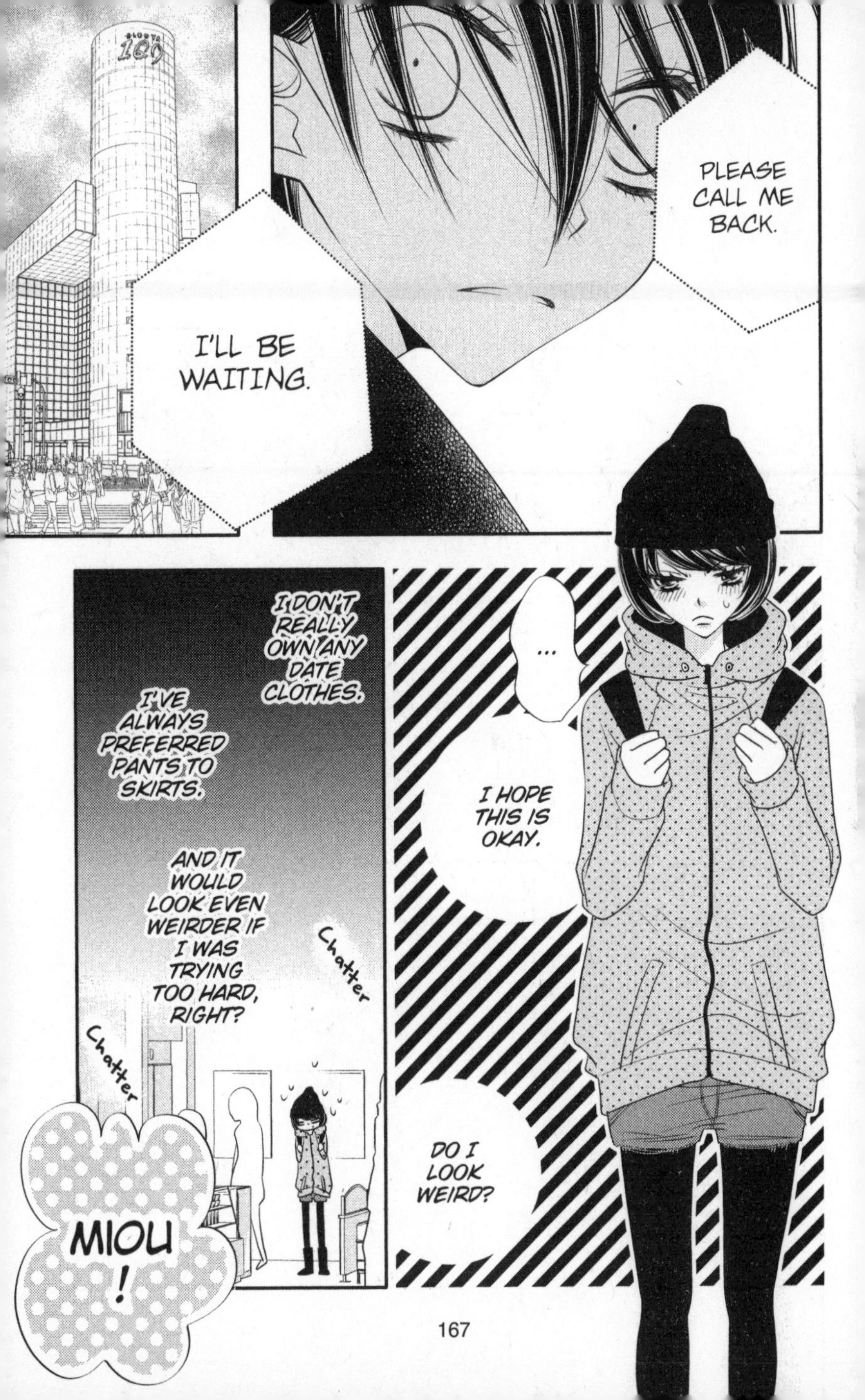
PLEASE CALL ME BACK.
I'LL BE WAITING.
...
I HOPE THIS IS OKAY.
DO I LOOK WEIRD?
I DON'T REALLY OWN ANY DATE CLOTHES.
I'VE ALWAYS PREFERRED PANTS TO SKIRTS.
AND IT WOULD LOOK EVEN WEIRDER IF I WAS TRYING TOO HARD, RIGHT?
Chatter
Chatter
MIOU!

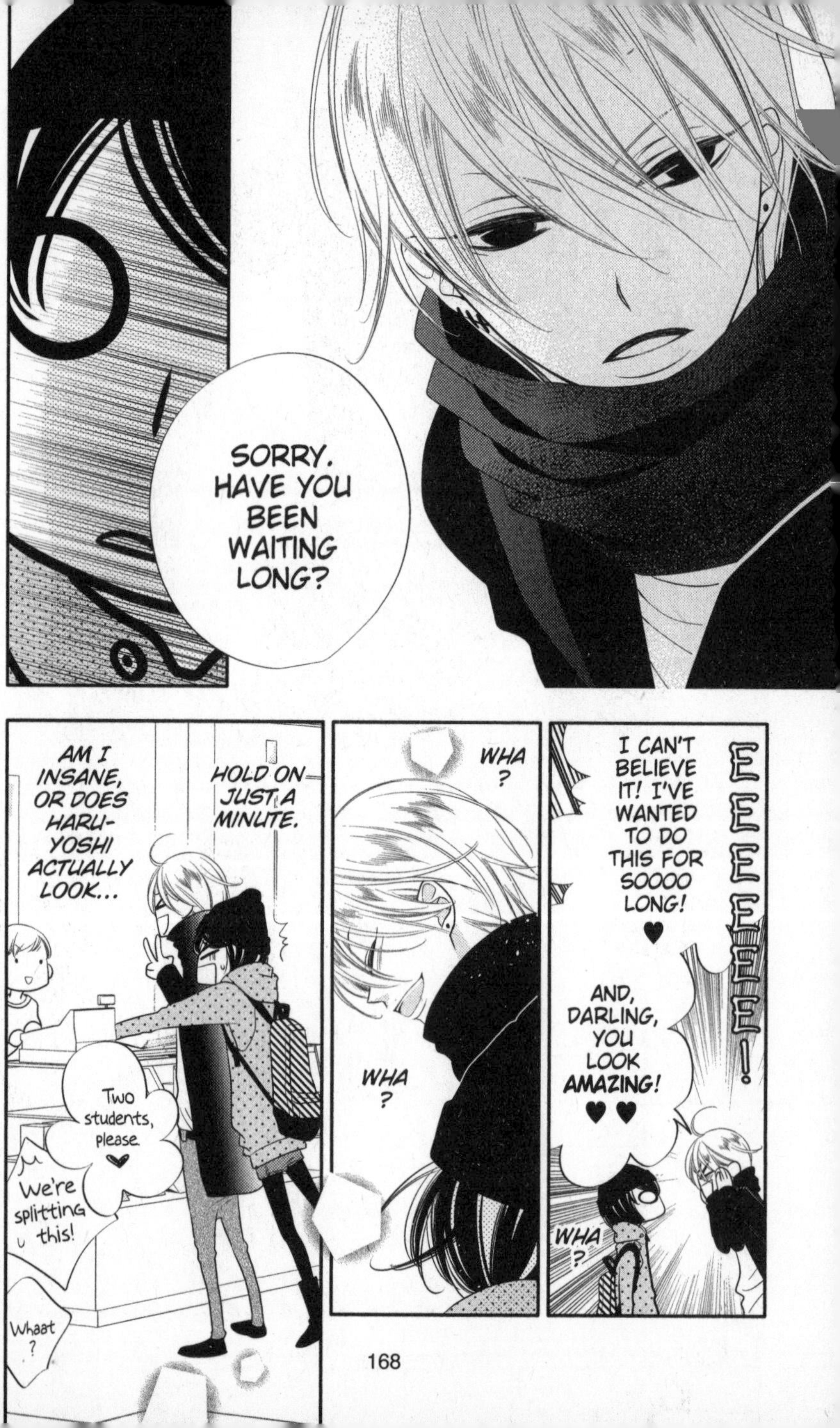
SORRY. HAVE YOU BEEN WAITING LONG?
EEEEEEE!
I CAN'T BELIEVE IT! I'VE WANTED TO DO THIS FOR SOOOO LONG! ♥
AND, DARLING, YOU LOOK AMAZING! ♥♥
WHA?
WHA?
WHA?
HOLD ON JUST A MINUTE.
AM I INSANE, OR DOES HARU-YOSHI ACTUALLY LOOK...
Two students, please. ♥
We're splitting this!
Whaat?

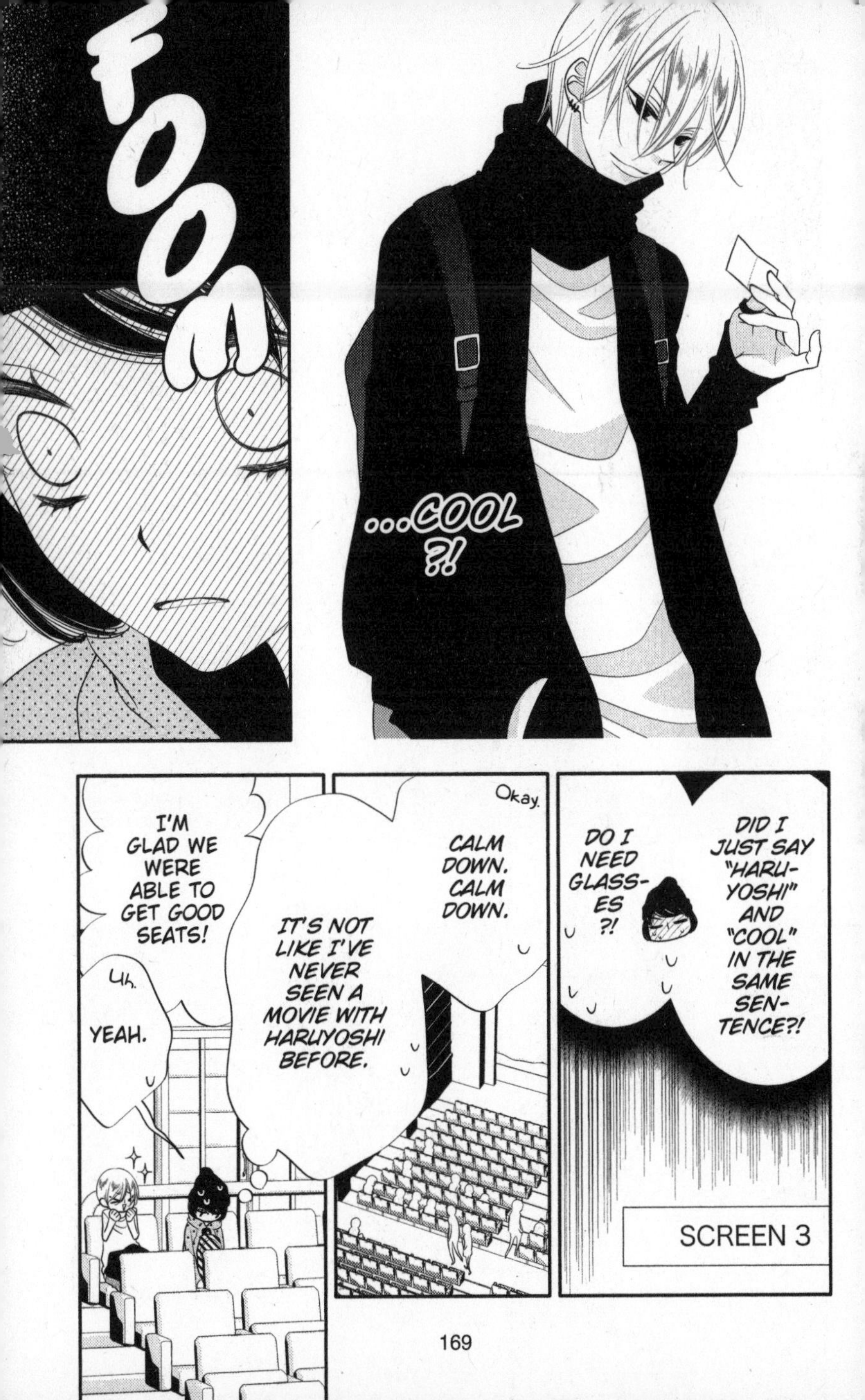
...COOL ?!
FOOOM
DID I JUST SAY "HARUYOSHI" AND "COOL" IN THE SAME SENTENCE?!
DO I NEED GLASSES?!
SCREEN 3
Okay.
CALM DOWN. CALM DOWN.
IT'S NOT LIKE I'VE NEVER SEEN A MOVIE WITH HARUYOSHI BEFORE.
I'M GLAD WE WERE ABLE TO GET GOOD SEATS!
Uh.
YEAH.

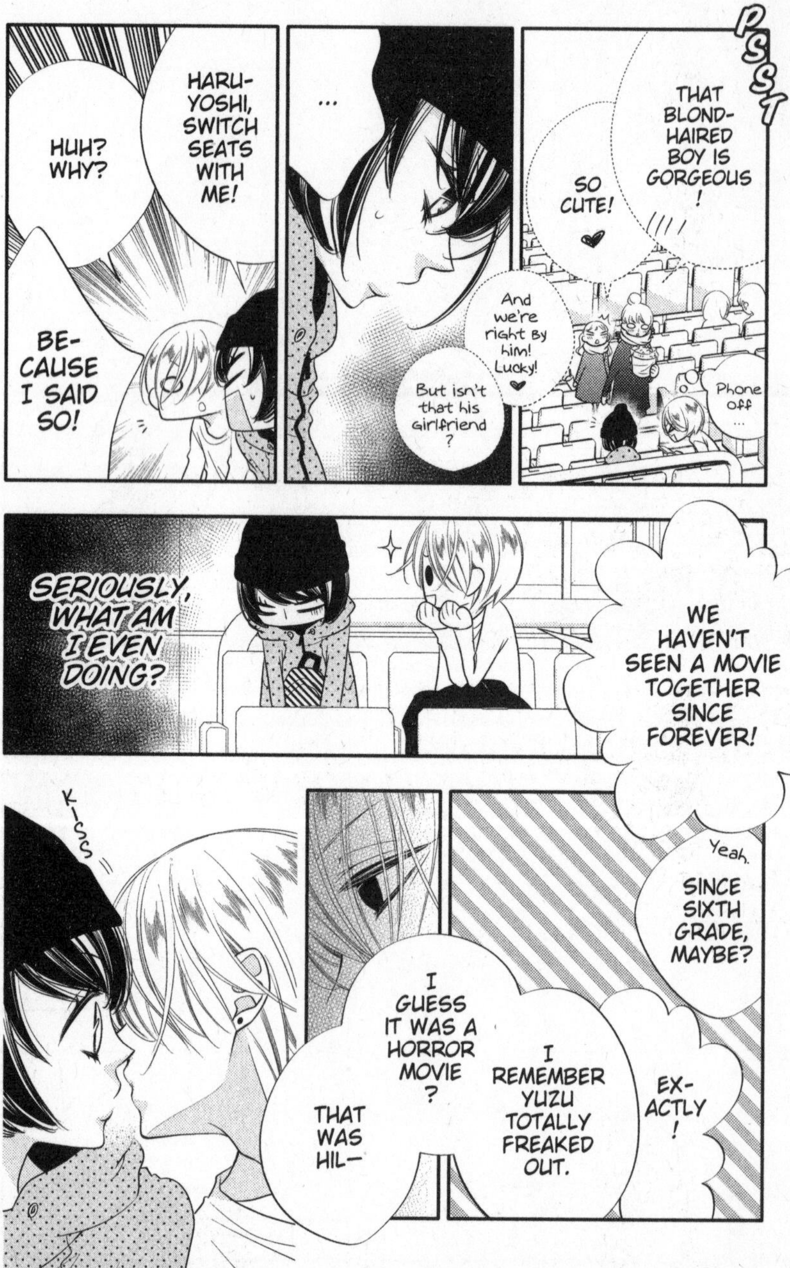
PSST
THAT BLOND-HAIRED BOY IS GORGEOUS!
SO CUTE!
And we're right by him! Lucky!
But isn't that his girlfriend?
Phone off...
...
HARU-YOSHI, SWITCH SEATS WITH ME!
HUH? WHY?
BE-CAUSE I SAID SO!
WE HAVEN'T SEEN A MOVIE TOGETHER SINCE FOREVER!
SERIOUSLY, WHAT AM I EVEN DOING?
Yeah.
SINCE SIXTH GRADE, MAYBE?
EX-ACTLY!
I REMEMBER YUZU TOTALLY FREAKED OUT.
I GUESS IT WAS A HORROR MOVIE?
THAT WAS HIL-
KISS

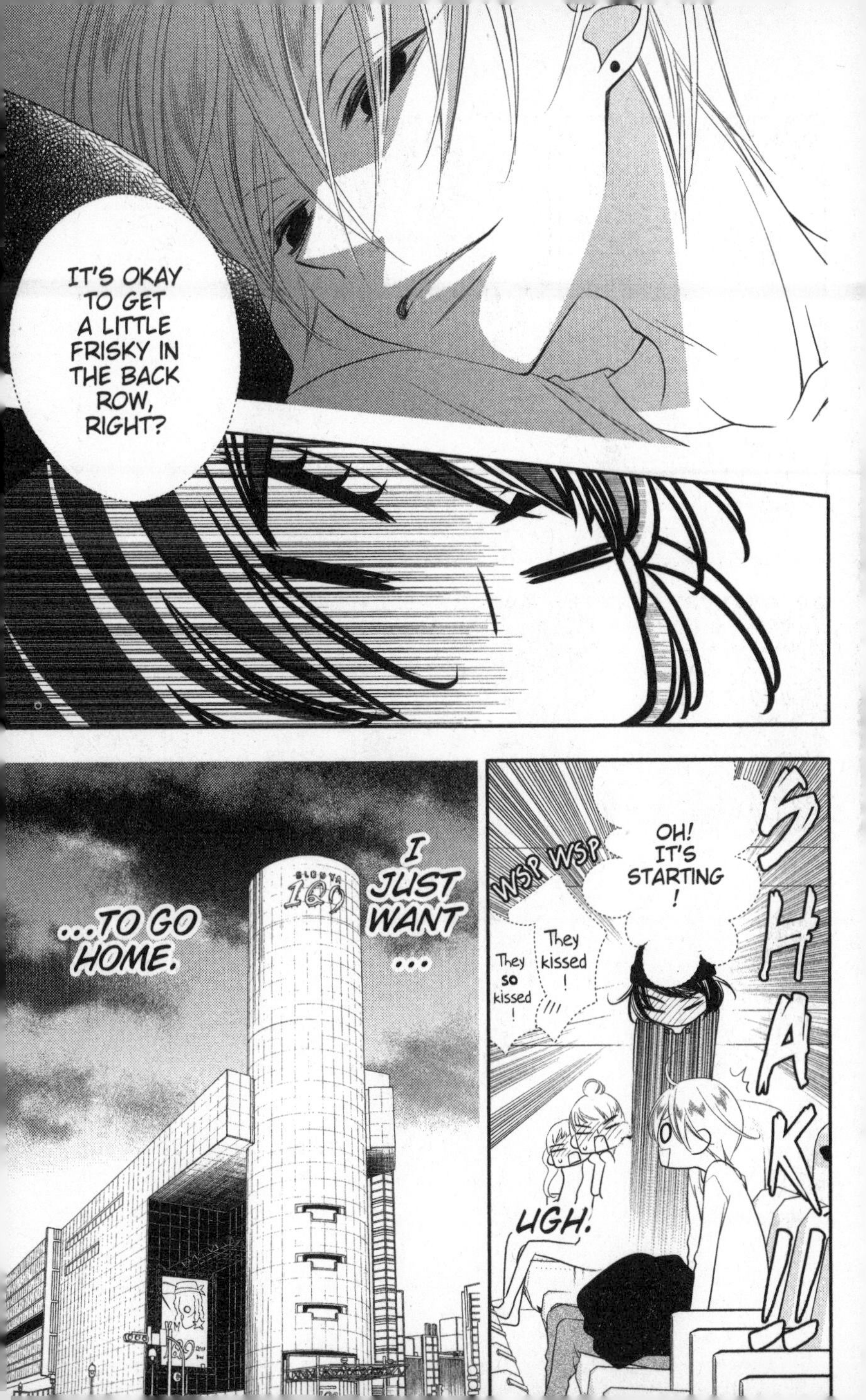
IT'S OKAY TO GET A LITTLE FRISKY IN THE BACK ROW, RIGHT?
SHAK
OH! IT'S STARTING!
WSP WSP
They kissed!
They so kissed!
UGH.
I JUST WANT...
...TO GO HOME.

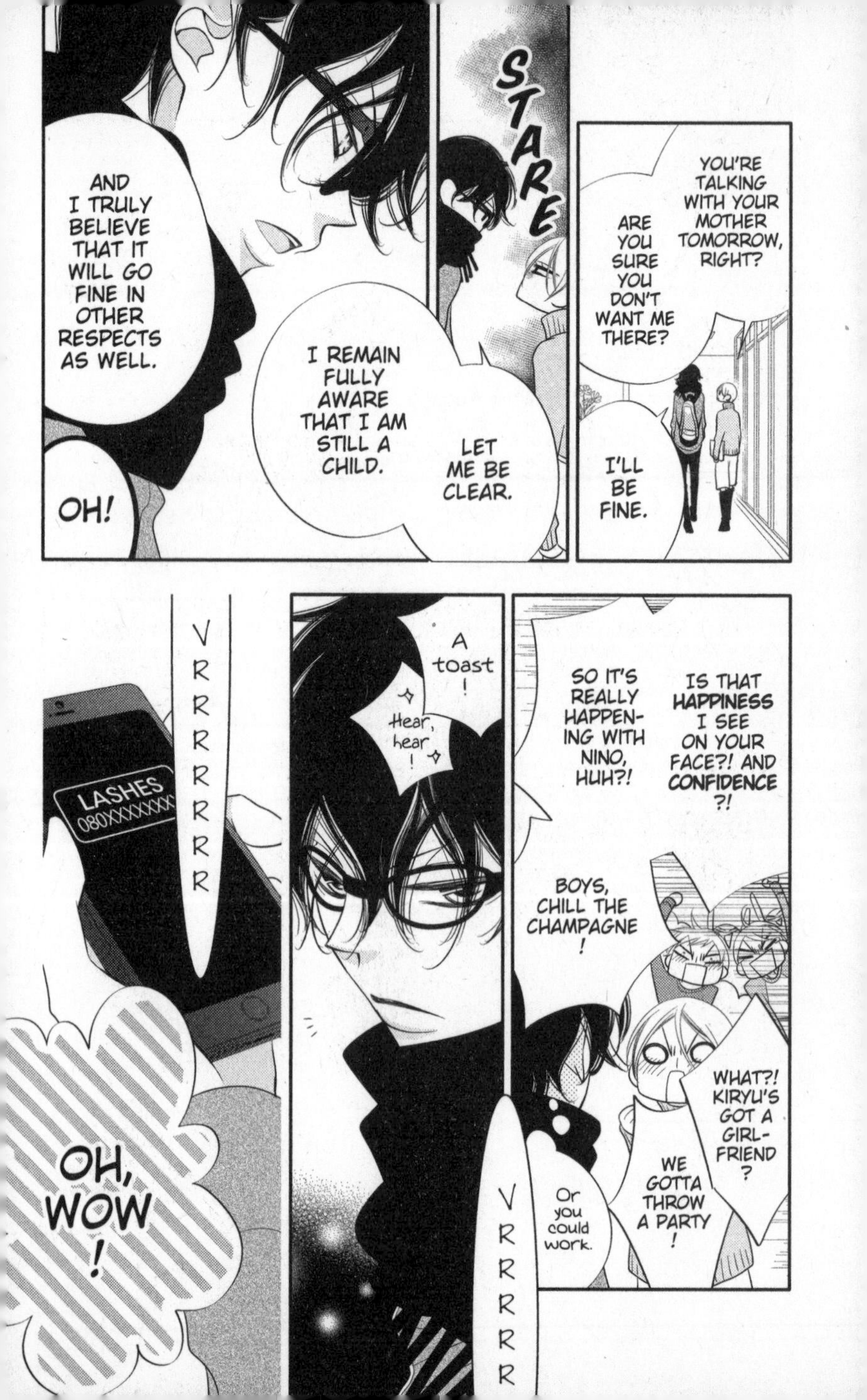
YOU'RE TALKING WITH YOUR MOTHER TOMORROW, RIGHT?
ARE YOU SURE YOU DON'T WANT ME THERE?
I'LL BE FINE.
STARE
LET ME BE CLEAR.
I REMAIN FULLY AWARE THAT I AM STILL A CHILD.
AND I TRULY BELIEVE THAT IT WILL GO FINE IN OTHER RESPECTS AS WELL.
OH!
IS THAT HAPPINESS I SEE ON YOUR FACE?! AND CONFIDENCE?!
SO IT'S REALLY HAPPENING WITH NINO, HUH?!
BOYS, CHILL THE CHAMPAGNE!
WHAT?! KIRYU'S GOT A GIRLFRIEND?
WE GOTTA THROW A PARTY!
Or you could work.
A toast!
Hear, hear!
VRRRR
VRRRRRRR
LASHES
080XXXXXXX
OH, WOW!

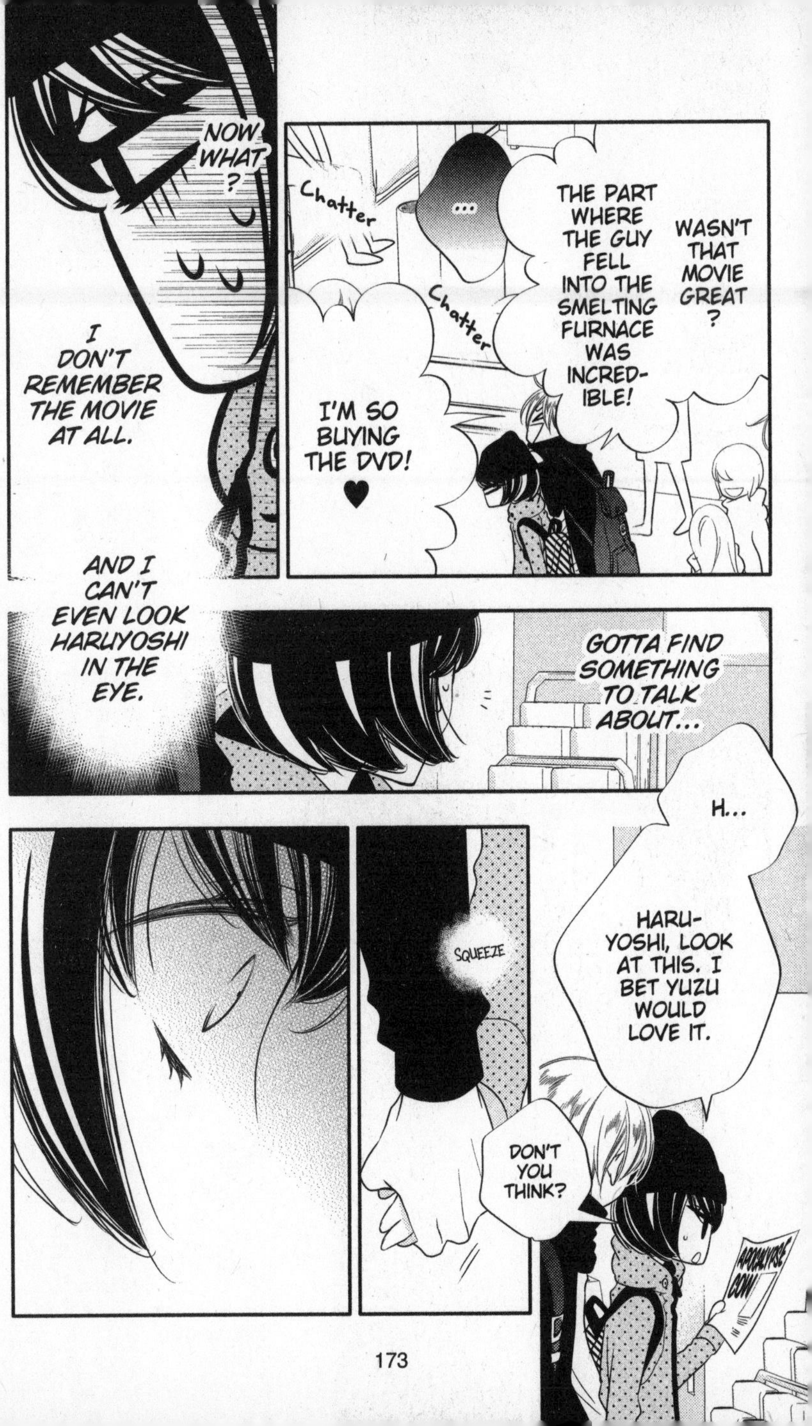
WASN'T THAT MOVIE GREAT?
Chatter
THE PART WHERE THE GUY FELL INTO THE SMELTING FURNACE WAS INCREDIBLE!
Chatter
...
I'M SO BUYING THE DVD! ♥
NOW WHAT?
I DON'T REMEMBER THE MOVIE AT ALL.
GOTTA FIND SOMETHING TO TALK ABOUT...
AND I CAN'T EVEN LOOK HARUYOSHI IN THE EYE.
H...
HARUYOSHI, LOOK AT THIS. I BET YUZU WOULD LOVE IT.
DON'T YOU THINK?
APOCALYPSE COW!
SQUEEZE

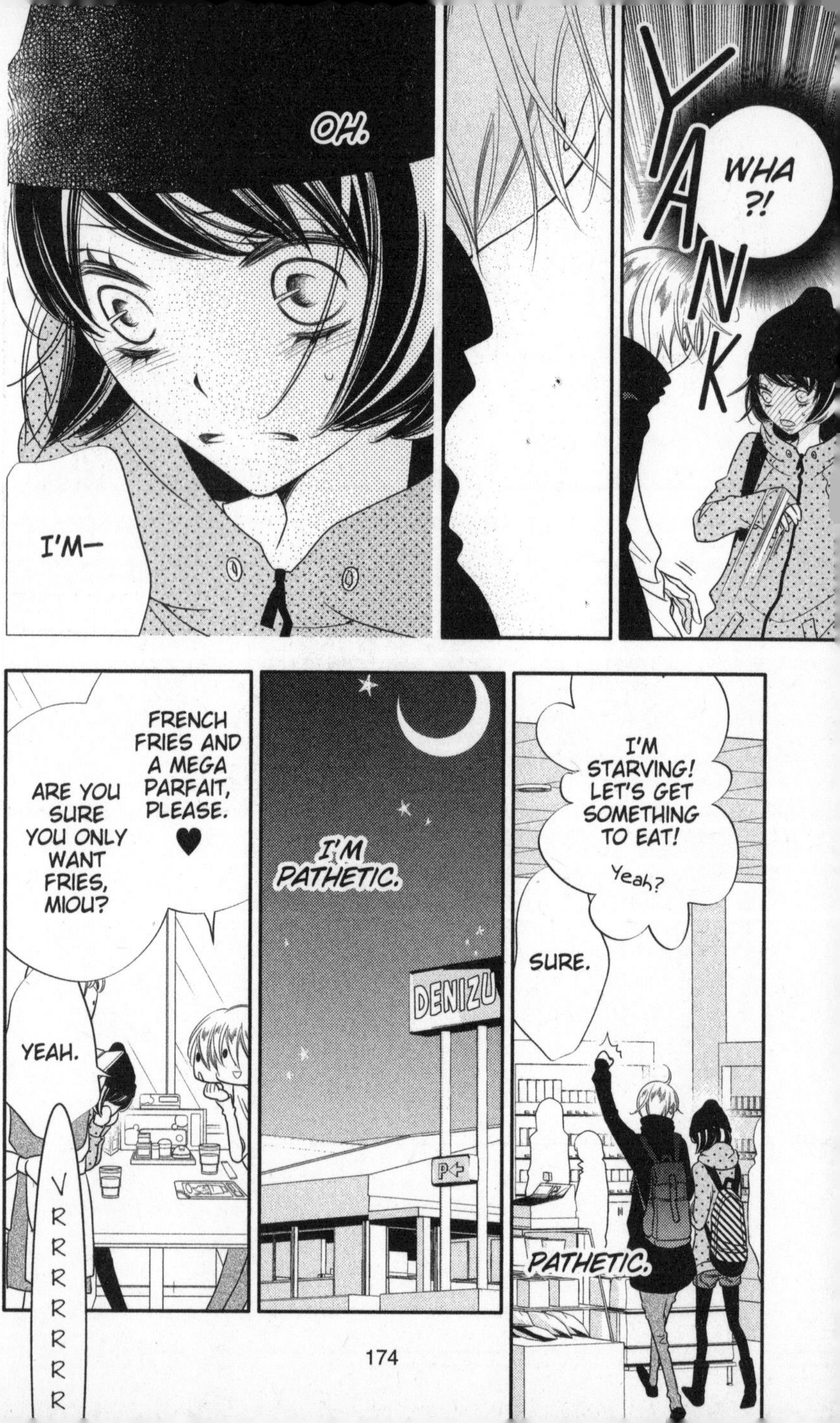
YANK
WHA?!
OH.
I'M—
I'M STARVING! LET'S GET SOMETHING TO EAT!
Yeah?
SURE.
PATHETIC.
I'M PATHETIC.
DENIZU
FRENCH FRIES AND A MEGA PARFAIT, PLEASE. ♥
ARE YOU SURE YOU ONLY WANT FRIES, MIOU?
YEAH.
VRRRRRRR

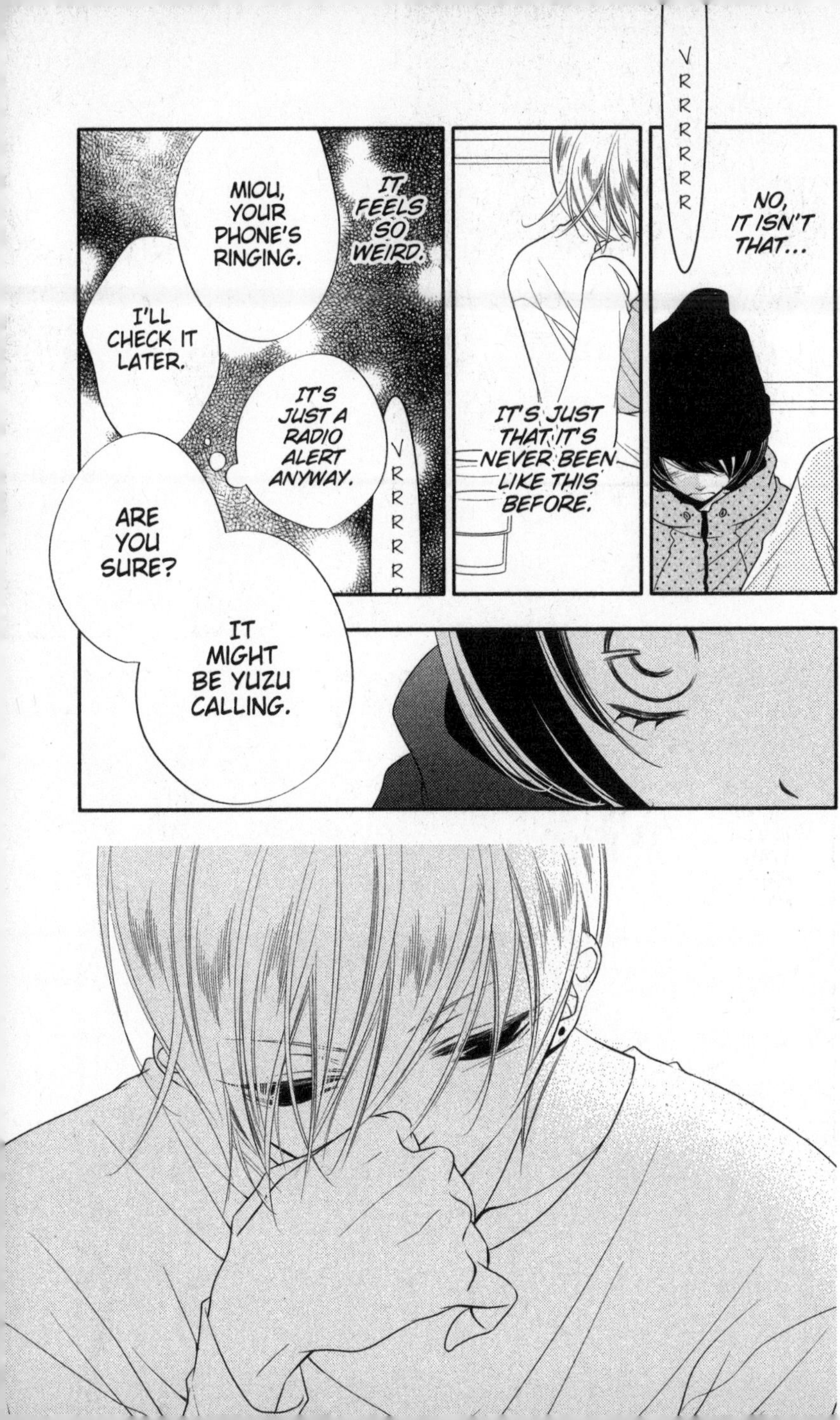
VRRRRRR
NO, IT ISN'T THAT...
IT'S JUST THAT IT'S NEVER BEEN LIKE THIS BEFORE.
IT FEELS SO WEIRD.
MIOU, YOUR PHONE'S RINGING.
I'LL CHECK IT LATER.
IT'S JUST A RADIO ALERT ANYWAY.
VRRRRR
ARE YOU SURE?
IT MIGHT BE YUZU CALLING.

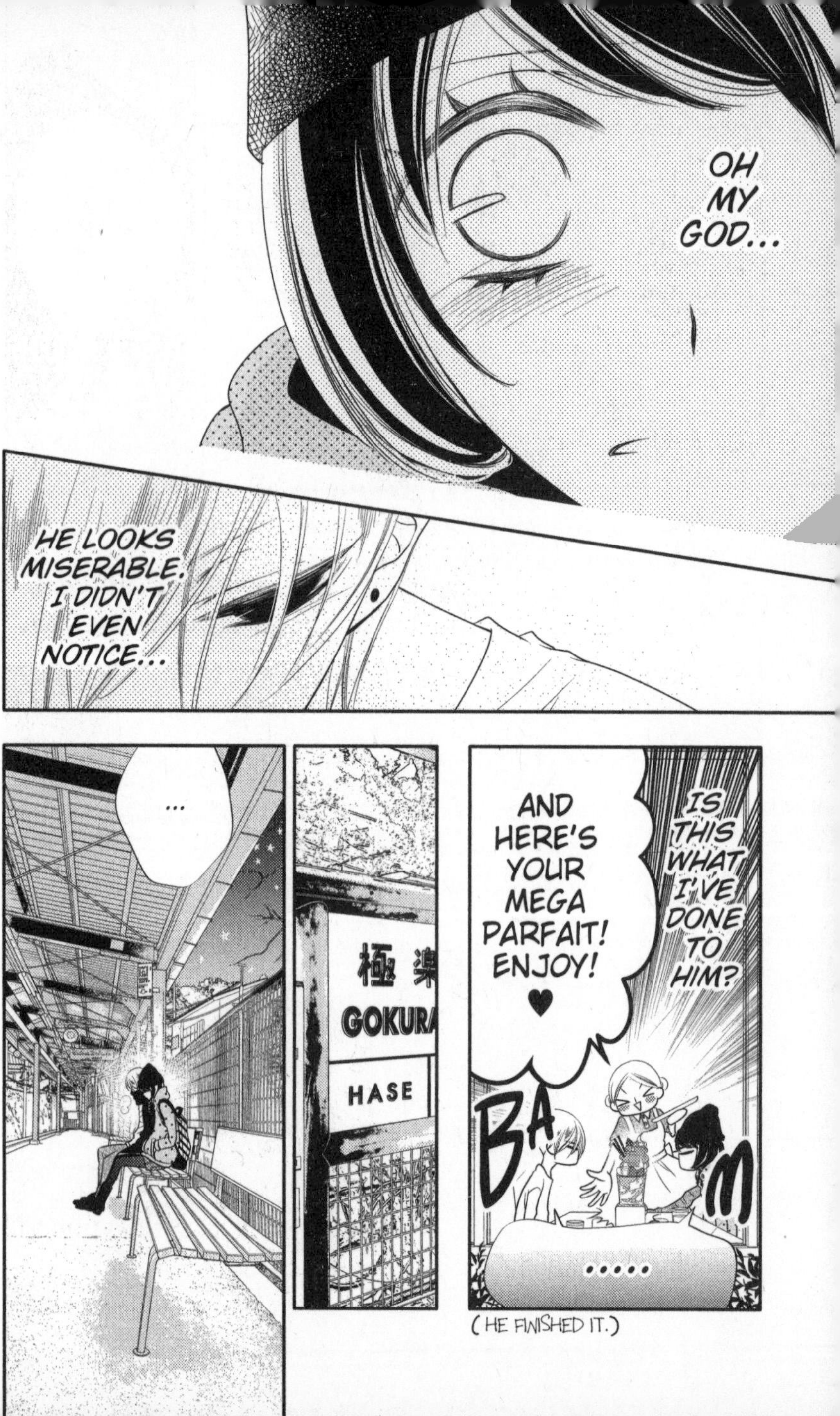
OH MY GOD...
HE LOOKS MISERABLE. I DIDN'T EVEN NOTICE...
IS THIS WHAT I'VE DONE TO HIM?
AND HERE'S YOUR MEGA PARFAIT! ENJOY! ♥
BAM
.....
(HE FINISHED IT.)
極楽
GOKURA
HASE
...

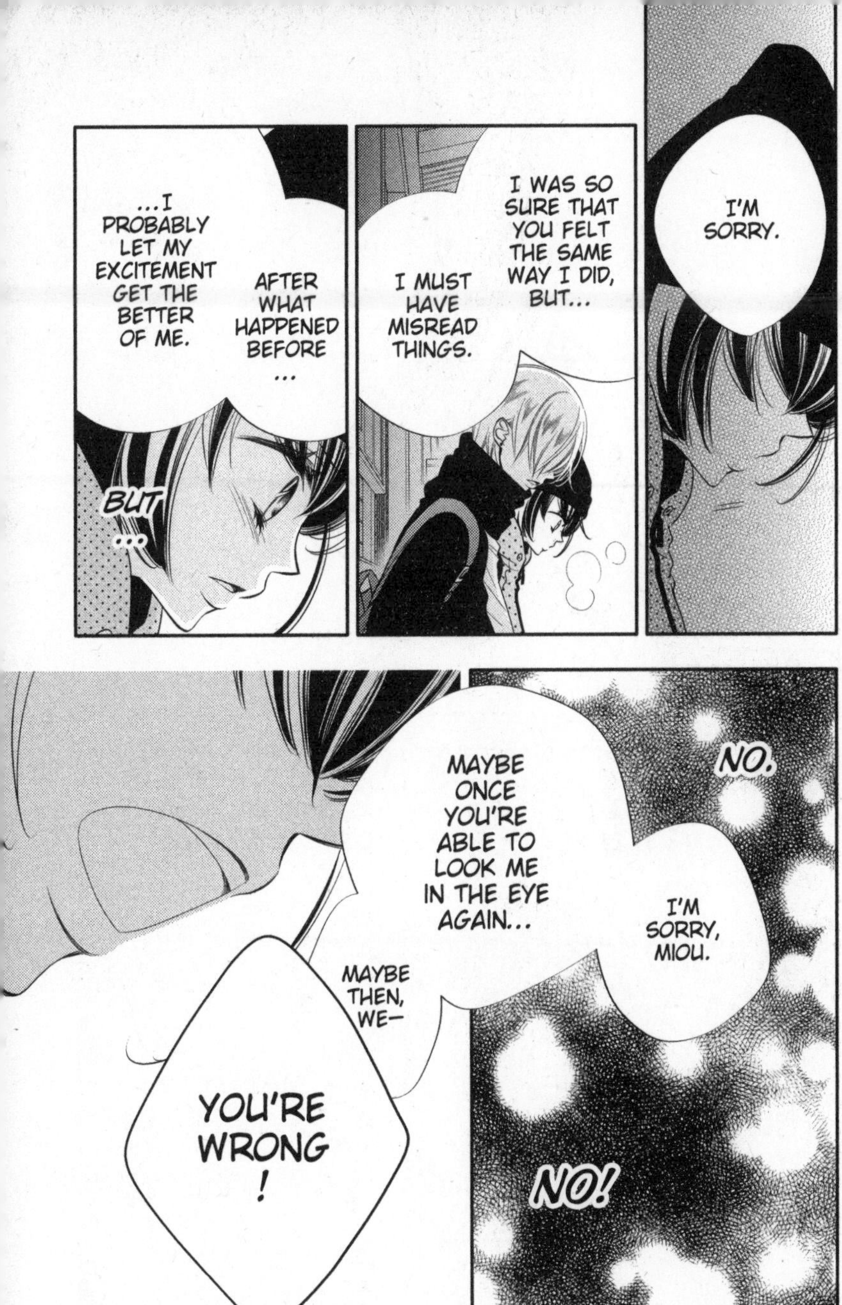
I'M SORRY.
I WAS SO SURE THAT YOU FELT THE SAME WAY I DID, BUT...
I MUST HAVE MISREAD THINGS.
AFTER WHAT HAPPENED BEFORE...
...I PROBABLY LET MY EXCITEMENT GET THE BETTER OF ME.
BUT...
I'M SORRY, MIOU.
MAYBE ONCE YOU'RE ABLE TO LOOK ME IN THE EYE AGAIN...
MAYBE THEN, WE—
NO.
NO!
YOU'RE WRONG!

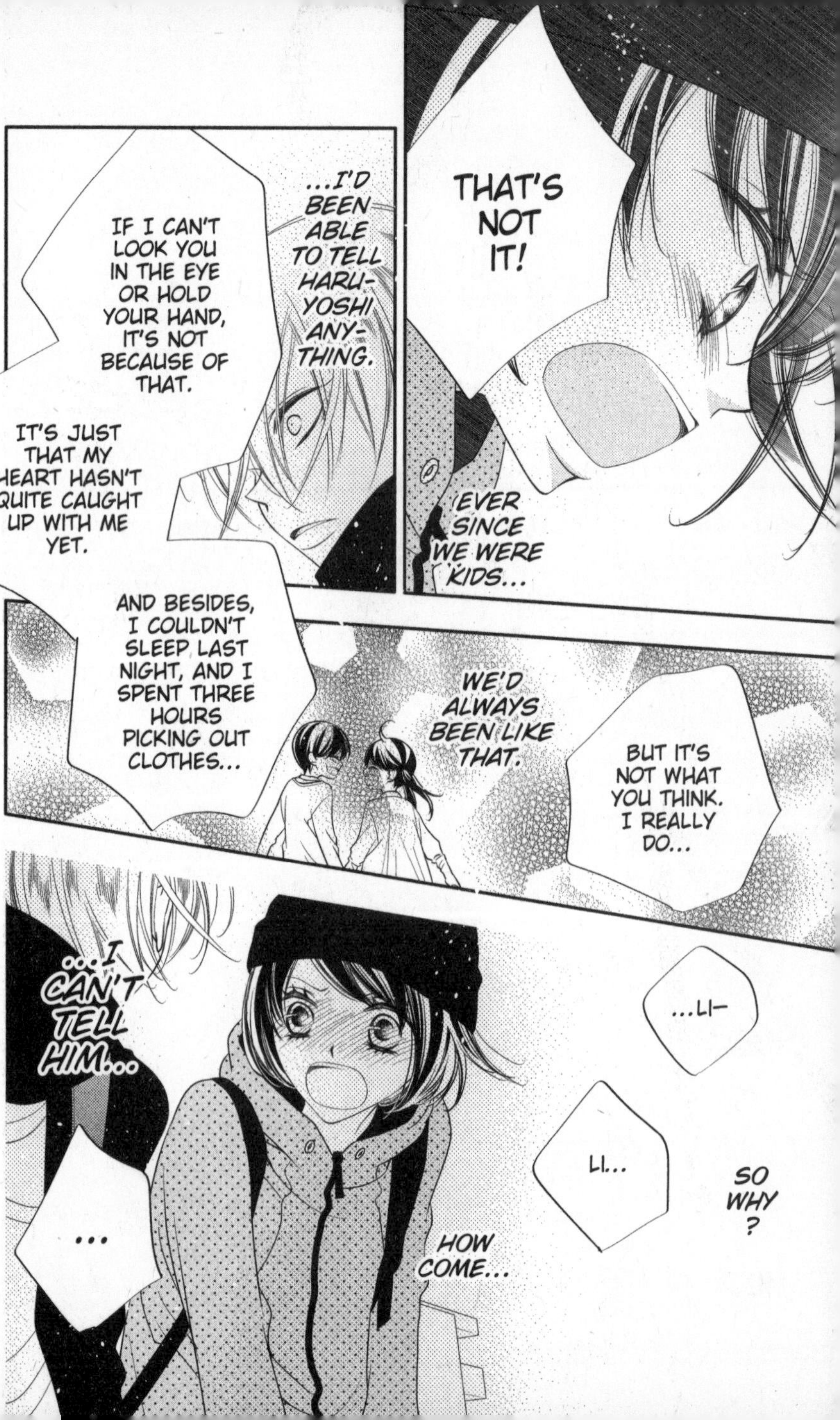
THAT'S NOT IT!
EVER SINCE WE WERE KIDS...
...I'D BEEN ABLE TO TELL HARUYOSHI ANYTHING.
IF I CAN'T LOOK YOU IN THE EYE OR HOLD YOUR HAND, IT'S NOT BECAUSE OF THAT.
IT'S JUST THAT MY HEART HASN'T QUITE CAUGHT UP WITH ME YET.
BUT IT'S NOT WHAT YOU THINK. I REALLY DO...
WE'D ALWAYS BEEN LIKE THAT.
AND BESIDES, I COULDN'T SLEEP LAST NIGHT, AND I SPENT THREE HOURS PICKING OUT CLOTHES...
...LI–
SO WHY?
LI...
HOW COME...
...I CAN'T TELL HIM...
...

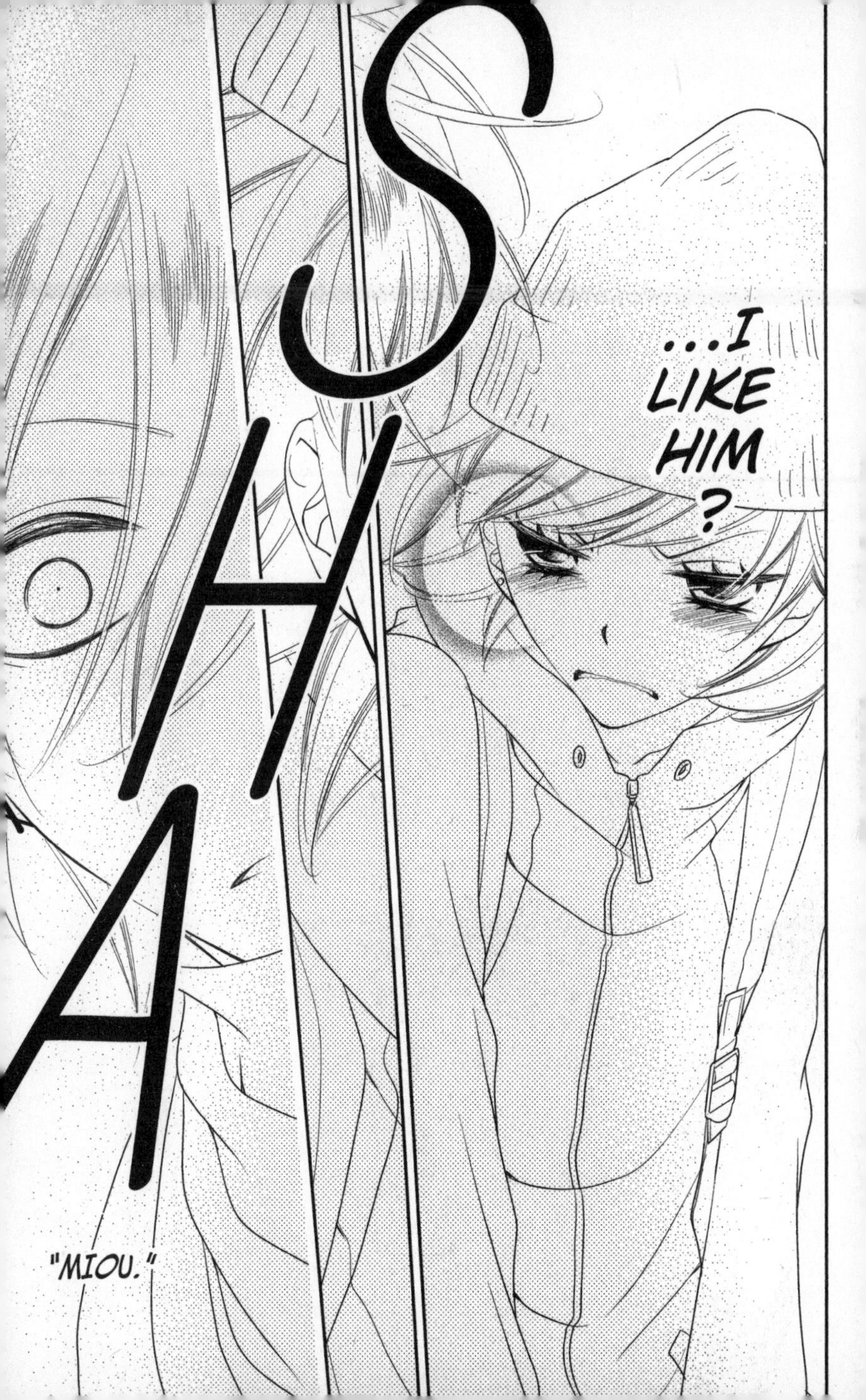
...I LIKE HIM?
SHA
"MIOU."

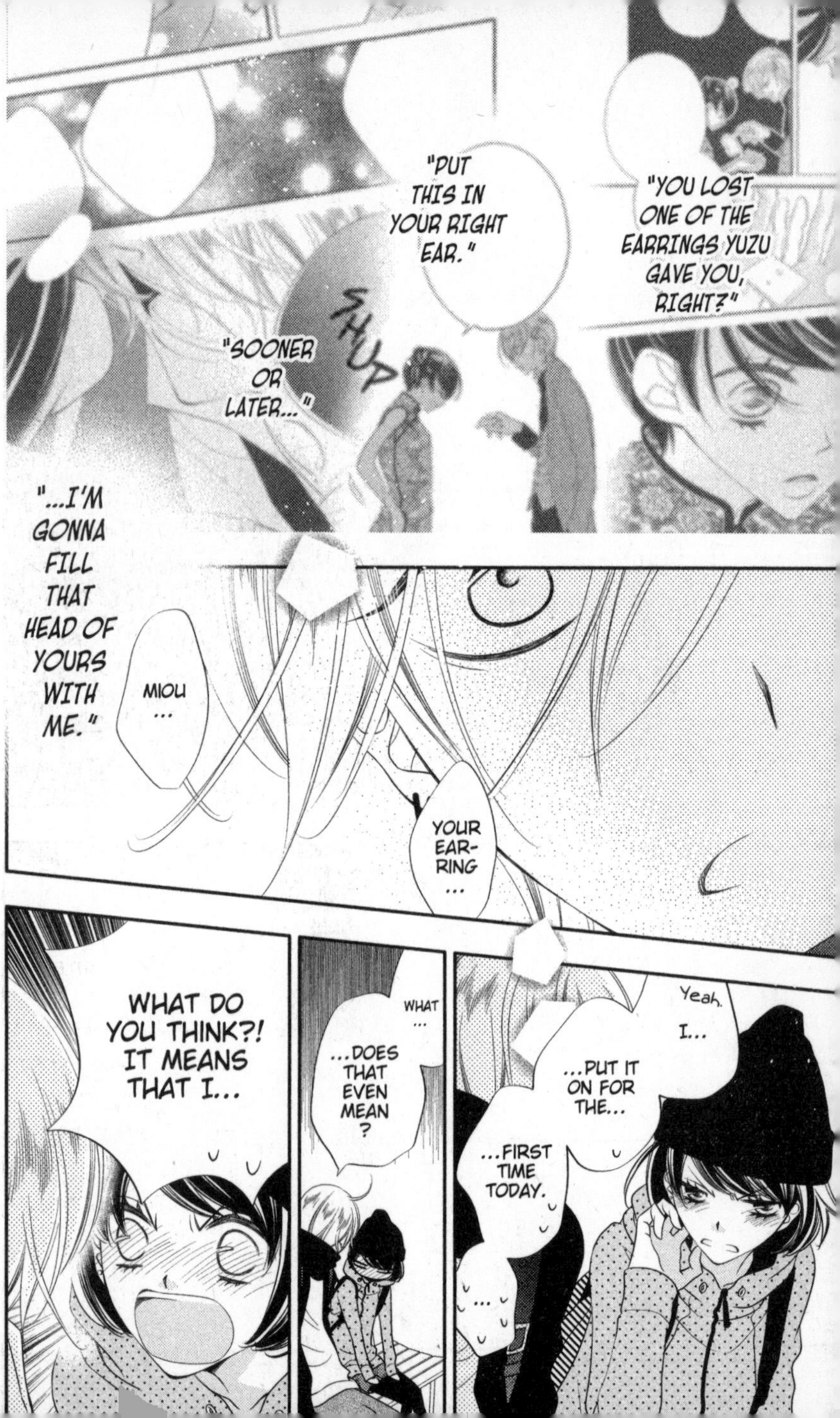
"YOU LOST ONE OF THE EARRINGS YUZU GAVE YOU, RIGHT?"
"PUT THIS IN YOUR RIGHT EAR."
SHUA
"SOONER OR LATER..."
"...I'M GONNA FILL THAT HEAD OF YOURS WITH ME."
MIOU...
YOUR EAR-RING...
Yeah.
I...
...PUT IT ON FOR THE...
...FIRST TIME TODAY.
...
WHAT...
...DOES THAT EVEN MEAN?
WHAT DO YOU THINK?! IT MEANS THAT I...

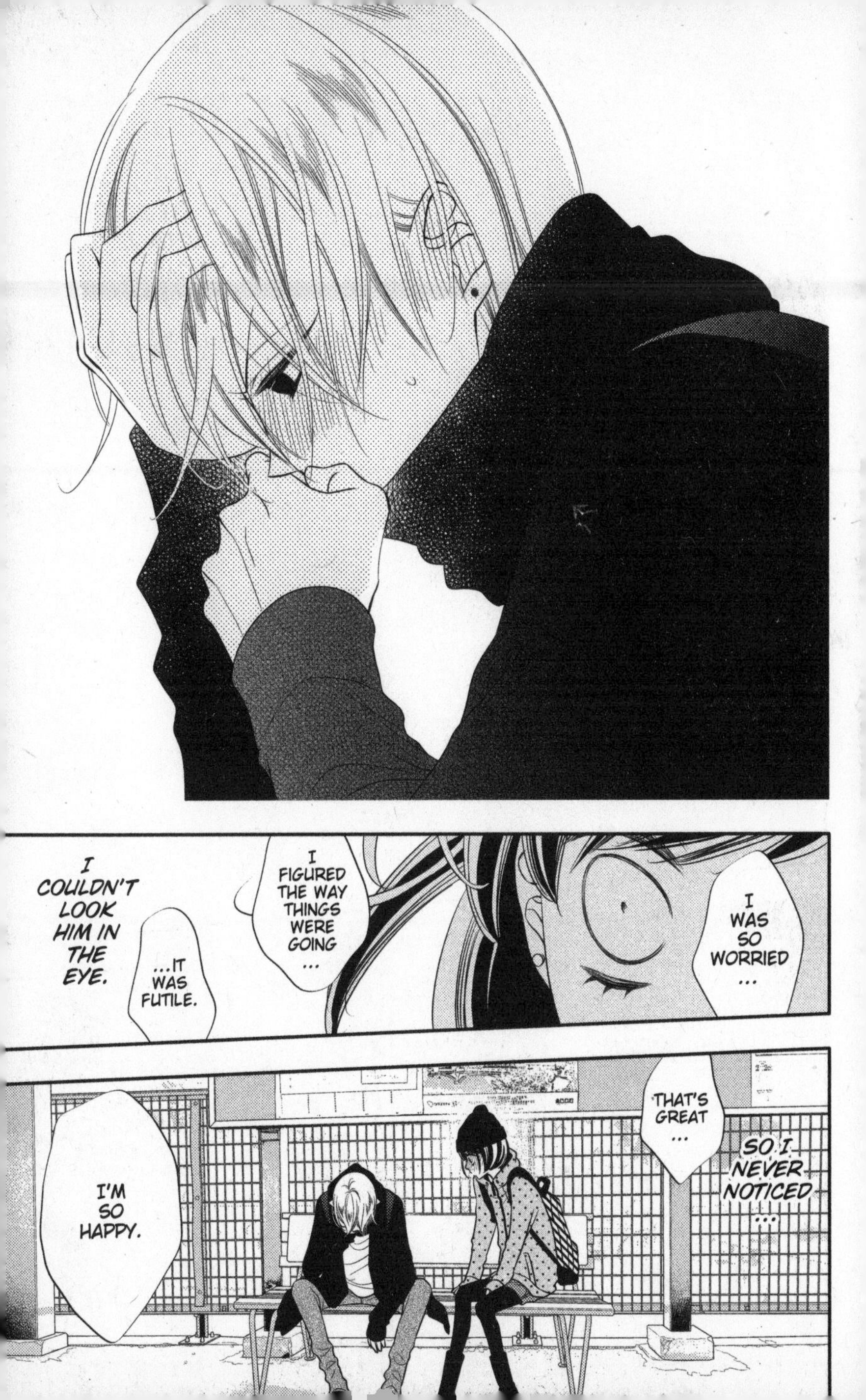
I WAS SO WORRIED ...
I FIGURED THE WAY THINGS WERE GOING ...
...IT WAS FUTILE.
I COULDN'T LOOK HIM IN THE EYE.
SO I NEVER NOTICED ...
THAT'S GREAT ...
I'M SO HAPPY.

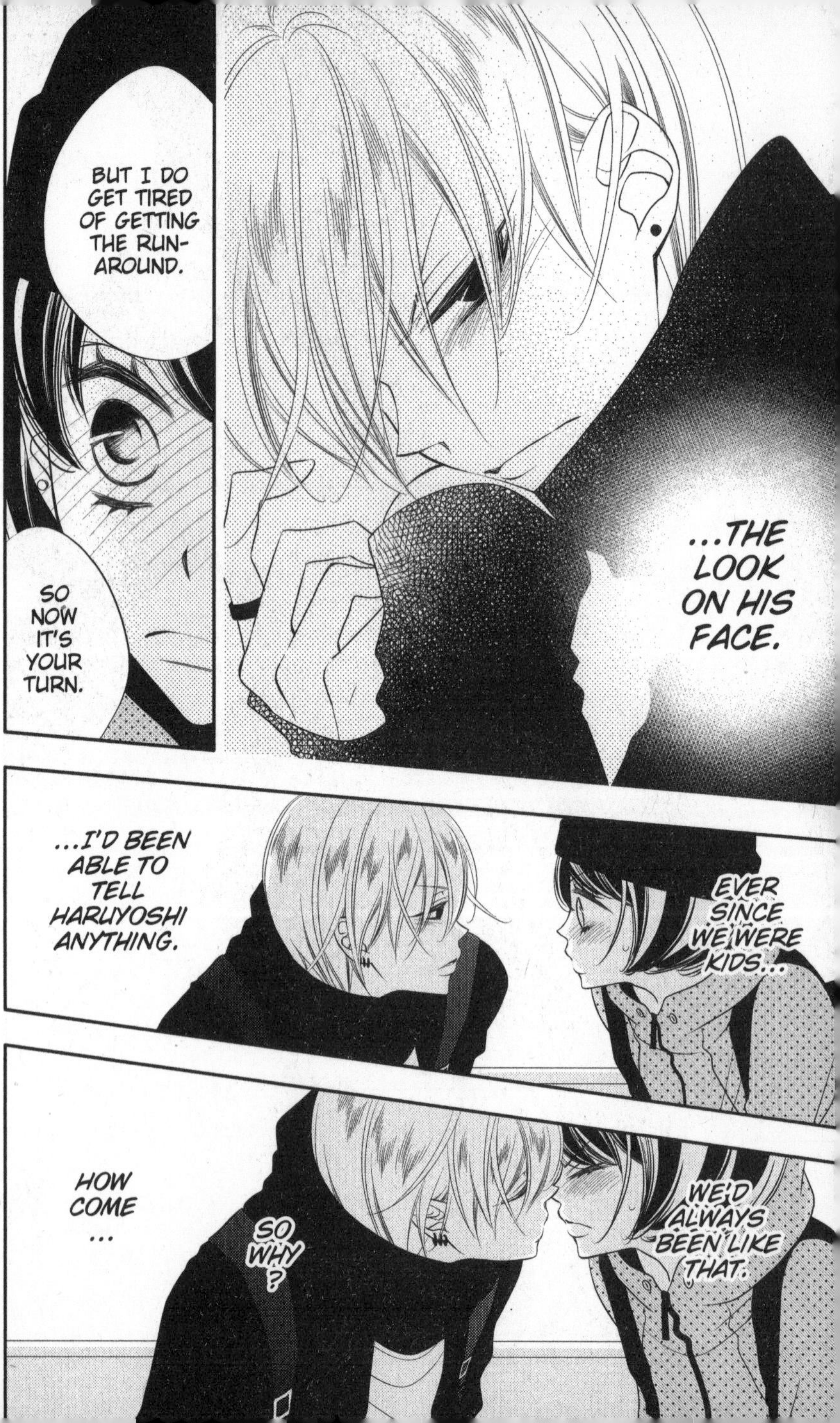

...THE LOOK ON HIS FACE.
BUT I DO GET TIRED OF GETTING THE RUN-AROUND.
SO NOW IT'S YOUR TURN.
EVER SINCE WE WERE KIDS...
...I'D BEEN ABLE TO TELL HARUYOSHI ANYTHING.
WE'D ALWAYS BEEN LIKE THAT.
SO WHY?
HOW COME ...

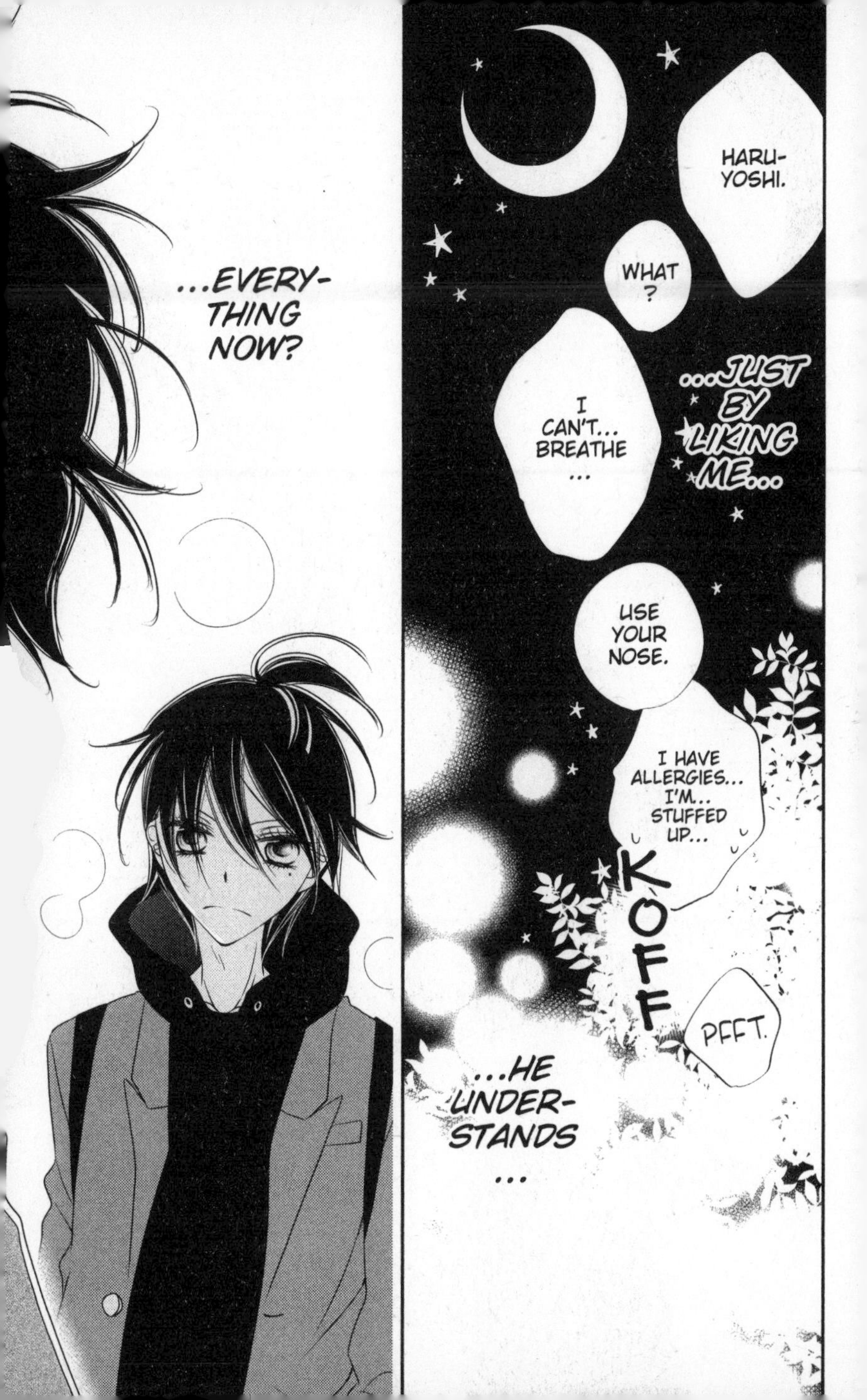
HARU-YOSHI.
WHAT?
...JUST BY LIKING ME...
I CAN'T... BREATHE...
USE YOUR NOSE.
I HAVE ALLERGIES... I'M... STUFFED UP...
KOFF
PFFT.
...HE UNDER-STANDS...
...EVERY-THING NOW?

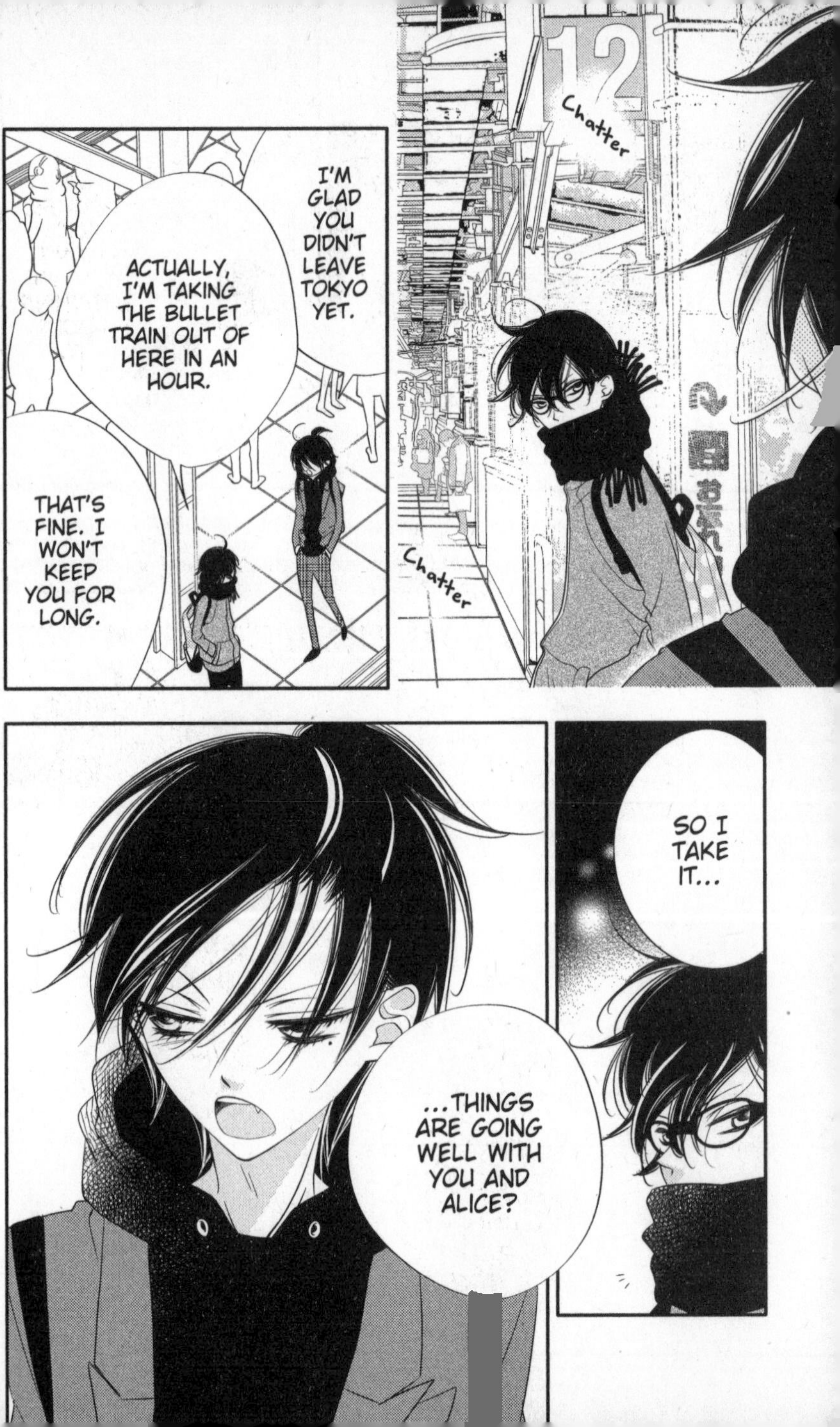
Chatter
Chatter
I'M GLAD YOU DIDN'T LEAVE TOKYO YET.
ACTUALLY, I'M TAKING THE BULLET TRAIN OUT OF HERE IN AN HOUR.
THAT'S FINE. I WON'T KEEP YOU FOR LONG.
SO I TAKE IT...
...THINGS ARE GOING WELL WITH YOU AND ALICE?

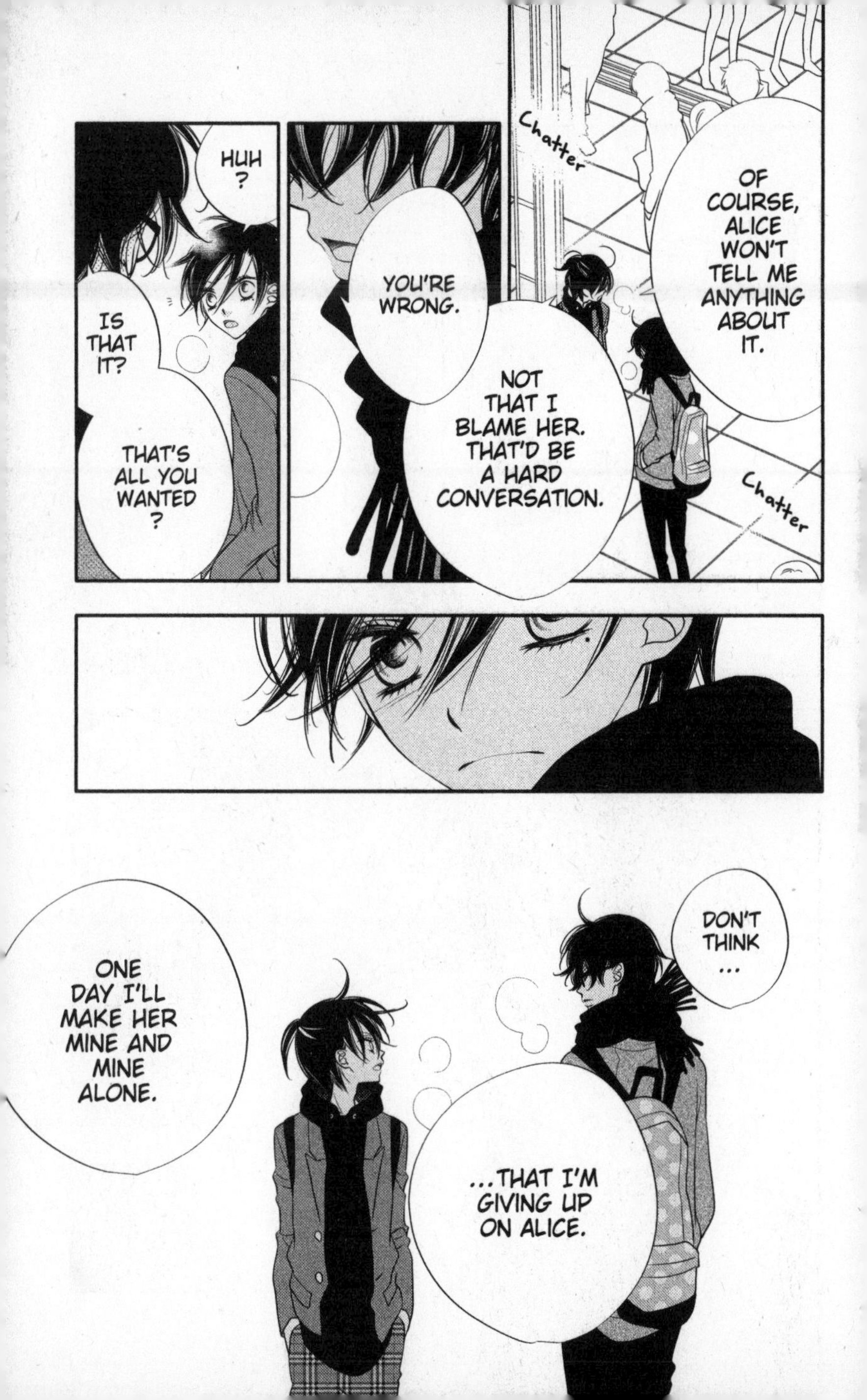
Chatter
OF COURSE, ALICE WON'T TELL ME ANYTHING ABOUT IT.
NOT THAT I BLAME HER. THAT'D BE A HARD CONVERSATION.
Chatter
YOU'RE WRONG.
HUH?
IS THAT IT?
THAT'S ALL YOU WANTED?
DON'T THINK...
...THAT I'M GIVING UP ON ALICE.
ONE DAY I'LL MAKE HER MINE AND MINE ALONE.

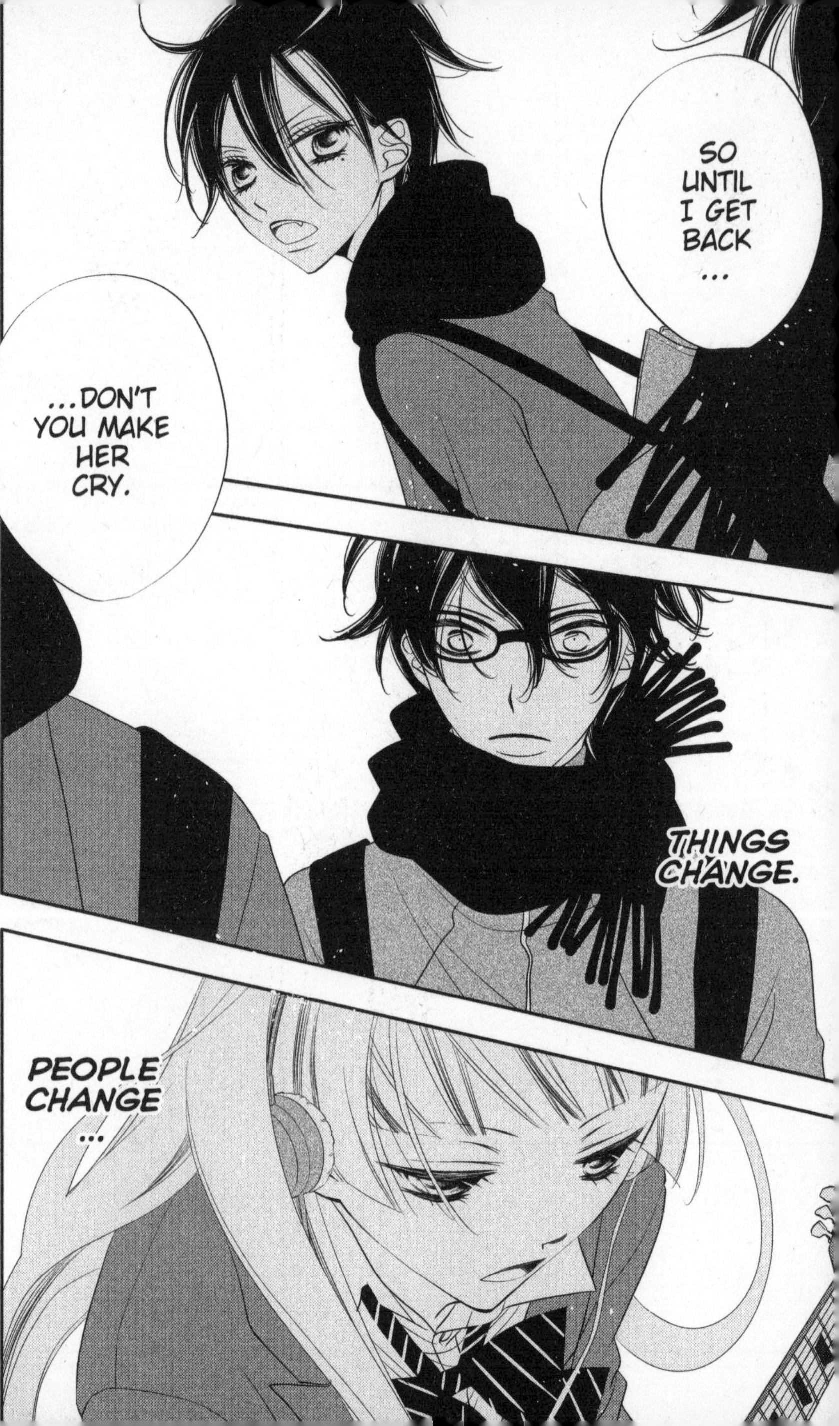
SO UNTIL I GET BACK ...
...DON'T YOU MAKE HER CRY.
THINGS CHANGE.
PEOPLE CHANGE ...

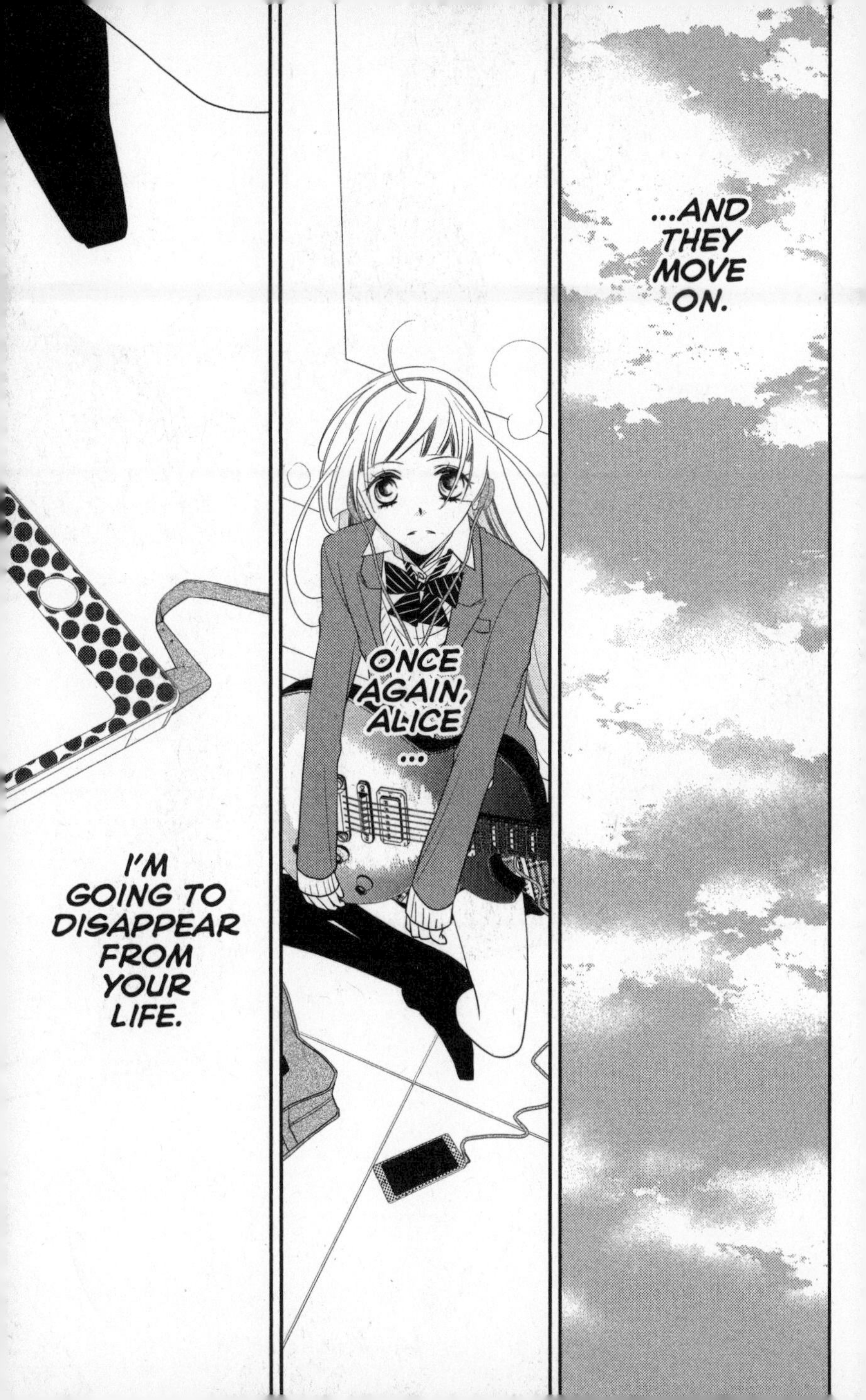
...AND THEY MOVE ON.
ONCE AGAIN, ALICE ...
I'M GOING TO DISAPPEAR FROM YOUR LIFE.

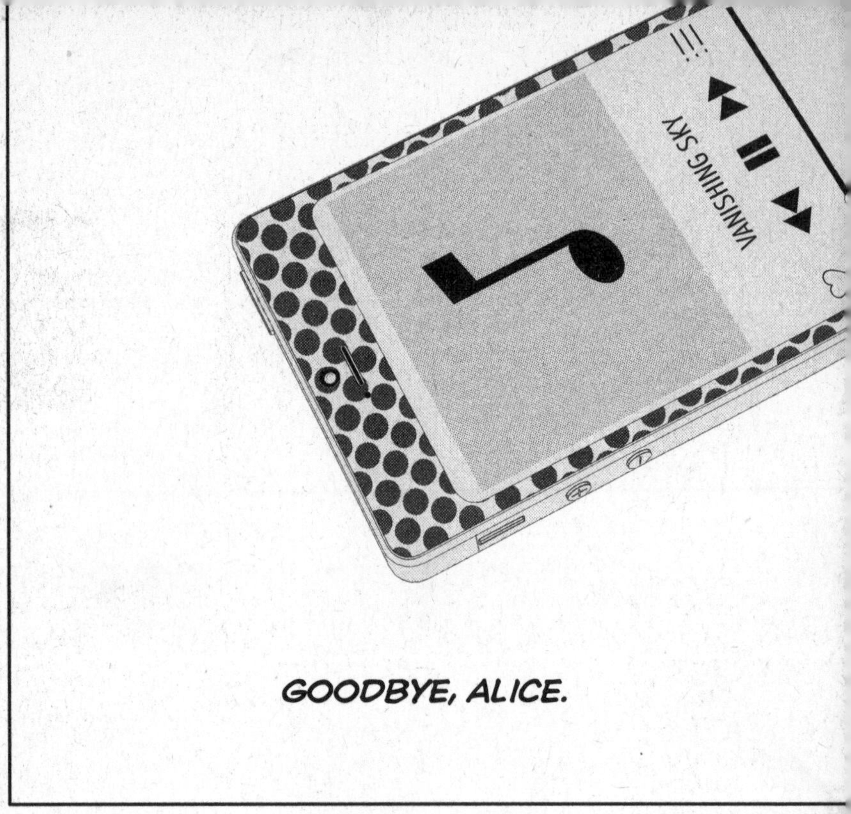
VANISHING SKY
GOODBYE, ALICE.

JUST FOR A LITTLE WHILE.

ANONYMOUS NOISE ⑪ / THE END

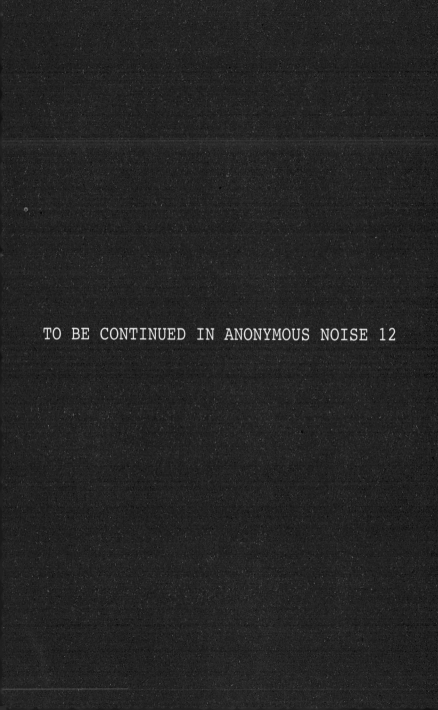

TO BE CONTINUED IN ANONYMOUS NOISE 12

When I debuted as a manga artist,
never in my wildest dreams could I
have predicted that my work would
be developed into both an anime and
a live-action film. I'd like to thank
you from the bottom of my heart for
making all this possible.

- Ryoko Fukuyama

Born on January 5 in Wakayama Prefecture in
Japan, Ryoko Fukuyama debuted as a manga
artist after winning the Hakusensha Athena
Shinjin Taisho Prize from Hakusensha's *Hana to
Yume* magazine. She is also the author
of *Nosatsu Junkie*. *Anonymous Noise* was
adapted into an anime in 2017.